INTRODUCTION TO COMPUTERS AND COMPUTER PROGRAMMING

SAMUEL BERGMAN
Temple University

STEVEN BRUCKNER
University of Pennsylvania

 ADDISON-WESLEY PUBLISHING COMPANY
Reading, Massachusetts
Menlo Park, California · London · Amsterdam · Don Mills, Ontario · Sydney

This book is published
under the editorship of Michael A. Harrison

ISBN 0-201-00552-2
FGHIJKL-AL-79

In Memory of
CELIA BERGMAN
RUTH BRUCKNER

PREFACE

This book is intended to serve as the text for an introductory computer programming course. It can be used for graduate students, undergraduates, and even high-school students. The approach employed differs considerably from most other texts in that the student first learns and programs in machine language, then assembly language, and finally in FORTRAN. In doing so, he follows the historical and logical development of programming complexity and is able to understand and appreciate the operation cycle of the machine, the assembly process, compilation, indexing, internal floating-point and character representations, and so forth. Such a course is, admittedly, more difficult than the ordinary FORTRAN course, but at the same time the student is left with the feeling that he has an understanding of what computers do and how they work, rather than merely the ability to communicate with them via some intermediary language. This course provides a sound foundation for further study of computer applications of any kind.

The course should be taught as a programming (rather than "computer appreciation") course. Students must be given the opportunity to actually write and debug *at least* six programs during the semester: one in machine language, two in assembly, and three in FORTRAN. Machine and assembly language programming is taught on the FACET computer, a small (1K) simulated decimal machine with character, floating-point, indexing, and debugging capabilities. The FACET simulator is written in FORTRAN and can be compiled on any machine with about 20K memory words (or overlays) available. FACET is supplied (at no cost) in machine-readable form by the authors. It is usually stored in a permanent file in compiled form, and called each time a user requires it (although other arrangements are possible). The student need not even be aware that a FACET computer does not physically exist. Student FACET programs generally cost about the same as student FORTRAN programs.

The FORTRAN presentation is more thorough than the standard approach because students who have completed the first part of the text can *already program* and are *already* familiar with the computer's operation. Students need only worry about the *syntax* of FORTRAN, since they will have already programmed similar problems in assembly language. This simplification of the FORTRAN learning process as well as the student's knowledge of computer operations allows the text to integrate material on FORTRAN implementation using FACET assembly language. Uniform, logical transitions are thereby established from machine language to assembly language and from there to FORTRAN.

Chapter 8 generalizes the picture of the FACET computer to "every computer," with emphasis on binary machines and octal/hexadecimal coding. Generalized input/output, data channels, I/O devices, and multiprogramming are presented. Indirect addressing, multiple general registers, and addressing schemes are also discussed.

This book grew out of "Engineering Science 110," a freshmen course at the University of Pennsylvania entitled "Numerical Solution of Engineering Problems by Digital Computer." The course, as it developed in the early 1960's, took on a twofold purpose: the explication of (a) operation and programming of computers and (b) solution of numerical problems (in FORTRAN). A simple decimal machine called INSECTS (INterpretive Simulator of an Educational Computer for Training Students) was simulated on an RPC-4000, and the Penn students were permitted hands-on operation. Dr. Thomas C. Lowe, then a graduate teaching fellow, developed INSECTS; Mrs. Amy Eliasoff Atlas, who also taught the course, developed a version of INSECTS for the IBM 7040. After learning some INSECTS machine language the students moved on to FORTRAN and numerical methods.

When we, as graduate teaching fellows at Penn, began teaching this course, we felt the lack of transition from INSECTS machine language to FORTRAN. Essentially, students could not see the connection between FORTRAN and INSECTS. What followed was first an INSECTS assembly language and finally a new machine—FACET. FACET was simple enough to be easily programmable and complex enough so that FORTRAN could conceivably be compiled into (and certainly explained in terms of) the FACET assembly language. The notes for this book were developed over a two-year period. Several thousand students at The Moore School of the University of Pennsylvania and at the School of Business Administration of Temple University used various versions of the notes before this volume was born.

There is no particular bias in the examples or explanations toward mathematical, scientific, or business applications of computers. Programming techniques are demonstrated using problems from various disciplines. The book can be used in a stand-alone or "dead-end" course, or as a first building block in an applications programming, information systems, or computer systems sequence. An Instructor's manual is available from the publishers.

We owe many thanks to Marc Specter who persuaded us to convert our skimpy notes into a book; to Mrs. Winnifred Franks who did wonders with our manuscript; to Drs. Leonard Garrett and Warren Seider who encouraged us and allowed us to experimentally use this approach with literally thousands of students;

to Mrs. Evelyn Gechman and Miss Thelma Jefferson for typing our scrawlings; and to the tens of instructors and the many students of U. of P. and Temple U. who suggested changes and discovered errors in our mimeographed notes.

Very special appreciation and thanks belong to Madeline Bergman, Sam's wife, who in love and friendship fed us and put up with our interminable work schedules during what seemed to be an interminable project.

Philadelphia   [SB]²
August 1971

CONTENTS

FOREWORD

We hear about computers constantly these days. They seem to be doing more and more in our society, relentlessly making inroads on tasks that are traditionally performed by man. It seems that once they merely performed calculations for us —complex scientific calculations and humdrum calculations in the world of business. Now they count us, tell us which political figures and policies we prefer, tell us whom we will elect before the election takes place, make our telephone connections, and run many of our factories; they are even teaching some of our schoolchildren, making out our paychecks, and finding us possible future mates. They compute our grades in universities and check up on our tax returns. The stock market would grind to a halt without them. It's about time we learned something about these computers.

The fact is that computers can't really do anything we don't tell them to do. Once we instruct a computer to do something, however, it does it with lightning speed—much faster than we ourselves could accomplish the same task. The process of telling a computer what to do and how to do it is called *programming*. It is the purpose of this book to introduce you to this activity. In the process you will learn more about the structure and capabilities of computers.

This book, at least in part, is a laboratory manual. In particular, you must actually write and run computer programs in order to proceed to later chapters. Experience has shown that computer programming is an activity which can be learned and appreciated only by participation. If you intend to read this book in a vacuum, in order to appreciate computers, you are making a mistake. This statement is true regardless of your talent or background. Increasingly, the text relies on your computer programming experiences. Without these experiences, the text will seem to become needlessly bogged down with details.

Computer programming is an activity that is not related to other activities in the academic, business, scientific, or industrial world. You needn't have very much of a background to study programming, or this book. You should know elementary school arithmetic, and some high-school algebra is helpful. Like many other subjects, some take to programming "like a fish to water," while others must work very hard to assimilate the material. In either case, the greater your involvement, the more you are likely to benefit.

Chapter 1

THE
FACET
COMPUTER
AND ITS
LANGUAGE

1.1 THE FACET COMPUTER

Because it is pedagogically sound to first study specifics and then generalize, we shall begin our study of the structure and programming of digital computers by discussing a specific computer. Our computer is called the FACET computer, so named because it is a

FAcility for Computer Education and Training

Although the FACET computer is similar to all digital computers in many respects, it also differs from these computers in many other respects (indeed, different computers differ from one another in general). Many of these similarities and differences will be pointed out after we have become familiar with many of the terms used in the computer world and after we have had some experience in programming the FACET computer. The terminology introduced in our study of the FACET computer is, generally speaking, standard terminology in use today. It is therefore important that we become familiar with it.

This book deals only with **general-purpose digital computers**. There are other kinds of computers, such as **analog** computers, **hybrid** computers, and **special-purpose digital** computers, but most of the computers you hear about are general-purpose digital computers. These include the ones which handle payrolls and billing, predict outcomes of elections, keep track of space satellites, handle data management systems, and keep bank records. We shall henceforth drop the adjectives "general-purpose digital" and speak of computers. When we do so, we always mean general-purpose digital computers.

1.2 WHAT COMPUTERS DO

Computers are machines which process information. "Information," however, is a very nebulous term, as are terms like "knowledge" and "ideas." Since computers are merely machines, they must deal in something concrete. Information is therefore **represented** by concrete objects called **symbols**. The computers then **process** and **manipulate** symbols, and we human beings **interpret** the symbols (that is, assign meaning to them).

For example, when a computer prints a paycheck for the employees of a certain firm, it doesn't in any sense "know" that the characters and digits it is printing on a check mean that a certain sum of money is being transferred to a certain individual. The computer is merely following a sequence of instructions to perform certain additions, multiplications, and so on, and to print the results of these manipulations onto check blanks in a certain format. Similarly, the computer doesn't "know" when it adds one and one (resulting usually in two) that "one" and "two" represent anything but arbitrary symbols which possess certain additive and other arithmetic properties.

Henceforth, and until chapter 8, we shall be concerned only with the FACET computer. However, all terms introduced and set in boldface type represent concepts important in all computers. Moreover, the terms used are the actual terms in use in the computer world. It is therefore especially important for you to understand these terms.

1.3 HOW THE FACET COMPUTER WORKS

In order to perform a task, the FACET computer must be supplied with:

a) *A set of instructions.* This tells it how (in great detail) to perform the task. The set of **instructions** is known as the **program**.

b) *A set of data.* This is the information to be processed.

The computer then goes about carrying out the instructions, manipulating the data according to these instructions, and finally emitting the results (often in printed form). These steps might be visualized as shown on the facing page. Basically, this is what all computers do. Today they perform these tasks at lightning speeds, many orders of magnitude faster than human beings. Yet it is always a human being who ultimately writes the program (or set of instructions) which defines explicitly the required task.

1.4 THE MEMORY

In order to perform all these tasks the FACET computer must be able to store the program (set of instructions) and the data given to it. It does so in the **memory**. The memory is a major part of the FACET computer. It consists of 1000 identical units called **memory registers**. Each memory register contains, at any given time, a sign followed by five decimal digits. Here are two examples of what a memory register might contain:

$$+ 0 0 0 0 5$$
$$- 3 0 4 9 2$$

Step 1

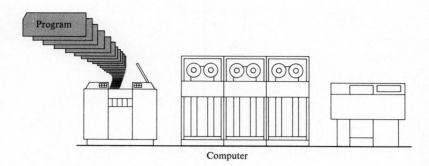

Computer

Step 2

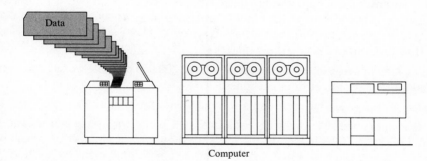

Computer

Step 3

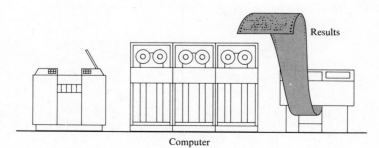

Computer

The contents of a memory register are known as a **word**. How many different possible words are there? Exactly 200,000 as follows:

$$
\begin{array}{l}
- \ 9 \ 9 \ 9 \ 9 \ 9 \\
- \ 9 \ 9 \ 9 \ 9 \ 8 \\
- \ 9 \ 9 \ 9 \ 9 \ 7 \\
\qquad \vdots \\
- \ 0 \ 0 \ 0 \ 0 \ 2 \\
- \ 0 \ 0 \ 0 \ 0 \ 1 \\
- \ 0 \ 0 \ 0 \ 0 \ 0 \\
+ \ 0 \ 0 \ 0 \ 0 \ 0 \\
+ \ 0 \ 0 \ 0 \ 0 \ 1 \\
+ \ 0 \ 0 \ 0 \ 0 \ 2 \\
+ \ 0 \ 0 \ 0 \ 0 \ 3 \\
\qquad \vdots \\
+ \ 9 \ 9 \ 9 \ 9 \ 8 \\
+ \ 9 \ 9 \ 9 \ 9 \ 9
\end{array}
$$

If we think of these words as integers (often written with leading zeros, such as +00001 meaning "one"), then every integer from -99999 to $+99999$ is represented uniquely, except for zero, which has two representations, +00000 and –00000. Note also that we cannot represent any integer less than -99999 or greater than $+99999$.

It is important to note at this time that:

a) each memory register may contain any of the 200,000 possible words, and it may contain different ones at different times;

b) each memory register must contain some word at all times.

A memory register might be visualized as a panel with six windows and six dials (Fig. 1.1): The window on the left may show only a plus (+) or minus (–), whereas each of the others may show one of the ten decimal digits 0, 1, 2, 3, 4, 5, 6, 7, 8, 9. Any sign and five-decimal digit combination may be set in the register.

How do we refer to these memory registers? Since there are 1000 identical registers, we must *name* them to differentiate among them. We do so by giving each one a unique three-digit name called an **address**. The register in Fig. 1.1 is number

Register No.

Figure 1.1

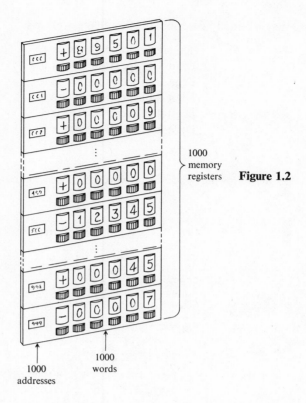

1000 memory registers   **Figure 1.2**

1000 addresses   1000 words

745. The 1000 addresses are the set of three-digit numbers: {000, 001, 002, ..., 998, 999}. The address of a register never changes; its contents (the word it contains) do.

Often we refer to registers as **locations**. In particular, when we refer to the contents of a register, we say "the contents of location such-and-such are so-and-so" —specifically we might say "the contents of location 745 are +38216." We abbreviate this by saying "C(745) = +38216."

The FACET memory is a sequence of these registers, beginning with the first one (location 000) and ending with the last (location 999), such as that depicted in Fig. 1.2. The following statements are true of the memory configuration shown in the figure:

$$C(000) = +89501$$
$$C(001) = -00000$$
$$C(002) = +00009$$

We further define **digit positions** within a word. The digits are numbered consecutively from left to right with numbers one through five. The sign position in a word is simply referred to as the **sign**. In the memory configuration illustrated above we may explicitly describe location 998 as follows:

The sign of location 998 is +.
Digit 1 of location 998 is 0.
Digit 2 of location 998 is 0.
Digit 3 of location 998 is 0.
Digit 4 of location 998 is 4.
Digit 5 of location 998 is 5.

Exercises 1.4

Assume that the following sequence of words has been placed into memory registers 625 through 635:

625	+	1	1	6	3	0
626	+	2	1	6	3	3
627	+	1	2	6	2	7
628	+	1	1	6	3	2
629	+	1	2	6	3	0
630	+	1	1	6	3	0
631	+	1	2	6	3	2
632	+	1	1	6	3	4
633	+	4	2	6	2	7
634	+	4	2	6	3	0
635	+	0	0	0	0	0

1. Complete the following:

   a) C(627) =
   b) C(630) =
   c) C(635) =

2. Complete the following:

   a) sign of location 629 =   b) digit 1 of location 634 =
   c) digit 2 of location 628 =   d) digit 3 of location 633 =
   e) digit 4 of location 635 =   f) digit 5 of location 630 =

3. Which of the following numbers can be represented in the FACET computer integer representation scheme?

   a) −439   b) 50   c) $\frac{3}{4}$
   d) 5 million   e) 99,999   f) 40,321
   g) 403,212   h) 0.005   i) π
   j) 5×10^{12}

4. How many different configurations can the FACET memory have? You may think of a memory configuration as a record of the entire contents of the memory. Two memory configurations are "unequal" if *any* sign or digit in some location of one is different from the corresponding sign or digit of the other. One possible configuration is that in which every register contains +00000. Another is where all contain +00000 except for location 745, which contains −38216.

1.5 THE ACCUMULATOR

The **accumulator** is another register in the FACET computer, structurally identical to the memory registers. It contains, at any time, one word (a sign and five digits).

```
ACC    | − | 0 | 0 | 0 | 7 | 0 |
```

Functionally, however, it is different from the memory registers. Let us first see how we intend to use the memory before further describing the accumulator.

We are interested in placing numbers into the memory, performing certain arithmetic and other operations on these numbers, obtaining new numbers as a result, and finally printing the results. For example, let us say that we have two numbers in memory, in locations 556 and 557, and we are interested in adding these together and placing the sum in location 558. If the memory registers of our computer were to perform this operation, *each* of the registers would have to be wired for addition (remember, the registers are identical). Similarly, they would each have to be wired for other desired operations. The cost would be exorbitant. Instead, we set up the memory so that we may only place words into it and copy words out of it. All other operations are performed in special registers. The accumulator is such a register. It is the register where arithmetic and certain other operations are performed. We may copy words from the memory into the accumulator, perform operations, and place the results back into the memory.

The situation is somewhat analogous to a man with an electric calculator. If he has many additions to perform, he comes with all pertinent numbers written on a sheet of paper (the "memory"). He then enters numbers of interest into the calculator (the accumulator), performs the operations, and copies the results onto his paper (again, the "memory").

Without further ado, let us write our first computer program. It will consist of a sequence of instructions to the FACET computer to print two numbers (from the memory), add them together, and print their sum. The two numbers are 15 and 33, and they are located in locations 200 and 300, respectively. We use two other registers in our program, location 400 and the accumulator. Their initial contents are not of concern to us (of course, they contain something—all registers do at all times).

We write the following instructions:

1. Print the contents of location 200.
2. Print the contents of location 300.

3. Load the contents of location 200 into the accumulator.
4. Add the contents of location 300 into the accumulator.
5. Store the contents of the accumulator in location 400.
6. Print the contents of location 400.
7. Halt.

Now we shall watch the contents of each of the registers of concern, as well as the printout paper, during the execution of this program.

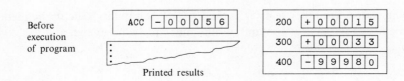

1. Print contents of location 200.

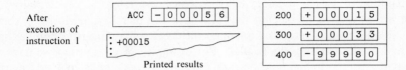

2. Print contents of location 300.

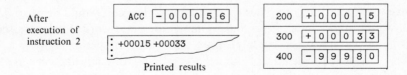

3. Load contents of location 200 into the accumulator.

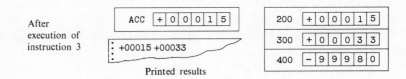

4. Add the contents of location 300 into the accumulator.

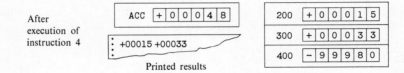

5. Store the contents of the accumulator in location 400.

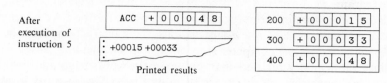

6. Print the contents of location 400.

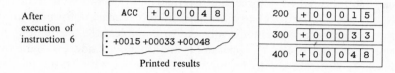

7. Halt.

You have probably noticed some very important points while following the execution of this program. We now state these points explicitly:

1. Every register contains some word (number) at all times. In particular, locations 400 and the accumulator contained numbers which were initially of no interest to us—they were probably left there during a previous calculation.

2. The contents of a register are unchanged unless some instruction explicitly changes them. When we print the contents of a register, those contents are printed on the paper, but they also remain in the register. The contents of the accumulator are not affected during printing. When we move a number from a memory register to the accumulator (**load** instruction) or from the accumulator to a memory register (**store** instruction), that number is merely copied. The source register (be it memory or accumulator) still retains the original number.

3. When a number is placed in a register, the previous contents of that register are destroyed. No trace of them remains.

4. We may print only the contents of a *memory* register. There is no instruction for printing the contents of the accumulator. If we want to print the number in the accumulator, we must first copy it into (store it in) a memory register.

5. The last instruction to be executed in a program must be the "halt" instruction.

Exercises 1.5

1. We have just introduced five types of instructions: print, load, add, store, and halt. Describe each of them explicitly. What does each cause the computer to do?

2. Using the five instructions we already know, write the following "programs":
   a) a program which computes two times the number in location 999, and then prints it;
   b) a program which (computes and) prints the sum of the numbers in locations 557, 693, and 842.

1.6 INSTRUCTIONS

In the program we have just written, we used five instructions: print, load accumulator, add, store in memory, and halt. In order for the FACET computer to follow a program or sequence of instructions, these instructions must be available to it. Where does the computer store them? In the memory, along with the data. Since the memory registers may only contain words (sign and five digits), we must **code** the instructions and place them into successive memory locations.

Instructions are coded as follows. Each instruction is coded as a two-digit **operation code** followed by a three-digit **operand**. The operation code defines the instruction (what is to be done), and the operand gives further information, such as the address of the memory register involved. An example is the instruction "print," whose operation code is 42. The operand is any three-digit address, signifying the location whose contents are to be printed. The instruction "print the number stored in location 200" is coded as +42200. Note that the operation code precedes the operand in the coding and that the sign is plus (+). Now we shall define all five instructions we have used explicitly, giving their operation codes (often known as **op-codes**), a three- or four-letter code representing the instruction, called a **mnemonic**† code, and a description of the behavior of the FACET machine while executing the instruction.

Instruction	Mnemonic code	Op-code	Description
Print number	PNUM	42	When the instruction +42nnn is executed (where nnn is any three-digit number), the contents of location nnn are printed as a signed five-digit number. The contents of location nnn are unchanged.
Load accumulator	LDAC	11	When the instruction +11nnn is executed (where nnn is any three-digit number), the contents of location nnn are loaded (copied) into the accumulator. The contents of location nnn are unchanged. The previous contents of the accumulator are lost.

† The word mnemonic (pronounced ni-mon'ik) means "helping, or meant to help, the memory." All sorts of words and codes are chosen mnemonically in computer programming, and the word "mnemonic" is used quite frequently by computer people. However, you might not catch it, since it is often mispronounced (as noo-mon'ik).

Add into accumulator	ADD	21	When the instruction +21nnn is executed (again, nnn is any three-digit number), the contents of location nnn, considered as an integer, are added to the contents of the accumulator, also considered as an integer. The sum is stored in the accumulator, replacing its previous contents. The contents of location nnn are unchanged.
Store accumulator in memory	STAC	12	When the instruction +12nnn is executed, the contents of the accumulator are stored in location nnn, destroying the previous contents of that location. The accumulator does not change.
Halt	HALT	00	When the instruction +00nnn is executed, the FACET computer stops executing the current program. The three digits nnn are ignored.

We are now ready to write the program in its encoded form:

Original program

1. Print contents of location 200.
2. Print contents of location 300.
3. Load C(200) into accumulator.
4. Add C(300) into accumulator.
5. Store accumulator in location 400.
6. Print contents of location 400.
7. Halt.

Coded program

+	4 2	2 0 0
+	4 2	3 0 0
+	1 1	2 0 0
+	2 1	3 0 0
+	1 2	4 0 0
+	4 2	4 0 0
+	0 0	0 0 0

Operands

Operation codes

Now we have **coded** the seven-instruction program into a sequence of seven FACET words. If the FACET computer is to **execute** the program, the program must be placed into the memory. Where in the memory? In any seven consecutive memory registers that do not include the registers in which data will be placed. There is plenty of room since the data will only occupy three memory registers—200, 300, and 400. This leaves locations 000–199, 201–299, 301–399, and 401–999. Let's arbitrarily choose locations 795–801. We must somehow get our program and data into memory as shown in Fig. 1.3.

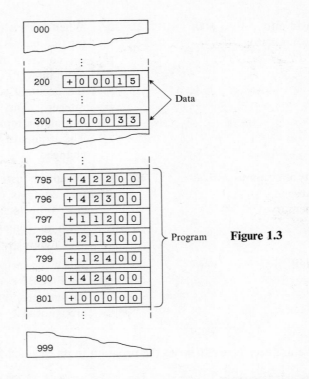

Figure 1.3

Note that although we do not place anything into location 400, that location will be used to store data during the execution of the program. The next obvious questions are "How do we get numbers into the FACET memory?" and "How do we tell it where the first instruction to be executed is located?" We deal with these questions in the next section.

Exercises 1.6

1. Following is some information about the contents of some memory location:

$$C(203) = +00045$$
$$C(499) = +00031$$
$$C(520) = -00030$$
$$C(603) = +00002$$

Write a program (sequence of instructions) using only these data to compute and print:

a) +00001   b) +00004   c) +00005
d) +00015   e) −00015   f) −00010

2. Write a program which prints the contents of the accumulator.

3. Write a program which copies the contents of location 753 into location 098. What would the accumulator contain immediately after the execution of this program?

4. Write a program which exchanges the numbers in memory registers 871 and 872.

5. Why should there be a HALT instruction at the end of a program?

6. Suppose the accumulator contains –50000 and location 217 contains +60055. What would these two registers contain after the instruction +11217 is executed?

7. Suppose C(Accumulator) = +00032 and C(560) = –00031.   If the instruction +12560 were executed, what would these two registers then contain?

8. C(900) = +11111 and C(Accumulator) = –22222. After the execution of instruction +42900,

   a) C(900) = ?   b) C(Accumulator) = ?

1.7 THE LOADER

The FACET machine has a special processor called the **loader**. It is the job of the loader to load (or place) words into the memory. These words are, of course, signed five-digit numbers, the only kind of object that the memory may contain. The loader reads these words from 80-column punched cards and places them into specified memory locations. Of course you must learn to use a keypunch machine in order to punch these numbers onto the cards. For example, let us take location 200, into which we want to place the word +00015. We then punch a card as follows:

Columns 1–3   the address, 200
Columns 4–6   blank
Columns 7–12   the word to be loaded into memory, i.e., +00015
Columns 13–14   blank
Columns 15–80   anything, comments, blanks, etc.

The card might look like Fig. 1.4 when punched.

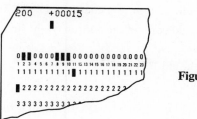

Figure 1.4

The loader does not differentiate between words which are intended to be instructions and words which represent data (numbers). So all words which are to be placed into the memory are punched on cards in a similar way. The order of the cards hardly matters, since each item has an address with it. When you have punched all nine cards, they might look like those shown in Fig. 1.5.

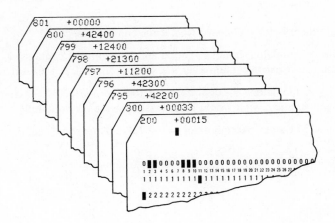

Figure 1.5

Now there are a few special cards that must be punched in order for you to *submit* your program to the computer. They are as follows:

a) *The* START. *card*

Columns 1–6 should contain the characters START. (including the period).

Columns 7–10 are left blank.

Columns 11–40 should contain your name.

Columns 41–70 should contain the name of your program.

Columns 71–78 should contain the bin number where your program should be returned (or left blank).

b) *The* LØAD. *card*

Columns 1–5 should contain LØAD. (including the period).

Columns 6–8 must be blank.

c) *The* EXECUTE. *card*

Columns 1–8 should contain the characters EXECUTE. (including the period).

Columns 9–11 should contain the address of the first instruction in your program (in our case, 795).

Columns 12–16 should be blank.

d) *The* FINISH. *card*

Columns 1–7 should contain FINISH. (including the period).

Column 8 should be blank.

e) *The* ENDJØB. *card*

Columns 1–7 should contain ENDJØB. (including the period).

Column 8 should be blank.

These special cards are often called **control cards**.

The START. card identifies you and your program. The LØAD. card tells the loader that the cards following it should be loaded into the FACET memory. The EXECUTE. card then tells the computer that the program it has just loaded should be executed beginning with location such-and-such. The FINISH. and ENDJØB. cards are placed at the end. Your entire **deck** now might look like that shown in Fig. 1.6.

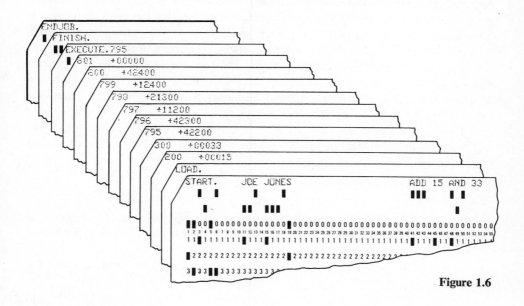

Figure 1.6

At your particular computer facility there might be a few more cards which must be placed at the beginning and end of the deck, but your instructor will either give them to you or tell you how to punch them. Their meaning should not concern you at this point; more will be said about such cards later. When you **submit** this deck to the computer it is called a **job** or task for the computer to do. At this point you should actually write, punch, and submit a program to the FACET computer.

Note. Your instructor might ask you to omit the ENDJØB. card from your program. If he does, it is very important that you comply. More will be said about this in Chapter 3.

Exercises 1.7

1. List at least two advantages of punching comments onto your program deck (in columns 15–80).

2. Write, punch, and submit a program to the FACET computer which computes and prints the sum of the three integers 1342, −987, and 469. Your work is not done until the program loads and executes properly.

1.8 YOUR JOB

When completed, your deck is placed into a **card reader**, which is a machine that reads punched cards into the computer. This is the **load phase** of your job. Words are placed mechanically into the memory. These words may or may not be instructions—they are signed five-digit numbers and are placed according to your specification into given memory registers. It is your responsibility as a programmer to make sure that among the words placed into the memory is a sequence of instructions, your program. The second phase of your job is the **execute phase**. During this phase, the FACET machine interprets certain words in memory as instructions and executes these instructions. If it encounters a word in the program sequence which is not an instruction, such as +98320, it will stop and print a message telling you that it encountered an **illegal instruction**. The computer is a machine and can never deduce "what you really mean" when you err in your program or when you mispunch a card. It will merely print a message that such-and-such an error was encountered—and it is up to you to correct the error and resubmit the job.

Exercises 1.8

1. What is the essential difference between these three programs? How do their printed results differ? Assume that locations 109 and 110 contain +00120 and +00256, respectively.

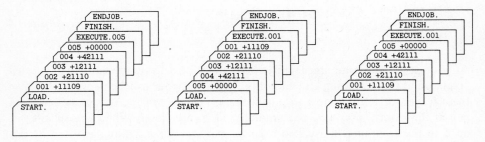

2. Describe and justify the need for two distinct phases during the running of your job by the FACET computer (i.e., the load phase and the execute phase).

1.9 DATA AND INSTRUCTIONS

Data and instructions are indistinguishable to the computer. To illustrate this, we shall write a few programs which use instructions as data and vice versa. The first program is a two-instruction program placed into locations 199 and 200 of the memory as follows:

199	+	4	2	1	9	9
200	+	0	0	0	0	0

If this program were, in fact, placed into the memory and executed, beginning with location 199, what would happen? The first instruction says, "Print the contents of location 199," but what are the contents of location 199? Why, the number +42199, and that is exactly what is printed. The next instruction says, "Halt," and so the machine halts. So this is a program for printing the number +42199 (which also happens to be an instruction). Note that if the program had been placed elsewhere in the memory, it would still have printed the contents of location 199, whatever they happened to be.

The next program is slightly more complicated. Before reading the explanation below, try to figure out what happens when this program is executed. The first instruction to be executed is in location 850.

850	+	1	1	8	5	0
851	+	2	1	8	5	3
852	+	1	2	8	5	3
853	+	3	1	0	0	1
854	+	0	0	0	0	0

The computer, of course, carries out this sequence of instructions very mechanically, no matter how silly it may seem to you. The instruction at location 850 says, "Load the contents of location 850 into the accumulator," so the number +11850 is placed into the accumulator. The next instruction is in location 851, and it states, "Add the contents of location 853 to the accumulator," and so +31001 is added to the accumulator, which already contains +11850, resulting in +42851 in the accumulator. Next is the instruction at location 852 stating, "Store the contents of the accumulator into location 853," and so +42851 is placed into location 853! Now the processor executes the instruction at location 853—the instruction *currently* at location 853, not the one which was there previously. The previous word is no longer there (nor anywhere, for that matter). The instruction at location 853 says, "Print the contents of location 851," since its code is +42851, and so +21853 is printed. Finally, location 854 contains the HALT instruction, and the processor terminates the program.

The lesson to be learned in the previous example is an important one. The computer slavishly goes through its cycle of interpreting instructions and carrying them out without questioning their meaning and without knowing what is data and what is program. Indeed, locations may contain words which are both. Data may be executed (if they are valid instructions), and instructions may be computed (as data) and placed into memory registers where they will be executed as instructions. The computer merely follows the ground rules. The rest is up to you, the programmer.

Programs which intermix instructions and data are the exception rather than the rule. Instructions and data are usually kept separated in the memory. However, this is the task of the programmer, not the computer. To the computer, all the memory registers look alike and each contains merely a word, a sign, and five digits. The "meaning" of a given word is unknown to the computer, until the time comes to execute it (in which case it is an "instruction") or to place it in the accumulator or operate on it in some other way (in which case it is "data").

Exercises 1.9

1. What determines whether the contents of a memory register will be used as an instruction or as data by the computer?

2. Write a FACET program which prints the number 102 (+00102). How short can you make this program? Can you have just two words loaded into the memory?

3. For the memory configuration of Exercise 1.4, what is printed if execution of the "program" begins at:

    a) location 635?   b) location 634?   c) location 632?

    d) location 630?   e) location 628?   f) location 625?

1.10 IN REVIEW

This book deals with the general-purpose digital computer. The first seven chapters will specifically discuss the FACET computer. However, the concepts dealt with and the terms introduced are general.

Both data and programs (sequences of instructions) are stored in the FACET memory. This memory consists of 1000 identical registers labeled from 000 to 999. These three-digit labels are called addresses. Each register, or location, contains (at any given time) a sign and five decimal digits called a word. A word may serve as an instruction, a piece of data, or both. Arithmetic operations are performed in a special register in the FACET machine called the accumulator. Data may be moved back and forth between the memory registers and the accumulator.

Five instructions available in the FACET computer are LDAC (load accumulator from memory), STAC (store accumulator in memory), ADD (add from memory into accumulator), PNUM (print number from memory register), and HALT. Their respective op-codes are 11, 12, 21, 42, and 00. An op-code (or operation code) constitutes the first two digits of an instruction as coded in a memory word. The other three digits are the operand.

A program to be executed in the FACET machine must first be punched onto cards, one word per card. This program together with some special cards called control cards constitute a deck. The deck is submitted to the computer, and it is called a job. The job passes through two phases: first is the load phase, during which the computer loads all the words in the deck into specified memory registers; second is the execute phase, during which the program now in memory is executed, beginning with the instruction at a specified location. The last instruction to be executed must be the HALT instruction.

The computer does all this mechanically, slavishly. It is merely a machine following a fixed sequence of operations. It is the programmer, you, who is responsible for submitting meaningful programs.

Chapter 2

LOOPS,
FLOWCHARTS,
AND
MORE
INSTRUCTIONS

2.1 INTRODUCTION

Key programming concepts will be presented in this chapter. Be sure that you understand this chapter well and that you have tried a number of the programming exercises before proceeding to succeeding chapters. We shall introduce ten new instructions (op-codes) and we shall discuss programming logic, loops and loop control, flowcharts (a pictorial method for representing programs), and algorithms. Debugging, or finding and correcting program errors, will also be discussed. By the end of this chapter you should be equipped to write fairly sophisticated programs for the FACET machine.

2.2 THE JUMP INSTRUCTION

Computers are often most useful when they do large repetitive tasks, such as payrolls or inventory control. The solution of complex systems of mathematical equations also requires many repetitive operations. Such tasks may be accomplished by programs in which sequences of instructions are executed again and again. In Chapter 1 we learned that instructions are executed from consecutive memory locations. In order to repeat a sequence of instructions, we must have an instruction which breaks this sequential order of execution. Such an instruction is the **jump** (also called the **transfer**) instruction.

In our FACET machine the JUMP instruction has op-code 31, and its three-digit operand specifies the location from which the next instruction is to be taken. For example, assume that the three-instruction program placed into locations 100, 101, 200, and 201 (location 201 does not contain an instruction) is as follows:

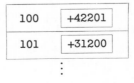

200	+00000
201	−00578

If we begin execution at location 100, then the following sequence is executed:

1. The instruction at location 100 is PNUM; the number at location 201 (it's −00578) is printed.

2. The instruction at location 101 is JUMP; take the next instruction from location 200.

3. The instruction at location 200 is HALT.

What do you think the following sequence of instructions accomplishes when executed beginning with location 980? Try it before reading the explanation below.

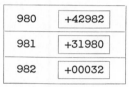

980	+42982
981	+31980
982	+00032

It prints the contents of location 982 (the number +00032) over and over again. Unless some person or device other than the FACET machine we have discussed so far intervenes, it will go on forever. Such a repetitive sequence of instructions is known as a **loop**. Before discussing how to "get out of the loop" we have another example. What does this program do? Execution begins at location 750.

750	+42755
751	+11755
752	+21755
753	+12755
754	+31750
755	+00001

Location 750 contains the print instruction; it prints the number in location 755 (it is +00001 to begin with). The next three instructions, locations 751 through 753 double the contents of location 755! They do so by adding the number in 755 to itself and storing the sum back in location 755. Finally, the JUMP instruction in location 754 starts the sequence over again. The second time +00002 will be printed, then +00004, +00008, +00016, and so on. The program prints nonnegative powers of two: $2^0, 2^1, 2^2, 2^3, \ldots$, and so on without end. It does so by executing a five-instruction loop.

Again, no provision has been made for halting. Most computers have some means of halting an endless loop—a timer, an operator who eventually pushes a stop button, and so forth. The FACET computer also has such devices, but they will be specified later. Actually, we are not interested in writing programs with endless loops, so we shall now discuss means of **exiting** from loops. Before we do so, we call your attention to one other item—one which you have probably already noticed. The largest number that a memory register can contain is +99999. Our program will print powers of two, which very quickly exceed that number:

1

2

4

8

16

32

64

128

256

512

1024

2048

4096

8192

16384

32768

65536

131072

After printing only 17 numbers, we already have computed one which is too large for the memory register. What happens when a sum requires more than five digits? The answer to that one is a bit complex, so we shall deal with such a situation separately in a section called **overflow**. Meanwhile, we can write programs which deal with data less than 100,000 in absolute value.

Exercises 2.2

1. What does this program print? Does it halt or stay in an endless loop? Explain.

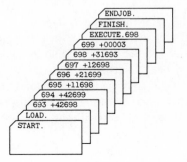

2. Can we get overflow by adding negative numbers to one another? by adding a positive number to a negative number?

3. What does this program print? Will it cause overflow? If it will, after how many times through the loop? Execution begins in location 440.

440	+11443
441	+21444
442	+31446
443	+00400
444	+00002
445	−00003
446	+21445
447	+12443
448	+42443
449	+31441

2.3 CONDITIONAL JUMPS—DECISIONS

The JUMP instruction causes an *unconditional* change in the sequence of instructions being executed. We now introduce three instructions which cause a change in the sequence of execution only under *certain* conditions. These instructions are called **conditional** jumps (or transfers). They provide means for **exiting** from a loop and for selecting one of several alternative steps in a process.

Instruction	Mnemonic code	Op-code	Description
Jump on negative accumulator	JNEG	32	Jump to the instruction whose address is given by the operand if the sign of the accumulator is minus (−). If the sign is plus (+), continue to the next instruction.
Jump on positive accumulator	JPØS	33	Jump to the instruction whose address is given by the operand if the sign of the accumulator is plus (+). If the sign is minus (−), continue to the next instruction.
Jump on zero accumulator	JZER	34	Jump to the instruction whose address is given by the operand if the accumulator is zero (either +00000 or −00000). Otherwise, continue on to the next instruction in the sequence.

Note that the effect of these instructions is determined by the condition of the accumulator.

The next example is a program which prints a number only under certain conditions. What are they? The program is executed beginning in location 600.

The number in question is in location 604 and is arbitrary. We have chosen –77777 as an example, but any number might have been chosen. What are the conditions?

600	+11604
601	+32603
602	+42604
603	+00000
604	–77777

The program says: Place the number in question into the accumulator and jump to the HALT instruction if the sign of the accumulator is minus (–). Otherwise execute the next instruction in the sequence (print the number) and *then* halt. So the program prints a number only if it is positive. If we had placed +77777 into location 604, it would have been printed. But with this example, nothing is printed.

Next we have a program which has a loop with an **exit**. It is a bit complicated, but again, try to figure out what it does before you read the explanation. Execution begins at location 000.

000	+42200
001	+11200
002	+21100
003	+34006
004	+12200
005	+31000
006	+00000

| 100 | +00001 |

| 200 | –00010 |

Did you figure it out? If we ignore the instruction in location 003, it is a simple loop for printing the number in location 200, adding one to it ("one" is stored in location 100), and then printing it again. Ordinarily this would be an endless loop. But each time we add one, we check if the number is zero (the instruction in location 003 checks if the accumulator is zero; if it is, we jump to location 006 and halt).

Since the number starts out at -10, we print -10, then -9, -8, through -1, and then halt. We have a loop with an exit.

Now we return to the program which prints (nonnegative) powers of two, and we insert an exit in the loop. How many powers of two are printed? Execution begins at location 750. Since op-codes are sometimes difficult to remember, we shall place the mnemonic code for the op-code next to each instruction henceforth.

750	+42758	PNUM
751	+11758	LDAC
752	+21758	ADD
753	+12758	STAC
754	+21759	ADD
755	+33757	JPØS
756	+31750	JUMP
757	+00000	HALT
758	+00001	(number)
759	−01000	(constant −1000)

The actual instructions are in locations 750 through 757, the data and **constants** are in locations 758 and 759 (location 759 contains a constant, a number which is used but never changed during the execution of the program). Location 758 contains the power of two, beginning with 1. The first four instructions (750 through 753) are as before, print the number, double it, and store it back into the memory. Now we get to location 754. Recall that the new number, now stored in the memory in location 758, is still in the accumulator as well, since the store instruction (STAC) leaves the accumulator unchanged. To this number we add -1000 (in effect, we subtract $+1000$). If the accumulator is *now* positive, the number originally there will have been greater than 999. In this case we jump to the HALT instruction. Otherwise we jump back to location 750 and repeat the sequence. The program therefore prints all nonnegative powers of two which are three digits or less. The first four-digit power of two will cause an exit from the loop and a halt.

Conditional jump instructions allow us to write programs in which **decisions** are made. These decisions pertain to which intruction is to be executed next, and are generally dependent on data. For example: "If number X is positive, do this," or "If number Y is negative, do that." Note that in the last program our decision was based on whether a certain number was greater than 999. Although the only instructions for decisions are JNEG, JPØS, and JZER, more complex decisions may be programmed by employing additional computations.

Exercises 2.3

1. If the accumulator contains zero, a JPØS instruction may or may not cause a jump to take place. Why?

2. The JZER instruction can be eliminated, and the same results can be achieved by substituting an appropriate sequence of other instructions, including JUMP, JPØS, and JNEG. This is a bit complicated, but if you assume that zero is represented only by +00000 (and never by −00000), the task becomes easier. Make this assumption and explain how you would then be able to eliminate JZER from a program.

3. Write and submit a program which prints the numbers from 100 down to zero and then stops: 100, 99, 98, . . . , 2, 1, 0.

4. The JPØS instruction is not really necessary for decisions. Programs using this instruction may be rewritten using other instructions which achieve the same result.

   a) Justify the statement above.
   b) Rewrite the program which prints one- to three-digit powers of two without using the JPØS instruction.

5. Assume that location 100 contains an arbitrary number which we shall refer to as N.

   a) Write a program which will print:
      i. +00001 if the sign of N is plus (+);
      ii. −00001 if the sign of N is minus (−).

   b) Write a program which will examine N and then:
      i. if $N > 200$, double N and print the result;
      ii. if $N \leq 200$, print N itself.
      The program then halts.

   c) Write a program which will examine N and then:
      i. if $N \geq 10$, print +00010 and halt;
      ii. if $-10 < N < +10$, print +00000 and then halt;
      iii. if $N \leq -10$, print −00010 and halt.

   The programs should work regardless of the value of the number in location 100.

6. Assume that the following has been loaded into the memory:

398	+11408	LDAC
399	+33403	JPØS
400	+31404	JUMP
401	+12408	STAC
402	+42408	PNUM
403	+00000	HALT
404	+21409	ADD
405	+34403	JZER
406	+32404	JNEG
407	+31401	JUMP
408	−00003	(number)
409	+00002	(number)

If the program begins execution at location 398, then:

a) Write down the instructions in the order in which they are executed. Write down each instruction *each* time it is executed.
b) What is printed?

2.4 FLOWCHARTS

It is rather cumbersome, to say the least, to look at a sequence of instructions and figure out what it does. As programs get longer and longer (and they do) the problem gets worse and worse. We now present a semipictorial way of representing a program. It is called a **flowchart**. A flowchart consists of a number of enclosures (rectangles, ovals) connected by arrows. It is a schematic method for representing the action performed by a program.

Instead of referring to specific memory registers in the flowchart, we shall refer to them by **names**, such as A, B, N, X, etc. We do this because it generally doesn't matter exactly where in the memory we store our data so long as they can be retrieved. For example, let us take the program in Chapter 1 in which we print two numbers, add them together, and print their sum. Recall that the numbers were 15 and 33, which were stored in locations 200 and 300, respectively. Our flowchart would look like that shown in Fig. 2.1.

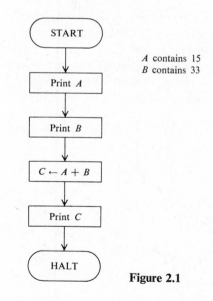

Figure 2.1

Everything in the flowchart is fairly self-explanatory except the box marked "$C \leftarrow A + B$." This is an abbreviation for "Add the contents of location A and location B, and store the results in C." In general, such notation is used whenever we change the value of some location. To the right of the arrow is some computation which results in the new number to be stored. To the left of the arrow is the name of the location into which the computed number is stored.

Flowcharts do not designate specific locations for either data or the program. Only when you actually write the program do you decide where in the memory to place instructions and data.

So far there are two kinds of boxes: the *oval*

for START and HALT, and the *procedure* box

for performing some operation.

A **procedure** box may correspond to one *or more* actual instructions. Each of the boxes stating "Print *A*" and "Print *B*" corresponds to a single instruction. The one stating "*C* ← *A* + *B*" corresponds to *three* instructions. **Mnemonically** (using the mnemonic codes) they may be written:

$$
\begin{array}{ll}
\text{LDAC} & \text{A} \\
\text{ADD} & \text{B} \\
\text{STAC} & \text{C}
\end{array}
$$

Figure 2.2 is a flowchart for one of the programs we have discussed. Try to determine which program before reading on. It is the program for printing powers of two, beginning with 1, 2, 4, 8, . . . , and continuing endlessly. Note that there is no HALT oval. The last box merely has an arrow back up to the "Print *N*" box, thereby closing the loop. Again, the box marked "*N* ← *N* + *N*" means "Add the contents of location *N* to the contents of location *N*, storing the results in location

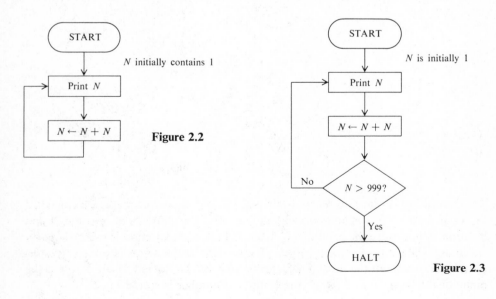

Figure 2.2

Figure 2.3

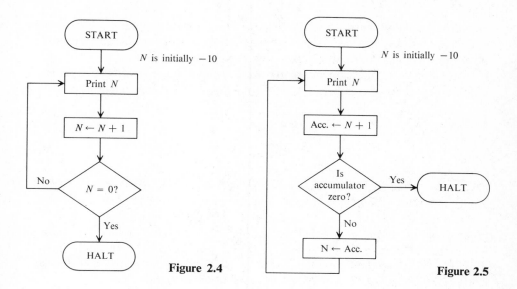

Figure 2.4   **Figure 2.5**

N"—or, in other words, "double N." Note that the value of location N does not change until after the computation to the right of the arrow is completed. Only then is the resulting number placed into the location named to the left of the arrow, namely N.

The arrows connecting the boxes depict the **flow** of your program; hence the name *flowchart*. Decisions usually mean that there are alternatives in the flowchart. These are implemented, you recall, with conditional jumps. Such instructions are also called **branch** instructions, since the flowchart **branches** at points where decisions are made. Figure 2.3 is a flowchart corresponding to still another program we have discussed. Again, try to determine which one before reading on. This is the program which prints nonnegative powers of two which are less than four digits. The diamond-shaped box is a **decision** box. The question asked in the decision box has a yes-no answer, and this answer determines the flow of the program, or the **branch** taken (and the next instruction executed). The question asked in the particular decision box in Fig. 2.3 is not one which corresponds to an actual instruction, so we must create a sequence of instructions which correspond to the question. Look at the powers-of-two program accompanying our original discussion and find that sequence of instructions. The question is "Is the number presently in N greater than 999?"

Now we shall draw the flowchart for the program which prints -10, -9, $-8, \ldots, -1$. We choose N as the location which contains the numbers to be printed. The flowchart is shown in Fig. 2.4. The actual instruction sequence does not follow the flowchart exactly. In the instruction sequence, after adding one to N, we first checked the accumulator to see if it was zero. If not, *then* we stored the result in location N (it was location 200 in the program) and looped back to continue. A more accurate flowchart would have been like that shown in Fig. 2.5.

However, such flowcharts only cloud the real issue, that is, what is going on—what is being computed and printed. We prefer never to mention the accumulator in flowcharts. We use the accumulator only during computations.

To summarize, decision boxes generally contain some statement asserting a relation between two numbers. All the following assert such a relation:

$$N = 0,$$
$$M < 5,$$
$$K + M - 2 > J,$$
$$A = B.$$

The question marks in the decision boxes ask, in effect, "Is this relation true?" Each decision box then has two exits: the first marked "yes" for the case in which the relation is true (i.e., that N *is* equal to 0, M *is* less than 5, $K + M - 2$ *is* greater than J, and A *does* equal B); the second is marked "no" for the case in which the relation is false (i.e., that N *is not* equal to 0, M *is not* less than 5, $K + M - 2$ *is not* greater than J, and A *does not* equal B). Other types of decision boxes are sometimes used, but we shall use only this type.

Exercises 2.4

1. Draw a flowchart corresponding to the program in Section 2.2 for printing the number 32 over and over again.

2. Draw a flowchart for a program which would print multiples of 7 in an endless loop: 0, 7, 14, 21, 28, 35, . . .

3. (a) Draw a flowchart for a FACET program which would print all multiples of 7 which are less than 1000. (b) Write and submit the program corresponding to this flowchart.

4. (a) Draw a flowchart for a program which computes $1 + 2 + 3 + \cdots + 50$. (b) Write and submit the corresponding FACET program. Of course, you know that

$$1 + 2 + \cdots + 50 = \sum_{n=1}^{50} n = \frac{50 \times 51}{2} = 1275,$$

so you can check to see whether the program worked.

5. Draw a flowchart for a program which prints 32 repeatedly 375 times.

6. Draw a flowchart for a program which prints the sequence 15, 14, 13, . . . through 3, 2, 1.

7. Draw a flowchart for a program which prints the number 15 fifteen times, then the number 14 fourteen times, and so forth, until it prints the number 3 three times, 2 twice, and 1 once. (*Hint:* you will need "nested loops," i.e., one loop inside another.)

8. Flowcharts are useful in problems other than straight numerical computation. For instance, Fig. 2.6 illustrates a flowchart for eating a meal in a restaurant. Can you follow it?

   Can you draw a similar one depicting Tom's scheme for traveling the 250 miles between his home and college by hitch-hiking, bus, or plane? Tom's choice depends on the weather, the amount of luggage he is carrying, his financial situation, and whether or

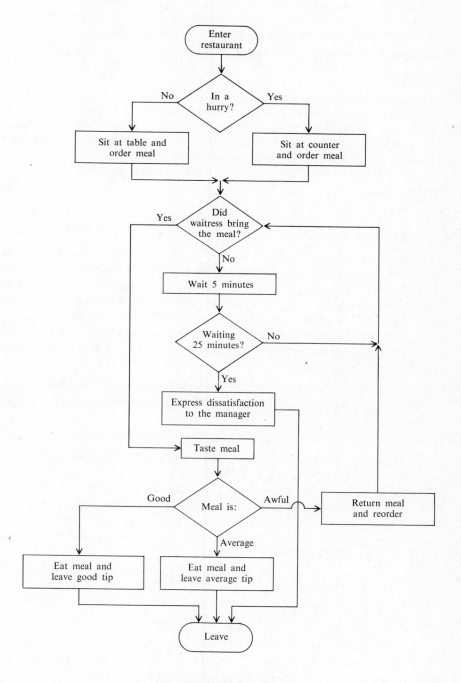

Figure 2.6

not his parents bought him tickets. Introduce conditions wherein Tom may travel part of the way by one mode of transportation and part by another. For instance, if he's waiting for more than ten hours for a hitch, he might take the bus.

9. Jimmy is a clockwatcher. He's always looking to see what time it is. As soon as it's exactly half-past the hour (every waking office hour) he performs the following actions in sequence:

   a) shaves if he hasn't shaved in more than seven hours;
   b) calls his wife if he hasn't seen a cute secretary within the past three hours;
   c) brushes his teeth if he hasn't called his wife in more than two hours or shaved in more than four—unless, of course, if he's seen a pretty secretary within the last hour, in which case he brushes his teeth regardless;
   d) gets a drink of water if he has not just shaved, brushed, or called.

   Draw a flowchart for Jimmy's actions on the half-hour. Construct the flowchart so as to eliminate unnecessary decisions.

2.5 INPUT AND OUTPUT

All the programs we have written so far have been written with specific data in mind; that is, we loaded the program *together* with the data on which the program was to operate, and then executed the program. In general, we want to write programs which operate on arbitrary data. Rather than writing a program which adds 15 and 33, we prefer to write a program which adds any two numbers. In order to do this we must be able to load the program and then have the program itself read data into the memory and operate on them. We gain a number of advantages by doing this:

1) The data, punched on cards, would not have to be assigned to specific memory locations. The program would take care of reading the data into appropriate locations.

2) Different sets of data could be operated on by the same program.

Here we introduce the instruction "Read a number." Its op-code is 41 and its mnemonic code is RNUM. The execution of the instruction +41nnn causes a single data card to be *read* and its contents deposited in location nnn in the memory. Let's write a program which reads two numbers, prints them, and prints their sum. The numbers will be stored in locations 100 and 200, their sum in location 300. We name these locations A, B, and C, respectively, for use in the **mnemonic program** written to the right of the actual program.

800	+41100	RNUM	A
801	+42100	PNUM	A
803	+41200	RNUM	B
804	+42200	PNUM	B
805	+11100	LDAC	A
806	+21200	ADD	B

807	+12300	STAC	C
808	+42300	PNUM	C
809	+00000	HALT	

Translated into English, the program says:

1. Read the first data card, store the number thereon in location 100.
2. Print the contents of location 100.
3. Read the next card, store the number thereon in location 200.
4. Print the contents of location 200.
5. Place the contents of location 100 into the accumulator.
6. Add the contents of location 200 into the accumulator.
7. Store the contents of the accumulator in location 300.
8. Print the contents of location 300.
9. Halt.

Data to be read by a program are punched, one to a card, in columns 1 through 6. The number 15, for instance, would be punched as shown in Fig. 2.7.

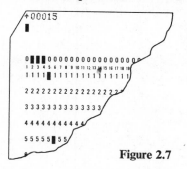

Figure 2.7

Place the data (to be read by your program) between the EXECUTE. card and the FINISH. card. These data must be in the order you expect them to be read. Every time a RNUM instruction is executed in your program, the *next* card is read. Once the card is read, your program cannot re-read it. Therefore, be careful to save the number just read in a memory location if it will be needed later in the program.

If your program attempts to read a card and there is none there (that is, it attempts to read the FINISH. card), the program will be terminated with an **error message**. The program should therefore be written so that it reads the right amount of data. Various examples throughout the rest of the chapter will suggest methods you may employ to accomplish this.

If, in fact, you were interested in adding 15 and 33, you might submit the job shown in Fig. 2.8. When you do this (and you might try it to see what happens), your **program** is loaded into the memory during the **load phase**—into specified

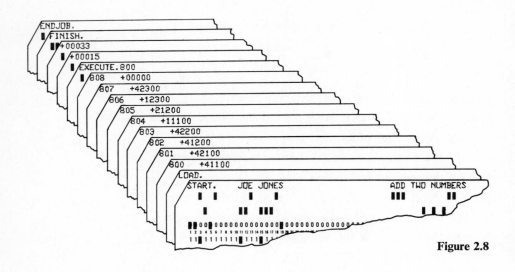

Figure 2.8

memory locations, of course. The **data** are read into the memory (by your program) during the **execute phase**. This program adds *any* two numbers, so those two data cards may be replaced by any other two data cards, and the program will operate on the two new numbers. Of course, there must be two properly punched data cards present after the EXECUTE. card. If more than two are present, the first two will be used and the rest ignored. If two aren't present, your program will terminate with a **reading error**.

All the data that are read into the memory during the execution of your program (in our case, by RNUM instructions being executed) are lumped under the general name **input**. The word *input* is also used as a verb ("to input data"), as well as a noun (to designate the process by which data are inserted into the memory under your program's control). **Output**, on the other hand, refers to the printing process (in our case) and can similarly be used as various parts of speech in computer jargon.

Exercises 2.5

1. You are given three consecutive data cards containing three numbers; let's call the numbers A, B, and C. Write a program which reads these three numbers and then computes and prints $3A + B + 2C$.

2. Write a program which reads five numbers from five consecutive data cards and then computes and prints:

   a) the sum of the first, third, and fifth numbers;
   b) the sum of the second and fourth numbers;

c) the sum of all five numbers;

d) twice the sum of the five numbers.

3. You have just been given a rather large deck of punched cards. Each card contains (punched in columns 1 through 6) a *positive* signed, five-digit integer. You want to print the list of numbers. You do *not* want to count the cards. If you write a FACET program to read and print the numbers, your program may try to read beyond the last card (causing error termination). To prevent this, you place another data card, a *negative* integer, at the back of the data deck. Detection of the negative number is used as a signal to exit from the loop. Draw a flowchart and write a program for printing the positive numbers in the deck and then halting.

2.6 LOADING VS. READING

You now know two methods of getting numbers into the computer: Numbers can be **loaded** into memory during the **load** phase. Numbers can also be **read** into the memory during the **execution** of your program. Each method has its characteristic use. Numbers which are loaded with a program are part of that program; their values are known at the time the program is written. Each time the program is used these numbers (their values unchanged) are again loaded with the program. Numbers which are read into the memory by your program are known as **data**. These are the values which are likely to change during different **runs** (instances of execution) of a program. Indeed, their values are usually unknown to you when you write the program.

Thus it is bad practice to have a number whose initial value never changes read in with the data. This number should be *loaded* with the program. Similarly, numbers which change during different runs of the program are data, and should be *read in* by the program.

Let's make these points more explicit with an example: We have written one program which adds 15 and 33, printing the sum; and another which reads two numbers, adds them, and prints their sum. If, in fact, we are interested only in the sum of 15 and 33, the first program is appropriate: In it 15 and 33 are loaded as part of the program. Of course that program will never do anything but add 15 and 33. On the other hand, we might be interested in a general program which adds *any* two numbers. In this case, the second program would be more appropriate, since the numbers to be added are data and may take on any two values.

The two programs are significantly different. When you write your programs, you should be careful to choose the more appropriate method for placing numbers into the memory.

Exercises 2.6

1. Discuss the differences between entering data at load time and at execution time. Enumerate and justify some instances in which loading data is "better," and some in which you would recommend the data be read.

2. What would the following program do? Discuss the implications of this example.

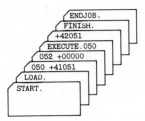

```
ENDJOB.
FINISH.
+42051
EXECUTE.050
052 +00000
050 +41051
LOAD.
START.
```

3. Which of the following data should be *loaded* with the program and which should be *read in* by the program at execution time?

   a) employee information in a payroll program;
   b) the constant π (3.14159...);
   c) student grades in a program for maintaining university records;
   d) the number 329.74, a constant in a mathematical computation;
   e) today's date, in an inventory report generating program.

2.7 LOOPS WITH A COUNTER

A loop with a counter is a loop which is **iterated** (repeated) some fixed number of times and is exited when the appropriate number of **iterations** is completed. One way to accomplish this is to have a special memory register which stores the number of times the sequence of instructions in the loop has been executed. Each time through the loop 1 is added to the contents of this register, which is called the **counter**. When we add 1 to the counter, we say that we **increment** the counter by one.

The next program we present is one which adds 20 numbers (these are data) and prints the numbers and their sum. The program will not read each number into a different location in the memory; the same location is used for each one. Look at the flowchart in Fig. 2.9 and see if you can figure out how it works. Note that there are three data locations used: N (a number from the list), S (the sum), and C (the counter).

The flowchart says:

1. Read the next number into location N (destroying the previous contents of that location).

2. Print the contents of location N.

3. Add the number in N to the number in S, storing the sum in S (S contains zero to begin with and thereafter contains a partial sum of the numbers read so far).

4. Increment the counter by one.

5. If the counter is 20, print the result (the sum S) and halt; otherwise go back to step 1.

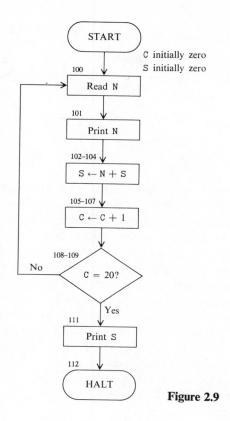

Figure 2.9

If we were to place this program into consecutive memory locations beginning with location 100, it might look like this:

100	+41113	RNUM	N
101	+42113	PNUM	N
102	+11113	LDAC	N
103	+21114	ADD	S
104	+12114	STAC	S
105	+11115	LDAC	C
106	+21116	ADD	(one)
107	+12115	STAC	C
108	+21117	ADD	(−20)
109	+34111	JZER	(location 111)
110	+31100	JUMP	(location 100)

111	+42114	PNUM S
112	+00000	HALT
113		(N) (initial contents arbitrary)
114	+00000	(S)
115	+00000	(C)
116	+00001	(constant 1)
117	−00020	(constant −20)

Each box in the flowchart is marked with the addresses of the memory locations containing instructions which correspond to the contents of that box, so you may compare the flowchart to the program. Note that when we load the program into memory, we will not place any number into location 113. The present contents of location 113 are immaterial, since that location is reserved for data which will be read in by the program during execution. If we actually keypunched and submitted this program, we would not punch a card for location 113.

Loops with counters are extremely important, and we shall be using such loops over and over again in different forms. The counters must not necessarily start at zero and be incremented by one until they reach a desired value. They may start at any value and may be either incremented or **decremented** (decreased) by one. For that matter, they may be incremented or decremented by any value, until a desired value is reached. In the previous example, for instance, we might have started the counter at 5 and incremented by 2 until 45 was reached. This would have given us 20 iterations also.

Exercises 2.7

1. Write a program which reads 20 numbers from 20 consecutive data cards, prints them, and then prints:
   a) the sum of the first, third, fifth, . . . , seventeenth, and nineteenth;
   b) the sum of the second, fourth, sixth, . . . , eighteenth, and twentieth;
   c) the sum of all twenty numbers.
   Note: All this is done by a single program.

2. You are given 50 data cards. Each card contains a signed, five-digit integer which is, of course, either greater than zero, equal to zero, or less than zero.

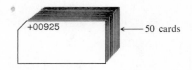

Write and submit a program which reads the data cards and computes and prints the *number* of cards containing numbers greater than zero, the number containing numbers less than zero, and the number containing zero. Note that your program prints *three* numbers.

3. All female rabbits belonging to a certain breed mature and are able to give birth for the first time exactly at the age of two months. At that time, and each succeeding month, a pair of these rabbits gives birth to another pair (a male and a female). Each newborn pair remains together and mates.

A newborn pair of such rabbits is placed on a certain uninhabited but congenial island. Naturally, they proliferate according to the abovementioned scheme.

Write a FACET program which will calculate and print the number of *pairs* of rabbits on this island for each of 18 consecutive months, starting with the month the first pair is placed there. Assume that there are neither fatalities nor other circumstances preventing the rabbits from breeding in their normal fashion during this period.

2.8 MORE INSTRUCTIONS

You have undoubtedly wondered why the only real arithmetic operation we have used so far is addition. The reason is that there were some important points to discuss before involving ourselves with other arithmetic operations. However, now we are ready for them.

Instruction	Mnemonic code	Op-code	Description
Subtract	SUB	22	When the instruction +22nnn is executed, the contents of location nnn (considered as an integer) are subtracted from the contents of the accumulator. The contents of location nnn are unchanged.
Multiply least significant	MLS	23	When the instruction +23nnn is executed, the contents of location nnn (five-digit integer) are multiplied by the contents of the accumulator (another five-digit integer). The resulting product is a *ten*-digit integer. The sign and five *least* significant digits (the five rightmost digits) are then placed into the accumulator. The contents of location nnn remain unchanged.
Multiply most significant	MMS	24	This instruction is similar to MLS, except that the sign and five *most* significant digits are placed into the accumulator.
Divide	DIV	25	When the instruction +25nnn is executed, the contents of the accumulator (considered as an integer) are divided by the contents of location nnn (again, con-

sidered as an integer). The integer portion
of the resulting quotient is stored in the
accumulator.   The fraction part (remainder) is discarded.   The contents of
location nnn are unchanged.

The subtract instruction is fairly simple. The two multiplication instructions,
however, are a bit confusing, so an example is in order. First, it is important to
note that if you mechanically multiply two five-digit numbers together, you get a
nine- or ten-digit product (answer). Try it—don't forget to carry along all leading
zeros. When the computer multiplies two five-digit numbers, it always produces a
ten-digit product, adding one leading zero if necessary. For example:

$$+35002 \times -02000 = -0070004000$$

If the accumulator contained +35002 and location 777 contained –02000, then the
execution of instruction +23777 (MLS) causes the sign and five least significant
digits of the product to be placed into the accumulator. The sign is minus. The
five least significant digits are 04000, so the accumulator will now contain –04000.
If instead we had executed the instruction +24777, the accumulator would contain
–00700, the sign and five *most* significant digits of the product. Whenever we deal
with integers which are small enough so that their product remains a five-digit
number, we use the MLS instruction only. This shall be the case in the next few
chapters.

The divide instruction is fairly simple. This sort of division is often called an
integer divide, since we divide two integers and get an integer result by dropping the
fraction part of the quotient. Here's an example: Say the accumulator contains
+00067 and location 200 contains –00005. If the instruction +25200 (DIV) is
executed, we get

$$\frac{+67}{-5} = -13.4.$$

The integer part is -13, so –00013 is placed into the accumulator.

We shall now use all these instructions in a program. We want to write a program
which finds and prints the divisors of 120. A *divisor* of a number is another number
which divides the first one evenly (i.e., without leaving a remainder). For example,
3 and 9 are divisors of 27, whereas 4 is not. How shall we do this?

We can find out whether 1 divides 120 (evenly), then whether 2 does, then
3, 4, and so on. Every time a number divides 120 (this means divides it evenly),
we print it; otherwise we do not. We try all numbers from 1 through 120. The
mathematical notation for a number (say n) dividing another (say m) is $n \mid m$. It is
read "n divides m" and means divides evenly. Be careful not to confuse the vertical
bar ($\mid$) with the division slash ($/$) just because they are similar in appearance.

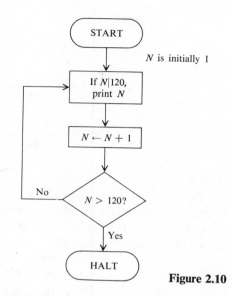

Figure 2.10

The flowchart is shown in Fig. 2.10. Note that we have a loop with a counter. The loop is iterated exactly 120 times. But this flowchart doesn't at all tell us how to write this program. That first box marked "if $N \mid 120$, print N" is fairly complicated in itself. So we see that procedure boxes in flowcharts need not contain operations which are in themselves very simple. We might even come across a flowchart which has a box like this:

Such flowcharts are known as **macro-flowcharts** since the details are not specified. They are often important in order to permit a view of the forest rather than lots of individual trees. Now let's take the box and further break it down. This helps a little:

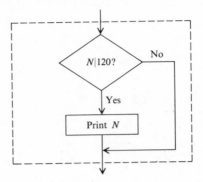

The dotted box can replace the box at the top of the flowchart. To find out if a number divides 120, we merely divide 120 by the number and multiply back by the quotient we obtain. Since we are using the **integer** divide, our result will be 120 only if the number does, in fact, divide 120. If this is confusing, let's look at a few examples. Bear in mind that we are using the **integer** divide.

$$10 \mid 120? \quad \tfrac{120}{10} = 12, \quad 12 \times 10 = 120: \quad \text{yes.}$$
$$50 \mid 120? \quad \tfrac{120}{50} = 2, \quad 2 \times 50 = 100: \quad \text{no.}$$
$$24 \mid 120? \quad \tfrac{120}{24} = 5, \quad 5 \times 24 = 120: \quad \text{yes.}$$
$$16 \mid 120? \quad \tfrac{120}{16} = 7, \quad 7 \times 16 = 112: \quad \text{no.}$$

We see that 10 and 24 do divide 120, but 50 and 16 do not. Now we can write the program. First we rewrite the flowchart, then we write the program, and finally we mark the boxes with the addresses of the corresponding instructions. Make sure you understand the program which follows *and* the flowchart shown in Fig. 2.11.

Mnemonic program		Actual program	
LDAC	(number 120)	000	+11014
DIV	N	001	+25015
MLS	N	002	+23015
SUB	(number 120)	003	+22014
JZER	006	004	+34006
JUMP	007	005	+31007
PNUM	N	006	+42015
LDAC	N	007	+11015
ADD	(number 1)	008	+21016
STAC	N	009	+12015
LDAC	(number 120)	010	+11014
SUB	N	011	+22015
JPØS	000	012	+33000

Mnemonic program	Actual program	
HALT	013	+00000
(number 120)	014	+00120
(*N*)	015	+00001
(number 1)	016	+00001

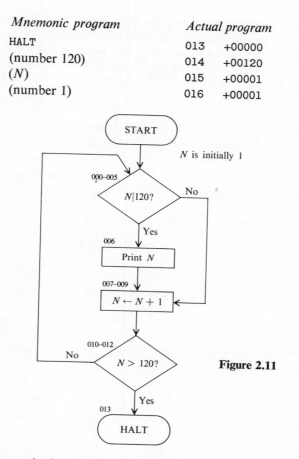

Figure 2.11

You may have noticed one possible problem in the last program. The 119th time through the loop we add one to N (getting 120), then subtract 120, and we expect an answer of +00000 so that we may go around the loop again. Is (+00120) − (+00120) = +00000? Maybe it's −00000! The answer is that whenever the result of an *arithmetic* operation in the FACET machine is zero, the accumulator is set to (plus) +00000. This is important to remember in exiting from loops. In other operations (such as LDAC, STAC, PNUM) the sign is not affected.

Exercises 2.8

1. Write a FACET program which reads two numbers from two data cards, then computes and prints the absolute value of their difference.

2. How would you check to see whether a number in a certain memory location is +00000 or −00000 (assume that you already know it is one of the two)?

3. Write a sequence of instructions which causes a jump to location 420 if the product of the numbers in locations 270 and 271 requires more than five digits. Remember, you don't know the signs of these numbers.

4. You are instructing a course in introductory programming. Naturally you wouldn't want to use any but the latest data processing techniques to compute your students' grade statistics. You have just given an exam, and have had the grades keypunched, one to a card, in the prescribed manner for the FACET machine. You then had one more card keypunched, the number of students in the class. This card you place in front of all the others.

Write a program which will:

a) read and print the number of students in the class;
b) read and print the grades of each of the students;
c) compute and print the highest, lowest, and average grades.

5. If you have a set of n student grades, $x_1, x_2, x_3, \ldots, x_n$, and you also know the mean (average) m, then the variance of the set is

$$ v = \frac{1}{n} \sum_{j=1}^{n} (x_j - m)^2. $$

Write a flowchart for computing the variance of a set of 33 student grades. Assume that the mean is 79, and that you have a data deck of 33 cards, each containing a student grade. Now write the program. Choose data which have a mean of 79.

6. You can write a program for computing the mean of a set of given numbers (exercise 4) and you can write one for computing the variance, given the mean (exercise 5). It is appreciably harder to write one which computes the variance without prior knowledge of the mean. This means you must compute the mean and variance in the same program, unless you devise another computation method. Discuss the problems involved in such a program. Draw a flowchart if you can.

7. Find the smallest positive integer which has 10 divisors. Use the FACET computer— it's easier to write the program than to try to find the number yourself.

8. Write a program which reads and prints the number on a data card and then prints the number with digit positions 2, 3, and 4 zeroed out. That is, if −87932 is the number, print both −87932 and −80002.

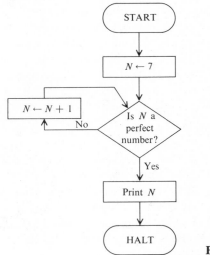

Figure 2.12

9. A **perfect number** is a number the sum of whose divisors is equal to twice the number itself. Six is a perfect number since the sum of its divisors (1, 2, 3, and 6) is $1 + 2 + 3 + 6 = 12$, which is twice six. Write a program which finds the next perfect number after six. Begin by drawing a detailed flowchart. (*Hint:* A macro-flowchart for this program might be as shown in Fig. 2.12.) Of course, the decision box requires expansion and detailing. The discussions of loops and the divides relation (|) should be helpful.

2.9 OVERFLOW

We have not yet discussed what happens when the result of an arithmetic operation is a six-digit number. This can happen only when we execute an addition or subtraction instruction (ADD or SUB). When a six-digit result occurs, a condition known as **overflow** is said to exist. The extra (sixth, leftmost) digit can be only a one. Here are some examples of additions and subtractions resulting in overflow:

1) $[+99999] + [+99999] = +199998$
2) $[-50000] - [+50000] = -100000$
3) $[+20101] - [-80010] = +100111$

There is a special indicator in the FACET computer called the **overflow indicator**. Whenever an addition or subtraction instruction is executed, the indicator is set to ØFF if no overflow occurs, and to ØN if it does. If overflow does take place, the sign and five least-significant digits of the sum (or difference) are placed in the accumulator. The following would be stored for examples 1 through 3 above:

1) +99998
2) −00000
3) +00111

Note that in example (2) the accumulator is set to −00000 after an arithmetic operation. This is because the result is not zero, but − 100000. The leftmost digit (which is always one when overflow occurs) is lost. However, there is a special instruction to test whether overflow has taken place as a result of the last ADD or SUB instruction executed.

The "jump on overflow" instruction has mnemonic code JØVF and op-code 35. When the instruction +35nnn is executed, and the overflow indicator is ØN, a jump to location nnn is executed (the next instruction is taken from location nnn). If the instruction is executed and the overflow indicator is ØFF, then the next instruction in sequence is executed. Note that the JØVF instruction does not change the overflow indicator.

To illustrate the overflow instruction, we shall write a program which prints nonnegative powers of two through the largest power of two that can still be stored in the FACET registers. Our exit from the loop will be a JØVF instruction. Execution begins at location 211. The flowchart for the program is depicted in Fig. 2.13;

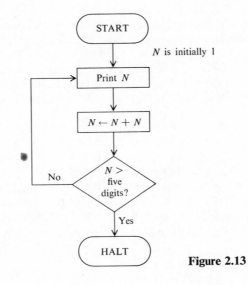

Figure 2.13

the program follows:

Mnemonic program		Actual program	
PNUM	N	211	+42218
LDAC	N	212	+11218
ADD	N	213	+21218
STAC	N	214	+12218
JØVF	217	215	+35217
JUMP	211	216	+31211
HALT		217	+00000
(N)		218	+00001

Exercises 2.9

1. Assume that your computer doesn't have the "jump on overflow" instruction. Write a sequence of instructions which causes a jump to location 682 if the sum of the numbers in locations 053 and 054 would cause overflow. Assume that both numbers in those locations are greater than zero. How is the problem complicated if they are not both greater than zero?

2. Discuss how you might use the JØVF instruction in place of the other conditional jump instructions (JNEG, JPØS, JZER) to control the counter of a loop. Specifically, say you had a loop which you wanted iterated 50 times. How might you set up the counter so that the loop exit is performed by the JØVF?

2.10 PROGRAM DEBUGGING

It is indeed seldom in the programming profession that one submits a program and finds that it has produced exactly the desired results on the very first try. Programs frequently have many errors. In fact, some programs in use today are so large and so complex that is unlikely that all their errors will ever be found. The process by which a programmer corrects his program is called **debugging**. Errors in a program are called **bugs**.

The problem is often a challenging one. A program usually reads some input, processes it, and then prints some output. Sometimes a processing error (due to a faulty program) will result in incorrect output; sometimes it will result in an error condition which terminates execution of the program and causes an error message to be printed. In either case, the actual cause of the error may be very obscure. A program error will probably initiate a chain of events resulting in an incorrect computation or an invalid instruction. However, there is often no direct way to trace this chain back to its source. Remember, the computer does what you *tell* it to do, not what you *want* it to do.

Since the only information you receive from the computer about its activities is *your* output or *its* error message, you won't know what happened in the computer at each intermediate step before the error occurred. Tracking down the intermediate step or steps causing the error frequently resembles a difficult detective game. You, as the detective, must use *all* the evidence at hand (error messages and output) to determine the probable cause of error. It is unwise to adopt the attitude "look what this arbitrary, fickle computer has done"—instead, remember the computer was, at every moment, slavishly following *your* instructions. The sensible attitude is to try to determine what action could possibly have initiated the sequence resulting in the evidence at hand.

Of course it may be that the evidence you have is insufficient to pinpoint the error. A suitable strategy would be to insert PNUM instructions at intervals throughout your program. This will help you follow the flow of execution of the program, and you may see if the program is doing what you expect it to do.

The FACET computer provides two additional facilities to aid you in debugging your program. Both may be used for debugging, but they should *not* be used in the final version of your program.

A program **trace** is a complete record of the contents of every pertinent register after the execution of every instruction in your program, every time it is executed. In other words, it is a sequential record of the execution of your program. During a program trace, the trace information is printed interleaved with the output of the program itself. On executing the ADD instruction, for example, the location of the instruction (this is contained in a special register called the **program counter** or PC), the instruction itself, the sum in the accumulator (after the addition is complete), the three-digit operand of the instruction, and the contents of the location named by the operand—*all* will be printed. Similar information is printed after the execution of each instruction. The trace is a powerful tool, but one which is extremely costly since it slows down the computer significantly. For this reason, you are limited (in the FACET machine) to tracing a maximum of 100 instructions. It is possible to restrict the trace by specifying two locations (addresses), say mmm and nnn. Only instructions between locations mmm and nnn will then be traced. The area of memory between (and including) locations mmm and nnn is known as the **trace-range**. Location mmm is called the begin-trace parameter and nnn is called the end-trace parameter.

When you want your program traced, insert a TRACE. card immediately following the START. card of your job (before the LØAD. card). The TRACE. card is punched as follows:

Columns 1–6   punch the characters TRACE. (including the period).

Columns 7–8   leave blank

Columns 9–11   punch the begin-trace parameter mmm (if you leave this blank, the begin-trace parameter is set to 000)

Columns 12–16   leave blank

Columns 17–19   punch the end-trace parameter nnn (if you leave blank, the end-trace parameter is set to 999)

Columns 20–24   leave blank

Columns 25–80   are ignored; they may contain anything.

If you have a rather small program, you might well leave the trace parameters blank and trace the entire program. However, if your program is large (say, from location 700 to location 950), an unrestricted trace might not help you very much, since 100 instructions will be traced well before your program nears its conclusion, and the portion of your program containing the error might not be executed until after tracing is suspended. In such a case, you might attempt to narrow the suspected trouble area by using different trace ranges. If you think the trouble is between locations 800 and 825, you might use the card:

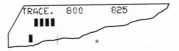

The second debugging aid is called the **memory dump**. When you request a dump, every location in the memory which was used or accessed by your program will be printed when the execution of your program ends. This occurs regardless of whether your program terminates normally (by executing a HALT instruction) or is terminated due to an execution error. The dump is especially helpful when your program is terminated by the computer due to some error before any output is printed. In this case you are guaranteed to get at least some "output" which will provide evidence as to what caused the error.

When a dump is desired, place the DUMP. card immediately after the START. card. The DUMP. card is punched as follows:

Columns 1–5   punch the characters DUMP. (including the period).

Columns 6–8   leave blank

Columns 9–80   are ignored and may contain anything.

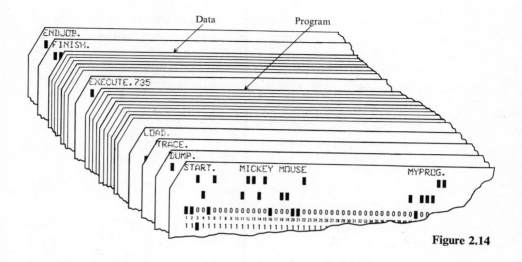

Figure 2.14

If both the trace and the dump are desired, the TRACE. and DUMP. cards may follow the START. card in any order. A program in which both the trace and dump options are requested might look like that shown in Fig. 2.14.

2.11 ALGORITHMS

When one has some sort of computational problem, he might think that the best way to solve it would be to give it to the computer. However, we know better—now that we have had a little bit of experience with the FACET computer. The first thing we must do is to figure out for *ourselves* how we would go about solving the problem. The computer cannot do anything for us that we cannot theoretically do for ourselves, were it not for our limited speed and accuracy. Of course, someone may have already solved the problem we're working on, or they may have written a program to do so. Or we might hire someone to solve our problem. But that's not the purpose of this book.

The actual conception and development of a **procedure** (often expressed as a set of instructions) for solving our problem can be done only by us humans. Such a procedure is often called an **algorithm**.

For a given problem there may be a number of different algorithms which may be used in its solution. Some of the algorithms may be more *efficient* than others; i.e., they may lead to a solution more quickly or require fewer computations. When given a computational problem (or any problem, for that matter), it is usually worth it to spend a good portion of the time allotted to its solution in discovering a good, easily implementable, efficient algorithm. You should compare a number of alternative approaches and choose the best. Only then should you begin working out the details of implementation (in the case of computation, writing a flowchart and then a program).

To illustrate this point, we shall choose a problem and demonstrate two algorithms which may be used in its solution. One of the algorithms will be vastly superior to the other, but it will also be far less obvious.

The problem is: Given two positive numbers, L (the larger of the two) and S (the smaller), find their greatest common divisor (gcd). Mathematically we may write:

Given L and S such that $L > S > 0$,
find the greatest integer D such that $D \mid L$ and $D \mid S$.
This integer D is known as the gcd of L and S.

(For example, the gcd of 30 and 18 is 6, because 6 divides both 30 and 18; yet there is no number greater than 6 which also does.)

Algorithm 1. Check to see whether S is the gcd we seek; i.e., if $S \mid S$ (of course it does) and $S \mid L$, then S is the gcd. If not, then we try $S - 1$ to see if it is the gcd (we ask, "$S - 1 \mid S$ and $S - 1 \mid L$?"), then $S - 2$, and so on until we finally find it. We are guaranteed to find the gcd, since every two positive numbers have a gcd (at worst it will be 1). We can now express this algorithm as shown in the flowchart in Fig. 2.15.

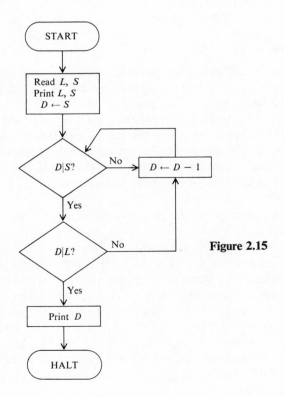

Figure 2.15

Now here's another algorithm. It's a well-known one called the **Euclidean algorithm**.

Algorithm 2 (Euclidean algorithm). [step 1] Divide L by S, obtaining a quotient and a remainder. If the remainder is zero, S is the gcd. [step 2] If not, replace L by S and replace S by the remainder, and go back to step 1.

In case this seems a bit confusing, let's look at a few examples. First, the gcd of 81 and 66:

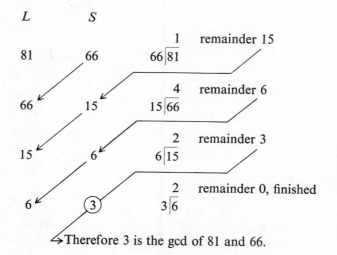

Therefore 3 is the gcd of 81 and 66.

Next, let's try 270 and 81:

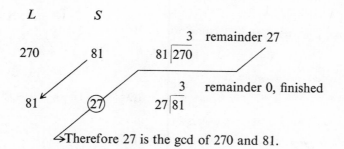

Therefore 27 is the gcd of 270 and 81.

The flowchart for the Euclidean algorithm is shown in Fig. 2.16. Note that in finding the gcd of 81 and 66, Algorithm 1 would have required 64 iterations. We would have tried 66 65, 64, ..., 4, 3. With Algorithm 2 we required four iterations.

In review, a given problem can usually be solved by any of a large variety of algorithms. However, it is worth while to spend a reasonable amount of time in search of an efficient one.

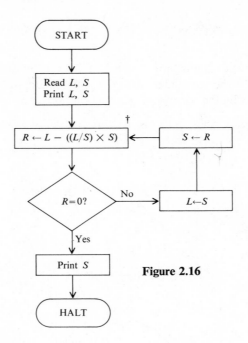

Figure 2.16

Exercises 2.11

1. Demonstrate (prove) that the expression $R \leftarrow L - [(L/S) \times S]$ (as it is used in the Euclidean algorithm flowchart) causes the remainder of L/S to be placed into R. Remember the *integer* divide.

2. Horner's method is an efficient algorithm for evaluating polynomials:

$$p(x) = a_n x^n + a_{n-1} x^{n-1} + \cdots + a_1 x + a_0.$$

The method employs the fully factored form of the polynomial:

$$(\ldots ((a_n x + a_{n-1})x + a_{n-2})x + \cdots + a_1)x + a_0.$$

Satisfy yourself, for example, that

$$3x^3 - 1x^2 + 5 \qquad \text{is the same as} \qquad ((3x + (-1))x + 0)x + 5$$

by multiplying out the factored expression.

a) Write a program which evaluates the above polynomial for $x = 2$. The values of x and the coefficients should be read in as data in the following order: x, a_3, a_2, a_1, a_0, or specifically,

+00002

+00003

−00001

+00000

and finally   +00005.

---

†   See exercise 1.

b) Generalize the above program to evaluate a polynomial of any degree n. This program should read $n + 3$ data cards during its execution in the following order:

(1) n (2) x (3) a_n (4) a_{n-1} $\cdots$ $(n + 2)a_1$ $(n + 3)a_0$.

Choose your own values for $n \geq 1$, x, and the a_1. Can your program also work for $n = 0$?

2.12 REVIEW OF INSTRUCTIONS

Mnemonic code	Op-code	Description
HALT	00	Halt.
LDAC	11	Load accumulator from memory register.
STAC	12	Store accumulator in memory register.
ADD	21	Add contents of memory register into accumulator. Turn overflow indicator ØN or ØFF depending on overflow condition.
SUB	22	Subtract contents of memory register from the accumulator. Turn overflow indicator ØN or ØFF depending on overflow condition.
MLS	23	Multiply memory register and accumulator contents, resulting in a ten-digit product. Place the sign and five *least* significant digits of product into the accumulator.
MMS	24	Same as MLS, retain sign and five *most* significant digits of product.
DIV	25	Divide accumulator by contents of memory register, place the integer portion of quotient into accumulator. Discard the fraction portion.
JUMP	31	Jump to instruction whose address is given by operand.
JNEG	32	Jump if sign of accumulator is minus (–).
JPØS	33	Jump if sign of accumulator is plus (+).
JZER	34	Jump if accumulator contains –00000 or +00000.
JØVF	35	Jump if overflow indicator is ØN.
RNUM	41	Read next data card. It must have a sign and five digits in columns 1 through 6. Place these into memory register given by operand.
PNUM	42	Print the contents of indicated memory register.

2.13 IN REVIEW

The jump instruction and a variety of conditional jump instructions allow the FACET computer to repeat (or iterate) a sequence of instructions a number of times. Such iterative programs or portions of programs are called loops. A conditional jump is used in exiting from such a loop. Sometimes a loop must iterate a fixed number of times; in such a case a counter keeps track of the number of iterations completed. Loops are extremely important in programming, since a frequent activity of computers is the performance of large repetitive tasks.

Flowcharts provide a semipictorial means of representing programs. They consist of a set of rectangular, diamond-shaped, and oval boxes connected with arrows. It is generally easier for humans to understand programs when they are represented as flowcharts. It is also easier to design programs by first drawing the flowcharts.

The read instruction (RNUM) allows data to be read into the memory during the execution of a program. This is important, since the data are usually not known at the time the program is written; furthermore, a program is usually written so that it can operate on a variety of data. Data that are read into the memory during the execution of the program are termed input. Output, on the other hand, is the term for what is printed during the execution of the program.

Arithmetic instructions (other than the ADD instruction) available in the FACET machine are subtraction (SUB), two multiplication instructions, (MLS and MMS), and division (DIV). The two multiplication instructions are needed, since the product of two five-digit numbers in the machine yields a ten-digit number. Either the five least significant digits (rightmost) or the five most significant digits (leftmost) of this product may be retained. The division instruction retains the integer portion of the quotient (discarding the remainder).

Two instructions, addition and subtraction, may cause a condition called overflow. This is the condition whereby a sum or difference computation results in a six-digit number. In this case the sixth (leftmost) digit is discarded and an overflow indicator is turned ØN. The condition of this indicator may be tested with the jump-on-overflow instruction (JØVF).

Bugs are errors in a program. Debugging is the process of finding and correcting errors. Two debugging aids available in the FACET machine are the trace and dump facilities. A program trace causes the computer to print the contents of all pertinent registers after the execution of each instruction. A memory dump is a printout of all memory registers used or accessed by a program. This occurs at the time execution terminates.

An algorithm is a procedure for solving a problem. A particular computational problem may have many algorithms leading to its solution. They may vary widely as to their efficiency or as to the number of computations required to obtain a solution. It is wise to spend a reasonable amount of time in search of an appropriate, efficient, and easily implementable algorithm for the solution of a problem.

Chapter 3

ASSEMBLY LANGUAGE

3.1 WHAT IS ASSEMBLY LANGUAGE?

By now we have a reasonable idea of how the FACET computer works and how we may program the computer using its **machine language**, the language of the machine itself. Machine language corresponds to the actual way in which the computer functions. Programming in this language, therefore, involves not only thinking through the solution to a problem, but also representing that solution in terms of machine functions; that is, you must not only choose an algorithm, but also represent your algorithm as a flowchart, translate the flowchart into machine language instructions, and so on. It should be obvious that there is a large gap between the way in which a human envisions the solution to a problem and the way that solution, or the algorithm leading to that solution, is presented to the machine. To help narrow this gap, we use **assembly language**.

Assembly language is a language which is somewhat closer to human thinking than machine language. It is a language in which many of the cumbersome details of machine language disappear. Once you master assembly language, you will probably never again use machine language. However, this does not relieve you of the responsibility of knowing and understanding machine language! The computer still operates *only* in machine language—those signed five-digit instructions placed into memory registers. That's the way the computer is constructed. How, you may ask, is it possible to program in a nonmachine language and have the computer execute those programs?

The answer may also have occurred to you: **Translate** the nonmachine language program into machine language. A processor which translates from assembly language to machine language is called an **assembler**. The FACET

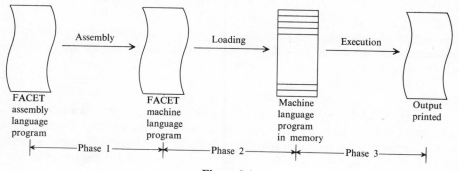

Figure 3.1

computer possesses an assembler. When you write a program in assembly
language, there are three phases through which it must go: **assembly**, loading, and
execution. See Fig. 3.1. Previously, we had only the latter two phases, since our
program was already in machine language. *Assembly* is the process of translation
from assembly language to machine language.

3.2 AN ASSEMBLY LANGUAGE PROGRAM

Following is an assembly language program. You can undoubtedly figure out
what it's for—we've written this program before in machine language.

Line	Label	Op-code	Operand
1		RNUM	A
2		PNUM	A
3		RNUM	B
4		PNUM	B
5		LDAC	A
6		ADD	B
7		STAC	C
8		PNUM	C
9		HALT	
10	A	LØC	
11	B	LØC	
12	C	LØC	
13		END	

This is the program for reading two numbers, printing them, and printing their
sum. Note that the assembly language program is written in three columns.
From left to right, these are called the **label** column, the **op-code** column, and the
operand column. In general, a line of the assembly language program corresponds
to one word in the machine language program.

The **names** in the label column (A, B, and C, appearing on lines 10 through 12)
serve to name locations, just as in machine language addresses name locations.
In assembly language, operands of instructions are names (again, like A, B, and C);
recall that in machine language operands are addresses.

Mnemonic op-codes in the op-code column are used instead of the two-digit
machine language op-codes. This is very helpful since, as you have doubtless
observed, it is difficult to remember the two-digit codes corresponding to the
instructions. A mnemonic op-code like ADD is easier to remember than a code
like 21.

An entry in the operand column usually designates the operand of some
instruction. As in machine language, this operand refers to some location by its
name. In machine language this name is a three-digit address, whereas in assembly
language it is a **symbolic name** like A, B, or C. For example, the operand of line 1

above refers to line 10, since line 10 has the label A and line 1 has an A in its operand column. All locations to which we want to refer *must* have names in the label column.

The assembler translates by making two assumptions: (1) that succeeding instructions will be placed in succeeding locations in memory, and (2) that the first instruction will be loaded into location 000. These assumptions and the two new op-codes LØC and END will be discussed on the following pages.

Let us examine how the assembler would translate the program we have been discussing.

Label	Op-code	Operand	Address	Contents
	RNUM	A	000	+41009
	PNUM	A	001	+42009
	RNUM	B	002	+41010
	PNUM	B	003	+42010
	LDAC	A	004	+11009
	ADD	B	005	+21010
	STAC	C	006	+12011
	PNUM	C	007	+42011
	HALT		008	+00000
A	LØC		009	
B	LØC		010	
C	LØC		011	
	END			

Assembly language program — Label, Op-code, Operand. *Machine language translation* — Address, Contents.

Note that the assembler assigns the first instruction to location 000 and assigns succeeding instructions to succeeding locations. It then constructs instructions corresponding to each line. The sign is plus (+). The two-digit op-code is constructed directly from the mnemonic op-code. Each name in the label column is associated with a three-digit address (A with 009, B with 010, and C with 011). These three-digit numbers replace the corresponding symbolic names when those names are used as operands. For example, RNUM A is translated to +41009, since 009 is associated with label A.

There are two new op-codes in this program: LØC and END. The LØC is used whenever we wish to name a location but are not interested in setting it to any value initially (when the program is loaded). This would be the case, for example, if numbers were to be read into a location: the initial contents of the location are immaterial because they are destroyed as soon as some other number is read into it. Since the location won't be set to a value at load time, no corresponding machine language word is generated.

The END op-code informs the assembler that this is the physical end of the assembly language program and that there are no more instructions to be assembled. There is only one END instruction per program.

Strictly speaking, LØC and END are not op-codes. They are **pseudo-operations** (or **psuedo-ops**), so called because they don't correspond to machine language instructions. Instead, they are instructions to the *assembler*. They tell the assembler to do something (name a location, finish assembling).

The final program which is *loaded* is

000	+41009
001	+42009
002	+41010
003	+42010
004	+11009
005	+21010
006	+12011
007	+42011
008	+00000

Although nothing is loaded into locations 009, 010, and 011, they are referred to in the program and will be used to store numbers during its execution.

Note that the assembly was done beginning with location 000—this is always the case. However, it is possible to have the program modified so it can be loaded elsewhere in the memory and still execute properly. This is called **relocation** and will be discussed later.

We are now in a position to appreciate the extent to which assembly language simplifies correction of program errors. You have most likely experienced the frustration of having to insert or delete an instruction in a machine language program. Did you not have to change *many* instructions each time a change was made? This was due to the use of actual memory addresses in the program. Thus a change in the length of the program (caused by insertion or deletion) caused all locations following the change and all instructions in the program referring to those locations to be ruined. In assembly language, a simple insertion or deletion is all that is necessary. The final correspondence between names and actual memory locations is not made until the assembly phase. At that time, actual addresses are assigned by the assembler.

Exercises 3.2

1. Why shouldn't the same symbolic name appear more than once in the label column of an assembly language program?
2. Why is there no operation or instruction in machine language corresponding to the LØC pseudo-op?

3.3 SYMBOLIC NAMES

We have named locations in the previous program using the letters A, B, and C. Called **symbolic names** (and often **labels**), they are used in place of addresses, which are the actual names of memory registers. We need not have confined ourselves to single-character names, as we shall see in the following rules for constructing FACET symbolic names.

A name or label must have between one and six characters. The first character must be alphabetic, that is, chosen from among the characters {A,B,C,...,Y,Z}. The remaining zero to five characters may be either alphabetic or numeric, that is, chosen from among the 36 characters {A,B,C,...,Y,Z,0,1,2,...,8,9}. Characters from among this set are sometimes known as **alphameric** (or **alphanumeric**) characters.

Thus the following are **valid** names:

LØØP	MINUS3
X12AB	AAA
C	Q555
ØNE	USA
TWENTY	MILYUN

The following are **invalid** names (they may *not* be used):

CØUNTER	999
A+B	X–RAY
3DATA	T(3)

Be sure you know why each of them is invalid. Sometimes a valid name is called a **legal** name, and similarly, an invalid one an **illegal** one.

These symbolic names are basic to assembly language. In writing machine language programs, our choice of machine addresses is usually arbitrary. The only reason for knowing the machine address of a location is to be able to refer to that location (as an operand) elsewhere in the program. Now that we use names, the assembler will relieve us of two tasks which we must perform when writing programs in machine language: assigning actual locations and using the proper three-digit numbers as operands of instructions.

Exercises 3.3

The digit *zero* and the letter *O* are often denoted by the same symbol in everyday use. This is confusing, since their meanings are different. Our output printers correct this problem by using different symbols, as you have seen when you received printed output from the FACET computer. The keypunch characters are also different. When you write them, however, they might well be indistinguishable. For this reason, programmers generally adopt some convention for distinguishing between the handwritten zero and the letter *O*. Often they slash the letter *O* like this: Ø. We shall use this convention throughout the book.

Decide whether each of the following is a *valid* or *invalid* assembly language name. If invalid, explain why.

a) GEØRGE

b) MICHAEL

c) TØM

d) THØMAS

e) THOMAS

f) 0Ø0Ø0Ø

g) ØØ0Ø0Ø

h) 000000

i) ØØØØØØ

j) X123456	k) X12345	l) START
m) START.	n) LØAD44	o) AB–79
p) 8EIGHT	q) 6	r) SIX
s) ZERØ	t) TWØ.5	u) FINISH
v) EXECUTE	w) (ABC)	x) PP1PPP
y) FDR	z) R	

3.4 MORE ASSEMBLY LANGUAGE PROGRAMS

We shall now write the program from Chapter 2 for adding 20 numbers together and printing their sum. This time the program will be in assembly language. The names used are changed slightly, for reasons you can probably figure out yourself. Look through the program and see if you can understand it.

```
BEGIN    RNUM    .NUMBER
         PNUM    NUMBER
         LDAC    NUMBER
         ADD     SUM
         STAC    SUM
         LDAC    CØUNT
         ADD     ØNE
         STAC    CØUNT
         SUB     TWENTY
         JZER    NEXT
         JUMP    BEGIN
NEXT     PNUM    SUM
         HALT
NUMBER   LØC
SUM      SET     +00000
CØUNT    SET     +00000
ØNE      SET     +00001
TWENTY   SET     +00020
         END
```

There are a number of items which you should note in the above program. First, instead of using the names N, C, and S for "number," "counter," and "sum," respectively, we use longer names for those locations. These names are mnemonic, since they give us a pretty good idea for what those locations are being used. The same is true of the two constants we use in the program, whose locations are named ØNE and TWENTY.

Second, we have introduced a new pseudo-operation, the SET pseudo-op. This pseudo-op is used when we want to place a number that isn't an instruction into some memory location during the load phase. The effect of this pseudo-op is to place into the assigned memory location the word in the operand column.

For instance, the location assigned to TWENTY would be loaded with +00020 and the one assigned to CØUNT would contain +00000.

The third item to note is that locations which contain instructions may also be given names, such as the two instructions in the above program, BEGIN and NEXT. Instruction names are usually needed as operands for jump instructions.

Let's look at the translation of this program to machine language, again beginning with location 000. Follow the translation through. Remember that the assembler first assigns consecutive locations to each line of the assembly language program (except for the END pseudo-op). It then translates op-codes, where applicable, and finally operands. The SET pseudo-ops merely get the entire word in the operand column assigned to their respective locations.

Assembly language program			Machine language translation	
BEGIN	RNUM	NUMBER	000	+41013
	PNUM	NUMBER	001	+42013
	LDAC	NUMBER	002	+11013
	ADD	SUM	003	+21014
	STAC	SUM	004	+12014
	LDAC	CØUNT	005	+11015
	ADD	ØNE	006	+21016
	STAC	CØUNT	007	+12015
	SUB	TWENTY	008	+22017
	JZER	NEXT	009	+34011
	JUMP	BEGIN	010	+31000
NEXT	PNUM	SUM	011	+42014
	HALT		012	+00000
NUMBER	LØC		013	
SUM	SET	+00000	014	+00000
CØUNT	SET	+00000	015	+00000
ØNE	SET	+00001	016	+00001
TWENTY	SET	+00020	017	+00020
	END			

It is important to remember that the assembler operates mechanically just like the FACET computer. It slavishly translates assembly language programs to machine language programs, not knowing whether the instructions it translates will, in fact, be used as instructions or as data. In the above program, for instance, we might have substituted the line

> SUM   HALT

for the line

> SUM   SET   +00000

This substitution would have resulted in the same translation, although it would have been more confusing for *humans* to read. To illustrate this still further, we offer an example which carries this idea of pure mechanical assembly to the limit. What does the following program do? Remember, it is assembled beginning with location 000.

```
HERE     LDAC    HERE
         ADD     THERE
         STAC    THERE
THERE    JUMP    HERE
         HALT
         END
```

You no doubt had difficulty unless you correctly translated this to the following machine language program:

```
000      +11000
001      +21003
002      +12003
003      +31000
004      +00000
```

Note that the first three instructions add two numbers, +11000 and +31000, storing the sum (+42000) in location 003. Then the instruction *currently* in location 003 is executed, printing the number in location 000 (that number is +11000). The next instruction is HALT. The lesson to be learned here is that the assembly language program tells us only what instructions (and data) are *initially* loaded into the various memory locations. After execution begins, the only one who can tell is the machine (and sometimes the astute programmer).

Here is still another program illustrating the mechanical nature of assembly:

```
BEGIN    LDAC    ØNE
         ADD     TWØ
         STAC    BEGIN
         SET     +42000
ØNE      SET     +00003
TWØ      SET     +00004
         END
```

Did you discover that this program adds three and four and then prints the result (seven)? Locations ØNE and TWØ contain the numbers +00003 and +00004, respectively. The fourth location (003) contains the PNUM instruction, and the third instruction stores the result of the addition in location BEGIN (000). Look at the translation of the assembler below:

```
BEGIN    LDAC    ØNE          000    +11004
         ADD     TWØ          001    +21005
         STAC    BEGIN        002    +12000
         SET     +42000       003    +42000
ØNE      SET     +00003       004    +00003
TWØ      SET     +00004       005    +00004
         END
```

Did you notice that the number three (+00003) also acts as the HALT instruction? Since its first two digits are 00, the "execution" of the constant three *as an instruction* causes the machine to halt!

You should not conclude at this point that it is sensible to write assembly language programs like these last two. The assembly language is meant to aid you in writing more understandable programs. But the assembler pays no heed to the logic of your program, nor do the mnemonic choices of the names mean anything to it. For example, when you need the constant six in your program, you may have the assembler place it in a location by writing

```
SIX      SET      +00006
```

or by writing any of the following:

```
ØNE      SET      +00006
TEN      SET      +00006
HARRY    SET      +00006
MINUS    SET      +00006
END      SET      +00006
SET      SET      +00006
HAHAHA   SET      +00006
```

All these are legal names, but the first name (SIX) is the most logical choice. It is considered good practice to write programs which can easily be understood by others—this means programs exhibiting clear logic and meaningful choice of names.

Exercises 3.4

1. Write a program in assembly language for printing powers of two. Restrict your program so that it contains only SET and END pseudo-operations (and nothing else). It should look something like this:

```
BEGIN    SET      . . .
         SET      . . .
          ⋮
         SET      . . .
         END
```

2. Does the following program halt, or does it remain in an endless loop? Is anything printed? Execution begins with the first instruction.

```
         LDAC     ABCD
ABCD     JUMP     ABCD
         STAC     ACBD
         PNUM     ACBD
         LDAC     ACBD
         STAC     ABCD
ACBD     HALT
         END
```

3.5 THE SYNTAX OF ASSEMBLY LANGUAGE

The **syntax** of a language is the form or grammatical correctness of a language. Roughly, a sentence in the English language is **syntactically** correct if it is grammatically correct.   The assembly language has certain syntax rules which must be obeyed if the assembler is to translate to machine language. A program violating these rules is said to have **syntax errors**; such a program cannot be assembled.   If you submit a program with syntax errors to the computer, the assembly will be terminated, and messages will be printed informing you that such-and-such syntax errors prevent assembly.   The following are syntax rules for the instructions and pseudo-ops discussed so far:

1. Instructions

    a) Label   An instruction may have a label in the label column, or the label column may be left blank.

    b) Op-code   A valid mnemonic op-code must appear in the op-code column.

    c) Operand†   The operand column may have either a valid name, a three-digit number (in which case those three digits are placed into the operand portion of the translated instruction), or may be left blank (in which case 000 is placed into the operand portion of the translated instruction).

2. Pseudo-op SET

    a) Label   The label column may contain a valid name or be blank.

    b) Op-code   The op-code column must contain SET.

    c) Operand   The operand column must contain a signed five-digit number.

3. Pseudo-op LØC

    a) Label   The label column may contain a valid name or be blank.

    b) Op-code   The op-code column must contain LØC.

    c) Operand   The operand column must be blank.

4. Pseudo-op END

    a) Label   The label column must be blank.

    b) Op-code   The op-code column must contain END.

    c) Operand   The operand column must be blank.

    d) Position   There must be exactly one END per program and it must appear as the last line in the program.

5. Names   Every name used as an operand must appear somewhere in the program in the label column. No name may appear more than once in the label column.

---

†   There are some instructions we have not yet studied which may receive only a three-digit operand. Two such instructions, TAB and CRGC, are discussed in Section 3.10.

3.6 SUBMITTING ASSEMBLY LANGUAGE PROGRAMS

When you have written an assembly language program, you punch it onto punched cards, one instruction (or pseudo-op) per punched card. The punched card contains four **fields**. A field is a sequence of contiguous columns which is defined for a specific application (such as for FACET assembly language). For our assembly language programs, the fields are:

1. Columns 1–8, the label field;
2. Columns 9–16, the op-code field;
3. Columns 17–24, the operand field;
4. Columns 25–80, the comment field.

The label (if any), op-code, and operand (if any) are punched in their respective fields **left-justified** and **right-padded** with blanks. Left-justified means that the characters in each of those fields are punched beginning in the first (leftmost) column of the field. Right-padded with blanks means that after whatever should appear in the field is punched, the remainder of the field is blank. The comment field can contain anything—it can be left blank or it may contain useful comments. Figure 3.2 is an example of a card from an assembly language program.

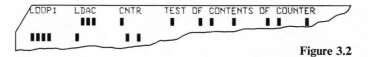

Figure 3.2

The control cards are very similar to those used in machine language programs except for one new one. The START. card is the same for both languages. The TRACE. card remains optional and is the same except that the begin-trace and end-trace parameters may be specified as labels as well as absolute machine locations. For example:

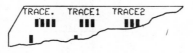

If TRACE1 and TRACE2 are labels in your program, the trace range will begin at the memory location corresponding to TRACE1 and will end at the one corresponding to TRACE2. If the begin- or end-trace parameter is left blank, it will be interpreted as location 000 or 999, respectively. The DUMP. card is unchanged.

A new card is required immediately preceding assembly language programs which tells the FACET machine that assembly is requested. The assembler is then called upon to assemble the program which follows. The card has no parameter and is punched with the characters A S S E M B L E . in columns 1 through 9. The rest of the card may contain anything, but is usually blank.

After the ASSEMBLE. card comes the program, ending with the END card.

If you also wish to have your program executed (rather than just assembled), then the program must first be loaded into the memory. You accomplish this by inserting a LØAD. card after the program and then an EXECUTE. card. The EXECUTE. card may have a parameter, either a three-digit address or a label in the program, indicating the first location of execution. If the first location of execution is also the first location of loading (000), the parameter may be left blank.

Thus, if you wanted your program assembled *only*, you might submit a job like that shown in Fig. 3.3. But if you wanted your program assembled, loaded, and executed, you might submit the job shown in Fig. 3.4.

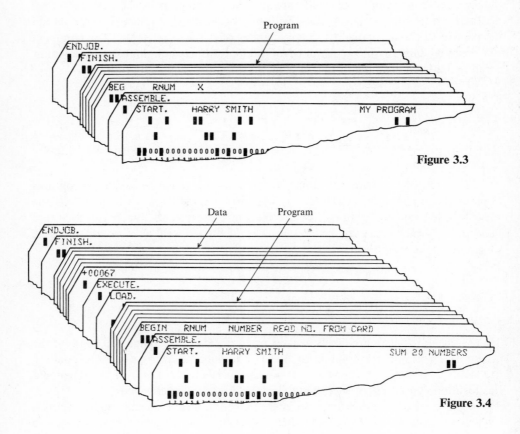

Figure 3.3

Figure 3.4

Note (in Fig. 3.4) that the EXECUTE. card does not have a parameter. This means that the first card in the program (in this case the card labeled BEGIN) is

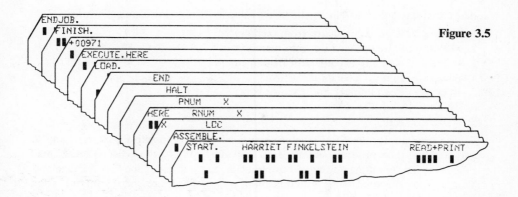

Figure 3.5

where execution begins. If you had a program (for reading and printing a number)
like

```
X       LØC
HERE    RNUM    X
        PNUM    X
        HALT
        END
```

then you would not want to start execution with the first card in the program.
You would want to start execution at location HERE. So you would submit a
program with the parameter HERE on the EXECUTE. card, as shown in Fig. 3.5.
This assures that execution begins at the location corresponding to the label
HERE.

Exercise 3.6

1. Write and submit a FACET assembly language program which reads 13 positive
   numbers from 13 consecutive data cards and prints those numbers which have a "9"
   in digit position 5, the rightmost digit. Don't forget to start by choosing an algorithm
   and drawing a flowchart. (*Hint:* Think about the special properties of the instruction
   MLS.)

2. Write one (or more) of the programs from the following exercise sets in Chapter 2 in
   assembly language (numbers in parentheses refer to exercise numbers):

   2.3 (3)   2.4 (4b)   2.7 (1)   2.7 (2)   2.7 (3)
   2.8 (4)   2.8 (5)   2.8 (7)   2.8 (8)   2.8 (9)

3. Submit any assembly language program with a DUMP. and TRACE. request. Then carefully
   look over the dump and trace to see exactly how they work. These are very important
   tools for future use; you should know exactly what everything printed by these
   facilities means.

4. Assume that you have a small computer (called General Educational Machine, or
   GEM). The structure and organization of GEM is identical to that of FACET, except

that GEM has only a few instructions available in its repertoire, and they are:

1. +11xxx   Load accumulator from memory.
2. +12xxx   Store accumulator into memory.
3. +21xxx   Add into accumulator from memory.
4. +33xxx   Jump if C(Acc.) is positive.
5. +41xxx   Read number into location xxx.
6. +42xxx   Print C(xxx).
7. +00xxx   Halt.

Write a program for the GEM machine which will read two positive integers, A and B, and compute their product (assume $A \times B < 100,000$). As the GEM is but a small FACET in its computing power, you can test-run the program on the FACET machine. You have implemented "soft" multiplication, very useful where "hard" multiplication is unavailable, as it, in fact, is on some machines.

3.7 MULTIPLE PROGRAMS

It is possible to submit a number of programs within a single job in the FACET machine. The FINISH. card actually indicates the end of a program (including the data), whereas the ENDJØB. card indicates the end of the entire job. When a multiple-program job is submitted, each program is written exactly like a single-program job, except that the ENDJØB. card is omitted. The ENDJØB. card appears only once, following the FINISH. card of the last program.

Both machine language and assembly language programs may be run together, intermixed, in a single job. Each new START. card indicates the beginning of a new program, and the subsequent LØAD. or ASSEMBLE. card indicates to the FACET machine whether that program is in machine or assembly language. Following is an illustration of the card sequence in a multiple-program job.

```
START.      ⎫
LØAD.       ⎪
  :         ⎬  First program (machine language)
  :         ⎪
FINISH.     ⎭
START.      ⎫
TRACE.      ⎪
ASSEMBLE.   ⎬  Second program (assembly language)
  :         ⎪
FINISH.     ⎭
START.      ⎫
LØAD.       ⎪
  :         ⎬  Third program (machine language)
  :         ⎪
FINISH.     ⎭
ENDJØB.
```

In some classes, the instructor may want to submit all student programs as *one* FACET job. Under this arrangement, it is very important that *no student use an* ENDJØB. *card.* Each student will hand in a program, complete from START.

card through FINISH. card. The instructor will be responsible for inserting the one ENDJØB. card after the last program. In either event, your instructor will inform you which is the proper arrangement.

3.8 THE ASSEMBLY PROCESS

At this point, let us examine the assembly process. We shall do so by examining how it might translate a simple program into machine language. We choose a program which reads a single number and prints its **absolute value**. The absolute value of a number, say M, is written in mathematical notation $|M|$ and is read, "the absolute value of M." It is defined as follows:

$$\text{If} \quad M \geq 0, \quad |M| = M,$$
$$\text{If} \quad M < 0, \quad |M| = -(M).$$

Our flowchart is shown in Fig. 3.6, and the assembly language program is as follows:

Card no.	Label	Op-code	Operand
1	BEGIN	RNUM	M
2		LDAC	M
3		JPØS	PRINT
4		MLS	NEG1
5		STAC	M
6	PRINT	PNUM	M
7		HALT	
8	M	LØC	
9	NEG1	SET	−00001
10		END	

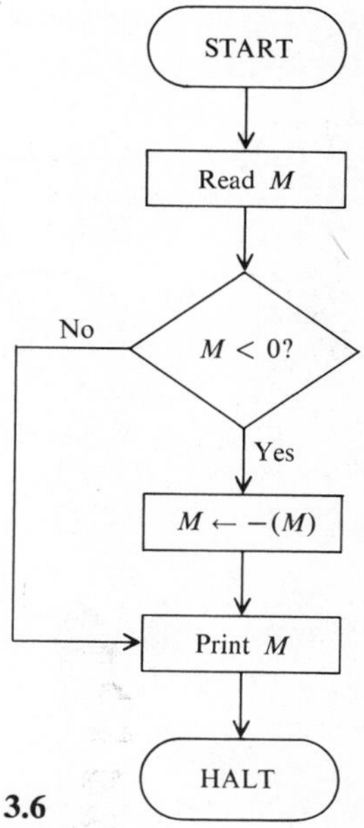

Figure 3.6

The assembler is activated by the ASSEMBLE. card, which comes immediately before card 1 in the deck. So far, none of the cards of the program have been read by the assembler. One strategy the assembler might attempt to use is to read the first card of the program, translate it, read the next card, translate it, and so on. Finally, the END card will be read and the translation will be complete. Let's see how this strategy works. Read the first card:

BEGIN   RNUM   M

Since the assembler assigns locations sequentially from 000, the name BEGIN will correspond to 000, and the translated instruction will be placed into that memory register. What is the op-code? +41 for RNUM. What about the operand? The assembler doesn't yet know which location to assign to M, since it must read a card on which M is the label to know this. This is card 8. Since it hasn't read any other cards yet, it cannot translate the first card for lack of information. Therefore this strategy fails.

A new strategy is needed. The strategy we shall use is called **two-pass assembly**. This means the assembler has to "look through the program twice." The first **pass** is used for assigning memory locations to the various instructions and pseudo-ops, and for substituting numeric op-codes for mnemonic op-codes. Pass two is used for substituting addresses for names in the operand column and thereby constructing operands for the instructions.

During the first pass, a table is constructed, called the **symbol table**. This table has each label in the program entered in it and the corresponding memory address next to each label. The symbol table is used in constructing operands during the second pass. After the first pass, the assembler has accomplished the following:

Assembly language program			*Translation*			*Symbol table*	
Label	*Op-code*	*Operand*	*Address*	*Contents*		*Name*	*Location*
BEGIN	RNUM	M	000	+41	M	BEGIN	000
	LDAC	M	001	+11	M	PRINT	005
	JPØS	PRINT	002	+33	PRINT	M	007
	MLS	NEG1	003	+23	NEG1	NEG1	008
	STAC	M	004	+12	M		
PRINT	PNUM	M	005	+42	M		
	HALT		006	+00	000		
M	LØC		007				
NEG1	SET	−00001	008	−00001			
	END						

Now the assembler makes its second pass. In essence, it must look at each symbolic operand in the assembly language program and construct the corresponding numeric machine language operand (where applicable). It does so by referring to the symbol table. For instance, on the first card, the operand is M. The symbol table tells us that M corresponds to location 007, so the numeric operand is 007, and the entire machine language word is +41007. Note that for LØC and SET pseudo-ops, nothing is done during the second pass. In the case of the LØC there is nothing to translate, and in the case of SET the entire machine word is already available during the first pass.

The completed translation is:

Address	Contents	Relocation
000	+41007	YES
001	+11007	YES
002	+33005	YES
003	+23008	YES
004	+12007	YES
005	+42007	YES
006	+00000	NØ
008	−00001	NØ

Note that location 007, into which nothing must be loaded, has disappeared from the program. This machine language program is now ready for loading. A new column called "relocation" has been added which is used for loading the program, beginning with some location in memory other than 000, and is explained in the next section.

3.9 RELOCATION

When given an assembly language program, the assembler produces a machine language program. It translates in such a manner that loading must begin at location 000 for the first instruction and continue into succeeding locations for subsequent instructions. It appears that all assembly language programs will be assembled and then loaded into the first memory registers, beginning with 000. There is no apparent harm in this. We stated earlier that one could, in fact, load a program anywhere in the memory that he chose. Why not let the assembled programs always be loaded beginning with location 000?

The situation in other, larger computers is such that there is often more than one program in memory at a given time. In these computers, the programmer is frequently not even permitted to decide where his program is to be loaded. Instead, the computer "decides" where to place the program in memory so it won't interfere with any other programs. For this reason, it is important for us to understand that assembled programs (such as the one just preceding) can be loaded starting from locations other than 000.

In the FACET computer it is the programmer who specifies the location at which his assembled program will be loaded. This address is specified as a parameter on the LØAD. card. Thus, if you wanted your program to be loaded starting with location 500, then the address 500 should appear in columns 9 through 11 on the LØAD card:

If columns 9 through 11 are blank, the loader uses load parameter 000. This is, in fact, what we have done so far. As you remember, the assembly was performed under the assumption that the program would be loaded starting with location 000. If the loader loaded the same program starting with location 500, most of the instructions would be incorrect because the operands refer to locations in a completely different region of the memory.

Let us now examine what adjustments are needed for loading an assembly language program at a location other than 000, and discover how these adjustments are made. Consider the final versions of the previous program for loading at locations 000 and 500, respectively.

Assembly language			*Loading at* 000		*Loading at* 500	
BEGIN	RNUM	M	000	+41007	500	+41507
	LDAC	M	001	+11007	501	+11507
	JPØS	PRINT	002	+33005	502	+33505
	MLS	NEG1	003	+23008	503	+23508
	STAC	M	004	+12007	504	+12507
PRINT	PNUM	M	005	+42007	505	+42507
	HALT		006	+00000	506	+00000
M	LØC		007		507	
NEG1	SET	−00001	008	−00001	508	−00001
	END					

The first instruction has been changed to

$$500 \qquad +41507$$

in place of

$$000 \qquad +41007$$

Both the address for loading and the operand have been changed. These changes have been effected by adding 500 (the load parameter) to the old address and operand, respectively. The parameter (500) is called the **relocation constant**. It represents the distance that the program must be displaced or **relocated** from address 000.

The sign and op-code, +41, remain unchanged in that first instruction. The operand was changed because it refers to location M, which now corresponds to address 507 instead of 007. If you check locations 500 through 505, you will see that the only change the loader must make is to increment both the address of the instruction and the operand portion of the instruction by the relocation constant, 500:

Old machine language instruction	0 0 0	+ 4 2 0 0 7
Add relocation constant	5 0 0	5 0 0
New machine language instruction	5 0 0	+ 4 2 5 0 7

Locations 506 and 508, however, do not have the operand portions of the instruction changed, because the corresponding instructions or pseudo-ops in the original assembly language program did not have label operands. The HALT instruction had a blank operand and the SET pseudo-op had a −00001 operand. Adding 500 to the translation of that SET pseudo-op would give us +00499, which would have ruined the program.

So we conclude that there are two types of words in a machine language program constructed by the assembler. One type requires two modifications during **relocation** (modification for loading at some point other than 000 in the memory); the other only requires one. The first type is modified by adding the relocation constant to both the address *and* the operand portion of the instruction. The second type requires modification of the address only. The memory word remains unchanged. Its operand is known as **absolute**.

Only those instructions with label operands (symbolic name operands) are classified as **relative** and therefore require operand modification. If an assembly language instruction has a three-digit operand, it is not changed by the loader. Thus an instruction

LDAC   001

in assembly language is translated as +11001, regardless of the relocation constant. Reasons for using such absolute operands and new instructions which require absolute operands will be introduced in the next section and in later chapters.

Those memory words whose operands require modification are marked YES in the relocation column of the assembler's output. Words with absolute operands (not requiring modification) are marked NØ. Satisfy yourself that the relocation column of the program on page 71 is correct. Following is another example. It is the program we wrote in Chapter 2 for computing powers of two. Note the relocation column.

Assembly language program			Assembler's translation			Loaded at location 750	
FIRST	PNUM	N	000	+42008	YES	750	+42758
	LDAC	N	001	+11008	YES	751	+11758
	ADD	N	002	+21008	YES	752	+21758
	STAC	N	003	+12008	YES	753	+12758
	ADD	CØNST	004	+21009	YES	754	+21759
	JPØS	SECØND	005	+33007	YES	755	+33757
	JUMP	FIRST	006	+31000	YES	756	+31750
SECØND	HALT		007	+00000	NØ	757	+00000
N	SET	+00001	008	•+00001	NØ	758	+00001
CØNST	SET	−01000	009	−01000	NØ	759	−01000
	END						

Exercise 3.9

Following is an assembly language program. It reads a single card, prints the number thereon, say *N*, and finally computes and prints the fifth power of *N*. Note that data storage locations are allocated right in the body of the instructions, instead of at the end of the program. This is not usual practice, but it is all right if we take care not to have these in the path of execution; i.e., if we don't have them executed. Look over the program:

```
START    RNUM    N
         PNUM    N
         JUMP    LØØP
N        LØC
ANSWER   SET     +00001
ØNE      SET     +00001
CØUNT    SET     +00004
LØØP     LDAC    N
         MLS     ANSWER
         STAC    ANSWER
         LDAC    CØUNT
         SUB     ØNE
         STAC    CØUNT
         JPØS    LØØP
         PNUM    ANSWER
         HALT
         END
```

a) Assemble the program relative to location 000 (of course). Include the symbol table and the relocation column.

b) Exhibit the program as it would look after relocation and loading from location 123.

3.10 PRINTED OUTPUT

By now you should be familiar with the input/output instructions RNUM and PNUM, and you should have written programs employing them. If you have actually submitted such programs and they were executed properly, then you know that the numbers were printed five to a line in fixed positions. They look something like this:

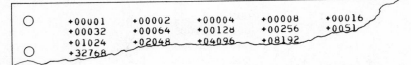

```
 ○    +00001    +00002    +00004    +00008    +00016
      +00032    +00064    +00128    +00256    +0051
      +01024    +02048    +04096    +08192
 ○    +32768
```

Sometimes other arrangements would be more desirable. For instance, you might have wanted to print the powers of two in a single column instead of as above; or maybe you would have liked to use a double column for printing corresponding x- and y-values for a function you computed. As the complexity of programming problems becomes greater, more carefully arranged printout becomes increasingly desirable. The FACET computer provides two instructions for controlling the printing of numbers.

Before introducing these instructions, we shall describe how the printer works. It is simplest to conceptualize the printer as a typewriter with the margins set to

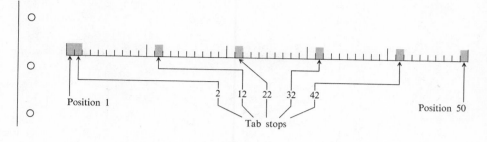

Figure 3.7

allow the printing of exactly 50 characters per line (including blanks, of course). The 50 character positions are numbered 1 through 50. When it is not printing, the printer is stationed at the character position immediately to the right of the last position in which it printed something. If it just printed its last character in position 17, the printer is positioned at 18.

The printer also has tabulator stops (or tab stops) set in five positions at 10-character intervals: positions 2, 12, 22, 32, and 42. See Fig. 3.7. These tab stops are fixed at these printing positions and cannot be adjusted. Used in a way similar to their use on a standard typewriter, tab stops provide a simple means to position the printer on a line and are commonly used for printing neat columns. We shall find that both you, the programmer, and several of the computer's printing instructions take advantage of these stops.

We are now in a position to understand how the PNUM instruction works. When execution of a program begins, the printer is set at position 1 on a line. A PNUM instruction causes the printer to

a) move to the *next* tab stop, and
b) print the number in the next *six* print positions.

Thus the first PNUM instruction would have the printer move from position 1 to the next tab stop (at position 2), and the number would be printed in positions 2 through 7. After completion of the printing, the printer would be positioned at position 8.

Similarly (assuming that no other print instructions have yet been used, other than PNUM), the fifth PNUM instruction would print a number in positions 42 through 47, inclusive. The sixth PNUM instruction would cause the printer to tabulate to the next tab stop—position 2 of the *next line*—and then print the number in positions 2 through 7. You should now be able to see how the repeated use of the PNUM instruction produces the columns of numbers visible in the illustration at the beginning of this section.

A sequence of contiguous character positions on the printer's paper is known as a **field** (similar to a field on the punched card). There are five numeric print fields in which the printer may print a number. These may be illustrated as shown in Fig. 3.8. The first instruction that controls the movement of the printer is the

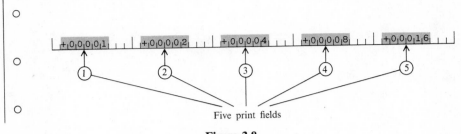

Figure 3.8

tabulation instruction, whose op-code is 45 and whose mnemonic code is TAB. When the instruction +45001 is executed, the printer moves to the next tab stop.

When the printer is in position	Instruction +45001 repositions the printer in position
1	2 of the same line
2–11	12 of the same line
12–21	22 of the same line
22–31	32 of the same line
32–41	42 of the same line
42–50	2 of the *next* line

When the instruction +45nnn is executed, nnn tabulations are performed (nnn is a three-digit number). Executing the instruction +45016 achieves exactly the same effect as executing the instruction +45001 *sixteen* times. Instruction +45016 will position the printer exactly three lines below the position it would have been set to if +45001 were executed. This is because each five additional tabulations (after the first) have the effect of moving down one line in the same print position.

The second instruction is used to control the starting of new lines. Called the **carriage control** instruction, its op-code is 46 and its mnemonic code is CRGC. Execution of the instruction +46nnn will do the following:

Value of nnn	Resulting action
000	Nothing
001	Printer is set to position 1 of the line immediately below the current line
002	Printer is set to position 1 of the line *two* lines below the current line
≥ 003	Printer is set to position 1 of the first line at the top of the next page.

Each of the 1000 possible operands for op-code +46 (CRGC) is thus a valid operand, despite the fact that CRGC may cause only three distinct actions. The numerical value of these operands has little bearing on what CRGC does; they are simply used to differentiate three different cases. Using different operands is analogous to setting the line feed to one, two, or three lines on the carriage control of a common typewriter. This would cause you to go to the beginning of the line, one, two, or three lines, respectively, below the line you were on when the carriage return was struck. Similarly, op-code +46 (CRGC) is basically used with its operand set to 001, 002, or 003. Every time it is executed with either 001 or 002, the printer positions itself at the beginning of the line, one or two lines below the current line. When the operand is set to 003, it positions itself at the beginning of the first line on the next page. Operands between 004 and 999 are the same as 003. A 000 operand does nothing.

Note that in these two instructions the operand portion is very different from the other instructions we have dealt with thus far. Previously, operands were always interpreted as addresses of memory registers, and instructions were always concerned with either the registers or with their contents. In the TAB and CRGC instructions, however, the three rightmost digits are *not* an address, but simply a three-digit number telling the FACET machine how to carry out the instruction. For this reason, a different specification of the operand is necessary in the assembly language. The operand must be a three-digit number. It would make no sense to say

TAB   A   or   CRGC   X

where A and X are labels in the program, since the actual three digits would then depend upon where in the memory the program (and hence A and X) was placed. One would instead write in assembly language, for example,

TAB   001   or   CRGC   002

When these are assembled, the relocation column is marked NØ so that the three-digit operand will not be altered during relocation. This may be seen in the following example of a program which prints the number +11111 in the *middle* of the line at the top of a new page:

Assembly language program			Machine language translation			Program loaded at location
Label	Op-code	Operand	Address	Contents	Relocation	500 *in memory*
CØNST	SET	+11111	000	+11111	NØ	500 +11111
BEGIN	CRGC	003	001	+46003	NØ	501 +46003
	TAB	002	002	+45002	NØ	502 +45002
	PNUM	CØNST	003	+42000	YES	503 +42500
	HALT		004	+00000	NØ	504 +00000
	END					
LØAD.	500					
EXECUTE.	BEGIN					

This number is an instruction with a label operand. It requires modification during relocation.

These numbers are *absolute* in that they require no change during relocation.

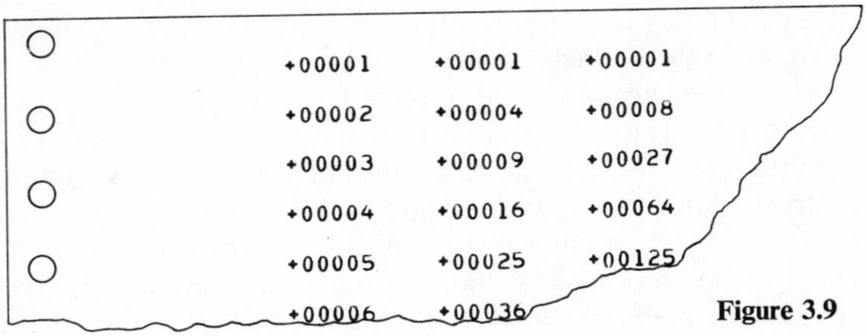

```
          +00001    +00001    +00001

          +00002    +00004    +00008

          +00003    +00009    +00027

          +00004    +00016    +00064

          +00005    +00025    +00125

          +00006    +00036
```

Figure 3.9

Each word marked NØ in the relocation column of the machine language translation is unaltered when loaded (this includes TAB and CRGC), but the PNUM instruction (which has a label as operand) is modified. Similarly, *any* operand which is specified in assembly language with three digits is considered absolute and will not be modified at the time of loading.

Let's look at an example which demonstrates how TAB and CRGC might be used in a program. Suppose that you wanted to print a table of numbers 1 to 20, their squares and cubes. Suppose, further, that you decide the best format for this table is three adjacent columns containing the numbers, their squares, and their cubes, respectively. You would like to use columns 2, 3, and 4 of the five possible columns which are used by the PNUM instruction. In addition, you wish to begin all this printing at the top of a new page to prevent any FACET computer messages from appearing on the same page as your output.

You might want the results to look something like that shown in Fig. 3.9. The flowchart for this program might look like Fig. 3.10, and the complete program might look like this:

```
START.       GEØRGE BRØWN                       SQUARES AND CUBES
ASSEMBLE.
ØNE     SET     +00001   CØNSTANT +00001
PLUS21  SET     +00021   CØNSTANT +00021
CØUNT   SET     +00001   CØUNTER, NUMBER TØ BE SQUARED, CUBED
A       LØC              LØCATIØN TØ CØNTAIN SQUARES AND CUBES
BEGIN   CRGC    003      SKIP TØ BEGINNING ØF NEW PAGE
LØØP    TAB     001      BEGINNING ØF LØØP. MØVE TØ PØSITIØN 2.
        PNUM    CØUNT    PRINT NUMBER IN SECØND CØLUMN
        LDAC    CØUNT
        MLS     CØUNT
        STAC    A        A CØNTAINS SQUARE ØF CØUNT
        PNUM    A        PRINT SØUARE IN THIRD CØLUMN
        MLS     CØUNT
        STAC    A        A CØNTAINS CUBE ØF CØUNT
        PNUM    A        PRINT CUBE IN FØURTH CØLUMN
```

```
           LDAC    CØUNT
           ADD     ØNE
           STAC    CØUNT    INCREMENT CØUNT BY ØNE
           SUB     PLUS21   TEST FØR EXIT
           JZER    DØNE     FINISHED IF ACCUMULATØR ZERØ
           CRGC    002      SKIP A LINE
           JUMP    LØØP     START AT TØP ØF LØØP AGAIN
   DØNE    CRGC    003      GØ TØ TØP ØF NEW PAGE AT END
           HALT
           END
   LØAD.   900
   EXECUTE.BEGIN
   FINISH.
   ENDJØB.
```

It is important to note that when PNUM is executed, a TAB   001 is automatically executed first, bringing it to the *next* tab stop. The tab occurs as part of the PNUM instruction. Note also that the comments on this program appear as they should be punched on cards and subsequently printed by the assembler. Such comments are valuable in documentation and as debugging aids.

Exercises 3.10

1. Without using the CRGC instruction, write a program which prints the numbers 1 to 20 in a single column.

2. Is the CRGC instruction superfluous? Can it be replaced entirely by the TAB instruction? What about CRGC   003?

3. Mnemonic op-codes may be used as symbolic names in assembly language programs. This is usually confusing but perfectly valid, since the assembler only considers as op-codes names that appear in the op-code column. What does the following program print when assembled, loaded from location 100, and executed?

```
           STAC    LDAC    SUB
           SUB     SUB     STAC
           PNUM    JPØS    SUB
           JPØS    STAC    STAC
           STØP    PNUM    STAC
           END     HALT    STØP
                   END
```

4. Write and submit a program which reads a single card containing a positive number, prints that number, and then computes and prints the square root of the number. If the square root is not an integer, the program will compute the integer part of the square root and print that. (E.g., if the number is 27, the "square root" printed is 5.) Try to find an efficient algorithm. An example of an inefficient one is the algorithm, "Try squaring successive integers 1, 2, . . . until one of the squares is larger than the number

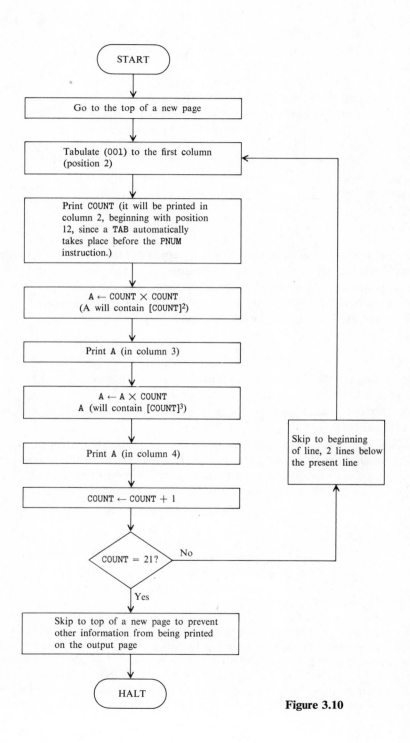

START

Go to the top of a new page

Tabulate (001) to the first column
(position 2)

Print COUNT (it will be printed in
column 2, beginning with position
12, since a TAB automatically
takes place before the PNUM
instruction.)

$A \leftarrow COUNT \times COUNT$
(A will contain [COUNT]^2)

Print A (in column 3)

$A \leftarrow A \times COUNT$
A (will contain [COUNT]^3)

Print A (in column 4)

$COUNT \leftarrow COUNT + 1$

COUNT = 21?   No

Skip to beginning
of line, 2 lines below
the present line

Yes

Skip to top of a new page to prevent
other information from being printed
on the output page

HALT

Figure 3.10

in question." Does your algorithm work for large (five-digit) numbers? Now modify your program so that it reads five successive numbers and finds the square root of each. It should print both the numbers and their square roots in two neat columns.

3.11 IN REVIEW

Assembly language is used in place of machine language to relieve the programmer of the need to assign and keep track of actual addresses while writing his program. A processor called an assembler translates such a program to machine language. An assembly language program submitted to the FACET computer for execution passes through three phases: assembly, loading, and execution.

Each line of an assembly language program contains three parts: a label, an op-code, and an operand. The op-code is mnemonic, such as ADD for addition. The label (whenever one occurs) is a symbolic name and represents a machine address. The operand is usually a symbolic name. Some of the lines of such a program do not correspond to machine language instructions. In these cases the op-code column contains a pseudo-operation or instruction to the assembler itself. The LØC pseudo-op merely names a location. The SET pseudo-op defines the initial contents of a location (which is not an instruction). The END pseudo-op marks the physical end of the program.

Symbolic names are chosen mnemonically by the programmer. Each must be 1 to 6 characters long. The first character must be alphabetic; the remaining characters are alphameric (either alphabetic or numeric).

The assembler translates (assembles) a program in two passes. During the first pass, consecutive addresses are assigned to lines in the program, beginning with 000. Also, mnemonic op-codes are converted to numeric op-codes, and a symbol table is constructed. During the second pass, operands are inserted, usually by reference to the symbol table. Each word is marked as either relative or absolute, so that the program may be loaded into any block of contiguous memory locations. The relative words must have their operands modified during loading, whereas the absolute words remain unchanged. Modification consists of adding the relocation constant (which is also the first location of loading) to the operand.

The assembly language has a set of rules called syntax rules which must be obeyed for assembly to take place. Violations of these rules are termed syntax errors and cause termination of assembly. Assembly language programs are punched on cards, one line of the program to a card. An additional control card needed (and inserted immediately preceding the program) is the ASSEMBLE. card, which calls upon the assembler. LØAD. and EXECUTE. cards then follow the program. DUMP. and TRACE. facilities are still available for debugging purposes.

It is possible to submit multiple-program jobs by placing a number of machine and assembly language programs in a sequence with the ENDJØB. cards omitted; that is, each program (with its data) ends with the FINISH. card. The ENDJØB. card is then placed at the end of the entire sequence.

Repeated use of the PNUM instruction causes numbers to be printed, five to a line, in fixed fields. Printout may be formatted differently by use of two new instructions, TAB and CRGC. The TAB instruction causes tabulation to fixed tab stops, one at the beginning of each print field. The CRGC instruction starts a new line, skips a line, or begins a new page. The operands of these two instructions may not be symbolic names, but rather three-digit numbers. They are always assembled as absolute words.

Assembly language is much easier to use than machine language. Insertions or deletions do not require changes elsewhere in the program, since all names are symbolic, rather than absolute machine locations. Although assembly language does not eliminate the need for knowing machine language (for debugging purposes and for understanding the operation of the machine), it is likely that a programmer will never again program in machine language once he becomes familiar with assembly language.

Chapter 4

ARRAYS
AND
INDEXING

4.1 INSTRUCTION MODIFICATION

Consider the following problem. You have written a large complex program in assembly language and you are still trying to debug it. The program trace proves ineffective because the error first appears after 100 instructions (maximum allowable number of traced instructions in the FACET machine) of each of the suspected sections of the program are executed. The dump is also found inadequate because it prints information only when execution terminates.

In order to help pinpoint the problem, you design something similar to the dump. It happens that all your data and constants are stored between locations A1 and XX34, inclusive. Note that we don't care how many words are actually located between A1 and XX34, but we shall assume there are many.

The program has been specified as follows:

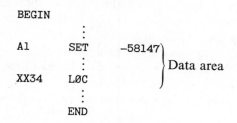

Suppose you decide that printing the contents of this data area (A1 through XX34) at several points in the program will locate the problem. This debugging method is sometimes called a **snapshot dump**, since we would be "taking a picture" of the data *during* the execution of the program. Since each location to be printed has its own label, you first suppose that the only way to do this is to have a sequence of distinct PNUM instructions, each with the name of one of the data locations. You would insert into the program the sequence

```
        PNUM    A1
        PNUM
          :       :
        PNUM    XX34
```

at each point in the program you want a snapshot dump. After debugging, these sequences could be removed. The program might now look like this:

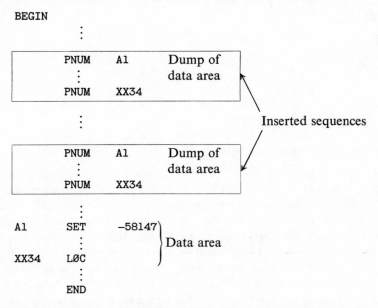

```
          BEGIN
                    ⋮
          ┌─────────────────────────────────────────────┐
          │     PNUM     A1      Dump of                 │
          │      ⋮                data area              │
          │     PNUM     XX34                            │
          └─────────────────────────────────────────────┘

                    ⋮                          Inserted sequences

          ┌─────────────────────────────────────────────┐
          │     PNUM     A1      Dump of                 │
          │      ⋮                data area              │
          │     PNUM     XX34                            │
          └─────────────────────────────────────────────┘

                    ⋮
          A1        SET      −58147 ⎫
                    ⋮                ⎬ Data area
          XX34      LØC              ⎭
                    ⋮
          END
```

However, if the data area is large (say 50 to 100 locations), this sequence is too long and bothersome for correcting a program.

A better technique is then discovered. Since A1 through XX34 constitute a contiguous block of memory locations, the addresses of consecutive data locations in the block differ by one. Thus, if we add one to the instruction PNUM   A1 at execution time and then execute the modified instruction, it would print the location immediately following A1 (another data location) and not A1 itself! For example, if A1 corresponds to location 534 and XX34 to 576, we might expect to see the following machine language sequence inserted for the dump.

```
                    ⋮
          221       +42534        Print location in data area.
          222       +11221 ⎫
          223       +21580 ⎬      Modify print instruction to print next
          224       +12221 ⎭      location in the data area.
          225       +11581 ⎫      Check loop termination: Print
          226       +22221 ⎭      instruction > dummy?
          227       +33221        No if + ; therefore repeat.  Yes if − ;
                    ⋮             continue regular program.
          534                     A1    ⎫
           ⋮         ⋮                  ⎬ Data area.
          576                     XX34  ⎭
           ⋮         ⋮
```

580	+00001	Constant one.
581	+42576	Dummy instruction to detect end of dump sequence.

The first instruction, +42534, prints the contents of A1. The next three instructions modify the contents of 221 by loading it, adding one to it (location 580), and storing it back in 221. The instruction in location 221 no longer prints A1 because it now is the instruction +42535 instead of +42534. This new instruction will print the location immediately following A1 when it is executed. The purpose of this loop is to modify the instruction in location 221 each time through the loop so first +42534 will be executed, then +42535, then +42536, and so on. We want to stop printing after XX34 has been printed. Therefore the last instruction in 221 we shall want to execute is +42576. In order to exit from the loop just after that instruction is executed, we placed a dummy instruction, also equal to +42576, in location 581. Note that this "dummy" is never executed. It is data and is used to detect when the instruction in location 221 has been modified from +42576 to +42577, an instruction we do not wish to execute. Note that the contents of location 221 is sometimes an instruction (when it is executed) and sometimes data (when it is being modified).

The same dump could be written in assembly language as follows:

```
MYDUMP    PNUM    A1        Print location in data area.
          LDAC    MYDUMP ⎫  Modify print instruction to print
          ADD     ØNE    ⎬  next location in the data area.
          STAC    MYDUMP ⎭
          LDAC    DUMMY  ⎫  Check loop termination; print
          SUB     MYDUMP ⎭  instruction.
          JPØS    MYDUMP    No if + ; therefore repeat.
            ⋮               Yes if − ; continue regular program.
ØNE       SET     +00001
DUMMY     PNUM    XX34
```

Which instruction is being modified here? It is the one labeled MYDUMP which is PNUM A1. Remember that the actual modification of this instruction does not occur until *execution time*. At this time, the assembly language version of the program no longer exists and the modifications are actually performed on the machine language translation of the program (as given in the first of the above two programs). Convince yourself that both the above sequences will print all locations between A1 and XX34, inclusive.

The technique used in the above programs is called **instruction modification**. Each time an instruction was modified, it referred to the next consecutive location. Instructions can also be modified in other ways; for instance, if we subtract one from an instruction, it refers to the location preceding the location it previously referred to.

Exercise 4.1

1. Write a FACET assembly language program which prints its own machine language equivalent. In other words, write a program that prints the sequence of machine words which result from its assembly (or its translation from assembly language to machine language). (*Hint:* Write a program which takes a snapshot of itself.)

4.2   ARRAYS

Up to now, data used in our programs have been stored in individually named locations. This coincides with the notion that we wish to refer to a number (actually, its location) by a single unique name. It is a frequent occurrence, however, that we operate on groups of numbers. For example, suppose that we are taking several different statistics on the intelligence quotients of a group of computer science instructors. Our program does not perform the calculations for all the different tests as it reads through the list of I.Q.'s for the first time. Instead, the I.Q.'s are processed for the first statistic, then for the second statistic, for the third, and so on. The reasonable way to implement this program is to read in the I.Q.'s once and store all of them in the memory. Then we can reference the I.Q.'s during each computation as often as necessary.

Let us suppose we are dealing with a group of 30 instructors. How shall these 30 I.Q.'s be stored in memory? A new memory structure called an **array** is used. An array is an arbitrarily long sequence of contiguous memory locations. A single name is usually associated with the entire sequence. In the FACET computer, the name refers to the *first* word in the sequence. A 30-word array named IQS could be constructed as follows:

$$
\begin{array}{ll}
& \vdots \\
\text{IQS} & \left.\begin{array}{l} \text{LØC} \\ \text{LØC} \\ \text{LØC} \\ \vdots \\ \text{LØC} \end{array}\right\} \text{30 cards} \\
& \vdots
\end{array}
$$

Here all 30 LØC's would be thought of as a unit with the name IQS. Individual numbers in the array could be referenced by instruction modification on instructions which have IQS as their operand. Specifically, the instruction RNUM   IQS would read the first number (datum) into the first location of array IQS. If this instruction were modified by adding one to it and then executed, it would read the second number from the data deck into the *second* location of array IQS.

Although this method of defining the array IQS can be generalized to create any array, it is very inefficient, since we have to punch as many cards as there are locations in the array. Instead, we introduce a new pseudo-op, ARAY. The ARAY pseudo-op requires a three-digit operand which specifies the length of the array.

For example,

$$\vdots$$

IQS   ARAY   030

$$\vdots$$

This single pseudo-op is equivalent to the sequence of 30 LØC instructions, the first of which has the label IQS.

In general, the instruction ARAY nnn allocates the next nnn consecutive locations (where nnn is a three-digit number). If the ARAY instruction has a label, then that label refers to the *first* location of the array. None of the nnn array locations is initialized to any specified value; that is, nothing is loaded into the array during the load phase. Only during execution can something be placed (usually read) into the array.

Below is a portion of the statistics program on the instructors' I.Q.'s. It reads in the 30 I.Q.'s into array IQS by applying the technique of instruction modification.

LØØP	RNUM	IQS	Read number into next location.
	LDAC	LØØP	⎫
	ADD	ØNE	⎬ Modify the RNUM instruction to read
	STAC	LØØP	⎭ into the next array location.
	LDAC	CØUNT	⎫
	ADD	ØNE	⎬ Modify Counter
	STAC	CØUNT	⎭
	SUB	THIRTY	⎫
	JNEG	LØØP	⎬ Check for loop exit.
NEXT			
	⋮	⋮	
IQS	ARAY	030	
THIRTY	SET	+00030	
ØNE	SET	+00001	
CØUNT	SET	+00000	

The instruction stored in location LØØP is the one which reads in numbers into successive array locations. It is modified each time it is executed. After it is modified the *thirtieth* time, the JNEG   LØØP instruction does *not* cause transfer, and we exit the loop.

Exercises 4.2

1. Are there certain types of problems in which an array *must* be used? If so, give an example of one. Discuss how you can tell when a computational problem cannot be solved by computer unless *all* the data are stored in the memory simultaneously.

2. Write and submit a FACET assembly language program which reads and prints a sequence of 30 numbers, finds two identical numbers in the sequence (there should be *exactly* two identical numbers), and determines the sum of the numbers between (but not including) those two numbers in the sequence. Here is an example:

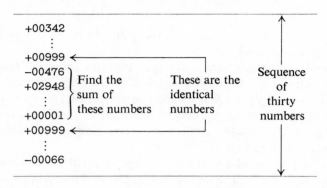

Does your program work when the two identical numbers are consecutive?

4.3 INDEXING

We have introduced a new structure for storing data, the array. In addition, we found the technique of instruction modification sufficient to enable the referencing of any location in the array. This was true despite the fact that the name of the array refers only to its first location. Unfortunately, this method is so cumbersome that complex programs become unwieldy. Often many different instructions must be modified. Sometimes instructions must be reset to their original value after modification. If you did exercise 4.2(2), you probably noticed many of the difficulties associated with instruction modification.

As a convenience, a new structure is added to the FACET computer to facilitate referencing of arrays. This new structure is called the **index register** (abbreviated XR). It contains three decimal digits (no sign); thus the index register may contain any number between 000 and 999. You should observe that these numbers can represent all possible memory addresses in the FACET computer. The index register may be visualized as shown in Fig. 4.1.

How is this register used? To understand this we must make explicit our intuitive notions of how the FACET computer executes an instruction (say, +21500). First, the op-code is taken to be the first two digits (in this case, 21). The operand is then taken to be the rightmost three digits (500 in the case of +21500). The operation (selected according to which op-code was present in the instruction) then uses the operand in the manner prescribed by the definition of the instruction. Either the three-digit operand itself is used directly, as with TAB or JUMP instructions; or the operand refers to a location whose contents are used by the operation, as in the case of STAC or the arithmetic instructions.

Figure 4.1

All the above is true, however, *only when the sign of the instruction is plus*. A different method is used to determine the operand when the sign of the instruction is minus. We now correct our originally oversimplified description of how the operand is determined. Note that in the discussion which follows, *operand* is still defined as digits 3, 4, and 5 of an instruction.

The instruction actually operates on the **effective operand**, which is determined as follows:

1. If the sign of an instruction is plus (+), then the operand (rightmost three digits of an instruction) becomes the effective operand directly.

2. If the sign of the instruction is minus (−), then the sum of the operand and the (contents of the) index register become the effective operand.

The following are some sample instructions and index register values with the effective operand values they determine:

Instruction	Index register	Effective operand
−12780	000	780
−11780	001	781
−22780	002	782
−41780	003	783
+31100	050	100
−31100	050	150
−11000	500	500
−42010	500	510

A discussion of what happens when the sum of the operand and the index register is greater than 999 appears in Section 4.8.

How is the minus sign placed into an instruction in order to invoke **indexing** (the use of an index register in the computation of an effective operand)? In machine language it is direct: Simply set the sign of the instruction to minus.

For example:

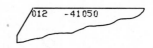

In assembly language an asterisk (*) is punched immediately following the mnemonic op-code. Thus, if

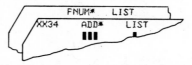

appeared in a program where LIST corresponded to location 150, then instructions −21150 and −42150 would be generated by the assembler, respectively. Since there is no meaningful way to translate an asterisk following a pseudo-op, the codes

$$\begin{array}{l} \text{ARAY}* \\ \text{L\O C}* \\ \text{END}* \\ \text{SET}* \end{array}$$

would be considered syntax errors if they appeared in the op-code column.

Exercise 4.3

1. Given that the index register contains 001, what would the execution of this sequence of instructions, beginning with location 003, cause to be printed? Does the program halt?

$$\begin{array}{ll} 003 & -42005 \\ 004 & +11004 \\ 005 & -22004 \\ 006 & +12006 \\ 007 & +31003 \\ 008 & +00000 \end{array}$$

4.4 INDEX REGISTER INSTRUCTIONS

A new register, the index register, has been introduced. Its introduction has been motivated by showing how it simplifies the referencing of arrays. We have further seen how any instruction may use the index register to determine an effective operand.

The index register is still useless to us until we learn how to set, modify, and test it. Specifically, data must be moved between the index register and memory as well as between the index register and the accumulator. Instructions are needed which perform arithmetic on the index register. In addition, conditional jump instructions are needed to test the contents of the index register. We now introduce the eight instructions used for operating on the index register.

Instruction	Mnemonic code	Op-code	Description
Load index register	LDX	13	When the instruction +13nnn is executed, digits 3, 4, and 5 of location nnn are loaded into the index register. Location nnn remains unchanged. The previous contents of the index register are destroyed.

(When the instruction −13nnn is executed, the effective operand is computed and used in place of nnn. This is done *before* the execution of the instruction, so the index register has not yet changed.)

Instruction	Mnemonic code	Op-code	Description
Store index register	STX	14	When the instruction +14nnn is executed, the contents of the index register are stored in location nnn (digits 3–5). The sign and digits 1 and 2 of location nnn are unchanged. The index register remains unchanged. The previous three digits in digit positions 3–5 of location nnn are destroyed.

(When the instruction −14nnn is executed, the effective operand is computed and used in place of nnn.)

Instruction	Mnemonic code	Op-code	Description
Place AC into index register	PACX	15	When instruction +15nnn is executed, digits 3–5 of the accumulator are placed into the index register. The accumulator remains unchanged; nnn is ignored.

(Note that the execution of −15nnn causes identical action; this is because indexing only affects the operand nnn, which is ignored in this instruction.)

Since nnn is ignored, it is considered a syntax error to use a label operand in assembly language. Usually, the operand column is left blank.

Instruction	Mnemonic code	Op-code	Description
Place index register into AC	PXAC	16	When the instruction +16nnn (or −16nnn) is executed, the contents of the index

Instruction	Mnemonic code	Op-code	Description

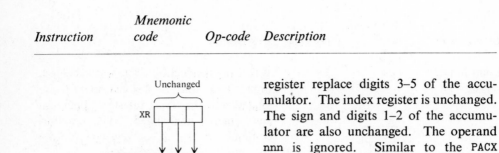

register replace digits 3–5 of the accumulator. The index register is unchanged. The sign and digits 1–2 of the accumulator are also unchanged. The operand nnn is ignored. Similar to the PACX instruction, the operand column is usually left blank for PXAC in assembly language.

The four instructions described above control the movement of data between the accumulator, the index register, and the memory. If we add the two instructions LDAC and STAC with which we are already familiar, we have a set of six data-movement instructions, which may be visualized as shown in Fig. 4.2.

To make certain you know how these instructions operate, see whether you obtain the same results (to the right) for the execution of the instruction (in the center) operating on the data (to the left) as we do.

	Before			Instruction executed		After		
	Loc.	Contents	AC	XR		Loc.	Contents	AC	XR
1.	750	−12345		005	(LDX) +13750	750	−12345		345
2.			+77777	001	(PXAC) +16000			+77001	001
3.	060	+19283		010	(STX*) −14050	060	+19010		010
4.			−11352	999	(PACX) +15333			−11352	352
5.	016	+31000		032	(STX) +14016	016	+31032		032
6.			+00000	357	(PXAC) +16000			+00357	357

Note that the effective operands of the PXAC and PACX instructions are superfluous to the definition of the instruction and are ignored. Be sure to remember that the sign and digits 1 and 2 of the accumulator and memory word are left undisturbed by the PXAC and STX instructions, respectively. Thus, if you wish to operate on the result of a PXAC or STX instruction, but you have not previously set the sign and digits 1 and 2 to +00, you may find yourself operating on some number quite different from the one (mistakenly) expected.

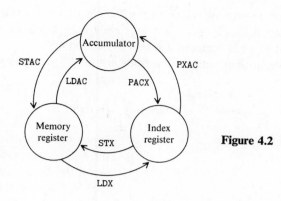

Figure 4.2

There are two instructions for modifying the index register:

Instruction	Mnemonic code	Op-code	Description
Increment index register	INCX	61	When the instruction +61nnn is executed, the number nnn (the three-digit operand) is added to the index register. Since nnn is not an address, the assembly language operand must be three digits. A label operand is a syntax error.
Decrement index register	DECX	62	When the instruction +62nnn is executed, the number nnn (the three-digit operand) is subtracted from the index register. Since nnn is not an address, the assembly language operand must, as in INCX, be three digits.

Following are the results of execution of several INCX and DECX instructions:

XR before execution	Corresponding instruction		XR after execution
	Assembly language	Machine language	
000	INCX 001	+61001	001
501	INCX 003	+61003	504
004	DECX 000	+62000	004
004	DECX 002	+62002	002

A problem arises if a four-digit sum or a negative difference is produced. If the index register contains 500 and we execute INCX   600 or execute DECX   600, the expected results are 1100 and −100, respectively. Since the index register cannot store four digits or a sign, something different must be done. The explanation of what happens appears in Section 4.9.

Two conditional jump instructions are used for testing the index register:

Instruction	Mnemonic code	Op-code	Description
Jump on index register zero	JXZR	36	When the instruction +36nnn is executed, the next instruction is taken from location nnn if the XR is zero. If it is not, then the next instruction in sequence is executed.
Skip on index register equal	SXEQ	37	When the instruction ±37nnn is executed, then: a) if the index register is *equal* to digits 3, 4, and 5 of the location indicated by the effective operand, the next instruction is *skipped*; b) if the index register does not equal digits 3, 4, and 5 of the location indicated by the effective operand, the next instruction in sequence is executed.

Instruction JXZR is similar to the other conditional jump instructions. If the condition is satisfied, i.e., if XR = 000, the next instruction to be executed is taken from the location whose address is the effective operand; otherwise the instruction *following* the JXZR instruction is executed next. SXEQ is different, however. The instruction tests for equality between the XR and digits 3, 4, and 5 of the memory location whose address is the effective operand. The effective operand does not specify a possible location of the next instruction as in the case of the other jump instructions. If the rightmost three digits of the location named by the effective operand are *not* equal to the XR, the instruction immediately following the SXEQ is executed. If they are equal, the instruction *two* locations after the SXEQ is executed next. Typically, the instruction immediately after the SXEQ is a JUMP instruction. This prevents the two cases from causing execution of the same instruction sequence. Typical uses of these two instructions are illustrated in Fig. 4.3. In these examples they are used for loop control.

Exercises 4.4

1. Assume that the index register contains 666 and the accumulator contains +11111 when each of the following instruction sequences commences execution. What are the

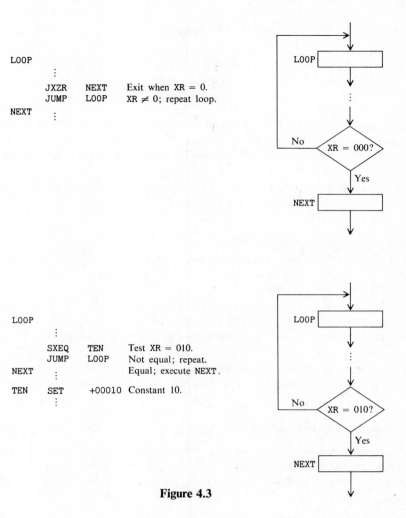

Figure 4.3

contents of these two registers *after* the execution of each of the sequences?

a)   PACX
       INCX   897
       PXAC

b)   STAC   X
       LDX   X
       DECX   002
       PXAC

c)   STAC   Y
       STX   Y
       SUB   Y
       JNEG   B
       STAC   Y
   B   LDX   Y

d)   STX   C
       SXEQ   C
       PACX
       PXAC
       ⋮
   C   LØC

2. There are eight index register instructions:

```
LDX     PACX
STX     PXAC
INCX    JXZR
DECX    SXEQ
```

If you were designing a FACET machine and were forced, for sake of economy, to implement only four of these instructions, which four would you choose? Remember, your choice should be such that the essential operation of the index register is not curtailed. Justify your choice.

3. Given that the index register contains 000, under what conditions will the instruction

```
SXEQ*    ABC
```

cause an instruction to be skipped?

4. Write a FACET assembly language program which reads a list of 43 numbers and prints the list backwards (that is, the last number read is printed first, and so forth), *omitting* the negative numbers.

5. What are the contents of the index register in the FACET computer immediately after the instruction −62990 is executed? Can the index register be set to zero with a *single* instruction which does not reference memory (or have a label operand in assembly language)?

6. Write a sequence of instructions which doubles the contents of the index register. Assume that the index register is less than 500. How short a sequence can you write?

4.5 USING THE INDEX REGISTER

There are many ways in which we may use the index register to advantage. One important use of the index register is its employment as a **pointer** to different words of an array. Suppose that we have defined a 30-word array named LIST with the pseudo-op

```
LIST    ARAY    030
```

There will probably be a number of instructions in our program which reference different locations in the array during different instances of their execution. By use of indexing, these instructions can refer to various array locations without being modified. For instance, the instruction

```
RNUM*    LIST
```

will refer to any of the 30 array locations if the index register contains any one of the 30 values 000, 001, 002,..., 028, 029. The index register acts as a pointer: If XR = 000, the instruction references the first location in LIST; if XR = 001, it references the second; if XR = 002, the third; and so on, until XR = 029, in which case the thirtieth location of array LIST is referenced. This is due to two facts:

1. LIST is the name of the *first* location of array LIST.

2. Indexing causes the contents of the index register to be added to the operand in the calculation of the effective operand of an instruction.

A pointer may be visualized as follows:

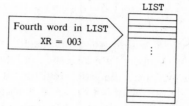

Discussion of arrays is simplified by formalizing a notation for naming array locations. From now on the ith location of an array X will be called X_{i-1}. Thus the first location of LIST will be $LIST_0$, and the last location (the thirtieth) of LIST will be $LIST_{29}$. Note that the subscript which refers to a particular location is the same as the index register value which points to that location. Thus $LIST_0$ is pointed to by XR = 000, $LIST_{29}$ by XR = 029, and, in general, for array position X_i, XR = i.

To better understand this notion of the index register's use as a pointer to array locations, we may consider the following analogy. Suppose that each single location in memory corresponds to a house on a street. Each of these is uniquely identified by its address. Suppose now that we also have an apartment house on the street (which corresponds to having an array defined in memory). Not only is the apartment house uniquely identified by its address, but each apartment in the apartment house is uniquely identified by its apartment number. In a similar way, we can consider any word contained in an array to be uniquely identified by a two-part address: one, the address of the array (actually the first word in the array), and two, its address within the array (actually the value in the XR). Whenever an instruction refers to a single location, it must merely name that location in the operand; e.g.,

$$\text{ADD} \qquad \text{AMØUNT}$$

or

$$\text{JUMP} \qquad \text{NEXT}$$

When we refer to some location within our array, we must also name the "apartment number" in the index register. We then name the array in the instruction operand, with indexing. For example:

LDX	TØM	Tom is the "apartment number."
STAC*	GEØRGE	George is the array name.

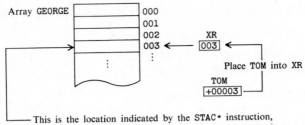

This is the location indicated by the STAC* instruction, since the index register (XR) contains that "apartment no."

Remember that the address within an array begins with 000. These "local addresses" or "apartment numbers" are also the "pointers" we have discussed.

Here is a program which uses the index register for pointing to the different locations in an array. The problem is to read in a sequence of 30 numbers into the array LIST and then print out the numbers in reverse order. The numbers will be read into $LIST_0$, $LIST_1$, ..., $LIST_{29}$, in that order. The numbers will be printed out in the order $LIST_{29}$, $LIST_{28}$, ..., $LIST_0$. The program follows:

```
BEGIN    LDX      ZERØ      Initialize XR to zero.
LØØP1    RNUM*    LIST      Read the next card into LIST [indexed].
         INCX     001       Increment XR by 1.
         SXEQ     THIRTY    Is XR equal to 30?
         JUMP     LØØP1     not equal, repeat first loop (read more).
LØØP2    DECX     001       XR = 030. Begin new loop. Decrement XR by 1.
         PNUM*    LIST      Print next number in LIST [indexed].
         JXZR     STØP      If XR = 000, jump to halt instruction.
         JUMP     LØØP2     If XR ≠ 000, continue printing.
STØP     HALT
ZERØ     SET      +00000
LIST     ARAY     030
THIRTY   SET      +00030
         END
```

Did you note how, in the first loop, the instruction

```
LØØP1    RNUM*    LIST
```

referred to $LIST_0$ through $LIST_{29}$ as the XR varied from 000 to 029? Each time the instruction was executed, a number was read into the *next* location of the array. The exit from the loop occurred when the XR was incremented to 030; it then pointed to $LIST_{30}$, which is beyond the last location in LIST. The instruction in LØØP2 then decremented the XR to 029, so it pointed to $LIST_{29}$, the last location in LIST. That location was printed, then $LIST_{28}$, $LIST_{27}$, until $LIST_0$ was printed. Immediately after $LIST_0$ was printed, the JXZR instruction detected that the XR was 000 and jumped to the halt instruction.

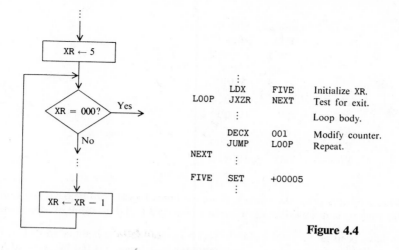

Figure 4.4

This program used the index register for two distinct purposes: It was used to point to the different locations in an array, and it was used as a counter to control the exit from the loop. Clearly, then, another common application of the index register is simply to serve as a counter for the control of loops. It is more efficient to use the index register as a counter than it is to use a storage location (memory location) because there is no need to load and store the index register whenever a modification or test is made. We might implement a single loop which is to be repeated five times as shown in Fig. 4.4.

Indexing works uniformly over the entire instruction set. That is, every instruction in the FACET machine may have indexing. Indexing may even be performed on index register instructions. It is performed as you would expect: The effective operand is determined and *then* used according to the definition of the instruction. Thus the LDX* instruction –13500, when XR = 004 and C(504) = –15324, first calculates the effective operand to be 504 (500 + 004). The XR is then reset to the digits 3 through 5 of location 504, so now XR = 324.

Exercises 4.5

1. Below is a program with a single loop. It is interesting in that it keeps two running computations, one in the accumulator and one in the index register. The results are stored in the memory for *printing purposes only*. Trace the loop a few times and then describe what the program does.

```
INIT    LDAC    ZERØ  ⎫
        LDX     ØNE   ⎬  Initialize XR and AC
LØØP    CRGC    001   ⎫
        STAC    A     ⎪
        STX     B     ⎬  This sequence prints the
        PNUM    A     ⎪  number in the accumulator
        PNUM    B     ⎭  and the XR on a new line
```

```
              INCX*  000
              ADD    ØNE
              SXEQ   PØS512
              JUMP   LØØP
              HALT
     ZERØ     SET    +00000
     ØNE      SET    +00001
     A        LØC
     B        SET    +00000
     PØS512   SET    +00512
              END
```

2. Explain how any program which will use the index register can be rewritten so that the index register is not used at all. Go into some detail. Try to think of all eventualities.

3. You have been given a deck of data cards representing the heights, in inches, of men in a certain graduating class. The heights range between 5 ft (60 inches) and 6 ft 8 in (80 inches). You, a FACET programmer, place another card at the back of the deck, containing +00000:

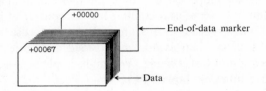

Write and submit a FACET program which reads and prints the data, computes the *median* height, and prints it. The median of a set of numbers is that number which has as many numbers greater than it as less than it. *Hint:* See the flowchart in Fig. 4.5.

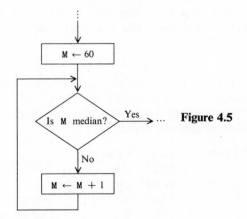

4. Explain the following: When the index register contains 944 and the instruction INCX* 010 (−61010) is executed, it results in an index register contents of 898.

5. What does this sequence of instructions do? Where would you use it to advantage in a program? (*Hint:* Assume that N will be between 1 and 5.) Invent a flowchart box that might be used to depict this sequence.

```
        ⋮
      LDX    N
L     JUMP*  L
      JUMP   A
      JUMP   B
      JUMP   C
      JUMP   D
      JUMP   E
        ⋮
```

6. Following is a program which reads 10 numbers, adds them, and prints the sum. This program doesn't always work; i.e., there is a bug in the program. Can you find it? Explain *exactly* what the problem is and why the program won't work under certain circumstances. State the circumstances explicitly.

```
          LDX    ZERØ
BEG       RNUM   NUMB
          LDAC   SUM
          ADD    NUMB
          STAC   SUM
          PXAC
          ADD    ØNE
          PACX
          SXEQ   TEN
          JUMP   BEG
          PNUM   SUM
          HALT
SUM       SET    +00000
ØNE       SET    +00001
TEN       SET    +00010
NUMB      LØC
ZERØ      SET    +00000
          END
```

4.6 LOOPS AND NESTED LOOPS

Nested loops constitute a more involved programming structure than we have examined so far. Although nested loops were already used in various exercises (e.g., the perfect number exercise in Chapter 2), a formalization of our intuitive notions concerning them will prove useful.

First we shall introduce terminology for describing loops. The **loop index** (previously called the counter) controls the number of repetitions of the loop. Before we enter a loop, the loop index must be **initialized,** that is, set to its initial

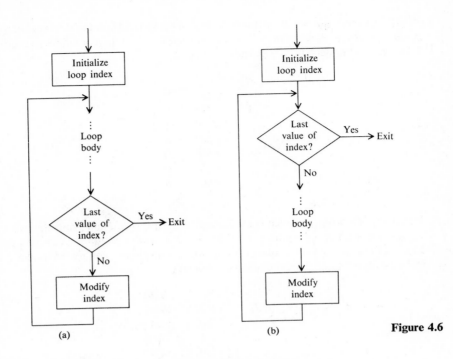

(a)   (b)   **Figure 4.6**

value. The loop is then entered, wherein three processes occur:

1. The **loop body** is executed. This is the main process we wish to have executed.
2. The loop index is **modified**.
3. The loop index is **tested** to determine whether the loop should be repeated or exited.

These three processes need not necessarily appear in the above order. For example, the test for exit may come after the loop body is executed, as shown in part (a) of Fig. 4.6, or it may come before the loop body, as in part (b). This difference may prove significant under the following circumstances: Suppose the loop index happened to be initialized to the termination value. In this case, the loop body should be skipped altogether. This can only be done if the test comes first. If the test comes after the body, as in part (a), the loop body must always be executed *at least* once. Such a problem might arise when we are updating inventory for items sold by several departments. Suppose we had a loop to update each department's inventory changes. If a certain department had no sales, we want the loop corresponding to it to be *skipped altogether*. In such case we would want a loop in which the test was performed before the body was executed.

Note another difference between the loops in parts (a) and (b). The tests are performed on *different* index values. In part (a) the test is, "Is this the last value of the index for which the body should be executed?" And in part (b) the question is, "Is this a value of the index *beyond* the range of values for which the body should be executed?" Look at the flowcharts and see why.

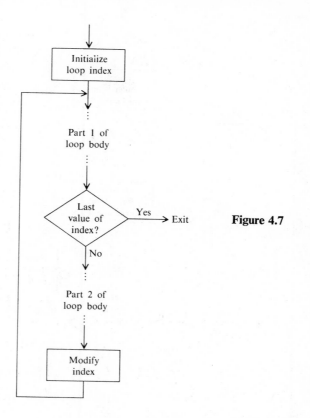

Figure 4.7

In some cases, you might want to place the test in the middle of the loop body; that is, place part of the loop body before the test and part after, as shown in Fig. 4.7. You would do this in case you want only part 1 of the body executed the *last* time through the loop.

A **nested loop** is a loop contained entirely within the body of another loop. A flowchart of a simplified nested loop arrangement is shown in Fig. 4.8. Note that all parts of the inner loop are within the loop body of the outer loop. More complex arrangements are obtainable by repeating this process. That is, at any point in the body of a loop, another loop may be inserted. If we have a set of nested loops, say $L_1, L_2, L_3, \ldots, L_n$, such that each loop contains all those with a greater subscript, then the set is said to be of **depth** n. Although we have discussed nesting of only depth 2, there are many programs requiring nesting depths of 10 or more.

Other nesting arrangements are possible. One alternative is shown in Fig. 4.9. Here the outer loop (Loop 4) contains two loops (Loop 2 and Loop 3). Loop 2, in turn, contains another loop (Loop 1). The nesting depth of this arrangement is three. This is because the largest set of *strictly* nested loops is three (Loop 4, Loop 2, Loop 1). In the next section we shall examine a process which requires nested loops.

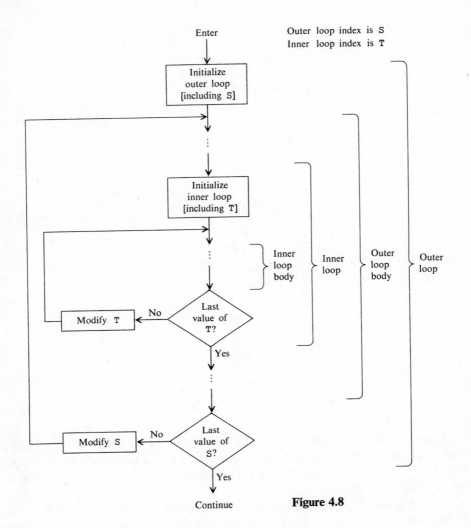

Figure 4.8

Exercises 4.6

1. Some loops always terminate; that is, when the loop is executed, it iterates (repeats) some number of times and then is successfully exited. We might call such loops **inherently terminating loops**. On the other hand, there are loops which never terminate; these may be called **inherently endless loops**. A third type of loop is one which may or may not terminate, depending on the values of certain registers which are, in turn, dependent upon the data being processed. The disposition of such a loop (whether or not it terminates) is termed **data dependent**.
   Exhibit and describe:

   a) an inherently terminating loop;
   b) an inherently endless loop;
   c) a loop whose eventual termination is data dependent.

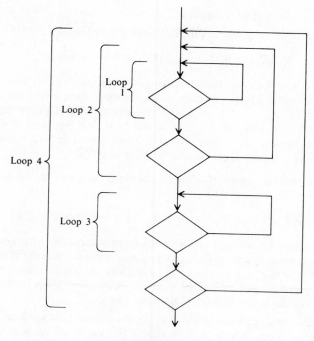

Figure 4.9

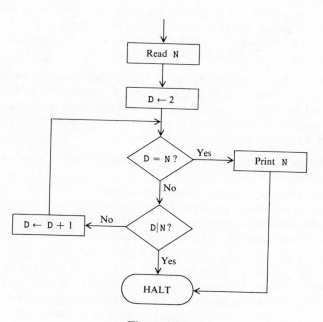

Figure 4.10

2. You are given a data deck containing:

a) on the first card—a number n, the degree of a polynomial

$$p(x) = a_n x^n + a_{n-1} x^{n-1} + \cdots + a_1 x + a_0;$$

b) on the next $n + 1$ cards—the coefficients $a_0, a_1, a_2, \ldots, a_n$, in that order. Write and submit a program which reads the data, then prints the coefficients in reverse order $(a_n, a_{n-1}, \ldots, a_1, a_0)$, and then computes and prints the value of the polynomial $p(x)$ for values of x: 1, 2, 3, 4, and 5. If your instructor does not supply a data deck, set up your own. Try several different sets of data to make sure that the program works. Does it work for $n = 1$? for $n = 0$?

3. A prime is a number greater than one whose only divisors are one and the number itself. In other words:

n is prime if and only if   a) $n > 1$,   b) if $d \mid n$ then $d = 1$ or $d = n$

a) Write and submit a program which reads a single number (positive, greater than one), tests to see whether it is, in fact, a prime, and prints the number if it is. The flow-chart in Fig. 4.10 on the previous page is one way to do this. It is an illustration of a simple algorithm. Test to see if any number between 2 and $n - 1$ (where n is the number) divides n. Note that the loop has two exits.

b) Write and submit a program which prints the primes between 2 and 30, inclusive. Use a nested loop. The inner loop should be exactly the same as that in part (a) above with the first instruction (the Read N box in Fig. 4.10) removed. The outer loop merely sets N to 2, 3, 4, . . . , through 30.

c) There is a more efficient way to compute primes which has to do with storing (in an array) all primes already computed, and using these in determining further primes. If you can think of such an algorithm, write and submit a program corresponding to it. Print all primes between 2 and 100.

General Hint: When programming nested loops, you might run into the problem of multiple index register use; that is, you want to use the index register as the loop index for both the outer and inner loops. In such cases, you must be careful to store the outer loop index (in the memory) when entering the inner loop and to bring it back to the index register after exiting the inner loop.

4. Write and submit a program which reads a sequence of numbers, all between 1 and 100, and then prints them in four columns:

All the numbers between 1 and 25 appear in column 1.
All the numbers between 26 and 50 appear in column 2.
All the numbers between 51 and 75 appear in column 3.
All the numbers greater than 75 appear in column 4.

For example, if the data were arranged as shown in Fig. 4.11(a), then your program might print the numbers as shown in part (b) of the figure. The last card of the data deck should be +00000, indicating end-of-data. The data should consist of no more than 50 numbers. Supply your own test data. Does your program work if there are *no* numbers in one or more of the categories? (*Hint:* The numbers need *not* be arranged in (either ascending or descending) order for this program.)

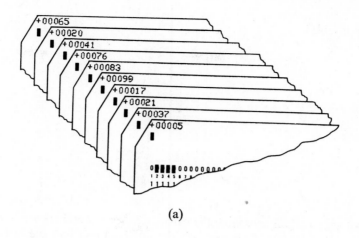

(a)

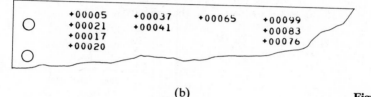

(b)

Figure 4.11

4.7 INTRODUCTION TO SORTING

Suppose we are given a sequence of 30 numbers and are asked to arrange them in order from the highest to the lowest. The process of arranging these numbers is known as **sorting**. Actually, *sorting* means arranging any set of objects according to some predetermined order. For the moment, we shall limit ourselves to sorting numbers into descending order (highest to lowest).

Let's assume that all 30 numbers have already been read into an array called XYZ. These numbers are to be rearranged so that the highest among them is in the first location of the array, the next highest in the second location, and so forth, until the thirtieth highest (the smallest) is in the thirtieth location of XYZ.

As we've said, many different things may be sorted. Alphabetization is the sorting of words into alphabetical order. Numbers may be placed into numerical order—**ascending** order if the first is the smallest and the last the largest, and **descending** order if the reverse—as we are, in fact, about to do.

Many different algorithms exist for sorting. Selection of more efficient algorithms becomes increasingly important as the number of items to be sorted increases. We shall present one commonly used algorithm. However, before we tackle the 30 numbers in array XYZ, let's try five numbers, written on cards and placed on a table:

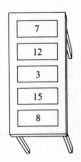

How shall we go about arranging the cards so that the numbers are in descending order? Here's one way: Scan through the numbers and find the largest; in this case it's 15. The order of the rest of the cards isn't important at the moment, so we just place card 15 at the top. We've now finished part of the job—we've got the first card in the right position (i.e., the *top* card):

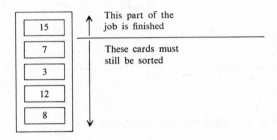

Now we ignore that top card and repeat the previous procedure on the remaining four cards. We find the largest (12) and place it at the top of that section of the table with which we are now dealing. This means that the 15 remains undisturbed.

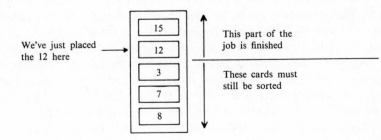

Now we have the top *two* cards in place. Next we shall do the same for the bottom three cards—find the largest (8) and place it at the top of the remaining section.

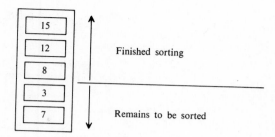

Then again for the last two cards:

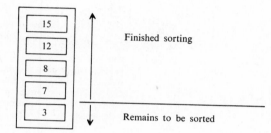

Of course, when one card remains in the "unsorted" section, we are finished, since there is no sense in rearranging a single card.

In working with our 30-number array, we shall do more or less the same thing. We'll find the largest number in the array and place it in the first position. Then we'll work with the "remaining section," which consists of the numbers in positions 2 through 30 of the array (remember, those are called XYZ_1 through XYZ_{29} according to our array notation—XYZ_0 is the first location). Figure 4.12 is a macro-flowchart for the sorting algorithm. When we've completed the loop with $N = 28$, then we've done the last section—the one with only two numbers, XYZ_{28} and XYZ_{29}. This means we're finished.

Now that we have a basic algorithm, we need a "sub-algorithm" to accomplish the placing of the largest number at the top of a section of the array. Let's go back to the tabletop analogy with the five cards and see how we can do it. We'll start with the original arrangement of the cards:

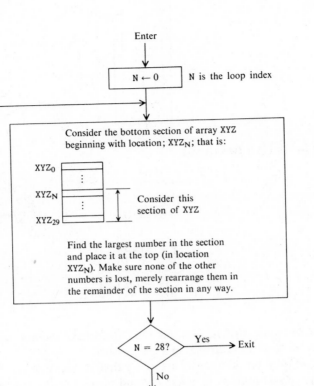

Figure 4.12

One thing we don't want to do is to scan through the cards remembering the largest number so far (and when we've finished scanning, we'll know the largest number), because we won't know where that largest number card is, and we'd have to scan through again to find it. To correct this, we could scan through the cards, remembering not only the largest number so far, but also the position of the card which contained that number. However, we'll do something else.

We shall use our left hand to point to the top card of the section with which we are dealing. In the following illustrations, we use pointers to indicate hands, like this:

Our right hand will begin by pointing to the next card below the top one in the section. This is how we start:

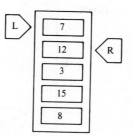

Step 1: We ask the question, "Is our right hand pointing to a number greater than the one our left hand is pointing to?" If so, exchange the cards; if not, leave them. In this case, we switch the 7 and 12:

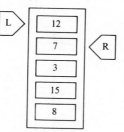

Step 2: Is the right hand at the bottom (pointing to the last card)? If so, we are finished. If not, we go on to step 3.

Step 3: Move the right hand down to the next card and go back to step 1.

So we go back to step 1 with the following configuration of cards and hands:

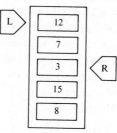

By the time our right hand is at the last card, we shall have placed the largest number at the top (next to our left hand). This is because each time we find a number larger than the one already at the top, we exchange it with the top one. This process allows us to always have the largest number encountered so far (by the right hand) at the top. When we finish scanning the cards, the largest number of them all is at the top. In our case, we have placed the card containing

15, the largest number, at the top. This is what the tabletop looks like at this point:

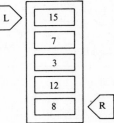

Now you can see how this fits into the larger algorithm. To accomplish the $N \leftarrow N + 1$ box in the flowchart, we merely move our left hand down one position in the array of cards on the tabletop and place our right hand one card below the left. Then we are ready to begin again at step 1:

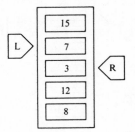

Each time the right hand completes scanning a section, we have placed the largest number in the section opposite the left hand. By the time the left hand gets to the bottom of the cards (actually, one card from the bottom), the *sort* is complete.

The actual writing (and testing) of a sorting program will be left to you as a (*very important*) exercise. It should not be extremely difficult, particularly if you understand how sorting is actually done (as described here), and if you are careful to put all the parts of the algorithm together carefully. However, there are some technical points which might cause difficulty, so we shall discuss them at this time.

When attempting to exchange two numbers (in two memory registers), you must be careful not to destroy one of them. The proper way to exchange the contents of two registers, say R1 and R2, is:

1) Move the contents of R1 to a temporary location, say T.
2) Move the contents of R2 to R1.
3) Move the contents of T to R2.

In assembly language, we would write

```
            ⋮
      LDAC    R1
      STAC    T
```

```
LDAC     R2
STAC     R1
LDAC     T
STAC     R2
  ⋮
```

Of course, the problem is somewhat more involved when the registers in question are located in arrays, since we have to worry about indexing.

The pointing right and left hands are, as you probably guessed, analogous to array pointers discussed previously (and implemented by use of the index register and indexed instructions). Since we have two pointers (left and right hand, or whatever), we must be sure that the correct pointer is in the index register at any time. Our program is actually a nested loop, the "left hand" being the loop index for the outer loop, and the "right" for the inner loop. Judicious use of the LDX and STX instructions can exchange pointers (we keep them in the memory when not in use).

Figure 4.13 is a flowchart for sorting (into descending order) the 30 numbers in array XYZ. The numbers are assumed to be in the array already. Remember

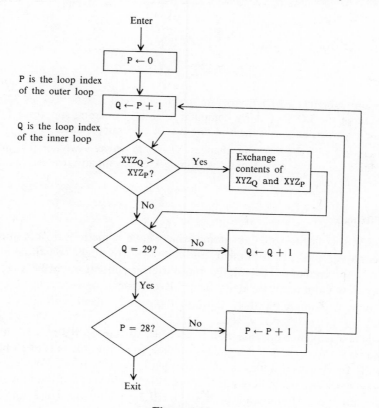

Figure 4.13

the notation:

XYZ_0 indicates the *first* location of XYZ.

XYZ_1 indicates the *second* location of XYZ.
  ⋮

XYZ_{29} indicates the thirtieth and last location of XYZ.

Exercises 4.7

1. Write an instruction sequence in FACET assembly language which adds the contents of the third and fourth locations in array XYZ, and then places the results in the fifth location.

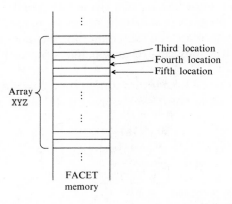

2. Write and submit a FACET program which will read a data deck of 30 numbers representing the I.Q.'s of thirty computer science instructors, sort these I.Q.'s into descending order, and print them. Choose your own sample data.

3. Do exercise 2 with the following changes: There are between two and fifty instructors (you don't know how many), and the data deck ends with an extra card containing a negative number.

4.8 MERGING

A **record** is a collection of data items which have something in common. For instance, name, rank, serial number, and date of birth might constitute a military record of a serviceman. The volume and butterfat content might be a record of a milk shipment from a certain dairy farm. Records can be very long or extremely short—such as a single number. The sorting exercise dealt with such very short records.

A **file** is a sequence or collection of records. If the records of a file have been arranged in some desired order by a sorting scheme, the file is said to be sorted. Frequently two (or more) files must be merged into one. If the files are unsorted, there is no problem, we merely put them together. However, if the files are sorted and we want the newly created file also to be sorted, we must use some kind of merge algorithm to accomplish this for us.

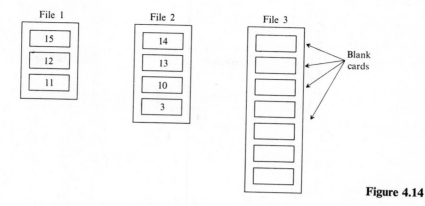

Figure 4.14

Let us assume that we have three tables, each not unlike the one we used for sorting cards. Two presorted files are arranged on the first two tables—the files consist of cards with numbers written on them and they are in descending order. Let's say one setup looks like that shown in Fig. 4.14.

How shall we proceed? We want to have the new file sorted in the order 15,14,13,12,11,10,3 on the table on the right when we finish. One way to accomplish this is as follows: We place a marker (pointer, finger) next to the first record in each file (files 1 and 2); then we ask, "which record should precede the other?" Card 15 should precede 14, so we copy it onto the first card in file 3. We also need a marker in file 3 to tell us where the next blank card is. After that, we move the appropriate markers down to the next card. When the first step is completed, our tables, with markers, are arranged as shown in Fig. 4.15.

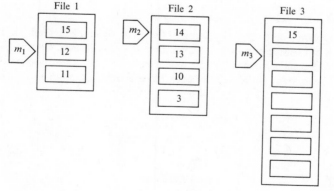

Figure 4.15

We iterate this process until one of the markers of either file 1 or file 2 moves beyond the end of the file (there must be some way to detect the end-of-file). Then we merely copy all the rest of the *other* file onto file 3.

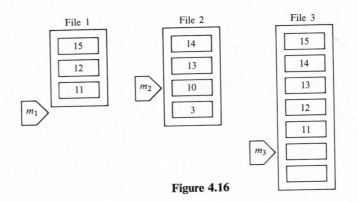

Figure 4.16

In our example, this situation occurs when our tables, cards and markers look like those shown in Fig. 4.16. File 1 has been completely transferred to file 3, since we have hit "end-of-file" (no more cards). Now we transfer the remainder of file 2 to file 3, and the merge is complete.

You probably already see the analogy between using tables, cards, and markers; and arrays, locations, and pointers. Let's write a flowchart for tables, cards, and markers (Fig. 4.17). *Note:* In the figure, (m_1) denotes the card which marker m_1 points to, as well as the number on that card. A similar convention is used with m_2 and m_3.

There are still a number of problems remaining, mostly having to do with storing pointers and reloading them into the index register when needed, but this will be left as an exercise.

Exercises 4.8

1. You will receive a data deck consisting of two files, F1 and F2. Each file will consist of a sequence of positive numbers, punched one to a card in FACET format and already sorted into *descending* order (largest first, smallest last). There are no more than 50 numbers in each file. At the end of each file is a card containing –00001 to mark the end of the file.

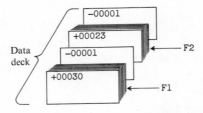

Write a FACET program which reads the two files into two arrays, merges the files into a third file, F3 (stored as a third array), and then prints F1, F2, and F3 in columns,

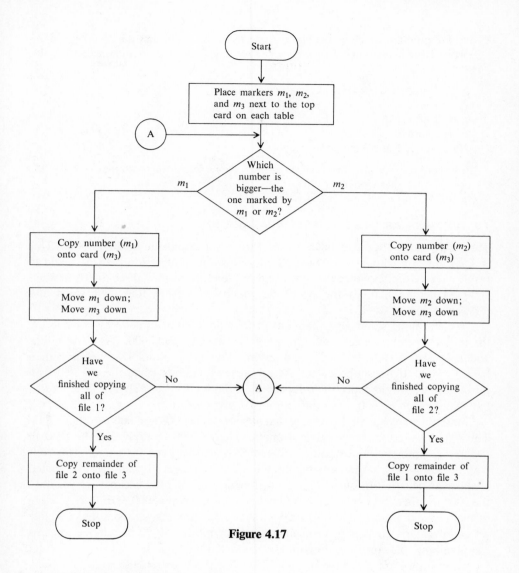

Figure 4.17

as shown in this example of output:

2. Write a program which works like exercise 1 above, except that the two files are unsorted. Read in files 1 and 2, sort them, and *then* merge them. Print intermediate results,
i.e.:

a) file 1 unsorted,
b) file 1 sorted,
c) file 2 unsorted,
d) file 2 sorted,
e) file 3 (files 1 and 2 merged).

Have your program use the same set of instructions for sorting both file 1 and file 2 (a
loop with two iterations).

4.9 ADDRESS ARITHMETIC AND WRAP-AROUND

The instructions INCX and DECX are performed in **arithmetic modulo 1000**. This
is a system of arithmetic in which all additions and subtractions can be made to
result in three digits. Since the index register contains exactly three digits, modulo
1000 arithemtic handles the problems which arise from four-digit sums and
differences.

We can understand what happens in modulo 1000 arithmetic by considering
the index register as a car's odometer. When new, it reads 000. As each mile is
added, it counts: 001, 002, 003, and so on. Finally it counts 998, 999, and then
back to 000. If we suppose that the odometer functions while the car is driven
in reverse, we would expect it to repeatedly subtract 1: ..., 521, 520, 519, and so
on. After reaching 000, the subtraction of 1 gives 999.

With the above analogy, we saw that $999 + 001 = 000$ and $000 - 001 = 999$.
Thus in this simple three-digit arithmetic scheme, 000 is equivalent to 1000 in
ordinary arithmetic, since usually $999 + 001 = 1000$ (not 000) and 1000 (not
000) $- 001 = 999$. Mathematically speaking, this special arithmetic is called
modular arithmetic. In our case, it is arithmetic *modulo 1000* because we use only
the 1000 numbers between 0 and 999, inclusive. Specifically, 000, 001, 002, ..., 999
forms the set of integers modulo 1000 we shall use. Any integer from the complete
set of integers is equivalent to a unique integer modulo 1000 in our set. Let us
examine how this corresponding integer (mod 1000) is found.

Suppose we are given the integer 1342. Since the arithmetic is modulo 1000,
we subtract 1000 from 1342 and see whether the result is between 0 and 999.
Since the result, 342, is between 0 and 999, we say that 342 is the integer in our set
equivalent to (**congruent to** for the mathematicians) 1342 (mod 1000). If the
number given was 4901, we would repeatedly subtract 1000 four times or simply
subtract 4000 to obtain the result that 901 was the integer in our set equivalent
to 4901 (mod 1000).

Negative numbers are treated in the same way except we *add* multiples of
1000 to obtain a result between 0 and 999. That is, given -480, we add 1000 to
it, obtaining 520. Therefore 520 is the integer corresponding to -480 (mod 1000).

For some additional examples:

Given number	Calculate	Equivalent number (mod 1000)
2949	$2949 - (2 \times 1000)$	949
1030	$1030 - (1 \times 1000)$	30
1000	$1000 - (1 \times 1000)$	0
42	$42 - (0 \times 1000)$	42
0	$0 - (0 \times 1000)$	0
-1	$-1 + (1 \times 1000)$	999
-2	$-2 + (1 \times 1000)$	998
-33	$-33 + (1 \times 1000)$	967
-998	$-998 + (1 \times 1000)$	2
-999	$-999 + (1 \times 1000)$	1
-1000	$-1000 + (1 \times 1000)$	0
-1001	$-1001 + (2 \times 1000)$	999
-4882	$-4882 + (5 \times 1000)$	118

Arithmetic modulo 1000 is used for all address arithmetic in FACET. Calculation of the effective operand works this way: If the instruction -11150 is executed when the XR equals 995, then its effective operand will be 145, since $995 + 150 = 1145$, which is equivalent to 145 (mod 1000).

Modular arithmetic also describes the operation of the INCX and DECX instructions. See whether you obtain the same results for their execution:

XR before execution	Corresponding Instruction		XR after execution
	Assembly language	Machine language	
100	DECX 010	+62010	090
100	INCX 990	+61990	090
000	DECX 001	+62001	999
000	INCX 999	+61999	999

We see from the above examples that DECX   010 is equivalent to INCX   990 and that DECX   001 is equivalent to INCX   999. This is so because -10 and -1 are equivalent to 990 and 999, respectively, modulo 1000. It should be obvious therefore that INCX and DECX are not both necessary. Instead of saying, "decrement the XR by 3" (or DECX   003), we could equivalently say, "increment the XR by -3" (or INCX   997). It is a matter of programming convenience and program readability that we are concerned with, and that is why both are provided.

Modulo 1000 arithmetic also describes what happens in the following situation: The instruction in location 999 of the FACET memory is executed, and it happens to be neither a HALT nor a transfer (jump) instruction. Which instruction is executed next? This question is similar to one we've already discussed: What is the effective operand when the sum of the operand and the index register is

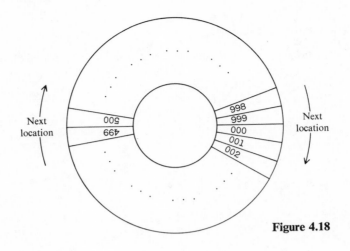

Figure 4.18

greater than 999? The usual answer to the first question (when the instruction is in a location other than 999) is "the next sequential location." But what is the next sequential location after 999? It is computed by adding one to 999,

$$1 + 999 = 1000,$$

but since this addition is performed modulo 1000, we get zero (location 000) instead.

This property of the computer is called **wrap-around**. The name suggests a visualization of the memory *not* as a list of FACET words with addresses from 000 to 999, but as a circular arrangement of locations wherein 000 follows 999. See Fig. 4.18.

Consider the following situation: you have written an assembly language program which, when assembled, requires 250 memory locations. Immediately following the program you place the card

Only the first 100 words (of the 250) may be loaded into the remaining memory, in locations 900 through 999. The rest must then be loaded in locations 000 through 149. The loader satisfactorily loads a program in this situation, relocating all words properly, with wrap-around. However, one should not get into the habit of using wrap-around too frequently. Although wrap-around exists on most computers, a user is rarely allowed to employ it. There are various reasons for this. One common reason is that a portion of the memory of many computers is reserved for special use and not available to the user. This section of the memory is usually a block of locations near the beginning, starting with location zero.

Exercises 4.9

1. Perform the indicated arithmetic operations in modulo 1000 arithmetic:

   a) 800 + 200
   d) 866 − 324
   g) 000 − 324
   j) 003 − 005

   b) 700 − 900
   e) 324 − 866
   h) 001 − 324

   c) 866 + 324
   f) 000 − 866
   i) 005 − 866

2. When the instruction in location 999 is SXEQ, and the index register is indeed equal to the three rightmost digits of the operand, from which location is the next instruction taken?

3. What happens if you fill the entire memory (all 1000 registers) with the word +11000, and then begin execution at location 000? Will the "program" halt? Is it stuck in an endless loop? Explain.

4. You may be interested in printing the contents of locations whose addresses are read in as data. For instance, if you read

you would want your program to print the *contents* of *location* 086. Write a program which reads five numbers (of which the sign and first two digits are +00) and then prints the contents of those locations. Run this program with a trace to make certain that you are printing the contents of the proper locations.

5. Does the following program halt or remain in an endless loop? If it halts, after how many iterations of the loop?

```
BEGIN    LDX     ZERØ
LØØP     INCX    003
         SXEQ    FIVE
         JUMP    LØØP
         HALT
FIVE     SET     +00005
ZERØ     SET     +00000
         END
```

6. Some computers have an instruction which does the following:

   a) If the index register is not zero, the index register is decremented by one and a jump is executed to a specified location.

   b) If the index register is zero, nothing is changed and the next instruction in sequence is executed.

   Describe how this instruction can be used in loop index control. Call the instruction DXJ (decrement index register and jump) and demonstrate how you would use it. Remember, the instruction works as follows:

   DXJ   AAA

   If the index register is zero, go to next instruction. If not, decrement it by one and jump to AAA.

4.10 OPERATION OF THE COMPUTER

The time has come to discuss exactly what happens in a computer during the execution of a program. We shall be looking at the FACET computer specifically, but you already know that similar things occur in other computers.

FACET is actually organized into four fairly separate entities:

1. the control unit
2. the memory
3. the arithmetic/logical unit
4. the input/output unit

The **control unit** essentially directs traffic. It causes the next instruction to be fetched from the memory, gets the arithmetic/logical unit to execute arithmetic and other related instructions, gets data from the memory, places results back into the memory, and activates the input/output unit when necessary. We are already familiar with the **memory**. The **arithmetic/logical unit** performs arithmetic and logical operations. (We shall discuss logical operations later.) The **input/ output unit** (**I/O** unit) supervises reading and printing.

There are a number of important registers used during the processing. We already know about two of them:

1. the accumulator (AC)
2. the index register (XR)

We shall discuss two others:

1. the program counter (PC)
2. the instruction register (IR)

The **program counter** (PC) is a three-digit register (like the index register) which contains the address of the next instruction to be executed. If you have used the trace option, you must have noticed a column labeled PC. The contents of the program counter is recorded in this column—namely the location of the instruction being executed. The **instruction register** (IR) contains the instruction currently being executed and, of course, has a sign and five digits.

Let's now recall that a computer is a machine which functions in a completely mechanical way. It merely shifts digits and signs around from register to register, sometimes changing digits, sometimes reading data from external devices (such as card readers), and sometimes printing characters on external devices (such as printers). There must therefore be some algorithm according to which it functions. Basically the algorithm works as shown in Fig. 4.19.

In order to execute a program, the machine "goes into a loop," executing instruction after instruction. Loop exit is caused by either a HALT instruction or some error condition (such as an illegal instruction or an attempt to read incorrectly punched data). The loop essentially consists of two phases—the **fetch cycle** and the **execute cycle**. During the fetch cycle, the next instruction to be executed is fetched from the memory and placed into the instruction register; then the op-code

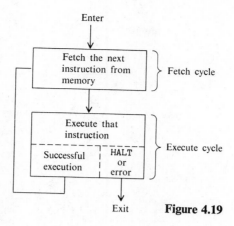

Figure 4.19

is decoded, the effective operand is computed, and finally the instruction is executed during the execute cycle.

Memory accesses (storing words into and retrieving words from the memory) are basic to the execution of an instruction. During the fetch cycle an access is always necessary, since the instruction itself must be fetched from the memory. During the execute cycle, memory accesses may or may not be required, depending on the instruction. The LDAC and STAC instructions require accesses during the execute cycle, for instance, whereas the PXAC instruction does not. Some instructions may even require a large number of accesses during a single execute cycle (e.g., PSYM, which we shall study in Chapter 5).

During the fetch cycle, the contents of that location whose address is in the program counter (PC) is fetched from the memory and placed into the instruction register (IR). Then the program counter is incremented by one, so it will be ready for the next fetch. Now the machine is ready to execute the instruction. The first two digits (the op-code) of the instruction in the instruction register (IR) are "decoded," so that the appropriate instruction may be executed. The effective operand is computed—we already know how that's done. Finally, the instruction is executed.

Instructions which do not require memory access during the execute cycle are said to have **immediate** operands. That means that the instruction operates on the actual three digits of the effective operand, rather than on the contents of the memory location whose *address* is the effective operand. An example of such an instruction is the JUMP. This instruction merely requires the effective operand to be copied into the program counter, so that the next instruction will be fetched from the appropriate location. We shall give some examples of all this shortly; first, let's look at a flowchart (Fig. 4.20) of the **operation cycle** of the machine.

To give you some insight into the execute cycle, we shall illustrate a few instructions. What actually happens is that there is a separate "path" for each instruction, and a "split" takes place in the flowchart or logic when the execution

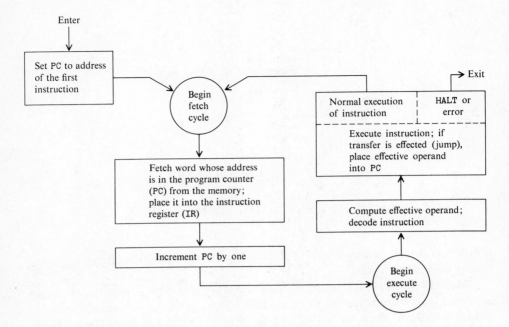

Figure 4.20

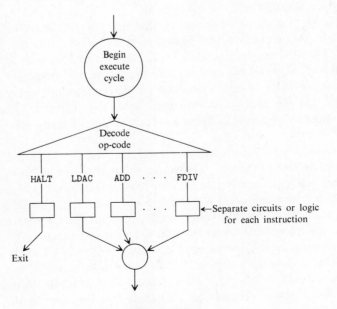

Figure 4.21

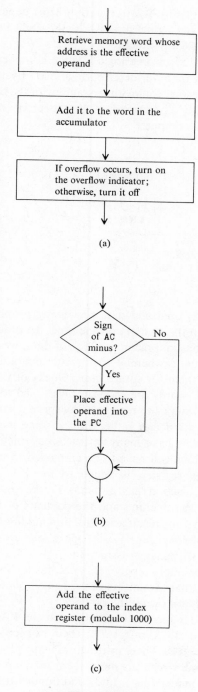

(a)

(b)

(c)

Figure 4.22

cycle begins, as shown in Fig. 4.21. Figure 4.22(a) depicts the flow of the ADD instruction; part (b) of the figure shows how the JNEG instruction might work; and part (c) depicts the INCX instruction.

Of course, the actual electronic logic is quite complicated; but behaviorally, it's no more complicated than our description above. Even the information we've presented here is not necessary for an understanding of the behavior of the machine. It is only important for understanding the inherent mechanical, completely deterministic nature of a computer.

Exercise 4.10

1. What is the effect, in FACET, of the card

Think in terms of registers.

4.11 IN REVIEW

Many types of computational and data processing problems require us to have large numbers of data in the memory at one time. In order to have our programs access successive locations in a memory block of data, we may employ instruction modification—a procedure whereby arithmetic operations are performed on instructions to change them for future use. Blocks of memory registers used to store sequences of data words are called arrays. The ARAY pseudo-operation in the FACET machine allows us to reserve array space during the assembly process.

Instruction modification is a rather cumbersome method to process arrays, in that complex programs have many instructions which must be modified, and so many more instructions will have to be employed to modify them. Instead, a new register, the index register, is added to the FACET machine. When a (machine-language) instruction has a minus in the sign position, the effective operand is the sum of the operand and the contents of the index register. This allows us to achieve the same result as instruction modification by merely changing the contents of the index register. Furthermore, one change in the index register serves to effectively modify many instructions.

When writing in assembly language, one indicates that indexing is desired in an instruction (that is, that a minus is desired in the sign position) by placing an asterisk (*) immediately following the op-code.

There are eight index register instructions in the FACET machine, LDX, STX, PACX, PXAC, JXZR, SXEQ, INCX, and DECX; their respective numeric op-codes are 13, 14, 15, 16, 36, 37, 61, 62. These instructions serve to move three digits between the memory and the index register, move them between the accumulator and the index register, test the index register and conditionally transfer, and finally change the index register by a set amount.

There are many uses to which the index register may be put. Two important uses are as loop indexes (formerly called counters), and as pointers to array locations. In many instances the index register may be used in both ways simultaneously.

Nested loops are loops appearing within other loops. Many programs require many degrees of nesting. In dealing with nested loops, one must be careful to keep track of the different loop indexes for the various loops. If the computer has only one index register (as is the case with the FACET computer), one must store away one index in the memory and place another into the index register at various points in the loops.

Sorting is the process of arranging an arbitrarily arranged sequence into a specified order. Examples of sorting are alphabetizing words and arranging numbers in either ascending or descending order. An algorithm for sorting numbers into descending order is discussed. Basically, the algorithm finds the largest number and places it at the top of the list or array. It then finds the next largest, or the largest in the remainder of the list, and places it immediately below the largest. This process continues until all the numbers are sorted.

Wrap-around is the property of the instruction-sequencing device, which considers location 000 to immediately follow location 999 in the memory. This allows a program which has been assembled to be loaded beginning with the "end" of memory (locations 990, 995, ...).

Chapter 5

SYMBOLS
AND
SYMBOL
MANIPULATION

5.1 THE NEED FOR SYMBOLS

We have already learned a sufficient number of instructions and programming techniques to write some fairly complicated programs. We have found prime numbers, perfect numbers and averages. We have evaluated polynomials and other algebraic expressions. We have sorted sequences of numbers. The limitations we face, in general, are those of time, memory size, and our ability to represent only those numbers which are integers less than 100,000 in absolute value (this last problem will be alleviated significantly in Chapter 6).

While programming these problems, and certainly as you program more and more complex problems, you will find it increasingly difficult to examine your printout. It is crowded with too many numbers representing too many different quantities. Time must be spent identifying and annotating the numbers printed. The time spent in deciphering and labeling the printout could be eliminated while the clarity of the output would be increased if, as part of the program, we could annotate the results of our computations.

Thus in Chapter 4, when we evaluated a polynomial at several values, we might have wanted to arrange our printout as shown in Fig. 5.1. Similarly, in the problem in Chapter 3 in which we computed and printed a table of numbers,

```
POLYNOMIAL DEGREE IS +00003

COEFFICIENTS ARE        +00002
                        +00000
                        -00015
                        -00346

             X          F(X)

          -00001       -00329
          +00000       -00346
          +00001       -00359
          +00002       -00?
          +00003
```

Figure 5.1

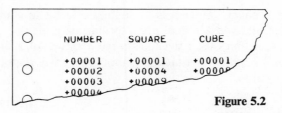

Figure 5.2

their squares and their cubes, we might have desired column headings like those shown in Fig. 5.2.

Such printouts are so much clearer than printouts of the same results without the annotation that there is hardly a program where a message-printing capability could not be used to advantage.

What additions must be made to the FACET computer, as we have defined it so far, to give it this capability? First we shall consider **hardware** additions, and then we shall discuss **software**. The hardware of a machine is the actual machine itself—its registers and interconnections and instruction set. The software is the collection of programs and programming techniques used with the machine.

We must first decide on some fixed set of characters that the printer will be able to print. Second, we must have some way of storing these characters in the machine. This latter requirement is known as the **internal representation** of characters. Finally, we need a way of having the machine examine a message stored in it and printing the message on the output paper. These three requirements would allow the FACET computer to be programmed to print messages along with the computed numbers.

5.2 THE CHARACTER SET

The FACET character set is already built into the machine. It has been chosen to include symbols most frequently needed by people programming the FACET computer. The character set is:

```
0  1  2  3  4  5  6  7  8  9
blank A  B  C  D  E  F  G  H  I
J  K  L  M  N  Ø  P  Q  R  S
T  U  V  W  X  Y  Z  )  *  (
/  =  ,  +  −  $  .
```

Of course, different symbols might be more suitable for other computers. A Russian computer would employ the Cyrillic alphabet, while the pound sterling symbol (£) would certainly be included in the character set of a computer in England.

Note that the **blank** symbol is included as one of the 47 characters in our set. This corresponds to the notion of having a key on the typewriter keyboard which, when depressed, will advance the paper one character position but will not leave any marks on the paper. Since it is sometimes difficult to count the number of blanks in a given message, we shall use ⊔ to indicate a blank. The symbols △, ƀ, and □ are also sometimes used to indicate the presence of a blank. Remember that when a blank is actually printed, an empty space will appear on the paper in that character position.

5.3 CHARACTER STRINGS

A **character string** (or symbol string) is a sequence of characters. Here are two character strings:

1. THE△ANSWER△IS
2. THEANSWERIS

These two strings are different; the first contains 13 characters, including two blanks, while the second contains 11 characters. We are particularly interested in character strings, since most of the messages we want printed consist of strings and not single symbols.

The **length** of a character string is the number of symbols or characters in it. What is the length of each of these character strings?

1. PØLYNØMIAL△DEGREE△IS

2. ⊔⊔⊔⊔⊔⊔⊔⊔⊔⊔X⊔⊔⊔⊔⊔⊔F(X)

3. △△△△△△△△△△NUMBER△△△△SQUARE△△△CUBE

If you counted the characters in each of the strings, you found that they contained 20, 22 and 33 characters, respectively (including all blanks). We say therefore that strings 1, 2, and 3 are of lengths 20, 22, and 33.

5.4 INTERNAL REPRESENTATION OF CHARACTERS AND STRINGS

How can we store the characters of our character set in the computer? The only facility for storing information is the memory, and yet we know that the memory can store only a sign and five digits in each of its registers.

One possibility is that we augment the registers so that each "window" of a register is able to contain any character from the set; and we could, for instance, have a memory register display such as

Unfortunately, this approach would greatly increase the complexity and cost of a memory register—between 50 and 100 percent of the original design. This is *not* the approach taken in the vast majority of computers, and it is *not* the approach used in FACET. Instead, the existing memory structure is left intact: The sign position can still have either a plus or minus (and nothing else), and each of the five digit positions can display one of the ten decimal digits (and nothing else). How, then, shall we represent characters?

The characters will be **encoded** as numbers. Since there are 100 different two-digit sequences (00,01,02,03,...,97,98,99), we can easily construct a code in which each of the 47 characters in our set corresponds to a single two-digit number or sequence. That leaves 53 unused codes. The FACET character code is as follows:

Character	Internal representation	Character	Internal representation
0	00	N	24
1	01	Ø	25
2	02	P	26
3	03	Q	27
4	04	R	28
5	05	S	29
6	06	T	30
7	07	U	31
8	08	V	32
9	09	W	33
blank	10	X	34
A	11	Y	35
B	12	Z	36
C	13	)	37
D	14	*	38
E	15	(	39
F	16	/	40
G	17	=	41
H	18	,	42
I	19	+	43
J	20	–	44
K	21	$	45
L	22	.	46
M	23		

Certainly any two-digit number can be stored in the FACET memory. However, further conventions are needed to prescribe exactly how and where in memory characters and strings can be stored.

Since two digits are used to represent each character, a maximum of two and one-half characters (five digits) can be stored in a single memory word. For uniformity and simplicity we adopt the convention that only two characters be stored in a single word. The first character is stored in digits 2 and 3; the second in digits 4 and 5. The sign and digit 1 are ignored by the character-handling instructions.

The following illustration shows memory register 600, which contains a representation of the two characters X=. Since the sign and first digit are ignored in internal character representation, any sign and digit can appear there. In this case, −3 appears.

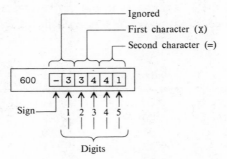

Character strings are stored in consecutive locations, two characters per location. When there is an odd number of characters, it is customary to put a blank (code 10) at the end of the string. This practice is sometimes called **padding with blanks** at the right.

Let's say we would like to store the string THE ANSWER IS in the memory, beginning with location 200. We would then encode the characters as follows:

Two characters		Their codes		The machine word	
T	H	30	18	200	+03018
E	␣	15	10	201	+01510
A	N	11	24	202	+01124
S	W	29	33	203	+02933
E	R	15	28	204	+01528
␣	I	10	19	205	+01019
S	␣	29	10	206	+02910

It is standard practice to have +0 in the sign and digit 1 positions of a word which represents two characters, however, it is not absolutely necessary. Later, when we discuss manipulation of characters, you will see that it is desirable to adhere to the +0 convention.

Exercises 5.4

1. What is the length of each of these strings?

   a) $43.29

   b) DØ␣NØT␣PASS␣GØ,␣DØ␣NØT␣CØLLECT␣$200.

   c) Q

2. Encode each of the following character strings as FACET machine words:

   a) PI = 3.14159

   b) ␣NAME␣␣␣GRADE

   c) CØST␣(AT␣$23.16/BUSHEL)−−

3. Decode each of the following sequences of words into character strings:

a) +01510	b) +01844	c) +01611
+04110	+01544	+01315
+02310	+02244	+03010
+01310	+02244	+01625
+02927	+02510	+02222
+03111	+01014	+01915
+02815	+02522	+02910
+01410	+02235	+01628
	+04610	+01929
		+01215
		+01529

5.5 PRINTING SYMBOLIC INFORMATION

There is an instruction in the FACET computer for printing a string of characters. It is the "print symbolic information" instruction and has numeric op-code 44 and mnemonic op-code PSYM. This instruction requires *two* items of information for its execution:

1. the length of the character string to be printed;
2. the memory location where the (encoded) string begins.

The effective operand of the PSYM instruction designates the location (address) of the beginning of the string to be printed. For example, if you had encoded the string THE ANSWER IS into seven consecutive memory locations beginning with location 200 (as we did in the previous section) and then, during the execution of the program, executed the instruction +44200, the printer would begin printing the message. Where does it end? The accumulator must contain the *length* of the string to be printed. If, in fact, the accumulator had contained +00013, then exactly THE ANSWER IS would have been printed in the *next* thirteen print positions of the line. When there is not enough room on a line for an entire string, it is continued on the next line, beginning with position 1.

In assembly language we might write PSYM   XXX, where XXX is the label of the first location of the encoded string in memory. Usually the instruction sequence for printing a message looks like this:

```
              .
              .
              .
         LDAC    LLL
         PSYM    XXX
              .
              .
              .
```

where LLL is a location containing the length of the string beginning in location XXX.

Let's say we have just executed these two instructions, and the printer has been positioned at position 42 of the line. Then this is what would be printed (assuming that the string at location XXX is THE␣ANSWER␣IS and that location LLL contains +00013):

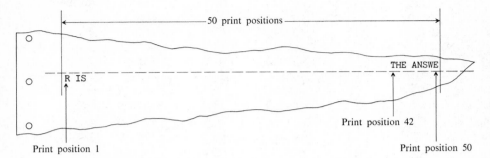

Of course, you would ordinarily be careful to have your messages and headings appear on one line, or at least not to have individual words split.

Can you now see how messages, headings, and other symbolic information can be interspersed among the numbers printed with the PNUM instruction by judicious use of the CRGC, TAB, and PSYM instructions? We can now have our results nicely formatted, labeled, and printed. For example, if we had just read in some information, printed this information, made some calculations, and were interested in printing the answer, we might want to print, in the center of a new line,

THE ANSWER IS   +00067

(assuming, of course, that 67 is indeed the answer). How might we have done this in an assembly language program? One way to do it is as follows:

	⋮		Read in the data, print the data and intermediate results, perform the computations, and place the answer into location ANSWER.
	CRGC	002	Perform two carriage returns.
	TAB	002	Tab to position 12 of the line.
	LDAC	THIRTN	Put +00013 into the accumulator.
	PSYM	MESSIJ	Print THE ANSWER IS in positions 12–24.
	PNUM	ANSWER	Print answer in positions 32–37.
	HALT		
THIRTN	SET	+00013	
ANSWER	LØC		
MESSIJ	SET	+03018 ⎫	
	SET	+01510 ⎪	Seven consecutive locations containing
	⋮	⋮	the encoded message THE ANSWER IS
	SET	+02910 ⎭	
	⋮	⋮	
	END		

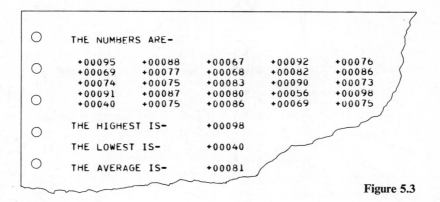

Figure 5.3

For another example, assume that we write a program which reads the grades of 25 students, prints those grades, then computes and prints the average grade, the highest grade, and the lowest grade. The results of this program would be a lot more readable if they were printed as shown in Fig. 5.3. In order to write this program we would have to encode the four messages as sequences of FACET words. Each sequence needs a name associated with the first word in the sequence. We choose the names MESSJ1, MESSJ2, MESSJ3, and MESSJ4 to represent the four strings. The program (omitting the portion in which the data are read in and the calculations are performed—i.e., most of the program) is as follows:

```
BEGIN   CRGC    003         Start on a new page.
        LDAC    LENGTH      Place string length +00016 in accumulator.
        PSYM    MESSJ1      Print THE NUMBERS ARE–.
        CRGC    002         Skip a line.
          ⋮                 Read in the 25 grades and print them; then
                            compute the average grade, the highest
                            grade, and the lowest grade; place
                            them into locations HIGH, LØW, and
                            AVRIJ, respectively.
        CRGC    002         Skip line.
        LDAC    LENGTH      +00016 into the accumulator.
        PSYM    MESSJ2      Print THE HIGHEST IS–␣ (columns 1–16).
        PNUM    HIGH        Print highest grade (columns 22–27).
        CRGC    002         Skip line.
        PSYM    MESSJ3      Print THE LØWEST IS–␣␣ (columns 1–16).
        PNUM    LØW         Print lowest grade (columns 22–27).
        CRGC    002         Skip line.
        PSYM    MESSJ4      Print THE AVERAGE IS–␣ (columns 1–16).
        PNUM    AVRIJ       Print average grade (columns 22–27).
        HALT
LENGTH  SET     +00016      Length of messages.
```

```
HIGH    LØC
LØW     LØC
AVRIJ   LØC
MESSJ1  SET     +03018   T H ⎫
        SET     +01510   E ␣ ⎪
        SET     +02431   N U ⎪
        SET     +02312   M B ⎬  Encoding of the character string
        SET     +01528   E R ⎪  THE␣NUMBERS␣ARE–.
        SET     +02910   S ␣ ⎪
        SET     +01128   A R ⎪
        SET     +01544   E – ⎭
MESSJ2  SET     +03018 ⎫
        SET     +01510 ⎪
         ⋮        ⋮    ⎬  Encoding of THE␣HIGHEST␣IS–␣.
        SET     +04410 ⎭
MESSJ3  SET     +03018 ⎫
        SET     +01510 ⎪
         ⋮        ⋮    ⎬  Encoding of THE␣LØWEST␣IS–␣␣.
        SET     +01010 ⎭
MESSJ4  SET     +03018 ⎫
        SET     +01510 ⎪
         ⋮        ⋮    ⎬  Encoding of THE␣AVERAGE␣IS–␣.
        SET     +04410 ⎭
         ⋮
        END
```

There are some important points you probably noticed in going through the program. They have been mentioned before, but we list them explicitly below:

1. The length of the printed string must be stored in the accumulator at the time the PSYM instruction is executed. It is not important how it got there. Note that in the preceding program we place +00016 into the accumulator just before printing THE HIGHEST IS–␣. The accumulator does not change thereafter, so that same number +00016 serves as the length for the next two PSYM instructions executed.

2. The four messages are actually of different lengths—two are of length 15 and one each of 14 and 16. The shorter messages were extended to length 16 (by padding on the right with blanks) so that the length in the accumulator would not have to be changed.

Exercises 5.5

1. You are an onion inspector in a soup factory. Your job is to grade each shipment of of onions. Grades, until now, have been based on a 0-to-100 scale; in fact, there is a punched-card file of the grades of various shipments. The first six columns on each

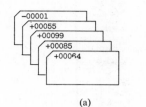

(a)

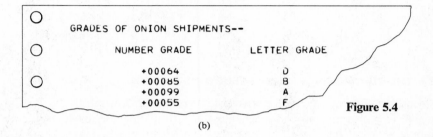

(b)

Figure 5.4

card contain a number representing the grade of a shipment. Your firm is converting to the six-letter alphabetic system. The conversion factors are:

Former grade (numeric):	90–100	80–89	72–79	63–71	less than 63
New grade (alphabetic):	A	B	C	D	F

Write and submit a program which reads a sequence of cards containing numeric grades and prints number and letter grades side by side in two columns. Use your own data deck. The end-of-data should be marked with a negative number at the back of the data.

If your data deck looks like that shown in Fig. 5.4(a), then your printout should be something like that shown in part (b) of the figure. Use at least 10 data cards.

2. Write and submit a program which prints:

```
SIMPLE SIMØN MET A PIEMAN
   GØING TØ THE FAIR
SAID SIMPLE SIMØN TØ THE PIEMAN—
   LET ME SEE YØUR WARE
SAID THE PIEMAN TØ SIMPLE SIMØN—
   SHØW ME FIRST YØUR PENNY
SAID SIMPLE SIMØN TØ THE PIEMAN—
   BUT I HAVENT ANY
```

Do not encode the jingle in its entirety. Each word or phrase which is repeated in the jingle (such as SIMPLE SIMØN, THE PIEMAN, SAID) should be encoded once only—the program should take care of having it printed the appropriate number of times and in the appropriate place. Do you have the spacing right?

3. Write and submit a program which prints an output as shown in Fig. 5.5. Employ a loop to perform the indentation. Encode the message FACET CØMPUTER only once.

(*Hint:* Store the blank symbol, and each time, on a new line, print that symbol the appropriate number of times; *then* print the message.)

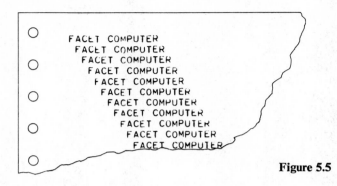

Figure 5.5

5.6 THE CHARACTER STRING PSEUDO-OPERATION

Encoding a string of characters is both tiresome and mechanical. Any process which is both tiresome and mechanical is a candidate for machine (rather than human) processing. So the character encoding process is delegated to the assembler. We must merely tell the assembler that we want a string of characters encoded, and it does so. We do this by using the pseudo-operation CHAR (for CHARacter string). This pseudo-op allows us to encode a character string of up to 56 characters with *one* assembly language statement (punched on *one* card).

Let's take the example in which we encoded THE ANSWER IS, of length 13, into seven machine words. We did this by writing

MESSIJ	SET	+03018
	SET	+01510
	SET	+01124
	SET	+02933
	SET	+01528
	SET	+01019
	SET	+02910

This entire sequence of assembly language pseudo-ops may be replaced by the single pseudo-op:

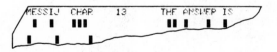

The effect of writing this pseudo-op is to set up a sequence of appropriate length containing the encoded character string. The first location of the sequence corresponds to the name in the label column (in this case MESSIJ). The length of the string is given in the operand column as a two-digit number (columns 17 and 18), and the string itself is punched beginning with column 25 (usually the comment field). When the string is of odd length, the extra character encoded is *blank.* Note that if there are less than ten characters in the string, then columns 17 and 18 still must contain a two-digit number (e.g., 07).

Those four long sequences of SET pseudo-ops for the four messages in the previous section may now be replaced by the four pseudo-ops:

```
MESSJ1    CHAR    16       THE NUMBERS ARE-
MESSJ2    CHAR    16       THE HIGHEST IS-
MESSJ3    CHAR    16       THE LØWEST IS-
MESSJ4    CHAR    16       THE AVERAGE IS-
```
               ↑   ↑   ↑   ↑— column 25
               │   │   └── column 17
               │   └──────── column 9
               └──────────── column 1

Of course, when the assembler finishes translating, the machine language program will actually contain the four sequences of machine words representing these character strings. It makes no difference whether you or the assembler does the encoding—the final program will be the same. Using the CHAR pseudo-op, however, does relieve us of doing the actual encoding—and for that matter, of remembering the two-digit codes.

Let's now write a program which prints the following:†

```
WERE SERGEANT PEPPERS LØNELY HEARTS CLUB BAND
WE HØPE YØU HAVE ENJØYED THE SHØW
SERGEANT PEPPERS LØNELY HEARTS CLUB BAND
WERE SØRRY BUT ITS TIME TØ GØ
SERGEANT PEPPERS LØNELY
SERGEANT PEPPERS LØNELY
SERGEANT PEPPERS LØNELY
SERGEANT PEPPERS LØNELY
SERGEANT PEPPERS LØNELY HEARTS CLUB BAND
```

Rather than store the entire verse, we'll store character strings *once* each, and perform repetition in the program. The program will begin with the data portion as follows:

```
L1      SET      +00005
M1      CHAR     05        WERE␣
L2      SET      +00024
M2      CHAR     24        SERGEANT PEPPERS LØNELY␣
L3      SET      +00016
M3      CHAR     16        HEARTS CLUB BAND
```

---

†   From "Sergeant Pepper's Lonely Hearts Club Band," Copyright © 1967 by Northern Songs Ltd., England. Reprinted by permission. All rights reserved. (Note the liberties taken with spelling due to the lack of an apostrophe (') in our character set.)

L4	SET	+00033	
M4	CHAR	33	WE HØPE YØU HAVE ENJØYED THE SHØW
L5	SET	+00024	
M5	CHAR	24	SØRRY BUT ITS TIME TØ GØ

Now we continue with the rest of the program:

BEGIN	CRGC	003	Start on new page.
	LDAC	L1	} Print WERE␣.
	PSYM	M1	
	LDAC	L2	} Print SERGEANT PEPPERS LØNELY␣.
	PSYM	M2	
	LDAC	L3	} Print HEARTS CLUB BAND.
	PSYM	M3	
	CRGC	001	New line.
	LDAC	L4	} Print WE HØPE YØU HAVE ENJØYED THE SHØW.
	PSYM	M4	
	CRGC	001	New line.
	LDAC	L2	} Print SERGEANT PEPPERS LØNELY␣.
	PSYM	M2	
	LDAC	L3	} Print HEARTS CLUB BAND.
	PSYM	M3	
	CRGC	001	New line.
	LDAC	L1	} Print WERE␣.
	PSYM	M1	
	LDAC	L5	} Print SØRRY BUT ITS TIME TØ GØ.
	PSYM	M5	
	LDAC	L2	} Initialize loop.
	LDX	ZERØ	
LØØP	CRGC	001	}
	PSYM	M2	} Loop to print SERGEANT PEPPERS LØNELY␣
	INCX	001	} five times, each time on a new line.
	SXEQ	FIVE	
	JUMP	LØØP	
	LDAC	L3	} Print HEARTS CLUB BAND.
	PSYM	M3	
	HALT		
ZERØ	SET	+00000	
FIVE	SET	+00005	
	END		

Did you notice that the text includes **trailing** blanks (blanks following a string of nonblank characters) where needed, as in the string WERE␣. Execution begins with the instruction labeled BEGIN.

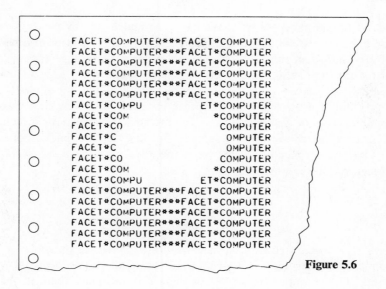

```
FACET*COMPUTER***FACET*COMPUTER
FACET*COMPUTER***FACET*COMPUTER
FACET*COMPUTER***FACET*COMPUTER
FACET*COMPUTER***FACET*COMPUTER
FACET*COMPUTER***FACET*COMPUTER
FACET*COMPUTER***FACET*COMPUTER
FACET*COMPU                 ET*COMPUTER
FACET*COM                   *COMPUTER
FACET*CO                     COMPUTER
FACET*C                       OMPUTER
FACET*C                       OMPUTER
FACET*CO                     COMPUTER
FACET*COM                   *COMPUTER
FACET*COMPU                 ET*COMPUTER
FACET*COMPUTER***FACET*COMPUTER
FACET*COMPUTER***FACET*COMPUTER
FACET*COMPUTER***FACET*COMPUTER
FACET*COMPUTER***FACET*COMPUTER
FACET*COMPUTER***FACET*COMPUTER
FACET*COMPUTER***FACET*COMPUTER
```

Figure 5.6

Exercises 5.6

1. Write and submit a program which prints, on a new page, the output shown in Fig. 5.6. Employ as few stored strings as possible (using the CHAR pseudo-op).

2. Write and submit a program which prints, in a column, the two-digit integers from 00 through 99:

$$00$$
$$01$$
$$02$$
$$\vdots$$
$$98$$
$$99$$

Do not employ stored character strings at all. Use a counter to compute the successive integers and to then *convert* the each integer representation to the character representation to the character representation of the two-digit integer. For example, when your program gets to 37, it computes

$$+00037$$

and then converts it to

$$+00307$$

which is the encoded character string 37 (of length two).

5.7 DIGIT AND SYMBOL MANIPULATION

Let's say we have been computing an amount of money (in pennies), and we would like to print the result in a format other than that which the PNUM instruction allows. For instance, if we have just computed +04592, we might prefer printing

$45.92 rather than +04592. We can accomplish this by clever manipulation of the digits of +04592, by rearranging them so that we can print a character string of *six* characters, namely $45.92. In order to rearrange these digits we shall introduce three new instructions especially designed for digit manipulation. At present, we have only arithmetic instructions available for actually changing the digits within a number—all the other instructions merely move words between registers without *changing* them. The arithmetic instructions are clumsy, and so some new instructions are warranted. But first, let's get back to our problem.

Instead of printing +04592 with the PNUM instruction, we want to print the sequence of three words (six characters)

$$
\begin{array}{ll}
+04504 & (\$4) \\
+00546 & (5.) \\
+00902 & (92)
\end{array}
$$

with the PSYM instruction. Since we don't know the outcome of the numeric computation (resulting in +04592) in advance, all we can do is take the last four digits of the computation (4592 in this case) and place them in the appropriate positions of the three-word sequence

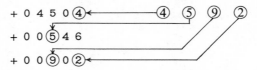

This can be accomplished by setting up the three-word sequence

$$
\begin{array}{c}
+\ 0\ 4\ 5\ 0\ \textcircled{0} \\[4pt]
+\ 0\ 0\ \textcircled{0}\ 4\ 6 \\[4pt]
+\ 0\ 0\ \textcircled{0}\ 0\ \textcircled{0}
\end{array}
$$

and then somehow extracting the individual digits of +04592, moving them over to the appropriate digit positions, and adding them onto the appropriate words in the three-word array.

To **extract** a digit (or some digits) from a word we use the *extract* instruction. Its numeric op-code is 53 and mnemonic op-code EXTR. This instruction operates on a word in the accumulator and allows us to specify any combination of digits we wish to save (extract); the remaining digits are set to zero (the sign is not affected). The operand of the instruction is the address of a word in memory known as a **mask**. For each digit in the mask which is zero, the digit in the accumulator in the *same digit position* is set to zero. For example, if we execute an EXTR instruction with mask +90530, then digits 2 and 5 of the accumulator are set to zero (since digits 2 and 5 of the mask are zero). If the accumulator had contained the word –07777, it would have contained –00770 after the execution of the instruction. Note that the other digits are not affected. When we set up the mask, it is easiest to use zeros and ones. So instead of +90530, we might have set the mask at +10110 with the same results.

The mask for the extract instruction is set up with the SET pseudo-op and usually remains constant throughout the program (although the programmer may use any mask he likes). In the case of extracting digits 1, 3, and 4 from the accumulator, we could write (in assembly language)

$$\vdots$$

```
          EXTR    MASK6
```

$$\vdots$$

```
MASK6     SET     +10110
```

$$\vdots$$

Now we know how to extract the second, third, fourth, and fifth digits, one at a time, from our result (+04592). We need a mask for each extraction:

```
DIGIT2    SET     +01000
DIGIT3    SET     +00100
DIGIT4    SET     +00010
DIGIT5    SET     +00001
```

In order to extract digit 4 from the accumulator, we must merely say

```
          EXTR    DIGIT4
```

Next, we must be able to move digits around within a word. We can already do this by arithmetic operations (multiplying and dividing by powers of 10), but a more direct way is to use the two instructions for **shifting** digits within a word (in the accumulator) to the left or right. The **shift** instructions in the FACET computer are LEFT (for shifting left) and RGHT (for shifting right). Their respective numeric op-codes are 51 and 52. Execution of the instruction +51nnn causes the five digits in the accumulator to shift left nnn positions. Similarly, the execution of +52nnn causes the accumulator word to be shifted right nnn digit positions.

As digits get shifted off the "end" of the word, they are lost. The "new" digits shifted in (from the other end) are zeros. The sign of the accumulator is never affected by either the LEFT or RGHT instruction.

Let's look at some examples. If the accumulator contained the word −90457, then:

The execution of instruction	Written in assembly language		Would result in the accumulator containing
+51000	LEFT	000	−90457
+51002	LEFT	002	−45700
+51004	LEFT	004	−70000
+51006	LEFT	006	−00000
+51855	LEFT	855	−00000
+52001	RGHT	001	−09054
+52003	RGHT	003	−00090
+52005	RGHT	005	−00000

Note that when the operand is greater than 004, the entire word gets shifted out and the digits are all replaced by zeros. The sign, however, is unaffected. You might visualize the shift instructions as follows:

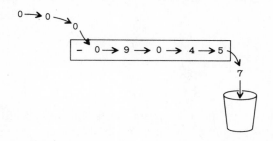

All three digit manipulation instructions, EXTR, LEFT, and RGHT, can be executed with indexing, in which case their effective operand is computed and used as you might expect. In such cases we would write EXTR*, LEFT*, or RGHT*.

Now we are ready to write the portion of the program which causes the printing of a four-digit number as a dollars-and-cents sum. We create the three word array

$$+04500$$
$$+00046$$
$$+00000$$

by using the CHAR pseudo-ops

```
DØLLR1    CHAR    02    $0
DØLLR2    CHAR    02    0.
DØLLR3    CHAR    02    00
```

Note that printing the six-character string beginning with DØLLR1 (before the changes are made) would cause $00.00 to be printed. Now we shall compute and add on the digits of our answer (stored in location ANSWER), as described before. Let's say we are at that point in the program where we have already computed the answer and stored it in location ANSWER. Assume also that the printer is positioned correctly and that any necessary messages have already been printed (or programmed). We now proceed to print $45.92 (or whatever the sum is to be).

```
    ⋮
    LDAC    ANSWER ⎫
    EXTR    DIGIT2 ⎪  Set up location DØLLR1 to contain the
    RGHT    003    ⎬  dollar sign ($), followed by the first
    ADD     DØLLR1 ⎪  dollar digit (4 in the case of our example).
    STAC    DØLLR1 ⎭
    LDAC    ANSWER ⎫
    EXTR    DIGIT3 ⎪  Set up location DØLLR2 to contain
    ADD     DØLLR2 ⎬  the second dollar digit (5 in our case),
    STAC    DØLLR2 ⎭  followed by a period (.).
```

```
           LDAC    ANSWER ⎫
           EXTR    DIGIT4 ⎪
           LEFT    001    ⎪ Set up DØLLR3 to contain the character
           STAC    TEMP   ⎬ codes for the two "cent" digits (9 and 2
           LDAC    ANSWER ⎪ in our case).
           EXTR    DIGIT5 ⎪
           ADD     TEMP   ⎪
           STAC    DØLLR3 ⎭
           LDAC    SIX    ⎫ Print the result; note that DØLLR1,
           PSYM    DØLLR1 ⎬ DØLLR2 and DØLLR3 must be consecutive.
           HALT
DØLLR1     CHAR    02      $0
DØLLR2     CHAR    02      0.
DØLLR3     CHAR    02      00
TEMP       LØC
SIX        SET     +00006
DIGIT2     SET     +01000
DIGIT3     SET     +00100
DIGIT4     SET     +00010
DIGIT5     SET     +00001
ANSWER     LØC
             ⋮
           END
```

There are many applications in which we would like to take a character string, that is stored in an array in the usual way (two characters per word) and **unpack** it. When information is **packed**, it is stored in relatively few registers, using up much of the available space in the registers. Our character strings are packed two characters per word, but other computers with longer registers can have four, six, or even ten characters packed in each word. Unpacking is the process of rearranging the information (characters in this case) so that less information (fewer characters) is contained in each register. Character strings are more efficiently stored when they are packed, but more easily handled when unpacked.

A packed character string like FE–FI–FØ–FUM is stored as:

```
+ 0 1 6 1 5      FE
+ 0 4 4 1 6      –F
+ 0 1 9 4 4      I–
+ 0 1 6 2 5      FØ
+ 0 4 4 1 6      –F
+ 0 2 7 2 3      UM
```

The 12-character string is stored in six locations. It could be unpacked into

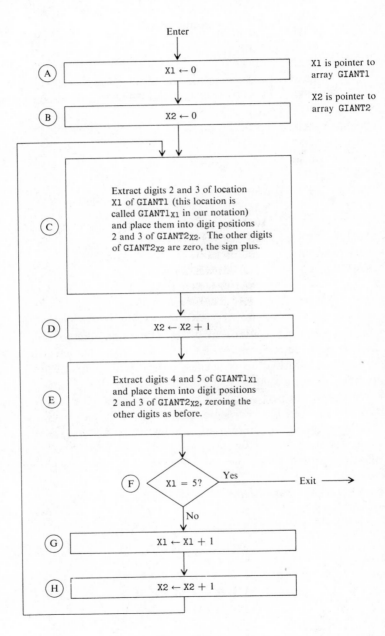

Figure 5.7

12 locations:

```
+ 0  16  0 0    F
+ 0  15  0 0    E
+ 0  44  0 0    -
+ 0  16  0 0    F
+ 0  19  0 0    I
+ 0  44  0 0    -
+ 0  16  0 0    F
+ 0  25  0 0    O
+ 0  44  0 0    -
+ 0  16  0 0    F
+ 0  27  0 0    U
+ 0  23  0 0    M
```

Let's say that FE-FI-FØ-FUM is stored in the first six locations of array GIANT1, and we would like to unpack it into the first twelve locations of array GIANT2. Assume that both arrays are longer than the particular string lengths with which we're dealing. A flowchart for this unpacking appears in Fig. 5.7. Essentially what we want to do is take the two characters in the first location of GIANT1 and place them into the first *two* locations in array GIANT2:

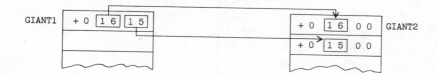

Next we want to place the next two characters, which are in the second location of GIANT1, into the third and fourth locations of GIANT2. We continue this procedure until the entire string is unpacked. The instruction sequence corresponding to the flowchart in Fig. 5.7 follows. Each section of the instructions corresponds to a box in the flowchart and is marked with the same letter (*A*, *B*, . . .).

```
LDAC    ZERØ
STAC    X1
```
A. Initialize pointer X1.

```
STAC    X2
```
B. Initialize pointer X2.

```
LØØP    LDX     X1      ⎫
        LDAC*   GIANT1  ⎪
        EXTR    DIG23   ⎬ C. Move first character to array GIANT2.
        LDX     X2      ⎪
        STAC*   GIANT2  ⎭

        INCX    001     ⎫
        STX     X2      ⎬ D. X2 ← X2 + 1.

        LDX     X1      ⎫
        LDAC*   GIANT1  ⎪
        EXTR    DIG45   ⎬ E. Move second character to array GIANT2.
        LEFT    002     ⎪
        LDX     X2      ⎪
        STAC*   GIANT2  ⎭

        LDX     X1      ⎫
        SXEQ    FIVE    ⎬ F. Test for loop exit.
        JUMP    CNTNUE  ⎪
        JUMP    NEXT    ⎭

CNTNUE  INCX    001     ⎫
        STX     X1      ⎬ G. X1 ← X1 + 1.

        LDX     X2      ⎫
        INCX    001     ⎬ H. X2 ← X2 + 1.
        STX     X2      ⎪
        JUMP    LØØP    ⎭

NEXT
          ⋮

FIVE    SET     +00005
DIG23   SET     +01100   Mask to extract digits 2 and 3.
DIG45   SET     +00011   Mask to extract digits 4 and 5.
GIANT1  ARAY    nnn      nnn ≥ 006.
GIANT2  ARAY    mmm      mmm ≥ 012.
ZERØ    SET     +00000
X1      LØC
X2      LØC
          ⋮
```

Printing an array such as GIANT2 is very simple—we must print one character at a time. To print the 12 characters of the string GIANT2, we merely write:

```
          ⋮
        LDX     ZERØ     Set pointer to first character of array.
        LDAC    ØNE      Set length of string to be printed to 1.
PRYNT   PSYM*   GIANT2   Print single symbol.
```

```
INCX   001     Increment pointer.
SXEQ   TWELVE  Test completion of 12 characters.
JUMP   PRYNT   Print more characters.
 :
```

We could not print the entire string with one PSYM instruction, since zeros are interspersed among the characters (in digits 4 and 5 of each of the first 12 words of array GIANT2), and these zeros (00 is the character code for 0) would be printed.

Exercises 5.7

1. A message may be encoded according to the following scheme: Substitute for each letter in the message the letter which appears three positions later in the alphabet. Thus D would be substituted for A, E for B, F for C, G for D, and so on. The exceptions are X, Y, and Z; A, B, and C would be used in place of X, Y, and Z, respectively. Such an encoding scheme is known as a substitution cipher. This particular substitution cipher can be illustrated as follows:

   for the character   A   B   C   D   E . . . W   X   Y   Z
   the character   D   E   F   G   H . . . Z   A   B   C   is substituted.

   Write and submit a FACET program which decodes and prints the message encoded (according to this scheme) in an array called SECRET, of length 15. Characters other than alphabetic are not changed. To test the program, place the following string into SECRET by using the CHAR pseudo-op:

   SECRET   CHAR   30   WKLV⌴LV⌴D⌴VHFUHW⌴PHVVDJH.

2. You are Pierre Q. Pumpernickel, the famous master-spy. You have been receiving your instructions in a special code which the enemy has been unable to crack. The code works as follows: You receive a list of five-decimal-digit numbers, all of which are positive except for the last, which is negative. You discard the negative number and write the others in the proper order in five columns (one for each digit). For instance, the other day you received the list of numbers:

$$
\begin{array}{r}
+11113 \\
+70000 \\
+12113 \\
+84293 \\
+31312 \\
+09565 \\
-20932
\end{array}
$$

   You write these numbers as follows (disregarding the last, negative number):

1	1	1	1	3
7	0	0	0	0
1	2	1	1	3
8	4	2	9	3
3	1	3	1	2
0	9	5	6	5

Now you begin picking off two-digit pairs, starting at the top of the rightmost column. When you finish a column, you move to the top of the next column to its left. In the above case, you would choose the pairs beginning as follows:

```
1    1    1    1 | 3 | ──→ 1st  pair  30
7    0    0    0 |⟍0 | ─↗  2nd  pair  33
1    2    1    1 |  3 | ↗   3rd  pair  25
8    4    2    9 | 3 | ↗   4th  pair  10
3    1    3    1 | 2 |↗         etc.
0    9    5    6 ⟍ 5 ↙
```

Finally, you end up with a list of pairs of digits. In the above case, this list is 30, 33, 25, 10, 19, 16, 10, 12, 35, 10, 24, 19, 17, 18, 30. You now decode the message by using the correspondence code:

$$10 = \text{blank}$$
$$11 = \text{A}$$
$$12 = \text{B}$$
$$\vdots$$
$$36 = \text{Z}$$

Note that this is the same code as that used in the FACET internal representation. This message is, for instance:

30	33	25	10	19	16	10	12	35	10	24	19	17	18	30
T	W	O		I	F		B	Y		N	I	G	H	T

It so happens that you, Pierre Q. Pumpernickel, recently stumbled upon an auction of surplus (authentic) James Bond equipment (on Sunset Blvd.) and you have outfitted yourself with the latest, including a FACET computer complete with assembler. As a result, you request your contact to supply you, in the future, with coded messages already punched on cards (sign and five digits in the first six columns). You are now about to write a FACET program (in assembly language, naturally) which will read the coded cards and print out the message. Decoding was never like this, but after all, a space-age spy ought to have a few amenities.

Write and submit this program. The (secret) message will be supplied by your contact (instructor) in the near future. Meanwhile, you can debug the program on contrived messages of your own choosing. *Note:* assume that no message will contain more than 100 characters.

5.8 READING SYMBOLIC INFORMATION

Frequently we would like our programs to process symbolic information not known to us at the time of writing; that is, we would like our programs to be able to *read* symbolic information, process it, and print results. At execution time, we would have to read sequences of symbols from an external medium (like a data deck) into the memory; then we would process these symbols as we have been doing. Examples of such programs are payrolls, cryptanalysis programs (for decoding or deciphering messages), inventory control programs, and billing programs. We must therefore add another instruction to the FACET instruction set—an instruction which reads symbolic information into the memory from data cards.

The read-symbolic-information instruction has the mnemonic op-code RSYM and the numeric op-code 43. The execution of the RSYM instruction causes the next data card to be read and a string of characters thereon to be encoded and placed into the memory in consecutive memory locations, beginning with the memory register whose address is the effective operand. The length of the string to be encoded (the number of symbols or characters in it) is specified in the accumulator in a manner similar to the PSYM instruction. The maximum length that may be read is 80 (the number of columns on a punched card). This allows us (potentially) to read all the information on a punched card. When a string of fewer than 80 characters is read, the string is taken from the beginning of the card. For example, if the accumulator contains +00012 and the instruction +43801 is executed, then the characters in columns 1 through 12 of the next data card are read into locations 801 through 806. If the card had contained

then the string THE␣QUICK␣BR would have been encoded and placed into the memory:

799		
800	⋮	
801	+03018	TH
802	+01510	E␣
803	+02731	QU
804	+01913	IC
805	+02110	K␣
806	+01228	BR
807	⋮	
808	Unchanged	
809	⋮	
810		

This is placed into the memory.

Furthermore, the data can no longer be accessed, so the rest of the information on the card is lost to the program. Each card can be read only *once* during the execution of the program, because the card reader is a sequential device, and once a card is read, it passes through the reading heads and into a bin. If we are not sure how much of the information on a card is really needed, we had better read in all 80 characters and decide at a later step in the program the actual disposition of the string.

When the RSYM instruction is executed, the accumulator must contain some number between +00000 and +00080 (otherwise the program terminates with an error message). The usual procedure is to load the accumulator with a number

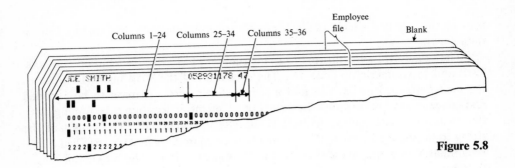

Figure 5.8

indicating the length of the string to be read *immediately* before each RSYM instruction, although this choice is really within the domain of the programmer.

Let's write a program. It will be a simple program to perform some calculations for a payroll. Our data will take the following form:

1. There will be a data card for each employee in the data deck.
2. The last card in the deck will be blank.
3. Each employee data card will contain:

   a) the employee's name in columns 1–24,
   b) his or her social security number in columns 25–33,
   c) the number of hours worked this week in columns 35–36.

This is an admittedly simplified payroll program. Assume that we pay $2.86 per hour to all the employees on this particular list. Such a list, by the way, is called a **file**, and each item (an employee card) is called a **record**. We want to write a program which will list all the employees in the file, together with their social security numbers, the number of hours worked, and the amount of pay they receive this particular week. We expect our employee file (the data deck) to look something like that shown in Fig. 5.8. Our printout will look something like that shown in Fig. 5.9.

The program is fairly simple. Most of the information read in (columns 1–34) is merely reproduced on the printout. The two (numeric) characters read from columns 35–36 must be converted to a FACET number, and the salary must then be computed. In the case of JØE SMITH, the characters are 47, which must

	NAME	S.S. NO.	HRS.	PAY
○				
○	JOE SMITH	052931178	47	$134.42
	JONATHAN JONES	063592701	40	$114.15
	TOM HARRIS	05924		

Figure 5.9

be converted to +00047. After the computation (resulting in a salary of +13442), the pay must be converted to a string of six characters (134.42) and then printed. The conversion techniques were discussed earlier in this chapter.

The program is a very simple loop: Each card is read. The first character is checked—if it is blank, we have hit the last card, and we exit the loop and program. If it is non-blank, it is a name, and the card must be processed. A flowchart for the program might be like that shown in Fig. 5.10.

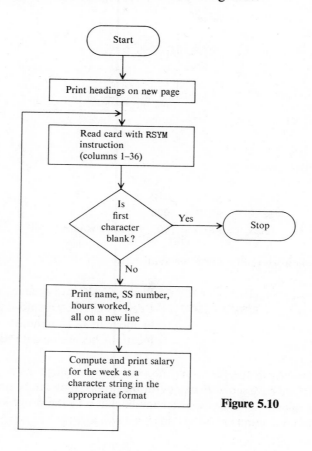

Figure 5.10

When we read a number of strings from different fields on a card, it is sometimes convenient to use consecutive arrays in the memory. In the previous problem, for instance, we read a card with:

1. a 24-character name   [12 FACET words]
2. a 10-character S.S. number (include blank)   [5 FACET words]
3. a 2-character number (hours worked)   [1 FACET word]

We might then allocate in our program 18 consecutive FACET words in three

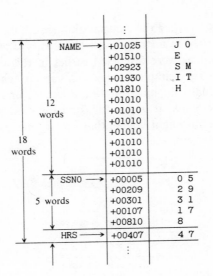

Figure 5.11

consecutive arrays:

NAME	ARAY	012
SSNØ	ARAY	005
HRS	ARAY	001	(equivalently, HRS LØC)

Then, when we read a card, we shall write

LDAC	THIRT6	Place +00036 into accumulator
RSYM	NAME	Read 36 characters into the
		memory in 18 consecutive
		locations beginning with NAME

The first card in the file would be read into the memory as shown in Fig. 5.11.

Since we have separate names for the arrays, they can be printed independently, without address or index register modification in the program. To print just the social security number, for instance, we would write

⋮

| LDAC | TEN |
| PSYM | SSNØ |

⋮

Since any character string (or part thereof) representing numbers can be converted to actual FACET numbers, we can process all sorts of mixed alphabetic and numeric information by computer. Standard instruction sequences for conversion are often used. These will be discussed in Chapters 7 and 9.

Exercises 5.8

1. If we had allocated the following arrays in our program,

$$\vdots$$

FIRST	ARAY	002
SECØND	ARAY	004
THIRD	ARAY	002

$$\vdots$$

and we had just read the card,

with the instruction sequence,

$$\vdots$$

LDAC	SIXTN	(+00016 into accumulator)
RSYM	FIRST	

$$\vdots$$

then what would be printed if:

a) +00010 were placed in the accumulator and we executed PSYM SECØND?
b) +00005 were placed in the accumulator and we executed PSYM FIRST?
c) +00001 were placed in the accumulator and we executed PSYM THIRD?
d) +00014 were placed in the accumulator and we executed PSYM FIRST?
e) +00007 were placed in the accumulator and we executed PSYM SECØND?

2. Write and submit a FACET program which reads a single data card (all 80 columns) and then determines and prints the number of occurrences of the character $. Do this by storing a dollar sign in some location, viz,

DØLR	CHAR	02	0$

and then checking each location of the 40-location array into which the card has been read. Don't forget to check both character positions in each word. Print the contents of the card also.

3. Write and submit the payroll program discussed in this section. Use your own data deck.

5.9 LOADERS AND ASSEMBLERS

Until now, we have vaguely referred to the loader and the assembler as "processors." In FACET, they are an integral part of the machine; however, this is not the case in other computers. If one has a general purpose digital computer, there is no reason why various "processors" cannot be software devices (programs). In fact, in other machines the loader and the assembler are usually programs. FACET's memory is too small to contain a complete loader or assembler; 1000 memory registers is not typical of today's computers—more typical is 8000 registers for a small computer and 250,000 registers in a large one.

How would one go about writing a loader for the FACET machine in machine language? First, we must recognize that the loader itself while operating, would occupy part of the memory. This implies that the entire memory would no longer be available to the program being loaded. If a loader in the FACET machine occupied locations 000–149, then programs could be loaded into locations 150–999 only.†

You can probably already imagine how a simple loader would work. It would read a card, all 80 columns, as a string of characters. Then it would check whether characters 1–3 constituted a three-digit address and whether characters 7–12 were a FACET word. If so, it would convert characters 7–12 to an actual FACET word and then place it (store it) in the appropriate register. When the loader comes across an EXECUTE. card, it converts the three digits to a FACET address (500 in this case) and *jumps* to that address (it has finished loading and is now allowing execution to begin).

Assemblers are more complicated. The actual translation from assembly language to machine language requires lots of work. The assembler must, if you recall, make two passes—first translating op-codes and numeric operands, while constructing a symbol table, and later plugging in the address corresponding to the labels in the program. Construction of these tables can be somewhat confusing. What would a symbol table look like in the FACET memory? Here is an example:

Label	Address
GEØRGE	003
X39	012
ØNE	112
FIFT5	113
⋮	⋮

In the FACET memory, a label must be stored in three registers, since it can contain up to six characters. The address requires another register. So an **entry**, such as GEØRGE 003 requires four locations. If we had chosen to place our entry in four consecutive locations, it might have been done as shown in Fig. 5.12. Our symbol table might then be an array where consecutive blocks of four words constitute the entries.

Without describing further points on the implementation of an assembler, you should begin to see how some very complex processors are programmed using techniques with which we are already familiar.

---

† Remember, this does not apply to the FACET computer, but it does to other computers.

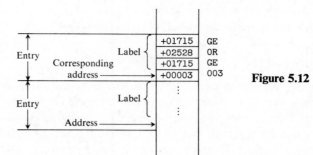

Figure 5.12

Exercises 5.9

1. Write a program in FACET which reads an assembly language (mnemonic) op-code
   in columns 9–12 of a card, and then prints it together with its corresponding numeric
   op-code. You may implement only a few op-codes (e.g., LDAC, STAC, ADD, PNUM,
   HALT). If the program reads

it should print

2. If assembly language is indeed so much better than machine language, is there any
   program that *must* be written in machine language? Explain.

3. **A relocative loader** is a loader which loads a program that is to be modified for relocation. Describe the activity of such a loader. How does this activity differ from that of
   an absolute loader? How does its input differ?

4. Describe an algorithm for checking a string of six characters to determine whether or
   not it is a valid FACET name (label). Draw a flowchart.

5. The following program is assembled and loaded beginning in location 313. What
   does it print? Does it halt?

```
           DECX*   999
           LDAC    GEØRGE
           LEFT    001
           STAC    GEØRGE
           LEFT    002
           STAC*   GEØRGE
           RGHT    004
   GEØRGE  CHAR    06        −V+X23
           END
```

6. Design and write a FACET loader.

7. Design and write a simplified FACET assembler.

5.10 IN REVIEW

A desirable feature in computers is a facility for printing symbols or characters other than numbers. Such a feature can be used, for instance, in labeling output. The FACET computer has such a facility. A character set of 47 characters has been chosen for use with the FACET machine—the 26 alphabetic characters, the 10 decimal digits, 10 other frequently used symbols, and the blank. Each character is assigned a two-digit code, so that two characters may be encoded in a single FACET memory word. Digits 2–5 of a memory word are used in the encoding; the other digit and the sign are ignored.

Symbolic input/output is achieved with two I/O instructions: read symbolic information (RSYM) and print symbolic information (PSYM), which have numeric op-codes 43 and 44, respectively. These instructions read and print entire strings of symbols (the length of the string is determined by the positive integer in the accumulator) from cards into memory arrays and from arrays onto the printer paper.

The CHAR pseudo-op is used to initialize a sequence of memory registers to the codes for a specified string of characters. It is especially useful for creating character string representations for specified messages to be printed with the output, i.e., for labeling output.

Individual digits of a memory word may be manipulated by use of the extract (EXTR, op-code 53) and the left and right shift (LEFT, op-code 51; RGHT, op-code 52) instructions. This facility is especially useful in moving characters, comparing characters in strings and alphabetizing words. These instructions also permit packing of information into a few registers and later unpacking this information for computation or printing. The character-manipulation instructions are also useful in converting character representations of numbers to their FACET numeric representations.

Loaders and assemblers are not usually built-in processors in most computers, although they are in FACET. In other computers, these processors are implemented as programs. Since the FACET computer has a much smaller memory than most computers today, it cannot contain a software loader or assembler; a loader or assembler implemented in software (as a program) would require more memory locations than are available in FACET.

Chapter 6

FIXED- AND FLOATING- POINT REPRESENTATION

6.1 INTRODUCTION

All the arithmetic problems we have dealt with so far have involved integers. Many problems, however, require us to handle fractions as well. Since the FACET registers cannot contain a decimal point, this presents a bit of a problem. But we've already seen that we can *represent* different kinds of objects in FACET memory registers—instructions, integers, characters. All we need is some convention for interpreting the sign and five digits, and we can have a memory word *mean* different things. In this chapter, we are concerned with having memory words represent numbers other than integers. There are different ways in which this can be accomplished; we shall examine two such methods: The first was used extensively a number of years ago, and is called **fixed-point** representation. The second, which has become wide-spread in recent years, is known as **floating-point** representation. We shall concentrate on the latter approach, although we shall briefly discuss fixed-point representation.

6.2 FIXED-POINT NUMBER REPRESENTATION

As programmers, we can actually "imagine" the presence of a decimal point in a FACET memory word. Until now, for instance, we have considered all FACET words which represent numbers as representing integers. In effect, therefore, we have imagined a decimal point at the extreme right of each of these words. When a register contained +00346, we considered the number to be 346 or 346.00. Let's say that we're now dealing with an arithmetic problem which involves only values less than 1000 (in absolute value). Further, let's assume that not all of the values are whole numbers. To be more concrete, let's say we want to add the numbers

$$33.4$$
$$4.26$$
$$15.0$$
$$496.82$$

We can do so in the FACET computer by adding the numbers

$$+03340$$
$$+00426$$
$$+01500$$
$$+49682$$

resulting in +54948. If we had considered these numbers as *representing* the original numbers by adhering to the convention that there is a decimal point between digits 3 and 4 of the words in the list, our result is correct, 549.48. Similar comments may be made concerning subtraction. Therefore we conclude that it doesn't really matter where we imagine the decimal point to be (when we perform addition and subtraction) so long as all the numbers are represented with the imaginary decimal point in the same fixed position. This sort of number representation is called fixed-point representation. The set of arithmetic operations employed with this representation is known as fixed-point arithmetic. When results are printed, we will have to know where the decimal point is to be inserted.

What about multiplication? Let's say we're again assuming that a decimal point exists between digits 3 and 4. We want to multiply 3.5 × 10.35; in our representation, that's +00350 × +01035. Shall we use MLS or MMS? Let's see—the 10-digit product of two five-digit numbers in FACET is

$$+\,0\,0\,3\,5\,0\ \times\ +\,0\,1\,0\,3\,5\ =\ +\,0\,0\,0\,0\,3\,6\,2\,2\,5\,0$$

5 most   5 least

significant significant

digits   digits

But 3.5 × 10.35 = 36.225. Or, using five-digit representation:

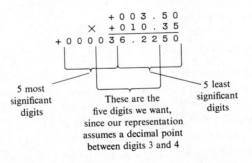

5 most   5 least

significant   These are the   significant

digits   five digits we want,   digits

since our representation

assumes a decimal point

between digits 3 and 4

To multiply two numbers in this representation, we must retain, as the product of two numbers, digits 4–5 of the five *most* significant digits, followed by digits 1–3 of the five *least*-significant digits. This is necessary to guarantee the position of the decimal point between digits 3 and 4 of the product. The multiplication therefore requires a number of machine language instructions. Let's say we want to multiply the numbers in locations NUM1 and NUM2 and place the product in location RESULT. We might then write this sequence of instructions:

```
LDAC   NUM1  ⎫  Compute leftmost 3 digits of 5 least significant
MLS    NUM2  ⎬  digits; place result in a temporary location
RGHT   002   ⎬  (in our case, the digits are 623).
STAC   TEMP  ⎭
LDAC   NUM1  ⎫  Compute sign and rightmost 2 digits of 5 most
MLS    NUM2  ⎬  significant digits (+03) and place them into sign
LEFT   003   ⎭  and digit positions 1–2 of accumulator.
ADD    TEMP     Add 3 rightmost digits of result, getting +03623.
STAC   RESULT   Store result +03623 into memory register.
```

Let's denote this fixed-point representation by XXX.XX, meaning that the decimal point is considered to be between digits 3 and 4. We may, in fact, have many different kinds of fixed-point representations. Some might be denoted:

$$.XXXXX$$
$$X.XXXX$$
$$XX.XXX$$
$$XXX.XX$$
$$XXXX.X$$
$$XXXXX.$$

But our integers could be representing *millions* or *billions* as well as *units*, as in, for instance, calculations of the gross national product of the U.S.A. So we might have fixed-point representations like this:

$$XXXXXxxxxx.$$

The X represents a FACET digit; the x represents a digit we cannot represent and will ignore. In such a representation +00003 would mean three million, since the decimal point is 6 places to the right of the 3.

A clever programmer might also handle a number of representations simultaneously. For instance, he might want to calculate 27.52 percent of 33 million. He might then represent

27.52 percent (or .2752) as +02752 in X.XXXX representation,

33 million   as +03300 in XXXXXxxxx. representation.

The multiplication could certainly be handled; we need know only the representation of the result and choose the appropriate five (out of ten) digits of the product. We would want the result to be

$$+00908 \qquad \text{(or 9.08 million)}$$

so it would coincide with our XXXXXxxxx. representation. We would take the ten

digit product

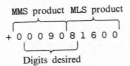

and "remove" the appropriate five digits (digits 2–5 of the MMS product followed by digit 1 of the MLS product).

Some other computers have an extra register, sometimes called the *MQ-register* or *multiplier-quotient* register, which stores the five least significant digits of a product; thus all ten (or however many, depending on the computer's register size) digits of the product are "produced" with one machine instruction. In many machines there are shift instructions which shift from one register to another, so the accumulator and MQ-registers can be considered as one for the operation:

In these cases fixed-point manipulations become easier. The FACET machine doesn't have an MQ-register, so all this doesn't apply directly.

We shall now write a short program to illustrate the use of fixed-point arithmetic (other than the pure integer arithmetic we have been using until now). Suppose, in a certain area, there is a 2.7 percent tax on food eaten in restaurants. The local tax office would like to distribute a table of taxes to all restaurants in the area. The office will compute the table on its FACET computer, for all plausible amounts from $1.00 to $100.00 (checks under $1.00 are tax-free). The computation will be performed in increments of 10 cents. How shall we write the program?

First, we must decide upon the number-representation scheme. Dollar amounts can be represented as

$$XXX.XX$$

and the percentage, 2.7% (or .027), can be represented as

$$.XXXXX$$

or as the FACET word +02700. The ten-digit product is

The five most significant digits are fine for our purpose; they give us three dollar-digits and two "cent"-digits. Here we have a case where the MMS instruction suffices for our computation. For example, if a bill were $51.30, we have

$$
\begin{array}{r}
051.30 \\
\times\,.02700 \\
\hline
001.3851000
\end{array}
$$

We want these 5
digits, the 5 most
significant

The solution we seek is +00138 or $1.38.

Now we write the program. The flowchart is shown in Fig. 6.1.

```
            CRGC    003     New page.
            LDAC    LENGTH ⎫
            PSYM    HEDING ⎬Print heading.
            LDAC    AMØUNT ⎫
    TAXTBL  MMS     PRCENT ⎬Compute tax.
            STAC    TAX    ⎭
            CRGC    001    ⎫
            PNUM    AMØUNT ⎪Print AMØUNT and TAX
            TAB     001    ⎬on a new line of table.
            PNUM    TAX    ⎭
            LDAC    AMØUNT ⎫
            SUB     DØL100 ⎬Check for end of table.
            JZER    FINISH ⎭
            LDAC    AMØUNT ⎫
            ADD     CENT10 ⎬Increment AMØUNT by ten cents.
            STAC    AMØUNT ⎭
            JUMP    TAXTBL
    FINISH  HALT
    AMØUNT  SET     +00100  Represents $1.00.
    PRCENT  SET     +02700  Represents 2.7% or .027.
    TAX     LØC
    DØL100  SET     +10000  Represents $100.00.
    CENT10  SET     +00010  Represents ten cents or $0.10.
    LENGTH  SET     +00025
    HEDING  CHAR    25      AMØUNT                    TAX
            END
```

The printout would look something like that shown in Fig. 6.2. We already know, from Chapter 5, that we can insert some extra steps in the program and have the results printed in a more acceptable (or more readable) format, like that shown in Fig. 6.3.

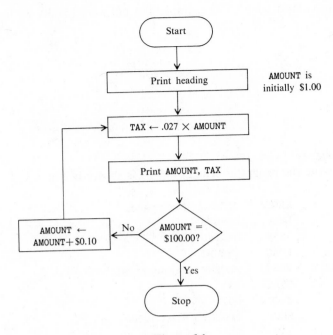

Figure 6.1

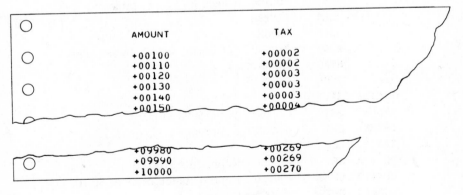

Figure 6.2

You might have noticed that all is not well with the calculation. For instance, 2.7 percent of $1.00 is 2.7 cents. If we do not want to carry fractions of a penny (or thousandths of a dollar), then we must change the 2.7 cents to either 2 cents or 3 cents. Our program **truncated** the fraction, that is, dropped it. We have another possibility. We can **round** it, or make it either 2 cents or 3 cents depending on whether the fraction is less than half a penny or greater than (or equal to) half a

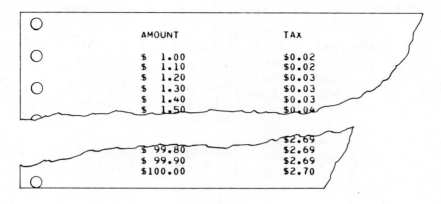

AMOUNT	TAX
$ 1.00	$0.02
$ 1.10	$0.02
$ 1.20	$0.03
$ 1.30	$0.03
$ 1.40	$0.03
$ 1.50	$0.04
	$2.69
$ 99.80	$2.69
$ 99.90	$2.69
$100.00	$2.70

Figure 6.3

penny. Here are some examples of **truncation** and **rounding**:

	Amount	*Truncated*	*Rounded*
To the penny	$10.234	$10.23	$10.23
	$10.235	$10.23	$10.24
	$10.236	$10.23	$10.24
To the dime	$ 5.44	$ 5.40	$ 5.40
	$ 5.45	$ 5.40	$ 5.50
To the dollar	$23.26	$23.00	$23.00
	$23.46	$23.00	$23.00
	$23.56	$23.00	$24.00

In the previous example on calculation of tax, we could have rounded the tax computation by finding the five least significant digits of the product and determining whether or not the first digit was

0–4   in which case we leave the original product, or

5–9   in which case we add 1 cent to the original product (+00001).

The instruction sequence corresponding to

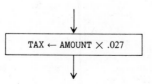

TAX ← AMOUNT × .027

could have been

```
            LDAC    AMØUNT  ⎫
    TAXTBL  MMS     PRCENT  ⎬ Compute tax.
            STAC    TAX     ⎭
            LDAC    AMØUNT  ⎫
            MLS     PRCENT  ⎬ Determine if next digit is 0–4.
            SUB     HALF    ⎬ If it is, go to NEXT, since tax
            JNEG    NEXT    ⎭ was correct.
            LDAC    TAX     ⎫
            ADD     ØNE     ⎬ Next digit is 5–9; increment
            STAC    TAX     ⎭ tax by one for rounding.
    NEXT    CRGC    001
            ⋮
    HALF    SET     +50000
    ØNE     SET     +00001
```

Exercise 6.2

1. Assume that you are using the fixed-point representation XXX.XX. Write a program which reads two numbers, m and n, and then computes and prints

$$m^2 + 2mn + n^2$$

Try it out for

$$m = 13.79, \qquad n = -27.5.$$

6.3 FLOATING-POINT REPRESENTATION

Keeping track of decimal points is sometimes a tedious and often a difficult job. In some cases, it is difficult to tell in advance what the magnitude of a result is. Since much energy must be devoted to tracking decimal points in complex problems, it would be useful to have the machine keep track of the decimal point for us. The scheme devised for this is called *floating-point* representation.

The idea behind floating-point representation is the following: We have a number of arbitrary magnitude. We want to store some of its leading (most significant) digits *and* also some indication of the position of the decimal point relative to those digits—two distinct items of information. Yet we want to store the entire number in a single memory register. We could do this by dividing the register into two portions:

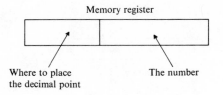

Memory register

Where to place   The number
the decimal point

One portion stores the number, and the other stores information regarding placement of the decimal point. Almost all medium-to-large computers today have built-in floating-point representation and arithmetic. Let's see how it works in FACET.

We shall divide a FACET word into three portions: the **sign**, the **exponent** (or **characteristic**), and the **mantissa** (or **fraction** portion). Let's choose a specific example:

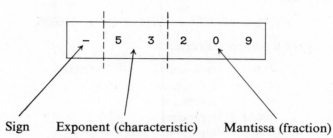

Sign   Exponent (characteristic)   Mantissa (fraction)

The mantissa represents some fraction between zero and 0.999. Add the sign to it to make it either positive or negative. In the example above we have −0.209. The exponent tells us where to move the decimal point to obtain the actual number being represented; 50 means, "don't move it at all." If the exponent is above 50, the decimal point is moved to the right; if below 50, to the left. Here 53 means 3 to the right, so the number becomes −209:

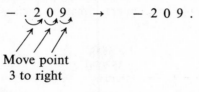

Move point
3 to right

The floating-point number

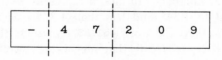

is −0.209 with decimal point moved 3 to the left (since 47 is 3 less than 50), so we get

$$- \,.0\,0\,0\,2\,0\,9$$

If the floating point-number is given symbolically by

$$s \quad d_1 \quad d_2 \quad d_3 \quad d_4 \quad d_5$$

Sign   Decimal
digits

then it represents the number

$$s.d_3d_4d_5 \times 10^{(d_1d_2-50)}.$$

For instance, +49107 represents

$$+0.107 \times 10^{49-50} = +0.107 \times 10^{-1} = +0.0107,$$

and –56976 represents

$$-0.976 \times 10^{56-50} = 0.976 \times 10^6 = 976000.$$

Do you see why the following are correct?

–42100	represents	-0.000000001
+48999	represents	0.00999
+51500	represents	5.0
–52627	represents	-62.7
+50999	represents	0.999
+57421	represents	4210000

Floating-point numbers are very different from integers. When we represented integers, we had exactly 199,999 different integers which could be represented, no more and no less. Each integer had a unique word which represented it, with the exception of zero. For instance, –00283 represented -283, and no other FACET word represented -283. Each floating-point number, on the other hand, represents an entire range of numbers (mathematicians, note: *real* numbers). For instance, +51135 represents

$$1.350000\ldots,$$
$$1.352090\ldots,$$
$$1.349762\ldots,$$
$$1.350051\ldots,$$

and an infinity of other numbers. In fact, it represents every number n which is greater than or equal to 1.345 and less than 1.355. So, for all n such that $1.345 \leq n < 1.355$, the FACET word +51135 represents them in floating-point representation. The difference is really that integers are discrete, while *real* numbers can be thought of as points on a *continuous* line:

Each of our floating-point numbers represents a *segment* of this line.

If we plot these floating-point numbers along the line, we find that as we get closer and closer to zero (from both directions), the points become more and more dense. This is so because there are exactly 900 floating-point numbers for *any* exponent, but the segment of the real line represented by *each* exponent is *one-tenth* the length of that represented by the next larger exponent. See Fig. 6.4.

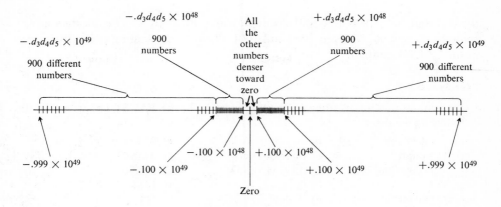

Figure 6.4

Unlike fixed-point representation, there are many floating-point numbers which do not have a unique representation. For instance, 1.0 can be represented as

$$+51100 \quad \text{and} \quad +52010 \quad \text{and} \quad +53001$$

Whenever this situation occurs, one of the representations is chosen as "preferred." Such a representation is known as the **normalized** representation. The normalized floating-point number is the one with a nonzero first digit in the mantissa. The normalized representation of *one* would be

$$+5\overset{\frown}{1}100 \qquad \text{This digit is nonzero}$$

This choice ensures three significant digits in each representation. If we allow leading zeros, then 5.13 might be

$$+51513 \quad \text{or} \quad +52051 \quad \text{or} \quad +53005$$

and significant digits would be lost.

The only exception to the normalization rule is zero; there are many ways in which we can represent zero:

$$+55000$$
$$-73000$$
$$+43000$$
$$-11000$$
$$\vdots$$

The normalized form chosen is +00000 for a number of reasons, the most important of which is that we now have the same representation for zero in both fixed- and floating-point representations. This allows us to use the JZER instruction when we are dealing with either fixed- or floating-point arithmetic.

You should be aware of the nature of floating-point numbers and the fact that each represents many actual numbers. One glaring example in FACET is the fact that both 1000 and 1001 are represented by +54100. This means that we cannot differentiate between 1000 and 1001 when we do floating-point arithmetic in the FACET computer.

Exercises 6.3

1. Find the normalized floating-point representation in the FACET computer for the following numbers:

   a) -43029 b) 5   c) 03.02476
   d) 15 billion   e) three-quarters f) 99.9999
   g) $-.000000000325$ h) 3.141592653589...   i) -0.5
   j) 73.6   k) 0   l) 1024
   m) 50,000.002   n) -8888 o) $12\frac{1}{3}$
   p) 23 × 10^{17}

2. Find a number represented by each of the following floating-point FACET words:

   a) +50123   b) −47201   c) −52112
   d) +59400   e) −30829   f) +58721
   g) −52594   h) −50520   i) +51314
   j) +49333   k) +48944   l) +51928
   m) −42700   n) +45314   o) +46555
   p) +54601

3. Normalize the following floating-point FACET words:

   a) +50023   b) −42001   c) +57095
   d) +69099   e) +23004   f) +42000

4. Give four possible interpretations for each of the following FACET words:

   a) −32746   b) +51829   c) +00000
   d) −51100   e) +62333   f) +44444

5. Describe a different floating-point representation that could have been used in the FACET machine instead of the one chosen: one which allows us to obtain *four* significant digits of precision.

6.4 ARITHMETIC OPERATIONS

There are four FACET instructions which allow us to perform arithmetic operations directly on floating-point numbers. They work very much like the fixed-point arithmetic operations in that the two numbers to be "operated on" are in the accumulator and in a memory register, and the result of the operation is placed into the accumulator. The instructions are as follows:

Instruction	Mnemonic code	Op-code	Description
Floating-point add	FADD	71	Add floating-point number at address denoted by effective operand to the floating-point number in the accumulator.

Instruction	Mnemonic code	Op-code	Description
			Round result to three significant digits and store floating-point result in accumulator.
Floating-point subtract	FSUB	72	Subtract floating-point number at address denoted by effective operand from the floating-point number in the accumulator. Round result to three significant digits and store floating-point result in accumulator.
Floating-point multiply	FMUL	73	Multiply floating-point number at address denoted by effective operand by the floating-point number in the accumulator. Round result to three significant digits and store floating-point result in accumulator.
Floating-point divide	FDIV	74	Divide floating-point number at address denoted by effective operand into the floating-point number in the accumulator. Round result to three significant digits and store floating-point result in accumulator.

The fact that the result of a floating-point arithmetic operation is **rounded** is important. (In some computers the results are **truncated** to the proper position.) Some examples of floating-point arithmetic as performed in the FACET computer are listed below:

Contents of accumulator before execution		Contents of location X		Instruction executed		Contents of accumulator after execution	
+51100	(1)	+52100	(10)	FADD	X	+52110	(11)
+51100	(1)	+52100	(10)	FMUL	X	+52100	(10)
+51100	(1)	+52100	(10)	FSUB	X	−51900	(−9)
+51100	(1)	+52100	(10)	FDIV	X	+50100	(0.1)
−46300	(−.00003)	−58300	(-3×10^7)	FMUL	X	+53900	(900)
−46300	(−.00003)	−58300	(-3×10^7)	FADD	X	−58300	(-3×10^7)
+52222	(22.2)	+50660	(.66)	FADD	X	+52229	(22.9)
+53100	(100)	+51300	(3)	FDIV	X	+52333	(33.3)
+51200	(2)	+51300	(3)	FDIV	X	+50667	(0.667)

Since we are dealing with representations (rather than the numbers themselves) when we perform these operations, peculiar things occur. In floating point,

$$1000 + 1 = 1000,$$

since adding +54100 to +51100 gives us +54100 (only the three most significant digits are retained).

Now we shall write a program employing the floating-point instructions. Let's compute the square root of some number. We shall choose an approximation formula which can be used repetitively to get better and better approximations of the square root. After all, we're only interested in an approximation to three significant digits. If we compute the square root of three, for instance ($\sqrt{3} = 1.732...$), then our result should be 1.73 or, in FACET floating-point, +51173. The formula is

$$X_{new} = \tfrac{1}{2}(X_{old} + N/X_{old}),$$

where N is the number whose square root we want, X_{old} is the old approximation, and X_{new} is the next, presumably better approximation of $\sqrt{N}$.

To see how this works, let's try to find $\sqrt{4}$ with this method. We need an initial approximation. We'll choose 1. (Of course, we know that $\sqrt{4} = 2$, but we're trying to see how this approximation method works.)

$$X_{old} = 1, \qquad X_{new} = \tfrac{1}{2}(1 + 4/1) = \tfrac{1}{2}(5) = 2\tfrac{1}{2}.$$

So $2\tfrac{1}{2}$ is the next approximation of $\sqrt{4}$, somewhat better than 1. Next let $2\tfrac{1}{2}$ be the old approximation, and we find a new one:

$$X_{old} = 2\tfrac{1}{2}, \qquad X_{new} = \tfrac{1}{2}(2\tfrac{1}{2} + 4/2\tfrac{1}{2}) = \tfrac{1}{2}(4.10) = 2.05,$$

which is pretty close; but let's try once more:

$$X_{old} = 2.05, \qquad X_{new} = \tfrac{1}{2}(2.05 + 4/2.05) = \tfrac{1}{2}(4.0012) = 2.0006.$$

The value 2.0006 expressed to three significant digits is sufficient for us, since that's 2.00.

Our program will read a floating-point number from a single card, print it, find its square root, and print it. We'll assume that the number is nonnegative, and we'll do four† new approximations, beginning with the initial approximation 1. Our flowchart is shown in Fig. 6.5.

Checking the flowchart, we see that we shall have to interpret all the numbers (except for the loop index CØUNT) as floating-point; e.g., if we read +51400, then

---

†   This algorithm is usually implemented with a *variable* number of approximations (iterations). The loop exit depends on a test such as

$$\left| \frac{N - X^2_{new}}{N} \right| < \varepsilon.$$

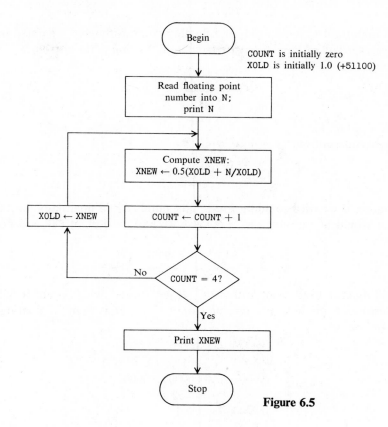

Figure 6.5

we'll print

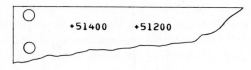

The flowchart is fairly straightforward so we shall just write the instructions for calculating XNEW, given XØLD and N:

```
          ⋮
      LDAC    N
      FDIV    XØLD        Compute N/XØLD.
      FADD    XØLD        Compute XØLD + N/XØLD.
      FMUL    HALF        Compute 0.5 (XØLD + N/XØLD).
      STAC    XNEW        Store result.
          ⋮
HALF  SET     +50500      Floating point 0.5.
```

It is important to keep fixed- and floating-point arithmetic separated in your programs. Certain of the data registers contain floating point numbers,

> XNEW
>
> XØLD
>
> N
>
> HALF

and others contain fixed-point numbers,

> ØNE
>
> CØUNT

For instance, if we tried to add a fixed-point number to a floating-point number, the result would be meaningless. Let's say we had fixed-point ØNE and floating-point HALF:

$$\begin{array}{llll} \text{ØNE} & \text{SET} & +00001 & (1) \\ \text{HALF} & \text{SET} & +50500 & (0.5) \end{array}$$

If we add them in fixed-point arithmetic, we get +50501 (which is either 50501 or 0.501 depending on how it's interpreted). If we add them in floating-point arithmetic, we get

$$(+50500) + (+00001)$$

or
$$0.500 + 0.001 \times 10^{-50}$$

or
$$0.500 + 0.00000\ldots00001$$
$$\overset{}{\mid\!\!\leftarrow 52 \text{ zeros} \rightarrow\!\!\mid}$$

or
$$0.5000000\ldots001$$

or
$$+50500$$

in FACET floating-point representation.

The rule of thumb is: when working with integers, use fixed-point arithmetic; when fractions are involved, use floating-point. You might ask, why use fixed-point arithmetic at all? There are two reasons: greater precision (more significant digits are carried) and economy (it is more expensive to use floating-point arithmetic since the operations take longer and so the programs take longer to run).

Exercises 6.4

1. Find the result of the indicated *floating-point* operations on the following FACET floating-point words:

a) +52100	+	+41000
b) +43259	÷	−44267
c) +00000	×	−42907
d) +52500	−	−51500
e) +50506	+	+50506
f) +35729	÷	−46908
g) −67801	×	−68333
h) +51100	×	+51100

i) −88302   +   +11111
j) +93201   ÷   +94402

2. Write and submit a FACET program which reads ten positive floating-point numbers and then computes and prints their square roots. Use the approximation method presented in this section. Let the initial approximation be the number itself (rather than 1, which we used in the example).

3. If location A contains +51234 and B contains +47105, what does the accumulator contain after the execution of *each* of the following instructions, in sequence?

```
LDAC    A
FADD    B
ADD     B
FMUL    A
SUB     A
FADD    B
SUB     B
FMUL    A
FADD    B
DIV     A
FSUB    A
```

4. In a program, you can check whether two words contain the same *characters* by the following procedure:

```
LDAC    A              LDAC    A
SUB     B    or        FSUB    B
JZER    X              JZER    X
```

If the floating-point subtract is employed, errors can sometimes be introduced. Assume that both locations A and B have +0 in the sign and first digit positions. Explain how these errors may be introduced.

Hint: Examine what the sequence does when A and B are initialized as follows:

```
A    CHAR    02    /D
B    CHAR    02    U/
```

6.5 SCIENTIFIC NOTATION AND FLOATING-POINT I/O

Very large and very small numbers are mostly used in scientific and mathematical applications. It is very inconvenient to write out these numbers with all their leading or trailing zeros, such as

$$64000000000000 \quad \text{or} \quad -0.0000000000984$$

Usually, a different convention is used, such as writing the number as some number between one and ten times some power of ten, like

$$6.4 \times 10^{13} \quad \text{or} \quad -9.84 \times 10^{-11},$$

where multiplying by 10^{13} is the same as moving the decimal point 13 positions to the right and, similarly, multiplying by 10^{-11} is equivalent to moving it 11 places to the left. This is sometimes known as **scientific notation**. In computer work, scientific notation is modified slightly, so that the number is expressed as a number between 0.1 and 1.0 times a power of ten. In this modified scientific notation, the two numbers above would be expressed as

$$0.64 \times 10^{14} \quad \text{and} \quad -0.984 \times 10^{-10}.$$

Convince yourself of the following equivalences:

$-3,842,000$	-3.842×10^6	-0.3842×10^7
$.0321$	3.21×10^{-2}	0.321×10^{-1}
43.7	4.37×10^1	0.437×10^2
0.0000009	9.0×10^{-7}	0.9×10^{-6}

Scientists and mathematicians generally prefer the scientific notation, i.e., a number between one and ten, times a power of ten, for instance,

$$4.72 \times 10^{12}$$

However, the modified scientific notation is more convenient for computer representation. The above number would be modified to

$$0.472 \times 10^{13}$$

i.e., a fraction between 0.1 and 1.0. The first portion corresponds to the mantissa while the power corresponds to the characteristic or exponent part of a floating point number:

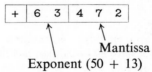

Since exponents are difficult to punch on cards or print on the printer, a further change is made. The three characters, $\times$ 10, are replaced by an E (for **exponentiation**), and the exponent itself (the power of 10) is written on the same line as the other characters (instead of as a superscript). This means that we would write

$$0.64 \times 10^{14} \quad \text{as} \quad 0.64E14$$

and

$$-0.984 \times 10^{-10} \quad \text{as} \quad -0.984E{-}10$$

The four numbers in our second example above would then be written

$-.3842 \times 10^7$	$-.3842E7$
$.321 \times 10^{-1}$	$.321E{-}1$
$.437 \times 10^2$	$.437E2$
$.9 \times 10^{-6}$	$.9E{-}6$

In FACET, we restrict the notation a bit further, insisting that each floating-point number consist of nine characters:

   a) a sign (+ or –)
   b) a decimal point
   c) three digits
   d) an E
   e) a sign (for the exponent)
   f) two digits (the exponent)

The four numbers above would then be written

$$
\begin{array}{ll}
-.3842 \times 10^7 & \texttt{-.384E+07} \\
.321 \times 10^{-1} & \texttt{+.321E-01} \\
.437 \times 10^2 & \texttt{+.437E+02} \\
.9 \times 10^{-6} & \texttt{+.900E-06}
\end{array}
$$

There are two FACET instructions dealing with reading and printing floating-point numbers in this E-notation. They are RFLT (read floating point) and PFLT (print floating point), with op-codes 47 and 48, respectively.

Instruction	Mnemonic code	Op-code	Description
Read floating-point number	RFLT	47	The next data card is read. The first nine columns on the card should contain a floating-point number in E-notation. It is converted to a FACET floating-point word and stored in the memory at the address indicated by the effective operand. An error message and program termination results if columns 1–9 on the data card do not contain a correct floating-point number.
Print floating-point number	PFLT	48	The word in the memory register indicated by the effective operand of the instruction is converted to E-notation. It is printed in nine character positions beginning with the next tabulation field on the output paper (that is, in columns 2–10, 12–20, 22–30, 32–40, or 42–50, whichever field happens to come next).

To illustrate these two instructions, we shall write a simple program for adding two floating point numbers:

```
AAA     RFLT    XX  ⎫
        RFLT    YY  ⎬ Read in the two numbers
        LDAC    XX  ⎫
        FADD    YY  ⎬ Compute their sum
        STAC    ZZ  ⎭
        PFLT    XX  ⎫
        PFLT    YY  ⎬ Print results
        PFLT    ZZ  ⎭
        HALT
XX      LØC
YY      LØC
ZZ      LØC
        END
```

If our data deck looks like

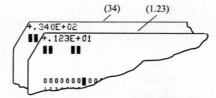

then after reading in the two cards, memory registers XX and YY will contain

XX | + | 5 | 1 | 1 | 2 | 3 |

YY | + | 5 | 2 | 3 | 4 | 0 |

After the computation, ZZ will contain

ZZ | + | 5 | 2 | 3 | 5 | 2 | (35.2)

When the results are printed, they will look like

```
○
     +.123E+01 +.340E+02 +.352E+02
○
```

Frequently, we will want to initialize locations at load time. We have been doing this all along with the SET pseudo-op. If we need the floating-point number one-half (0.5) in our program, we can write

```
HALF    SET     +50500
```

but it is more convenient to use the E-notation. Therefore we have another pseudo-op, FSET (floating-point SET), which works exactly like SET, except that in columns 17–25† of the card we write the number in E-notation, which in our example would be

HALF   FSET   +.500E+00

Both of these statements will cause the memory register corresponding to HALF to be loaded with +50500. Note that FSET uses column 25 of the card.

Exercises 6.5

1. Write the following numbers in FACET E-notation:

a) 33

b) 0

c) −.000329

d) 5 million

e) 73.9 billion

f) −8.07

g) 0.0000009

h) 28.4×10^{-10}

i) 9.4×10^{35}

j) $\frac{2}{3}$

2. Write and submit a FACET program which reads ten floating-point numbers, $X_1, X_2, \ldots, X_{10}$, and then computes and prints $f(X_1), f(X_2), \ldots, f(X_{10})$, where

$$f(X) = 3.2X^2 - 5.77X + 2.$$

Have the results printed something like this:

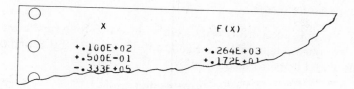

3. Write one (or more) of the programs given in following previous exercises, using floating-point numbers and arithmetic (numbers in parentheses refer to exercise number):

2.3 (3)   2.7 (3)
2.4 (4b)   2.8 (4)
2.7 (1)   2.8 (7)
2.7 (2)   2.8 (9)

4. Your FACET computer's floating-point arithmetic and I/O are broken, and yet you simply *must* do some floating-point computations. You must write an instruction sequence which adds the (floating-point) numbers in locations X and Y, storing the sum in Z. Do this. Test the sequence by inserting it in the following program:

RNUM   X
RNUM • Y

---

† This is a slight incursion on the comment field in this one special case, but the rest of the card (columns 26–80) is still available for comments.

```
                    ┌─────────────────┐
                    │  Your sequence  │
                    └─────────────────┘

                     PNUM    Z
                     HALT
                 X   LØC
                 Y   LØC
                 Z   LØC
                     END
```

5. Assume that the FACET machine has no floating-point arithmetic instructions (FADD, FSUB, FMUL, FDIV) but still has floating-point I/O (RFLT and PFLT). Write a program which reads two floating-point (*E*-notation) numbers and prints the larger of the two. Assume that the numbers are normalized.

6.6 ROUNDING ERRORS

Since all our floating-point calculations are performed to three significant digits, we must expect that certain errors will creep into the results. Actually, calculations are performed to four significant digits and the results are rounded to three. In order to see this, let's perform the following two calculations:

a) $(0.666 + 0.666) - 0.666$

b) $0.666 + (0.666 - 0.666)$

Remember, the machine performs the computations to four significant digits of precision, but only retains a three-significant-digit result (by rounding). The calculations would be performed as follows:

a) $0.6660 \longleftarrow$ Add fourth digit for computation
    $+0.6660 \longleftarrow$
    $\overline{1.332}$
     $\underbrace{}$
    Retain three digits

    $1.330 \longleftarrow$ Add zero for four-digit computation
    -0.666
    $\overline{0.664}$
     $\underbrace{}$
    Retain three digits   *Result:* 0.664

b) 0.6660
    -0.6600
    $\overline{0.000}$

    0.6660
    $+0.0000$
    $\overline{0.6660}$
     $\underbrace{}$
    three digits   *Result:* 0.666

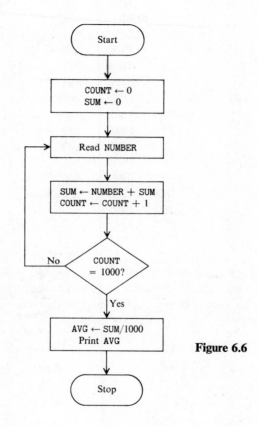

Figure 6.6

So seemingly trivial differences in algorithms can affect the results of a floating-point calculation, since only a certain number of significant digits are retained in the intermediate steps. This is true in all computers, although many have longer registers than FACET, and therefore can retain 6, 10, or even 15 significant digits.

In the above calculations, we would prefer the result in (b), namely, 0.666. The result 0.664 has an error of 2 in the third significant digit. This type of error, known as a **rounding error**, is due to the fixed size of registers. In certain types of computations rounding errors can add up to produce errors in the second and first significant digits as well. We shall now illustrate this possibility in an extreme case.

Let's say we want to write a program which finds the average of 1000 floating-point numbers. Assuming that each is punched on a single card in the correct format, we might think of performing the calculation as shown in Fig. 6.6.

In the program, the COUNT will be kept in the index register and the running SUM in the accumulator. Note that the loop exit is determined when the index register goes from 999 to 000, indicating that 1000 numbers have been read.

```
              LDX     ZERØ
              LDAC    ZERØ
     LØØP     RFLT    NUMBER
              FADD    NUMBER
              INCX    001
              JXZR    NEXT
              JUMP    LØØP
     NEXT     FDIV    THØU
              STAC    AVG
              PFLT    AVG
              HALT
     ZERØ     SET     +00000
     THØU     FSET    +.100E+04
     NUMBER   LØC
     AVG      LØC
              END
```

Everything seems in order, and the program should work under ordinary circumstances. But what if the 1000 numbers were all the same, namely, 0.333? Of course, the average is 0.333. Let's compare this with the results of the actual program. It begins by adding the 1000 numbers:

	0.000	
1	+ 0.333	
	0.333	
2	+ 0.333	
	0.666	
3	+ 0.333	
	0.999	
4	+ 0.333	
	1.33②	⟵ Drop this digit in rounding
5	+ 0.333	
	1.66③	⟵ Drop
6	+ 0.333	
	1.99③	⟵ Drop
⋮	⋮	
	9.91	
31	+ 0.333	
	10.24③	⟵ Drop these two digits in rounding
32	+ 0.33③	⟵ Drop this digit since arithmetic is carried to four digits
	10.5③	⟵ Drop

```
   33          +   0.33Ⓝ◄─────── Drop
                 ─────────
                   10.83
    ⋮               ⋮
                   99.9
  331          +   0.33Ⓝ◄─────── Drop
                 ─────────
                  100.Ⓝ◄─────── Drop
  332          +   0.3ⓃⓃ◄─────── Drop
                 ─────────
                  100Ⓝ◄─────── Drop
    ⋮               ⋮
                   100.
 1000          +   0.3ⓃⓃ◄─────── Drop
                 ─────────
                  100Ⓝ◄─────── Drop
```

Final sum = 100

After our running sum reaches 100, each succeeding addition of 0.333 leaves that sum unchanged, since 100.333 rounded to three significant digits is merely 100. Our final sum, then, is 100, and the average is

$$100/1000 = 0.100,$$

rather than 0.333, which it should be.

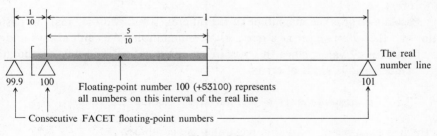

Figure 6.7

We can visualize the reason why the repeated addition of 0.333 to 100 remains 100. Recall our representation of floating-point numbers as marks on a continuous line. Consider 100, the floating-point number just before it (99.9), and the one just after it (101), as shown in Fig. 6.7. Note that the length of the real line between 99.9 and 100 is $\frac{1}{10}$, whereas the length between 100 and 101 is 10 times greater, or 1. There are no other floating-point numbers between 99.9, 100, and 101. Therefore the floating-point number 100 represents any real number which is located between the square brackets. These brackets are placed at the halfway distance to the next point which marks the boundary between round-off to the left or right point.

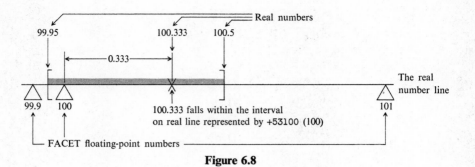

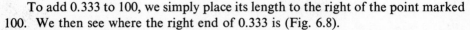

Figure 6.8

To add 0.333 to 100, we simply place its length to the right of the point marked 100. We then see where the right end of 0.333 is (Fig. 6.8).

The right end of 0.333 still appears within the brackets! Therefore the number 100.333, which appears at the X, must be represented in floating-point by 100. We can now see the problem of addition and subtraction of very large with very small numbers in floating-point representation. The difficulty lies with the different densities of floating-point numbers on the real line. The lesson to be learned is that rounding errors can mount up and actually ruin the result, even in the first significant digit. This is especially true in iterative processes.

Rounding errors are but one kind of error that we encounter when dealing with numerical calculations on computers. Other errors, such as those inherent in the numerical methods themselves also exist, although they will not be discussed in this text.

Absolute error is the magnitude of the difference between the "real" or desired value and the value we get as a result of a computation. We can't always find the "real" or "true" value, since this requires a computation, and any computation can include various kinds of errors.

$$\text{absolute error} = |\text{actual value} - \text{computed value}|$$

In the first example of rounding, recall that we computed

$$(0.666 + 0.666) - 0.666 = 0.664.$$

The actual or desired value is .666, whereas the computed value is .664. The absolute error is then

$$\text{absolute error} = |0.666 - 0.664| = 0.002.$$

In our second example, we computed the average of 100 numbers, all identical (0.333); our answer was 0.100, whereas we "desire" 0.333. So we get

$$\text{absolute error} = |0.333 - 0.100| = 0.233$$

Relative error is the magnitude of the absolute error divided by the actual value:

$$\text{relative error} = \left| \frac{\text{actual value} - \text{computed value}}{\text{actual value}} \right|$$

In the two cases above we get:

a) $\text{relative error} = \left| \dfrac{0.666 - 0.664}{0.666} \right| = 0.003,$

b) $\text{relative error} = \left| \dfrac{0.333 - 0.100}{0.333} \right| = 0.6997.$

Relative error, when expressed as a percentage is called **percentage error**. In the above two cases we would get:

a) 0.3%,
b) 69.97%.

Although we cannot entirely escape errors in our computer computations (regardless of which computer we use), when dealing with floating-point arithmetic, we can keep them within reasonable bounds. An engineer computing a desired thickness of a supporting beam doesn't particularly care if his computational errors are less than 0.01 inch, since it will not affect his structure. Similarly, an accountant might not mind a dollar amount error of 0.001 cent. Errors are inherent in the structure, but quite tolerable if small; however, someone must make sure they remain below this tolerance level. At this point, you should at least be very aware of the existence of such errors. Later, in Chapters 8 and 10, we shall discuss a few remedies for intolerable errors. These include modification of floating-point representation to increase the number of significant digits we store.

Exercises 6.6

1. Perform the following calculations according to the FACET floating-point arithmetic scheme, and then find the rounding errors in each calculation—the absolute error, the relative error, and the percentage error:

a) $(0.620 \times 231) \div 231$
b) $(0.888 + 13.5) - 13.5$
c) $0.88 + (13.5 - 13.5)$
d) $(69.7 + 325) \times 11.4$
e) $12^3 - 11^3$
f) $93^2 - 41^3$
g) $2.5^3 - (12.3 + 3.32)$

6.7 TWO FLOATING-POINT PROGRAMS

You should not get the idea that these annoying rounding errors preclude your using floating-point arithmetic. Floating-point arithmetic is often invaluable. It is true that the three significant digits of precision available in FACET are somewhat limiting for many real-life situations, but remember that FACET is essentially a "practice" computer, and many "real-life" computers have larger (longer) registers, which afford us greater precision.

To illustrate the use of floating-point arithmetic, we shall write two programs, both of which will seem rather deep and complex. However, both are fairly trivial, since we are not developing algorithms, but rather using standard formulas.

In the first program we shall compute a sine table for angles from 0° through 90° in steps of 5°. Recall that the sine of our angle A is defined by drawing a right triangle with A as one of the angles:

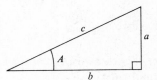

The sine of angle A (written sin A) is the ratio a/c. If angle A is expressed in radians, rather than degrees (to convert from degrees to radians, multiply by $\pi/810$, $\pi = 3.14159\ldots$), then we have a formula for sine:

$$\sin A = A - \frac{A^3}{3!} + \frac{A^5}{5!} - \frac{A^7}{7!} + \frac{A^9}{9!} - \frac{A^{11}}{11!} + \frac{A^{13}}{13!} - \frac{A^{15}}{15!} + \ldots,$$

where 3! is read "three factorial" and means $1 \times 2 \times 3$, or 6. Similarly, $5! = 1 \times 2 \times 3 \times 4 \times 5 = 120$, $7! = 1 \times 2 \times 3 \times 4 \times 5 \times 6 \times 7 = 5040$, and so forth.

Our program looks something like that shown in Fig. 6.9. Angles and sines will be expressed in floating-point representation. Since we're only interested in computing sines to three significant digits, the truncated formula

$$\sin A = A - \frac{A^3}{3!} + \frac{A^5}{5!} - \frac{A^7}{7!}$$

suffices. So we have:

$$\sin A = A - \frac{A^3}{3!} + \frac{A^5}{5!} - \frac{A^7}{7!} = A - \frac{A^3}{6} + \frac{A^5}{120} - \frac{A^7}{5040},$$

$$\sin A = A\left(1 + A^2\left(-\frac{1}{6} + A^2\left(\frac{1}{120} - \frac{A^2}{5040}\right)\right)\right),$$

$$\sin A = A(1 + A^2(-.167 + A^2(.0083 - .000198A^2))).$$

Once we have A in radians, then the box

Compute sin A

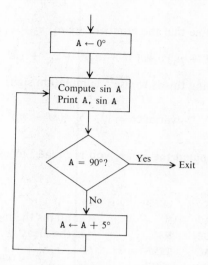

Figure 6.9

is fairly easy to implement:

LDAC	A	A
FMUL	A	A^2
STAC	ASQ	
FMUL	CØNST1	$-.000198\ A^2$
FADD	CØNST2	$.00833 - .000198\ A^2$
FMUL	ASQ	$A^2(.00833 - .000198\ A^2)$
FADD	CØNST3	$-.167 + A^2(.00833 - .000198\ A^2)$
FMUL	ASQ	$A^2(-.167 + A^2(.00833 - .000198\ A^2))$
FADD	ØNE	$1 + A^2(-.167 + A^2(.00833 - .000198\ A^2))$
FMUL	A	$A(1 + A^2(-.167 + A^2(.00833 - .00198\ A^2)))$
STAC	SINA	

$$\vdots$$

CØNST1	FSET	$-.198E{-}03$
CØNST2	FSET	$+.833E{-}02$
CØNST3	FSET	$-.167E{+}00$
ØNE	FSET	$+.100E{+}01$

$$\vdots$$

Now the whole program is fairly simple. You can complete it yourself and even check to see if the sine table generated corresponds to the one you can find in a trigonometry book (to three significant digits).

The second program is one which finds the mean and variance of a sequence of numbers. Assume that there are 50 numbers. You can read them into an array, add them up, and divide by 50. This gives you the mean (average). The variance is defined as the sum of the squares of the differences between the numbers and the mean divided by the total number of numbers. If this is confusing, then here it is mathematically (assume that the numbers are $n_1, n_2, \ldots, n_{50}$ and the mean is M):

$$\text{variance} = \tfrac{1}{50}\left[(M - n_1)^2 + (M - n_2)^2 + \ldots + (M - n_{49})^2 + (M - n_{50})^2\right].$$

Another way of writing this is to use a summation sign:

$$\text{variance} = \frac{1}{50} \sum_{i=1}^{i=50} (M - n_i)^2$$

Once you have computed the mean, you are ready to use a loop to compute the variance.

```
            ⋮
          LDX     ZERØ        XR ← 0
LØØP      LDAC    M           M contains the mean.
          FSUB*   N           N is the array of numbers.
          STAC    TEMP        M − nᵢ
          FMUL    TEMP        (M − nᵢ)²  } Compute (M − nᵢ)².
          FADD    SUM
          STAC    SUM
          INCX    001     ⎫
          SXEQ    N50     ⎬   Increment XR; check for loop exit.
          JUMP    LØØP    ⎭
          LDAC    SUM     ⎫
          FDIV    FIFTY   ⎬   Compute variance.
          STAC    VAR
            ⋮
SUM       FSET    +.000E+00
ZERØ      FSET    +.000E+00
FIFTY     FSET    +.500E+02
N50       SET     +00050
            ⋮
```

The "standard deviation" (usually denoted σ) is the square root of the variance. You already know how to compute square roots.

We shall point out again that the applicability of FACET floating-point arithmetic depends on whether or not three significant digits are sufficient for your computational needs. If greater precision is required, you must go on to more advanced techniques, which we shall discuss in a later chapter.

Exercises 6.7

1. Complete and run the sine program.

2. Complete and run the variance program.

3. Write a program which reads a single fixed-point number, prints it (with PNUM), and then *converts* it to the corresponding floating-point number and prints that. When you've finished, put the whole program in a loop to read, convert, and print ten such

numbers. Sample output:

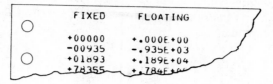

```
         FIXED       FLOATING

  ○      +00000      +.000E+00
         -00935      -.935E+03
  ○      +01893      +.189E+04
         +78355      +.784E+0
```

4. Write a program which computes and prints a cosine table for five-degree increments from 0° to 90°.

6.8 OVERFLOW AND UNDERFLOW

Recall that in fixed-point addition and subtraction the term *overflow* refers to the condition where the result of one of these arithmetic operations is a number which is either too large (greater than +99999) or too small (less than –99999) for the accumulator to contain. In such cases the overflow indicator is turned on. (Otherwise it is turned off). A similar situation occurs in floating-point arithmetic.

What numbers are "too large" or "too small" for the accumulator to hold? The largest number (in magnitude) that can be represented in FACET normalized floating point is $\pm.999 \times 10^{49}$; the smallest (excluding zero) is $\pm.100 \times 10^{-50}$. Whenever a calculation results in a floating-point number larger (in magnitude) than $.999 \times 10^{49}$, **overflow** is said to have occurred. Similarly, when a calculation results in a number (other than zero) smaller than $.100 \times 10^{-50}$ (in magnitude), **underflow** is said to have occurred. In practice, this hardly ever happens, since even the numbers which astronomers, physicists and chemists generally deal with are in the range 10^{-50} to 10^{+49}. Usually when a floating-point overflow or underflow occurs, it is due to some programming error. Yet, the possibility of overflow or underflow exists, and can be detected with the JØVF instruction. In fact, any of the four floating-point arithmetic instructions can cause overflow *or* underflow. Each of these instructions *always* sets the overflow indicator either ØN or ØFF, as the case warrants, as the ADD and SUB instructions do in fixed-point arithmetic.

Let's look at some FACET computations which cause overflow or underflow:

$$(0.300 \times 10^{29}) \times (0.200 \times 10^{28}) = 0.600 \times 10^{56}: \qquad \text{overflow}$$
$$(0.100 \times 10^{-40}) \div (-0.500 \times 10^{+45}) = -0.200 \times 10^{-85}: \qquad \text{underflow}$$
$$(0.998 \times 10^{49}) + (0.305 \times 10^{49}) = 0.130 \times 10^{50}: \qquad \text{overflow}$$
$$(0.123 \times 10^{-40}) \times (0.456 \times 10^{-30}) = 0.561 \times 10^{-71}: \qquad \text{underflow}$$
$$(0.500 \times 10^{49}) - (-0.500 \times 10^{49}) = 0.100 \times 10^{50}: \qquad \text{overflow}$$

Overflow or underflow sometimes occurs when one accidently operates on two numbers, one represented in fixed point, the other in floating. Of course, this is a programming error.

When overflow or underflow does occur, the program continues executing, the only change being that the overflow indicator is ØN. You might wonder therefore what *result* is actually computed in such cases. The answer is that the result is correct in the sign and the mantissa and incorrect (± 100) in the exponent. For instance, if we compute

$$+0.900 \times 10^{65},$$

then

a) the mantissa should be (and is) 900;
b) the sign should be (and is) $+$;
c) the exponent should be $65 + 50 = 115$; it is set to $115 - 100 = 15$;
d) the result in the accumulator is +15900.

Similarly, if we get -0.123×10^{-70}, then

a) mantissa is 123;
b) sign is $-$;
c) the exponent should be -20, but is set to $-20 + 100 = 80$;
d) the result is therefore –80123.

Exercises 6.8

1. Write a program which causes overflow or underflow. Run it with a program trace and follow the actual arithmetic. Try using a JØVF instruction with floating-point overflow/underflow.
2. Write a FACET program which computes and prints floating-point powers of two. Keep on computing and printing until overflow occurs. The program is similar to the one in Chapter 2, except that you can get many more powers of two printed. Why? How large is the error of the largest power printed?

6.9 IN REVIEW

Fixed-point arithmetic is mechanized arithmetic in which a decimal point is assumed to appear in some fixed position of each word. By clever programming, one can perform all sorts of intricate manipulation of the decimal point, and one can keep track of several different fixed-point representations simultaneously. However, this work is tedious and difficult. By and large, fixed-point arithmetic is used only for integers today. Whenever fractions are involved, a different internal representation is employed—floating-point representation.

In the FACET computer, a number may be represented as a word consisting of a sign, a two-digit exponent part (or characteristic), and a three-digit fraction part or mantissa. This gives only three significant digits, but allows a wide range of numbers to be represented, from very small (10^{-50}) to very large (10^{49}). There are four floating-point arithmetic instructions: FADD, FSUB, FMUL, and FDIV for floating-point addition, subtraction, multiplication, and division, respectively. Their respective opcodes are 71, 72, 73, and 74.

Scientific notation allows us to represent a number by some number between one and ten times some power of ten. A modification of this notation, which we call E-notation, is used in computers. Two floating-point instructions in the FACET computer allow us to use this notation in input/output: RFLT (read floating-point) and PFLT (print floating-point), with respective opcodes 47 and 48.

Overflow is the condition wherein the result of an arithmetic operation is too large in magnitude for representation in a FACET word. Similarly, if the result of a (floating-point) operation is too small in magnitude, underflow occurs. In either case, an overflow indicator is set ØN. It can be tested, as in fixed-point operations, with the JØVF instruction. Overflow rarely occurs except when a programming error occurs, since FACET can represent a wide range of floating-point numbers, and most computations of interest fall in this range.

Chapter 7

SUBPROGRAMS

7.1 A SIMPLE SUBPROGRAM

Consider the following problem. You have written the program discussed in Sections 3.10 and 5.1 which prints a table of numbers between 1 and 20, their squares and their cubes. The output of the program was:

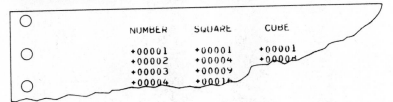

However, you are dissatisfied with the way the PNUM instruction always prints the plus sign and leading zeros. Instead, you would prefer to print the output with plus signs and leading zeros **suppressed** (omitted):

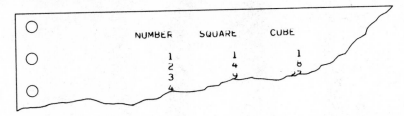

You like the idea so much that you decide to print integers in this format in all future FACET programs. Therefore you decide to write a sequence of instructions which prints any integer with its leading zeros and plus sign suppressed. You design this instruction sequence so that it can be substituted for the PNUM instruction wherever it appears in a program. This sequence will print

0		+00000
−0		−00000
5		+00005
−43	instead of	−00043
349		+00349
−9999		−09999
32197		+32197
−72103		−72103

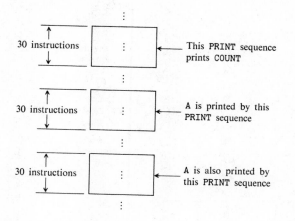

Figure 7.1

The substituted numbers are printed in the same six print positions that the PNUM instruction uses. If fewer than six characters actually appear, the field is left-padded with blanks (e.g., ⊔⊔⊔–43).

This substitution is accomplished by examining the number to be printed, digit by digit, and printing the sign and digits as *characters* using the PSYM instruction. The instruction sequence that does this, which we shall call sequence PRINT, requires some thirty instructions and seven pseudo-operations.

The original program (Section 3.10) for printing squares and cubes contains three PNUM instructions:

⋮

PNUM   CØUNT   Print the number.

⋮

PNUM   A   Print its square.

⋮

PNUM   A   Print its cube.

⋮

We can alter the previous program by substituting the sequence PRINT each time the PNUM instruction appears. The new program is shown in Fig. 7.1. While removing three PNUM instructions from our program, we have now added some 90 instructions and some 7 pseudo-operations.

Each of the three PRINT sequences uses virtually the same 30 instructions. The only difference among the three is the one instruction which determines whether CØUNT or A is to be printed. Here we have the same 29 instructions repeated three times. This repetition of PRINT wastes keypunching time, wastes debugging time (making each correction three times), wastes program assembly time, and adds a distracting clutter of instructions which basically do no more than print a number. If we could find some means to have this PRINT sequence appear *only once* in the program instead of three times, then we could eliminate these undesirable characteristics.

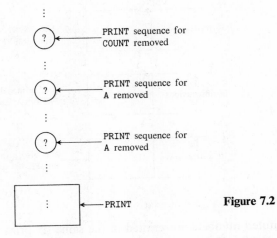

Figure 7.2

How can we make do with only a single appearance of PRINT? Suppose we remove the PRINT sequence from the three places it appears and place it, once, at the end of the program. Such a sequence is called a **subprogram**† because it is no longer part of the main instruction sequence. See Fig. 7.2.

A technique must be found which permits the program to use the PRINT sub-program at the end, yet still behave as though the original three sequences were present. In other words, when the program reaches the point where one of the PRINT sequences *used to be* (where a question mark now appears in Fig. 7.2), the program must still execute PRINT even though it is in a different position. This can be done by inserting the instruction

JUMP   PRINT

where each of the three question marks appear. If PRINT is the label marking the beginning of the PRINT sequence, then the program will execute it whenever PNUM would have been executed in the original program. The program would now be as shown in Fig. 7.3.

It is reasonably clear how the three JUMP PRINT instructions initiate PRINT at the proper moment. The question, however, is what should be done when the program gets to the end of PRINT? We must arrange to preserve the original program's instruction sequence as though all three PRINT sequences were present. For the first JUMP PRINT, see Fig. 7.4. The dotted line indicates where JUMPs take

---

†   For those already familiar with this area, *subprograms* are often called *subroutines*. We refrain from using that terminology because we do not wish to confuse it with the subroutine and function constructs in FORTRAN.

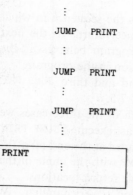

Figure 7.3

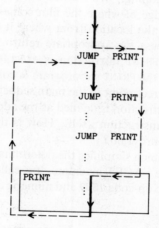

Figure 7.4

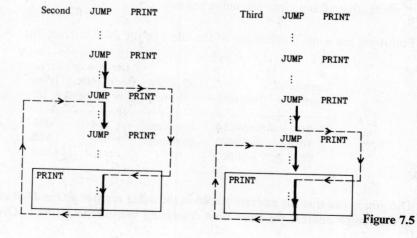

Figure 7.5

place. The solid line shows the sequence in which the instructions are executed. Note that the PRINT sequence returns to the next instruction following the first JUMP PRINT, so that the program behaves as though the PRINT sequence were actually in its original position in the program.

Execution of the second and third JUMP PRINT instructions lead to similar situations, as shown in Fig. 7.5.

We observe that in each of the three cases we wish to return to the location immediately following the last executed JUMP PRINT instruction. We must find an instruction which can be placed at the end of PRINT to implement all three returns. We cannot simply write JUMP with the name of the return location as its operand, since there are three possible return locations.

The basis of the solution is very familiar. We use the same method which enables us to get back the pictures from a mail-order developer to whom we have sent a roll of film for developing. We include our **return address** with the order. Without any prior knowledge of where the film comes from, the developer, uses this address to return it to the location from where it came. Similarly, the main instruction sequence can pass the appropriate return address to the PRINT subprogram before the JUMP PRINT instruction is executed. After the JUMP PRINT instruction is executed and the PRINT subprogram is completed, PRINT can use this address to return to the correct point in the main sequence. The return address for a particular JUMP PRINT instruction is defined as the address of the next instruction following the JUMP PRINT instruction itself. How is this address determined and how is it passed to the subprogram?

A special instruction which simplifies the determination and the passing of this address exists as part of the FACET machine. It is called the jump-to-subprogram instruction, with mnemonic op-code JSUB and numeric op-code 38. This instruction does two things:

1. performs a jump to the location given by the effective operand;
2. determines the address of the location following the JSUB instruction itself and places that address into the index register.

Following are some illustrations of the effect of the JSUB instruction:

Location of instruction	instruction	XR-index register	Location of next instr. to be executed	New XR
058	+38114	anything	114	059
101	+38023	anything	023	102
055	−38200	010	210	056

Did you notice that the address placed in the index register by the JSUB instruction is the return address we have been discussing relevant to PRINT? Given some machine language sequence, we see that

$$\vdots$$

| 058 | +38114 | Jump to subprogram. |
| 059 | | Next instruction. |

$$\vdots$$

| 114 | | First instruction of subprogram. |

$$\vdots$$

where 059 is the location of the next instruction to be executed upon return from the subprogram starting at 114. The JSUB instruction causes a jump to location 114 to begin the subprogram and passes the return address, 059, to the subprogram via the index register.

We can now substitute the JSUB PRINT for the JUMP PRINT instruction appearing in our example.

$$\vdots$$

JSUB   PRINT

$$\vdots$$

JSUB   PRINT

$$\vdots$$

JSUB   PRINT

$$\vdots$$

PRINT

$$\vdots$$

Thus when it begins execution, PRINT would assume that the correct return address will be found in the index register. Let us see how PRINT uses this address to return. Suppose the last instruction in PRINT was

JUMP*   000

What would its effective operand be? Since the instruction is indexed, it would be the sum of the operand and the index register. The operand of JUMP* 000 is 000. The index register contains the return address (059 in the previous example). The effective operand is the sum of the two:

$$
\begin{array}{r}
000 \\
059 \\
\hline
059
\end{array}
$$

And this is the return address itself. So this instruction effectively says, "jump to the location designated by the index register," or better, "return to the main sequence of the program, to the instruction immediately following the JSUB." Our new arrangement would be:

$$\vdots$$

JSUB   PRINT

$$\vdots$$

JSUB   PRINT

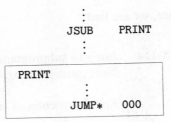

Make certain you understand how the JSUB instruction works and how it interacts with the JUMP* instruction to return control to the appropriate point in the main sequence.

We have not yet considered how the PRINT subprogram will print the contents of CØUNT on one occasion and the contents of A on the others. It is undesirable to do this by inserting instructions in PRINT which make the subprogram dependent on this particular program, that is, for printing either CØUNT or A. PRINT is general enough to be useful in other programs; it follows that it is preferable not to modify PRINT for each program in which it is used. This further implies that the labels CØUNT and A should not appear in PRINT, because they are defined in the main part of the program.

Instead, every time we initiate PRINT, we can pass it the *number* we wish to have printed. A simple technique for doing this is to pass the number through the accumulator; that is, when we wish to have CØUNT printed, we would say

```
        LDAC    CØUNT
        JSUB    PRINT
```

Similarly, to print A:

```
        LDAC    A
        JSUB    PRINT
```

Thus when the subprogram PRINT begins, it expects to find the number to be printed in the accumulator. PRINT can then print that number without ever "knowing" whether the number was originally contained in CØUNT or A. This is significant because PRINT is now independent of the rest of the program and, in fact, could be used without modification in *any* program to replace the PNUM instruction.

The PRINT subprogram would probably store the number found in the accumulator into some location as a first step. This frees the accumulator for other uses. Similarly, PRINT would save the return address found in the index register in some location if the index register is needed for other purposes. The final program (showing only the essential instructions for calling, returning, and passing information) would look something like that shown in Fig. 7.6.

Note that the subprogram stores the number in the accumulator into location PRO7. This number is known as the **parameter** or **argument** of the subprogram. Regardless of whether this number was originally in location A or location CØUNT, subprogram PRINT treats it identically. Note also that CØUNT and A are **input parameters** to the subprogram. The subprogram receives this value and uses it in

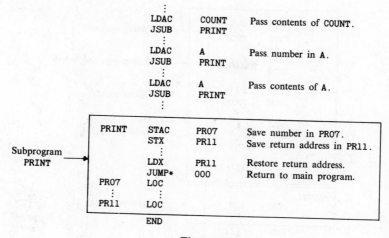

Figure 7.6

performing its function. Often subprograms produce certain values as a result of their computations; these values must be passed back to the main program as **output parameters**.

We now present a possible version of the PRINT subprogram:

PRINT	STAC	PRO7	Store argument in PRO7.
	STX	PR11	Store return address in PR11.
	TAB	001	Perform tab (automatically done by PNUM).
	LDX	PR10	Initialize loop counter.
PRO1	LDAC	PRO7	
	RGHT*	000	⎫ Search for leftmost nonzero digit.
	JZER	PRO5	Is digit zero?
PRO2	LDAC	PRO7	No; take care of signs.
	JNEG	PRO3	If negative, jump to PRO3.
	LDAC	PRO9	
	PSYM	PR12	⎫ Positive; print a blank.
	JUMP	PRO4	
PRO3	LDAC	PRO9	
	PSYM	PR13	⎫ Print a minus sign.
PRO4	LDAC	PRO7	
	RGHT*	000	
	EXTR	PRO9	⎫ Extract digits from left and prepare them for printing.
	LEFT	002	
	STAC	PRO8	
	LDAC	PRO9	
	PSYM	PRO8	Print the digit.
	JXZR	PRO6	Entire number printed? If yes, jump to PRO6.
	DECX	001	No; continue on to next digit.
	JUMP	PRO4	

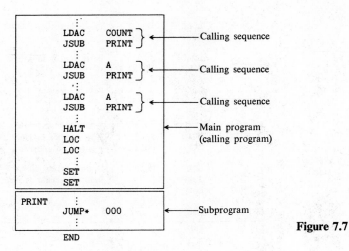

Figure 7.7

PR05	LDAC	PR09	} Print a blank.
	PSYM	PR12	
	DECX	001	Decrement digit count.
	JXZR	PR02	} Determine whether or not this is the rightmost digit.
	JUMP	PR01	
PR06	LDX	PR11	Restore return address to index register.
	JUMP*	000	Jump back to next instruction in main program.
PR07	LØC		
PR08	LØC		
PR09	SET	+00001	
PR10	SET	+00004	
PR11	LØC		
PR12	CHAR	01	⊔ The single character "blank."
PR13	CHAR	01	− The single character "minus."

That portion of the total program which does not include the subprogram is called the **main program**. If the main program **calls** a subprogram, it is also known as a **calling program**. The specific sequence of instructions which calls the subprogram is known as a **calling sequence** (see Fig. 7.7). Even if you don't work through the subprogram in detail, the mechanism used for passing the parameters and return address, as well as how the subprogram saves and uses these, must be understood. The remaining sections in this chapter depend on this understanding.

Exercises 7.1

1. Here is a subprogram which receives a parameter in the accumulator, as does the PRINT subprogram. What does this subprogram do?

```
XXX      STAC    XXX1
         FMUL    XXX1
         FMUL    XXX2
         STAC    XXX1
         PFLT    XXX1
         JUMP*   000
XXX1     LØC
XXX2     FSET    +.314E+01  ← This is 3.14, the constant π.
```

2. Write and test a subprogram called CARRG which receives an input parameter n in the accumulator, skips n lines, and returns. Does the program work properly when n is zero? What happens when n is negative? when n is 30000?

3. Can you think of any methods we might use to have a subprogram return a computed value to the main program? Write a subprogram which, when called, reads a floating-point number from the next data card, divides it by 59.7, and returns the result to the main program. Test out this subprogram.

7.2 MULTIPLE PARAMETER SUBPROGRAMS

In the previous section we examined PRINT—a subprogram with one input parameter and no output parameters. The single argument was passed to the subprogram in the accumulator. Suppose now we wish to write a subprogram with several parameters. Clearly, they can't all be stored in and passed through the accumulator. A more universal convention is needed for passing parameters to and from subprograms.

One technique used widely is to have the calling program form a list of the parameters in memory. The location of this **parameter list** is then passed to the subprogram when it is called. The subprogram, knowing where the list is found in memory, uses this information to obtain the arguments in the parameter list.

In the FACET computer this can be done quite simply. Why not also use the address passed by the JSUB instruction (in the XR) as the address of the parameter list? This address is the address of the location immediately following the JSUB instruction itself. The parameter list can therefore appear as a block of locations immediately following the JSUB instruction. In this parameter list will be the input parameters and the output parameters. The "return address," or rather the instruction to be executed immediately after return from the subprogram, will follow the parameter list in the memory. For example, if we had five parameters for subprogram X, X beginning in location 543 in the memory, and if we called X from location 250, the parameters would be stored in locations 251–255 and the next instruction (return address) would be in location 256, as shown in Fig. 7.8.

For example, suppose that we are to write a subprogram, QRØØT, which will find the two roots of the quadratic equation of the form

$$ax^2 + bx + c = 0.$$

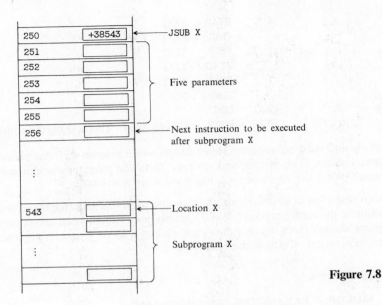

Figure 7.8

(This subprogram assumes that the equation has real roots only; adjustments must be made for complex or imaginary roots.) Subprogram QRØØT will have five parameters:

1) a, the coefficient of the x^2 term; ⎫
2) b, the coefficient of the x term;   ⎬ Input parameters
3) c, the constant term;   ⎭
4) r_1, the first root;   ⎫ Output parameters
5) r_2, the second root.   ⎭

QRØØT is to receive the values for a, b, and c, and is to compute and return values r_1 and r_2, according to the formulas

$$r_1 = \frac{-b + \sqrt{b^2 - 4ac}}{2a}, \qquad r_2 = \frac{-b - \sqrt{b^2 - 4ac}}{2a}.$$

Note that we don't want this subprogram to read anything or print anything. This subprogram is designed to perform a calculation for the **calling** program. Naturally, the calling program is the program which calls QRØØT and thereby "requests" the calculation. QRØØT merely performs the calculation and returns the results to the calling program, in the locations reserved for output parameters.

QRØØT "knows" where the parameters are, because it receives the "address" of the parameter list in the index register. The actual number in the index register is the address of the first parameter, one more than that is the address of the second parameter, and so on. For instance, if QRØØT begins and finds 251 in the index register, then it "knows" that:

1) a is in location 251;
2) b is in location 252;
3) c is in location 253;
4) r_1 should be placed into location 254;
5) r_2 should be placed into location 255;
6) a jump should be executed to location 256 after completion of the calculation.

Let's say that at some point in your program you have computed three numbers, n_1, n_2, and n_3; and that these three numbers are stored in locations R, S, and T, respectively. Let's also say that you want to find the roots of the quadratic equation

$$n_1 x^2 + n_2 x + n_3 = 0.$$

Since you already have subprogram QRØØT written, you must merely set up n_1, n_2, and n_3 in a parameter list and call upon QRØØT to perform the calculation. The results (the roots) will be placed into the fourth and fifth positions of the list by QRØØT. So you would write:

	LDAC	R	Put n_1 into the first position	
	STAC	X1	in the parameter list.	
	LDAC	S	Put n_2 into the second position	
	STAC	X2	tion in the parameter list.	
This is	LDAC	T	Put n_3 into the third position	
a calling	STAC	X3	in the parameter list.	
sequence for				
subprogram	JSUB	QRØØT	Jump to subprogram.	
QRØØT				
X1	LØC		First argument (parameter).	
X2	LØC		Second argument (parameter).	The
X3	LØC		Third argument (parameter).	parameter
X4	LØC		Fourth argument (parameter).	list
X5	LØC		Fifth argument (parameter).	

$\vdots$ The next instruction.

Now that the arguments are successfully stored in the parameter list, we must develop a technique for the subprogram to get at them. It cannot use the labels, X1, X2, or X3 directly because if the subprogram were called again from some other location in the calling program, a different parameter list with different labels would be used. That is, elsewhere we might find QRØØT being called to find the roots of $m_1 x^2 + m_2 x + m_3 = 0$, where m_1, m_2, and m_3 are stored in locations

U, V, and W, respectively. In this case we would write another calling sequence:

```
        LDAC    U        ⎫ Place m₁ into first position in the
        STAC    Y1       ⎭ parameter list.
        LDAC    V        ⎫ Place m₂ into second position in the
        STAC    Y2       ⎭ parameter list.
        LDAC    W        ⎫ Place m₃ into third position in the
        STAC    Y3       ⎭ parameter list.
        JSUB    QRØØT
  Y1    LØC              ⎫
  Y2    LØC              ⎪
  Y3    LØC              ⎬ The parameter list
  Y4    LØC              ⎪
  Y5    LØC              ⎭
        ⋮                  Next instruction executed after QRØØT.
```

Since the subprogram cannot use the labels in the parameter lists directly, the subprogram can instead *construct* the required addresses of parameter list locations each time it is called. This is a simple task because of the indexing capabilities of the machine. Consider the first case, where we are interested in constructing the addresses of X1, X2, and X3. When the subprogram QRØØT is called, the JSUB instruction places the address of X1, the first parameter in the list, into the index register. Let's say that this address is 251. To access X1, subprogram QRØØT uses an instruction like

$$\text{LDAC∗}\quad 000\qquad(\text{assembled as } -11000)$$

Since this instruction is indexed, its effective operand is

$$
\begin{array}{rl}
000 & \text{(operand)}\\
+251 & \text{(contents of index register)}\\
\hline
251 & \text{(effective operand and address of X1)}
\end{array}
$$

and so X1 is loaded into the accumulator. When the subprogram must refer to X2, it uses an indexed instruction with 001 as the operand, since

$$
\begin{array}{rl}
001 & \\
+251 & \\
\hline
252 & \text{(address of X2)}
\end{array}
$$

Similarly, LDAC∗   002 would load X3 into the accumulator. We are now using indexing in a different way than we have previously. Before, an indexed instruction generally had an address of an array or block of locations as the *operand*, while the address within the array (000, 001, 002, ...) was in the *index register*. We now have the address of the block in the *index register* (251 in this case) and the address within the block (000, 001, ...) as the *operand* of the instruction. Note that we think of the parameter list as a contiguous block of memory just like an array.

Instructions like

$$\begin{array}{ll} \text{LDAC*} & 001 \\ \text{ADD*} & 000 \\ \text{FMUL*} & 002 \\ \text{STAC*} & 004 \end{array}$$

would be used to refer to the parameters of the subprogram. So long as the appropriate parameter "block" address remains in the index register, these instructions will refer to the correct locations in the parameter list.

If there are five arguments, then instructions which refer to those arguments will have operands 000, 001, 002, 003, or 004. The return address is the location immediately following the parameter list, and we can jump to it by executing

$$\text{JUMP*} \qquad 005$$

which causes a return from subprogram QRØØT to the correct location in the calling program.

Here is one possible way of writing subprogram QRØØT:

QRØØT	STX	QRT1	Save return address in index register.
	LDAC	QRTFP4	4
	FMUL*	000	$4a$ ⎱ Compute $4ac$.
	FMUL*	002	$4ac$
	STAC	QRT2	$QRT2 \leftarrow 4ac$
	LDAC*	001	b ⎱ Compute $b^2 - 4ac$;
	FMUL*	001	b^2 this is argument for
	FSUB	QRT2	$b^2 - 4ac$ SQRT (square root)
	STAC	QRTP1	$QRTP1 \leftarrow b^2 - 4ac$ subprogram.
	JSUB	SQRT	Jump to SQRT subprogram. ⎱ Compute $\sqrt{b^2 - 4ac}$
QRTP1	LØC		Input parameter ($b^2 - 4ac$). using SQRT
QRTP2	LØC		Output parameter ($\sqrt{b^2 - 4ac}$). subprogram.
	LDX	QRT1	Restore parameter list address to index register.
	LDAC*	001	b
	FMUL	QRTFM1	$-b$
	FADD	QRTP2	$-b + \sqrt{b^2 - 4ac}$ Compute first
	FDIV	QRTFP2	$(1/2)(-b + \sqrt{b^2 - 4ac})$ root, r_1.
	FDIV*	000	$(1/2a)(-b + \sqrt{b^2 - 4ac})$
	STAC*	003	Store r_1 into fourth parameter list position.
	LDAC*	001	b
	FMUL	QRTFM1	$-b$
	FSUB	QRTP2	$-b - \sqrt{b^2 - 4ac}$ Compute second
	FDIV	QRTFP2	$(1/2)(-b - \sqrt{b^2 - 4ac})$ root, r_2.
	FDIV*	000	$(1/2a)(-b - \sqrt{b^2 - 4ac})$

```
        STAC* 004          Store r₂ into fifth parameter list position.
        JUMP* 005          Return to calling program.
QRTFP4  FSET  +.400E+01    Floating-point 4.
QRTFP2  FSET  +.200E+01    Floating-point 2.
QRTFM1  FSET  -.100E+01    Floating-point -1.
QRT1    LØC            ⎫
QRT2    LØC            ⎬ Temporary storage locations
                       ⎭
```

As you look through the above program, you will no doubt note that another subprogram, SQRT, is called from within the QRØØT subprogram! This square root subprogram requires two parameters in its parameter list: first, a floating-point number greater than zero whose square root is to be found; second, the location in which the answer is to be returned. Note how, immediately upon return from the SQRT subprogram, the index register is reloaded with the previously saved quantity in QRT1. Do you see why that was necessary? Think about what the JSUB instruction does to the index register.

Sometimes the calling sequence of a subprogram can be simplified. This occurs when the location permanently holding the number to be stored in the parameter list can actually be placed in the parameter list itself. Recall that at one point we wanted to find the roots of

$$n_1x^2 + n_2x + n_3 = 0,$$

where n_1, n_2, and n_3 were in locations R, S, and T. Let's assume that we needed those two roots in two locations RØØT1 and RØØT2. We might have written

```
                    ⋮
            JSUB    QRØØT
    ₹       LØC
    S       LØC
    T       LØC
    RØØT1   LØC
    RØØT2   LØC
                    ⋮
```

instead of actually transferring the parameters to and from the parameter list like this:

```
                    ⋮
            LDAC    R
            STAC    X1
            LDAC    S
            STAC    X2
            LDAC    T
            STAC    X3
            JSUB    QRØØT
    X1      LØC
```

```
X2        LØC
X3        LØC
X4        LØC
X5        LØC
          LDAC      X4
          STAC      RØØT1
          LDAC      X5
          STAC      RØØT2
            :
R         LØC
S         LØC
T         LØC
RØØT1     LØC
RØØT2     LØC
            :
```

The first calling sequence is far easier to program than the second one because there is no longer a need to explicitly load locations RØØT1 and RØØT2 with the results, nor to store R, S, and T into the parameter list. However, we cannot always use this approach. For instance, if R is an argument of a number of different calling sequences (to either the same or different subprograms), it cannot permanently be stored in the parameter list of more than one subprogram.

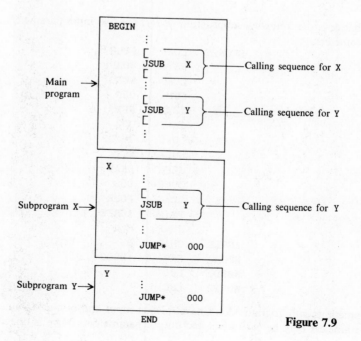

Figure 7.9

A subprogram may call another subprogram. In such a case the first subprogram acts as the calling program for the second, and there would be a calling sequence among its instructions. Complex interconnections among subprograms may then arise. Remember that the **main program** is that portion of the entire program within which execution begins. What happens in Fig. 7.9? Note that both the main program and subprogram X act as calling programs for subprogram Y at different times.

Exercises 7.2

1. What does the following subprogram do? It has two input parameters and two output parameters. Recall that an indexed instruction with

   operand 000 refers to first input parameter,
   operand 001 refers to second input parameter,
   operand 002 refers to first output parameter,
   operand 003 refers to second output parameter,
   operand 004 refers to return address.

   The subprogram is

WHAT	LDAC*	000
	FADD*	001
	STAC*	002
	LDAC*	000
	FSUB*	001
	STAC*	003
	JUMP*	004

2. What does the following subprogram do? It has two input parameters and no output parameters.

SECRET	LDAC	FØUR	
	RSYM	WØRD1	
	LDAC	WØRD1	
	SUB*	000	
	JZER	NEXT	
	JUMP*	002	
NEXT	LDAC	WØRD2	
	SUB*	001	
	JZER	ØKAY	
	JUMP*	002	
ØKAY	LDAC	FØUR	
	PSYM	AGREE	
	JUMP*	002	
AGREE	CHAR	04	YES.
FØUR	SET	+00004	
WØRD1	LØC		
WØRD2	LØC		

3. Sometimes subprograms don't have distinct input and output parameters; i.e., some parameters may be *both* input *and* output parameters. Here is one such, with three

arguments in its parameter list. What does it do?

```
FIB     LDAC*    001
        STAC*    000
        LDAC*    002
        STAC*    001
        ADD*     000
        STAC*    002
        JUMP*    003
```

Hint: A program which computes the Fibonacci sequence, 1, 1, 2, 3, 5, 8, 13, 21, . . . , wherein each term is the sum of the previous two terms, can use this subprogram.

4. In Chapter 6 we wrote a program to calculate the sine of an angle (given in radians) by calculating the first few terms of the infinite series,

$$x - \frac{x^3}{3!} + \frac{x^5}{5!} - \frac{x^7}{7!} + \cdots$$

The series for $\cos(x)$ in radians is

$$\cos(x) = 1 - \frac{x^2}{2!} + \frac{x^4}{4!} - \frac{x^6}{6!} + \frac{x^8}{8!} - \cdots$$

Write a subprogram with one input and one output parameter which computes $\cos(x)$. Use the first four terms of the series.

5. Why can't a subprogram call itself? Even if we could find some use for such a call (there *are* uses), why wouldn't it work if we employed the conventions we have been discussing?

6. Write the subprogram called ABS. It has two parameters, one input and one output. It finds the absolute value of its input parameter and returns that value as the output parameter.

7. Write a subprogram FLØAT which converts a fixed-point number to its floating-point equivalent. Use exercise 6.7(3) as a guide. It should have one input parameter and one output parameter. FLØAT should not print anything.

8. Write a subprogram IFIX which converts a floating-point number to its fixed point (integer) equivalent by truncating the fraction part. If the magnitude of the floating-point number is too great, set the output parameter to +00000 and turn on the overflow indicator. This subprogram has one input and one output parameter.

Both FLØAT (exercise 7) and IFIX are very important subprograms which find frequent use in FORTRAN, as we shall see in Chapters 9 and 10.

7.3 ARRAY PARAMETERS

All the subprograms we have discussed have had arguments which were single FACET words. All we had to do in order to pass these words back and forth between the calling program and the subprogram was to place them in a block of memory whose whereabouts is known to both. Until now, the subprogram calling process could have been viewed as a three-step operation, as depicted in Fig. 7.10.

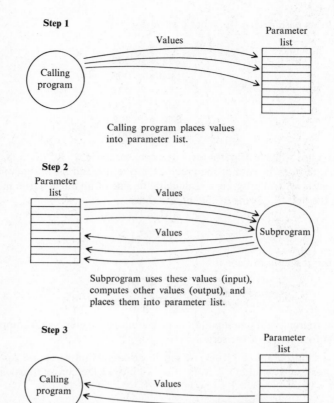

Figure 7.10

Sometimes we are interested in passing an entire array to a subprogram as a parameter. This could occur in many applications. For example, subprograms which might require arrays are merge subprograms, subprograms which find the median or variance of a list of numbers, and subprograms which search an array for the presence of a specified number. Another example is a subprogram which sorts the elements of an array into ascending (or descending) order. You might suppose that we could pass an array to the sorting subprogram by placing every element of this array on the parameter list, as depicted in Fig. 7.11. The problem with this method is that arrays can get so long that it is difficult, if not prohibitive, to pass an entire array, element by element, in a parameter list.

Instead of passing all the elements of an array in the parameter list, we can use a different technique, one used by almost all instructions in the FACET computer. Consider the following instruction:

$$+42222 \quad (\text{PNUM}).$$

Array elements stored on input parameter list

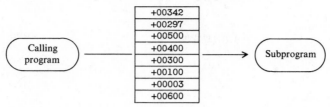

Array elements reordered on output parameter list (the same list)

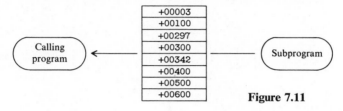

Figure 7.11

Its operand is the *address* 222, which causes the *contents* of 222 to be printed. However, if we printed the same number by calling the subprogram PRINT (Section 7.1), we would *not* have passed the address 222 to the subprogram, but the *contents* of 222. It should be apparent therefore that we could have passed the address 222 instead of its contents as a parameter to the subprogram. The subprogram would then have used the address to get at the contents of 222 just as the computer does when executing +42222.

When the *contents* of some location are passed as a parameter, that parameter is said to be passed **by value**, because the parameter's value is passed. When the *address* of a parameter is passed, it is said to be passed **by name**, since the address serves as the name of a location. Up to this point all parameters have been passed by value because it is a simpler technique for the passing of single-word arguments.

Arrays, however, can be passed more efficiently by name. This is done by storing the address of the array (i.e., the address of its first location) in the parameter list. The subprogram uses this address to access any location in the array.

We must be cautious and point out that many computers have special hardware features to simplify the passing of parameters by name. For such machines, parameter passing by value loses its comparative advantage. Passing parameters by name is used for passing both array and single-location parameters in such machines. For this reason, it is important to understand what is involved with both methods. One of the hardware features affecting the passing of parameters by name is discussed in Chapter 8 (indirect addressing).

Let's examine the technique for passing an array argument by name. We'll look at the machine language calling sequence first, since it is more illustrative of what is actually happening. Assume that we have a subprogram, beginning in location

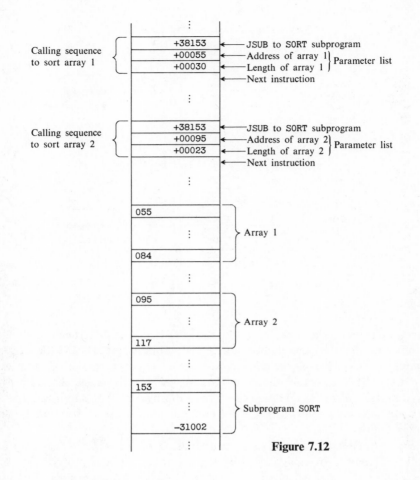

Figure 7.12

153, for sorting an array. This subprogram has two parameters:

a) the *address* of an array (the address of its first location), and
b) the length of the array (passed by *value*).

The main program has two arrays which it must have sorted at different times—one begins in location 055 and has 30 elements, and the other begins in location 095 and has 23 elements (we'll call them array 1 and array 2, respectively). We could sort them as shown in Fig. 7.12. Note that the subprogram can obtain the *address* of the array (055 in one case and 095 in the other) which it must somehow manipulate to retrieve and work on the elements of the array.

We must now examine how, in assembly language, we can place the address of an array into the parameter list. To do this, a special pseudo-operation exists in the FACET assembly language. It is the **address pseudo-operation**, with mnemonic ADRS. Its operand is any label appearing in the program. The assembler sets that

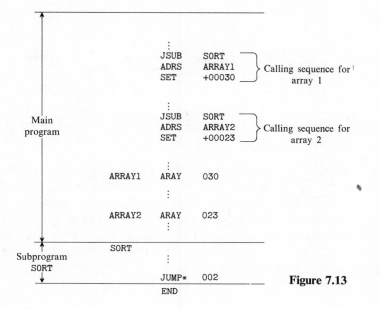

Figure 7.13

location to the address corresponding to the label. For example, the calling sequences in assembly language for sorting the two arrays might be as shown in Fig. 7.13. Note that pseudo-op

ADRS   Q

is translated to +00nnn, where nnn is the address assigned to Q by the assembler.

Let us now examine how we might go about writing a subprogram SØRT. Our subprogram receives two important items of information in its parameter list: the address of the first element in the array and the length. How shall these be used most effectively?

Suppose we wish to sort ARRAY1, a 30-word array beginning in location 055. If we were writing an ordinary program to do this (no subprograms), we would have indexed instructions with operand ARRAY1, with an appropriate address within the array (a pointer) in the index register. Typical instructions might be:

Machine language	Assembly language	
−11055	LDAC*	ARRAY1
−22055	SUB*	ARRAY1
−12055	STAC*	ARRAY1

When these instructions are executed, the index register will presumably contain some value between 000 and 029, addresses within block or array ARRAY1. For instance, if the index register contains 004 and we execute LDAC*   ARRAY1, then the fifth location in the array is loaded into the accumulator (Fig. 7.14). This can be thought of as a two-part addressing scheme with half of the address in the

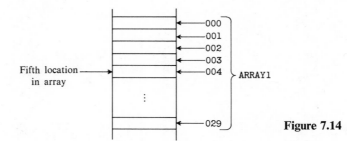

Figure 7.14

operand and half in the index register. The two parts are added together to give the actual address shown in Fig. 7.15. We see that 055 (address of ARRAY1) + 004 (address within block ARRAY1) is 059 (address of location in question).

When we write the subprogram we don't know the name (or address) of the array being sorted, so we must devise a method for *inserting* the appropriate address at execution time. Let's suppose we start by writing subprogram SØRT by writing a sequence of instructions for sorting a fictional array Z:

```
            ⋮
       LDAC*    Z
            ⋮
       SUB*     Z
            ⋮
       STAC*    Z
            ⋮
```

Let us now attach a label to each location which refers to this fictional array, and leave out the name of the array:

```
                   ⋮
       INST1    LDAC*    000
                   ⋮
       INST5    SUB*     000
                   ⋮
       INST12   STAC*    000
                   ⋮
```

At the beginning of the subprogram we will write a sequence of instructions for storing the appropriate array address in the operand portion of *all* locations referring to the array. We can do this with the STX instruction, since that instruction only affects the operand (digits 3–5) and does not affect the sign or the op-code. We start by getting the address of the array into the index register. See Fig. 7.16. Note that the major portion of the subprogram is essentially the same as an ordinary program for achieving the same result. References to a specific array name are deleted, and supplied at execution time whenever the subprogram is called. Each

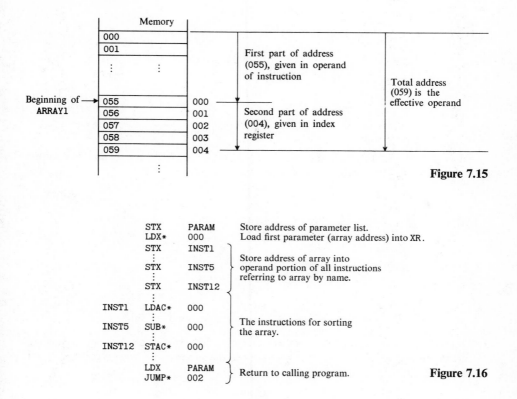

Figure 7.15

```
        STX    PARAM     Store address of parameter list.
        LDX*   000       Load first parameter (array address) into XR.
        STX    INST1     ⎫
         ⋮               ⎪  Store address of array into
        STX    INST5     ⎬  operand portion of all instructions
         ⋮               ⎪  referring to array by name.
        STX    INST12    ⎭

INST1   LDAC*  000       ⎫
         ⋮               ⎪  The instructions for sorting
INST5   SUB*   000       ⎬  the array.
         ⋮               ⎪
INST12  STAC*  000       ⎭
         ⋮
        LDX    PARAM     ⎫  Return to calling program.
        JUMP*  002       ⎭
```

Figure 7.16

call causes a new, possibly different, address to be inserted in all the pertinent instruction operands.

The essence of this section is the definition of passing parameters by value and by name, and the presentation of some appropriate differences in comparative efficiencies between the two techniques, based on hardware differences among computers. For this reason, it's important for your ideas surrounding each to remain flexible. Try writing some FACET subprograms in which parameters (particularly array parameters) are passed by name, but bear in mind that techniques might differ somewhat in different computers.

Exercises 7.3

1. Assemble the following program (by hand) and trace through its execution to figure out what it does. If this is difficult, punch and submit the program with a trace, and follow what happens as it executes:

```
        LDX    A
        LDX*   000
        LDX*   000
        LDAC*  000
```

```
                        STAC    E
                        PNUM    E
                        HALT
                A       ADRS    B
                B       ADRS    C
                C       ADRS    D
                D       SET     +00325
                E       LØC
                        END
```

2. This is a subprogram which has one input parameter (passed by name) and one output parameter (passed by value). What does it do?

```
        WHEN    STX     WH2
                LDX*    000
                LDAC*   000
                JPØS    WH1
                MLS     WH3
        WH1     LDX     WH2
                STAC*   001
                JUMP*   002
        WH2     LØC
        WH3     SET     −00001
```

3. This is a subprogram which has two parameters. The first is an array, passed by name, and the second is passed by value. What does the subprogram do? Which are input parameters and which are output parameters?

```
        HAHAHA  LDAC*   001
                STAC    HAHA3
                INCX    002
                STX     HAHA2
                LDX*
        HAHA1   RFLT*
                LDAC    HAHA3
                SUB     HAHA4
        HAHA2   JZER    000
                STAC    HAHA3
                INCX    001
                JUMP    HAHA1
        HAHA3   LØC
        HAHA4   SET     +00001
```

4. Write a SØRT subprogram which receives two parameters: the name (address) of an array, and a number—the number of numbers in that array. Upon return to the calling program, the array should be sorted into descending order.

7.4 INDEPENDENT SUBPROGRAM ASSEMBLY

An important advantage of subprograms is that many of them perform universal processes which can be used in more than one program. Examples of this type of program are PRINT, SQRT, and QRØØT. PRINT could be used to advantage with any program containing a PNUM instruction. QRØØT and especially SQRT can be used in programs with scientific applications. Other examples of useful subprograms are sine, cosine, absolute value, sort, merge, median, variance, convert floating point to integer, and convert integer to floating point.

These processes are so useful that an important design goal for subprograms becomes their usability in any program which needs them. A criterion for judging "usability" of a subprogram is that the calling program need to know as little information as possible about the subprogram itself. We have already seen what that minimum amount of information is:

1. The calling program must know the name of the subprogram.
2. The calling program must know
   a) the number of parameters,
   b) the type of each parameter (fixed or floating point; or character),
   c) the type of call to each parameter (by name or by value),
   d) the order in which the parameters appear.

Once these things are known, we should expect that subprograms written by different people could be used without further communication in a single program. This would aid the writing of large, complex programs. Also, many programming systems and programming languages provide a library of subprograms accessible to anyone using that system or language. Since this interchangeability of subprograms is so important, we must ask whether anything might interfere with it. The answer is yes, and the problem revolves about labels.

Subprograms should be self-contained. Therefore they should not attempt to share storage or constants with a calling program or another subprogram. The following subprogram RTN would not be independent of its calling program:

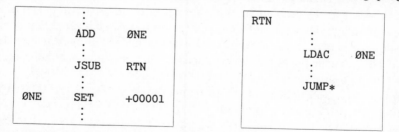

The operand ØNE in subprogram RTN and the operand ØNE in the calling program both refer to the label ØNE defined in the calling program. This prevents the direct use of RTN with some other program because the error message—**undefined operand**—would be generated for ØNE; +00001 should be defined both in the calling program and in RTN. Of course, the label ØNE could not be used in both places because that would be a syntax error, since the same label may not appear more than once in the program. This syntax error is often called **duplicate label**. A useful technique for generating labels in subprograms is to use a prefix abbreviating

the name of the subprogram on each label. We might rewrite subprogram RTN
above like this:

```
RTN
            ⋮
          LDAC      RT1
            ⋮
          JUMP*
            ⋮
RT1       SET       +00001
```

Subprogram RTN is now self-contained because it does not refer to labels defined
elsewhere.

A major difficulty with the use of labels in subprograms is the avoidance of
duplicate labels. We maintain that a good practice for avoiding multiple definition
of labels is to use a prefix for every label in the subprogram. The prefix could be
some abbreviation of the subprogram's name. This practice was evident in the
PRINT and QRØØT subprograms:

PRINT *labels*	QRØØT *labels*
PRINT	QRØØT
PRØ1	QRTP1
PRØ2	QRTP2
⋮	QRTRL4
PR13	QRTRL2
	QRTRM1
	QRT1
	QRT2

All the labels in PRINT have the prefix PR, and all the QRØØT labels use QRT. This
technique resolves the problem of duplicate labels, for all practical purposes. After
all, how often will the same prefix be used? However, we indicated that some subprograms are part of larger systems used by thousands of programmers. In such
cases, "all practical purposes" is insufficient. A comprehensive solution which
removes the possibility of duplicate labels is required.

Specifically, we might have the program shown in Fig. 7.17. The label ØNE
appears both in the main program and in the subprogram, and is a syntax
error—a duplicate label error. We would like the operand ØNE (1) to refer to
label ØNE (2) and operand ØNE (3) to refer to label ØNE (4). It would be desirable,
however, to have a facility in which duplicate labels are allowed. A label could
appear a number of times in a program, but only once in each subprogram and
once in the main program. An operand would then refer to the label within its own
subprogram (or the main program). The assembler and loader would somehow
have to keep track of these duplicate labels and the subprograms in which they
belong. In other words, a reference to a label in a particular subprogram must
refer to the definition of that label in that subprogram alone and no other. In

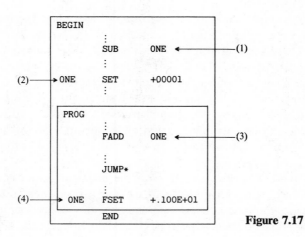

Figure 7.17

effect, fences must be constructed about the main program and about each sub-program to limit the scope of definitions appearing inside them so that they will not conflict with one another. Although this facility, which is known as **independent assembly** of subprograms, is not used in FACET, it is used in most programming languages. It will therefore be discussed in some detail even though you cannot practice using it in FACET.

Basically, this process involves the assembly of the main program and each subprogram comprising the entire program *independently* of one another. Consider the program in Fig. 7.17 with its one subprogram PRØG. The label ØNE is defined in both the main program and the subprogram. Of course, in FACET the multiple definition of ØNE would be considered a syntax error. To provide for the new independent assembly technique, additional END statements would have to be inserted. These now mark the end of each subprogram and the main program. It would now read as shown in Fig. 7.18.

Figure 7.18

The assembler would then perform the assembly process, as described in Chapter 3, on the main program from BEGIN through the *first* END. In this way, label ØNE would cause no error because the assembler has not yet encountered the second appearance of label ØNE. The resulting machine language translation of the main program is stored by the assembler. It then clears its symbol table and proceeds to assemble PRØG through its END statement. Again there is no problem with the label ØNE because the assembler now has an entry for the second ØNE in its symbol table and no entry for the first. The operand ØNE for the instruction FADD ØNE is therefore resolved correctly. The assembler also stores the machine language translation of the subprogram PRØG.

When the LØAD. card is read, both the main program and subprogram PRØG are loaded into consecutive blocks of memory. If you remember, the loader had to increment absolute address operands by the relocation constant when the program was loaded from a location other than 000. Similar adjustments must be made under the new technique except that the main program and each subprogram now has its own relocation constant associated with it, the location from which each is being loaded.

The problem of duplicate labels is completely solved. You may have observed, however, that a new problem has been created by this solution! The self-containment demanded of each subprogram is absolute. We indicated earlier that this was preferable, but there exist some cross-references between subprograms which cannot be eliminated. These are the calls to a subprogram from the calling program. They appear as the instruction JSUB PRØG in Fig. 7.19. Here PRØG is an operand in the main program but is not defined in it. Operand PRØG refers to the label PRØG in the subprogram. It should be clear that this cross-reference cannot be avoided. A technique must therefore be provided to permit

```
BEGIN
         ⋮
         SUB      ONE
         ⋮
         JSUB     PROG
         ⋮
ONE      SET      +00001
         ⋮
         END
```

```
PROG
         ⋮
         FADD     ONE
         ⋮
         JUMP*
ONE      FSET     +.100E+01
         END
```

Figure 7.19

the resolution of such cross-references where necessary. In other words, we need a "hole in the fence" that we just constructed, through which necessary information can be passed. So, along with the independent assembly of subprograms, two new pseudo-operations must be added. One, commonly called EXTERNAL, has a label as its operand and says that the label is defined in some *other* subprogram. The main program would be:

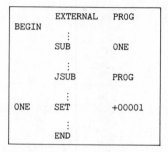

The EXTERNAL pseudo-op tells the assembler that PRØG will be defined in some other subprogram. This prevents the assembler from saying that PRØG is an undefined operand (an operand which does not appear as a label). When the machine language instruction corresponding to JSUB PRØG is generated, the operand is left blank because the assembler still does not know where PRØG will be located. Instead, the assembler creates a reminder in a **control dictionary** stating that the label PRØG is still unresolved and that it is an operand in such-and-such locations. The above, translated, could be as shown in Fig. 7.20.

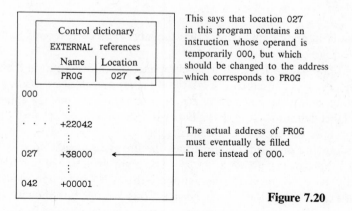

Figure 7.20

Before execution can take place, the address corresponding to PRØG (defined in another subprogram) must be substituted for the operand of the instruction in location 027. In assembly language, this instruction was JSUB PRØG. The machine language translation combined with the control dictionary is called an **object module**.

The other new pseudo-operation, called ENTRY, also has a label operand. It specifies that its operand is a label defined in the subprogram and referred to by another subprogram (or the main program). The assembler saves the location of that label in the control dictionary. In subprogram PRØG we might write:

```
            ENTRY    PROG
PROG
            ⋮
            FADD     ONE

            ⋮

            JUMP*
ONE         FSET     +.100E+01
            END
```

This would be translated as expected, except for the addition to the control dictionary. It might appear as:

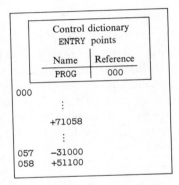

This control dictionary entry states that the label PRØG corresponds to location 000 in the subprogram.

When the separate assemblies are complete, the information in their respective control dictionaries is used to resolve the remaining unresolved operands. This is called **linking** and is carried out by a processor called the **linkage editor**. Its task is to link label definitions appearing under the ENTRY statements with the operands appearing under the EXTERNAL statements.

The following program demonstrates the linkage process. The program contains two subprograms, FUNCT and SIN. The main program calls both FUNCT and SIN directly, let us assume. Further, suppose the FUNCT subprogram also calls SIN. We might expect to see the relevant instructions arranged as shown in Fig. 7.21.

The assembler might then produce three object modules which appear as shown in Fig. 7.22.

Note that control dictionaries also contain the length or number of machine locations needed to load that object module. This assists the linkage editor in determining the address at which loading will start for each module. In this example, since the lengths of the three modules are 170, 56, and 41 words, re-

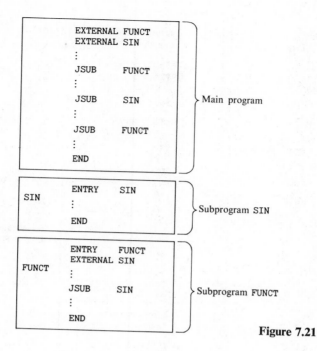

Figure 7.21

spectively, the relocation constants for the three modules would be 000, 170, and 226, respectively. These constants are found by adding together the lengths of all previous modules.

The linkage editor processes the object module and outputs a **load module**. This load module contains no control dictionaries, since all the EXTERNAL references have been resolved. In addition, the linkage editor will adjust the addresses of instructions as well as all nonabsolute operands. These operations will generally require two passes. On the first pass the following composite control dictionary could be formed:

Defined at:	*Name*	*Referenced at:*
170	SIN	072, 254
226	FUNCT	058, 109

Note how the addresses have been adjusted by their relocation constants. For example, SIN is referenced at location 028 in the third object module whose relocation constant is 226. Therefore 254, which equals 226 + 028, is entered in the table. FUNCT, defined at location 000 of the third module, is also adjusted by 226 to produce its load module address, 226.

The load module could then be arranged as shown in Fig. 7.23.

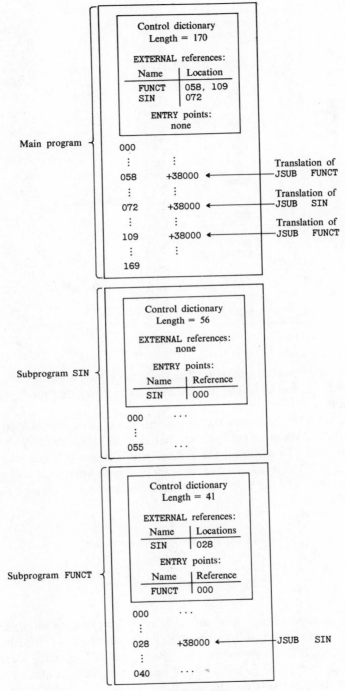

Figure 7.22

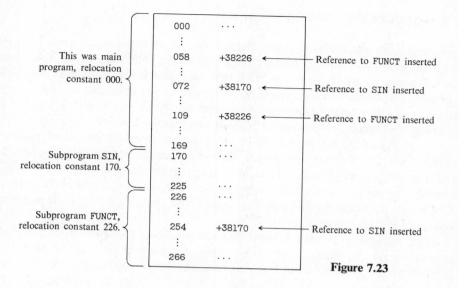

Figure 7.23

    The addresses and operands have been adjusted as though the entire program was assembled at once. This output resembles the output of the FACET assembler. Although not shown in the figure above, you may have realized that associated with each word is an indication of whether its operand is absolute or relative. Only relative operands need be adjusted in loading. These indications are placed by the assembler and left intact by the linkage editor. This procedure permits the loader† to load the program at some location in the memory other than 000. If the program is to be loaded from location 200, then 200 becomes the relocation constant for the entire load module.

    In summary, let us review those processes used by most assemblers and other translators to ensure interchangeability of subprograms. Each subprogram is translated independently of each other subprogram. The assembler or translator produces an object module which is the machine language form of the program together with a control dictionary containing information pertaining to the ENTRY and EXTERNAL pseudo-ops. The linkage editor uses this information to link together all the separately assembled subprograms into one relocatable machine language program with all address references resolved. This is sometimes called a load module. The loader can now load this load module into memory for execution.

---

†   A *typical* procedure has been described here; in actuality, there are many schemes followed. Frequently, for instance, the linkage editor is part of the loader itself. Sometimes the control dictionary is saved with the load module for debugging and other purposes.

7.5 MODULAR DESIGN OF PROGRAMS

We have now introduced a new programming construct—the subprogram. As with any new programming tool we must explore the valid reasons for its use and the advantages we hope to realize from that use. This is especially necessary with subprograms because their advantages, although very significant, are not always obvious. In fact, many experienced programmers take insufficient advantage of subprograms precisely because they do not understand their full worth.

At this point, something should be mentioned to those whose sole exposure to subprograms has been via this chapter. Most programming languages have simpler techniques for specification and calling of subprograms than are found in FACET assembly language. You should therefore not take the complexity of their use in FACET as characteristic of other languages. You should also not let it prejudice you against their use.

One advantage of subprograms has already been discussed as our original motivation for the PRINT subprogram. Subprograms provide a means to reduce the number of instructions in our program when the same instruction sequence appears at more than one point in the program. Savings in keypunching time, assembly time, debugging time, and storage are obtained, as well as an increase in the clarity of the program. These improvements increase in significance as the number of calls to the subprogram increases.

Many other advantages relate to the property of subprograms which makes them largely independent of the programs in which they are used. Assuming independent assembly of subprograms, the only contact between a program and one of its subprograms is through the parameter list. Based on this property, a subprogram written by one person can be used by many. Some subprograms, commonly supplied by computer manufacturers, are used daily by thousands of programmers. It is therefore worth your while to take advantage of this property by abstracting general processes used in your programs and programming them in their general form as subprograms. You may be able to get multiple use out of them.

We can also use this property advantageously when programming long, complex programs. These programs can be broken down into parts and specified in terms of subprograms. Each subprogram can be assigned to a different programmer. When all parts are completed, they can then be brought together to function as a single program.

Another advantage of subprograms becomes evident if we break a problem down into smaller parts and implement the parts by using subprograms. Any one piece of the problem is simpler than the whole problem. Thus, if we program one subprogram at a time, the amount of logical complexity we are dealing with at any given time decreases. This makes the writing simpler and less prone to error.

Directly related to the advantage mentioned above of programming smaller, less complex parts of a problem is the debugging and checking out of those parts. The idea is to debug at most one subprogram at a time by executing it only with already debugged subprograms. Thus we can assume that any error will be contained in the non-debugged subprogram; whereas if we are checking an entire non-debugged program, the error may be anywhere in the program. We check out a program by testing it with all possible inputs and examining whether the outputs are correct. If all possible inputs cannot be tested because there are too many, then we test those inputs we believe to be most critical. It should be obvious that the total number of critical inputs to be tested with a subprogram is usually much less than the number to be tested with the entire program.   Thus better program checkout is possible using subprograms.

Subprograms also form a physical "outline" of the processes contained in a program. This helps in the writing of more logically organized programs because the very act of looking for those parts of the solution which make good subprograms is an important part of the problem solving process. By looking for and using subprograms you are automatically carrying out necessary analytical steps to solve your problem which you might ordinarily skip if you were not using subprograms.

This same "outline" characteristic also makes a program more understandable because the presence of subprograms simplifies the identification of the processes found in the program. Once the processes are understood, their interrelationships can be determined, thereby leading to an understanding of the entire program.

We expect that you can accept the presence of good, logical organization as an advantage in a program. It is probable though, that you cannot see just how important these things are, because the problems given in this introductary book are not complex enough to demonstrate these principles. Good, logical organization does not emerge as a vital necessity until we need it to help us deal with complexity. Our intellects are not capable of handling arbitrarily complex phenomena. It is only through the perception of unifying relationships and their expression in a logically organized way that we can make complex phenomena manageable. To make these points better understood, we shall discuss a "complex" problem.

Suppose you are writing a program to construct the index of a book. A simplified index will be sufficient. Let's say we want an entry for *every* word in the book, followed by *all* the numbers of the pages on which that word appears. Such an index has several undesirable characteristics, but we shall not be concerned with them. We may further suppose that the text of the book is punched onto cards.

The algorithm for constructing the index is straightforward. Examine each word in the book in turn. If it is the first appearance of that word, enter it in the index with its page number. If the word has already been entered in the index, add its page number to that entry.

We can now begin constructing the algorithm. There are many details. Among these is deciding how the index will be stored in memory. This is a complex problem because we do not know how many words there will be or on how many pages each word will appear. Without getting deeper into these details, let us return to the algorithm statement and find subprocesses contained in it which can be written as subprograms.

First, we are to examine each word in the book in turn. A useful subprogram would be one called NEXTWØRD (pardon the extra characters in the subprogram name), whose output parameter is the next word in the book. Note that the output parameter is different each time. The main program could now ignore this task. The subprogram itself must read in cards and scan the characters until it finds a character which separates two words. Such characters include blanks, commas, and periods, as well as other marks of punctuation.

The design of NEXTWØRD could be simplified further by introducing a subprogram NEXTCHARACTER which would return the next character each time it was called. After it returned the eightieth character on a card, it would read the next card. NEXTWØRD would simply accumulate the characters returned by NEXTCHARACTER till a whole word was formed, which it would return to its calling program.

The algorithm then calls for determining whether this word is already in the index. A subprogram called SEARCH might be useful. Its input parameter would be the next word of text. SEARCH would then interact with that part of the index accumulated thus far to find the word. SEARCH would return as output an indication of whether or not the word had previously been encountered, and if so, where.

Based on the response of SEARCH, we must enter a page number if the word is already in the index, and enter both the word and the page number if it is not. These steps can be carried out by subprogram WØRDENTER and subprogram PAGENTER. If the word is already in the index, the main program could call PAGENTER with the location of the word and its page number as input parameters. It would then insert the page number. If the word is not already in the index, WØRDENTER could enter the word in the correct alphabetical position. WØRDENTER could then call on PAGENTER to insert the page number of the new word.

We might characterize this subprogram structure as shown in Fig. 7.24. Note that subprogram PAGENTER can be called by either SEARCH or WØRDENTER.

The design of this program heavily uses the subprogram construct. Look it over and think how you would implement it. Despite the fact that the major details concerning how to represent the index in memory are missing, you should still see that the subprogram approach is beneficial in crystallizing the approach to the program's implementation.

We have not as yet mentioned any disadvantages of subprograms. Their principal disadvantage is the extra time spent by the machine language program in executing the calling sequence and passing parameters. This disadvantage is proportional to the number of times the subprogram is called. The more times the subprogram is called, the more time is spent in executing the calling sequence and the more inefficient it is. The significance of this disadvantage depends on the relative importance of execution speed versus the other advantages of subprograms. In most cases, the execution speeds of current machines are so fast that you need not be concerned with this disadvantage. Certainly do not assume that the only measure of a program's efficiency is its execution speed. The programmer's time is also important and costs money. Subprograms save programmer's time by improving the design, debugging, and checkout of the program and make future modifications easier.

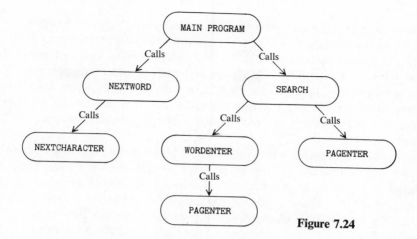

Figure 7.24

7.6 IN REVIEW

Frequently a sequence of instructions must be repeated a number of times in the same program. The sequence might operate on different data each time it appears. It is possible to have this sequence appear once in the program, possibly at the end of the main sequence of instructions. Each time the sequence is to be executed, control can be transferred to it with a JUMP instruction. Such a sequence is termed a subprogram. The JSUB instruction, jump to subprogram (op-code 38), is a special instruction for use in calling subprograms. It causes the "return address" to be placed automatically into the index register.

The set of values with which a subprogram is expected to work is called the argument list or parameter list of the subprogram. The arguments may be different each time the subprogram is called. There is usually a convention used in passing these arguments back and forth between the calling program and the subprogram. One such convention is described for use with FACET.

The parameter list may contain either values (in which case the parameters are said to be passed *by value*) or addresses where the values may be found (in which case they are passed *by name*). Arrays are usually passed by name, since one address then suffices for the entire array. The address pseudo-op ADRS is used in passing the address of some argument in the parameter list.

Subprograms may be called from various points in the main sequence of instructions (called the main program) or from other subprograms. They may themselves call other subprograms. Once the conventions for passing parameters are established, different programmers may work on different subprograms for the same program.

In FACET, the entire program, including all subprograms, is assembled as one large program. In order to avoid duplication of labels, a convention of employing prefixed labels in subprograms may be used. Under this convention, every label in a subprogram begins with the same first two or three characters. Some computers have more sophisticated assemblers which assemble subprograms independently. In such cases the assembler creates, together with each subprogram (and the main program), a control dictionary, which contains information as to addresses that must be filled in at load time. Those are addresses in other subprograms. The control dictionary also contains a table of labels and addresses which are referred to by other subprograms. At load time the loader uses these control dictionaries to complete the interconnections between the separately assembled parts of the program.

The use of subprograms is very important in programming and offers a number of advantages, particularly in large or complex programs. Among them are: the elimination of repeating a sequence of instructions a number of times in the same program, the creation of universal subprograms which are useful in many different programs, the possibility of having different programmers work simultaneously on different parts of a program, independent debugging and checkout of parts of a program, and division of a logically complex entity into a number of simpler parts.

One possible disadvantage of the subprogram approach to programming is that programs so designed take somewhat longer to execute, particularly if a subprogram must be called hundreds or thousands of times. This disadvantage is usually offset by the advantages listed above, the overall saving in programming time, and the high speed of today's computers.

Chapter 8

A
LOOK
AT
OTHER
COMPUTERS

8.1 INTRODUCTION

FACET is just one example of a computer, and it is a rather small and simple one at that. However, if you understand the organization of the FACET machine, and if you are able to program in FACET machine and assembly language, then you have progressed a long way toward understanding digital computers in general. At this point, we shall take a second look at the concepts we have introduced and see how their implementation differs from computer to computer. This should not be very difficult to grasp, since the similarities of computers are much greater than their differences.

8.2 NUMBERS AND DECIMAL NUMBER REPRESENTATION

Numbers are abstract concepts. They don't really exist in the sense in which apples and elephants do. However, we use the number concept so frequently that we often feel that numbers are physical entities. Most of us, when shown a "5," think we are looking at a "five" as in "five apples" or "five elephants"—that is, at the **number** five. Of course, we're not. The **numeral** "5" is merely a representation of the abstract concept "five," just like the character string "APPLE" represents the fruit. The Roman numeral "V" also represents the same number. FACET represents five not by a single character, but by a string of six characters: in fixed-point representation by +00005, and in floating-point representation by +51500. In E-notation we write +.500E+01.

All the representations of five we have just discussed (with the exceptions of the character string FIVE and the Roman V) are based on **decimal arithmetic**. We often think of numbers and **decimal numbers** as synonymous, but in fact decimal numbers are merely representations of numbers.

One way to visualize the set of numbers (the **real** numbers) is by drawing a straight line and marking off equal intervals (for the whole numbers or integers):

Each point on the line, both on and between the integer marks, represents a number. Now we have a way of representing numbers without giving them explicit names: we can refer to a number by saying "that point on the line" and pointing. Every number is (potentially) represented so long as we have a way of extending the line as far as we please.

The decimal system is a method of naming these numbers. Certain character strings represent certain numbers. We can't represent all the numbers with strings of finite length (there are too many), but we can represent enough to serve our purposes. We use the character set

$$+ \quad - \quad . \quad 0 \ 1 \ 2 \ 3 \ 4 \ 5 \ 6 \ 7 \ 8 \ 9$$

Thus we write strings like 988 and -67.023 and $+100.3$ and many others. In this decimal **number representation system** we use ten **digits**, 0 through 9. A digit can mean different things, according to its **position** in the string. We can think of all the decimal numbers as being written in imaginary columns. The digit to the extreme right of the string (in the case of integers) or immediately to the left of the dot (in case fractions are also involved) is considered to be in the one's column. The column to its left is the ten's column, then the hundred's column, and so forth. To the right of the dot (if there is one) is the tenth's column, the hundredth's column, and so forth. The dot is known as the **decimal point**. Some decimal numbers with the columns illustrated explicitly are shown in Fig. 8.1.

The numbers for which the columns are named ($\cdots$0.001, 0.01, 0.1, 1, 10, 100, 1000, $\cdots$) are called the **columnar weights**. So the columnar weight of the hundred's column is one hundred, the ten's column is ten, and one's column is one, etc. The magnitude of a number is equal to the sum of the products of its digits with their respective columnar weights. For instance, 741 is

	seven times its columnar weight (a hundred)	=	700
plus	four times its columnar weight (ten)	=	40
plus	one times its columnar weight (one)	=	1
or	seven hundred forty one		741

Similarly, 39.06 is

$$\begin{aligned} & 3 \times 10 \\ + \ & 9 \times 1 \\ + \ & 0 \times \tfrac{1}{10} \\ + \ & 6 \times \tfrac{1}{100} \end{aligned}$$

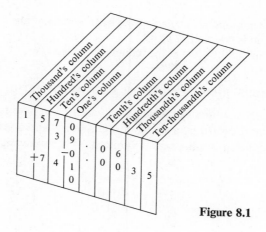

Figure 8.1

You probably already know that the columnar weights are powers of ten:

$$\cdots, \quad 10^{-2} = 0.01, \quad 10^{-1} = 0.1, \quad 10^0 = 1, \quad 10^1 = 10, \quad 10^2 = 100, \quad \cdots$$

This is essentially why we call our representation system **decimal** or **base ten**.

The FACET computer is constructed with registers which contain decimal digits, and so is suited for decimal (or base ten) representation of numbers. FACET is not the only machine constructed with decimal registers; however, most computers today employ a different number representation system—**binary** or **base two**. This is chiefly due to the fact that it is cheaper, simpler, and more reliable to construct electronic devices which have two states instead of ten states. The states of a two-state device can be made to correspond to the two binary digits, 0 and 1; ten-state devices would be best for representing the decimal digits, 0, 1, 2, $\cdots$, 8, 9. Base-two (or binary) representation of numbers is very similar to decimal representation. The two major differences are:

1. There are only two binary digits [0, 1] as opposed to ten decimal digits.
2. The columnar weights in binary representation are powers of two (not ten).

Of course, we who have been trained in and have employed decimal arithmetic for many years might find it difficult to adjust to binary. When you are building a computer, however, the efficiency requirements outweigh the "adjustment" considerations. Therefore the decision of builders of computers has been base two.

Exercises 8.2

1. Describe "five"—what do you visualize when you think of the *number* five? How about other numbers? What is a number?

2. In this (decimal) number,

$$38721.094,$$

a) what is in the ten-thousand's column? the tenth's column? the one's column?
b) in which column is the digit 7? 9? 4?
c) what is in the million's column? the millionth's column?

8.3 BINARY NUMBER REPRESENTATION AND ARITHMETIC

A "base-two number" is a number which is represented in base two. An integer is represented as a sign followed by a string of digits (zeros and ones). Sometimes, as in decimal representation, a plus sign is omitted. The following are *binary* (base two) numbers:

$$+0$$
$$-1101101$$
$$101110$$
$$1$$
$$-111$$
$$+10111011110$$

We can compute the value of a binary integer just like we "computed" the value of a decimal integer—each digit is multiplied by its columnar weight and all these products are summed. The columnar weights begin with 1 for the rightmost digit; then as we move left 2, 4, 8, 16, 32, and so on. These columnar weights correspond to 2^0, 2^1, 2^2, 2^3, 2^4, 2^5, etc.

The six numbers above can be written with their digits labeled with appropriate columnar weights as follows:

2^{11}	2^{10}	2^9	2^8	2^7	2^6	2^5	2^4	2^3	2^2	2^1	2^0
2048	1024	512	256	128	64	32	16	8	4	2	1
											+ 0
					– 1	1	0	1	1	0	1
						1	0	1	1	1	0
											1
									– 1	1	1
	+ 1	0	1	1	1	0	1	1	1	1	0

To compute the value of a binary number, multiply each of its digits by its columnar weight and add them up. Of course, we usually express the "value" of a number by its decimal representation, since that's what we're used to.

The last number in our table above, $+10111011110$, is actually

$$
\begin{aligned}
1 \times 1024 &= 1024 \\
0 \times 512 &= 0 \\
1 \times 256 &= 256 \\
1 \times 128 &= 128 \\
1 \times 64 &= 64
\end{aligned}
$$

$$
\begin{aligned}
0 \times 32 &= 0 \\
1 \times 16 &= 16 \\
1 \times 8 &= 8 \\
1 \times 4 &= 4 \\
1 \times 2 &= 2 \\
0 \times 1 &= 0 \\
\hline
&\ 1502
\end{aligned}
$$

When we represent numbers in different bases on the same page, it is often useful to parenthesize the numbers and add, in the subscript, the base of representation. We would write, for instance,

$$
\begin{aligned}
(0)_2 &= (0)_{10}, \\
(-1101101)_2 &= (-109)_{10}, \\
(101110)_2 &= (46)_{10}, \\
(-111)_2 &= (-7)_{10}.
\end{aligned}
$$

Fractions are represented in binary as you might expect. The columnar weights continue to the right of the dot; those weights are 1/2, 1/4, 1/8, 1/16, and so on. The dot is called the **binary point**. These are binary numbers:

$$
\begin{aligned}
&101.1101 \\
-&10.001 \\
&111110.0 \\
&10010.10101 \\
&0.00001
\end{aligned}
$$

Written with the columnar weights of the digits, they are:

2^5	2^4	2^3	2^2	2^1	2^0		2^{-1}	2^{-2}	2^{-3}	2^{-4}	2^{-5}
32	16	8	4	2	1		$\frac{1}{2}$	$\frac{1}{4}$	$\frac{1}{8}$	$\frac{1}{16}$	$\frac{1}{32}$
			1	0	1	.	1	1	0	1	
			$-$ 1	0	0	.	0	0	1		
1	1	1	1	1	0	.	0				
	1	0	0	1	0	.	1	0	1	0	1
					0	.	0	0	0	0	1

Note that the columnar weights are (positive and negative) powers of two. Have you figured out the decimal equivalents to these binary numbers? Try it before you look:

$$
\begin{aligned}
(101.1101)_2 &= (5\tfrac{13}{16})_{10} = (5.8125)_{10}, \\
(-10.001)_2 &= (-2\tfrac{1}{8})_{10} = (-2.125)_{10}, \\
(111110.0)_2 &= (62.0)_{10}, \\
(10010.10101)_2 &= (18\tfrac{21}{32})_{10} = (18.65625)_{10}.
\end{aligned}
$$

Not only are numbers represented in binary in most computers, but arithmetic also is done in binary. The addition and multiplication tables are very simple:

Addition				Multiplication		
	0	1			0	1
0	0	1		0	0	0
1	1	10		1	0	1

Here's how the decimal numbers 18.25, 12.5, and 13.125 are added in binary arithmetic:

$$
\begin{array}{r}
10010.010 \\
1100.100 \\
+\quad 1101.001 \\
\hline
101011.111
\end{array}
$$

which is 43.875 in base 10. Here we multiply 21.375 by 10.5:

$$
\begin{array}{r}
10101.011 \\
\times \quad\quad 1010.1 \\
\hline
10101011 \\
00000000 \\
10101011 \\
00000000 \\
10101011 \\
\hline
11100000.0111
\end{array}
$$

which is the decimal number 224.4375. Work through the above examples and see whether you obtain the same results.

If that went a bit fast for you, let's try it again. Let's say we want to add:

$$
\begin{array}{r}
10.110 \\
1.111 \\
+11.101
\end{array}
$$

First, as in decimal arithmetic, we begin with the first (rightmost) column of digits:

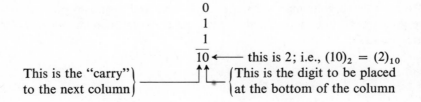

$$
\begin{array}{r}
0 \\
1 \\
1 \\
\hline
10
\end{array}
$$ ← this is 2; i.e., $(10)_2 = (2)_{10}$

This is the "carry" to the next column } ↑↑ { This is the digit to be placed at the bottom of the column

We'll write the zero at the bottom of the column, and carry the one:

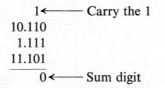

Now we add the next column:

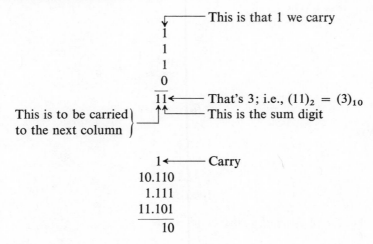

That third column (from the right) is now added:

```
                    1←——— The carry from the previous column
                    1
                    1
                    1
                   ——
                  100 ←——— That's 4; i.e., (100)₂ = (4)₁₀
10 is carried to the        ⎫  ↑↑↑
next column—(10)₂ = (2)₁₀  ⎭ └──┘ └——— The sum digit
```

We now have

```
              ⎛———— Carried
         ⑩
         10.110
          1.111
         11.101
         ——————
          0.010
```

We add the next column:

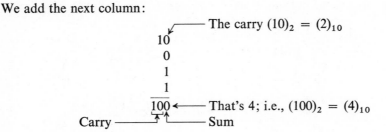

And now we have

$$
\begin{array}{c}
\textcircled{10} \\
\downarrow \\
10.110 \\
1.111 \\
11.101 \\
\hline
0.010
\end{array}
$$

and finally:

$$
\begin{array}{r}
10.110 \\
1.111 \\
11.101 \\
\hline
1000.010
\end{array}
$$

A quick check assures us of a correct addition:

Base 2		Base 10
10.110	=	2.750
1.111	=	1.875
11.101	=	3.625
1000.010	=	8.250

The process is really very much like decimal addition—you add one column at a time, get the (binary) result, take the rightmost digit as the sum for that column, and the remaining digits as the "carry" to the next column on the left. The other arithmetic operations are also quite similar to their decimal counterparts. Let's take an example in division. We'll divide 1011010 by 1001:

$$1001 \,\overline{)\,1011010}$$

We can see that 1001 goes into 1011 once, since $(1001)_2$ is $(9)_{10}$ and $(1011)_2$ is $(11)_{10}$, so we write

$$
\begin{array}{r}
1 \\
1001 \,\overline{)\,1011010} \\
1001\downarrow \\
\hline
100
\end{array}
$$

Now 1001 goes into 100 zero times, so we continue:

$$
\begin{array}{r}
10 \\
1001\ \overline{)\ 1011010} \\
1001\ \downarrow \\
\hline
1001
\end{array}
$$

The next digit in the quotient is obviously a one:

$$
\begin{array}{r}
101 \\
1001\ \overline{)\ 1011010} \\
1001 \\
\hline
1001 \\
1001 \\
\hline
00
\end{array}
$$

The final quotient is 1010:

$$
\begin{array}{r}
1010 \\
1001\ \overline{)\ 1011010} \\
1001 \\
\hline
1001 \\
1001 \\
\hline
00 \\
00 \\
\hline
\end{array}
$$

And we check:

$$(1001)_2 = (9)_{10}$$
$$(1011010)_2 = (90)_{10} \quad \text{and} \quad (90)_{10} \div (9)_{10} = (10)_{10}$$
$$(1010)_2 = (10)_{10}$$

At this point you should have some understanding of binary number representation and arithmetic. Can you now see that any number can be represented in binary? It is easy to see that any *integer* can be so represented. Fractions in binary, as in decimal, can be expressed to any given **precision** (number of digits). Let's take $\frac{1}{3}$—how is it represented? We already know that in decimal representation we have $0.33333 \cdots$ Any partial representation, such as 0.33, is the best approximation of $\frac{1}{3}$ by *a certain number of significant digits*. It's the same in binary. A third is represented by

$$0 . 0\ 1\ 0\ 1\ 0\ 1\ 0\ 1\ 0\ 1 \cdots$$

Alternatively, this can be written $.\overline{01}$ where the digits under the horizontal bar are to be repeated indefinitely. We may represent one third in binary to whatever precision we wish. The same holds for any other fraction. One tenth, for instance, is

$$0.000110011001100110011 \cdots \quad \text{or} \quad 0.0\overline{0011}$$

Exercises 8.3

1. Perform the indicated arithmetic operations in binary arithmetic:

   a) 1.101 + 101.110
   c) 111101100 × 1000111
   e)   11.11001
        10.10111
      +11.01111

   b) 1011101 − 1001
   d) 1011010 ÷ 1011

2. Convert the following decimal numbers to binary representation:

   a) 45   b) −437   c) 23.75
   d) 100   e) 2.625   f) 256
   g) −1000   h) 2.1875   i) $\frac{2}{3}$
   j) 0.2

3. Convert the following binary numbers to decimal representation:

   a) 101010101   b) 0.010101   c) −11111.1
   d) 1000000001   e) 1001111001   f) 10111011.10001
   g) 11011.11   h) −1010111.011   i) 1000010001.0110
   j) 1011

4. Any fraction that can be expressed exactly in binary representation can also be expressed exactly in decimal, e.g., $(0.11)_2 = (0.75)_{10}$; the reverse is not true—there are fractions which can be expressed exactly in decimal representation but not in binary. Prove this statement. If you cannot give a proof, try to *explain* why it is true.

8.4 OTHER NUMBER REPRESENTATION SYSTEMS

The binary and decimal number representation systems are just two of many possible systems called **fixed-radix**, **positional number-representation** systems. In fact, any positive integer greater than one can serve as the **radix** or **base** of such a system. All that is required is a set of symbols known as digits. These digits represent the integers from zero through one less than the radix. In base 2 (binary) representation we need two digits, 0 and 1. In base 10 (decimal), we need 10 digits,

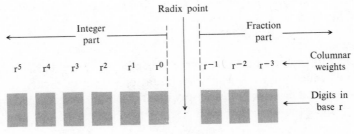

Figure 8.2

0, 1, 2, 3, 4, 5, 6, 7, 8, 9. Similarly:

If we were using a fixed radix positional system with radix	then we would require digits to represent these integers
2	0, 1
3	0, 1, 2
4	0, 1, 2, 3
5	0, 1, 2, 3, 4
6	0, 1, 2, 3, 4, 5
7	0, 1, 2, 3, 4, 5, 6
8	0, 1, 2, 3, 4, 5, 6, 7
9	0, 1, 2, 3, 4, 5, 6, 7, 8
10	0, 1, 2, 3, 4, 5, 6, 7, 8, 9
11	0, 1, 2, 3, 4, 5, 6, 7, 8, 9, 10
12	0, 1, 2, $\cdots$, 11
$\vdots$	$\vdots$
16	0, 1, 2, $\cdots$, 15
$\vdots$	$\vdots$
360	0, 1, 2, 3, $\cdots$, 359
$\vdots$	$\vdots$

Note that each digit in a particular number representation system is a single symbol, not a string. So in base 12, we need 12 distinguishable digit symbols. If we use the 10 symbols we already have from the decimal system (0, 1, 2, $\cdots$, 8, 9), then we only need two more, one for the integer 10 and one for 11. We could use A and B or t and e, or any other two symbols as digits, for that matter.

We represent an integer in some radix system by writing a string of digits in that system, as we do in binary or decimal. These digits are viewed as falling into imaginary columns, again as in binary or decimal representation. Other numbers, with fraction parts, can be represented by placing a dot (radix point) after the integer portion of the string, and writing some more digits. The columnar weights for our arbitrary radix r are as shown in Fig. 8.2. Let's look at some examples. Recall that when a number is placed in parentheses, the subscript denotes the radix of representation:

$$(100.11)_2 \quad \text{base 2}$$
$$(93.74)_{10} \quad \text{base 10}$$
$$(45.01)_7 \quad \text{base 7}$$

This last example, $(45.01)_7$, represents

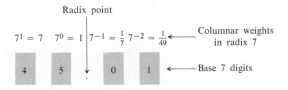

which is

$$
\begin{aligned}
4 \times 7 &= 28 \\
5 \times 1 &= 5 \\
0 \times \tfrac{1}{7} &= 0 \\
1 \times \tfrac{1}{49} &= \tfrac{1}{49} \\
&= (33\tfrac{1}{49})_{10} = (33.020408\cdots)_{10}
\end{aligned}
$$

Let's try $(20321.32)_4$, which is

$4^4 = 256$	$4^3 = 64$	$4^2 = 16$	$4^1 = 4$	$4^0 = 1$		$4^{-1} = \frac{1}{4}$	$4^{-2} = \frac{1}{16}$
2	0	3	2	1	.	3	2

or

$$
\begin{aligned}
2 \times 256 &= 512 \\
0 \times 64 &= 0 \\
3 \times 16 &= 48 \\
2 \times 4 &= 8 \\
1 \times 1 &= 1 \\
3 \times \tfrac{1}{4} &= \tfrac{12}{16} \\
2 \times \tfrac{1}{16} &= \tfrac{2}{16} \\
&= (569\tfrac{7}{8})_{10} = (569.875)_{10}
\end{aligned}
$$

A radix greater than ten is somewhat peculiar in that there are strange symbols representing integers which we don't expect to have single-digit representation. Let's look at base thirteen. It requires 13 digits to represent integers zero through twelve. Let's use $0, 1, 2, \ldots, 9, A, B, C$, where

$$
\begin{aligned}
A &\quad \text{represents} \quad 10, \\
B &\quad \text{represents} \quad 11, \\
C &\quad \text{represents} \quad 12.
\end{aligned}
$$

Our imaginary columns would look like this in base 13:

13^2	13^1	13^0		13^{-1}	13^{-2}
$\cdots$			.		$\cdots$

The number $(A8B.2C)_{13}$ represents

$$
\begin{array}{llll}
A \times 13^2 & \text{or} & 10 \times 169 = & 1690 \\
8 \times 13^1 & & 8 \times 13 = & 104 \\
B \times 13^0 & & 11 \times 1 = & 11 \\
2 \times 13^{-1} & & 2 \times \tfrac{1}{13} = & \tfrac{26}{169} \\
C \times 13^{-2} & & 12 \times \tfrac{1}{169} = & \tfrac{12}{169} \\
& & = (1805\tfrac{38}{169})_{10} & = (1805.22485\ldots)_{10}
\end{array}
$$

Arithmetic in a radix other than decimal or binary is quite simple in theory, although one tends to get confused in practice. Each radix has its own addition and multiplication table. For instance, radix 7:

+	0	1	2	3	4	5	6
0	0	1	2	3	4	5	6
1	1	2	3	4	5	6	10
2	2	3	4	5	6	10	11
3	3	4	5	6	10	11	12
4	4	5	6	10	11	12	13
5	5	6	10	11	12	13	14
6	6	10	11	12	13	14	15

Each time an addition or multiplication is performed, we "perform it" in base 10 and convert back to the base in which we're working (unless we memorize these tables). So if we perform

$$(3A)_{13} \times (58)_{13}$$

we write

$$\begin{array}{r} 58 \\ \times\, 3A \\ \hline 2 \end{array}$$

and carry the 6, because $(A)_{13} \times (8)_{13} = (10)_{10} \times (8)_{10} = (80)_{10} = (62)_{13}$. Similarly,

$$(A)_{13} \times (5)_{13} = (10)_{10} \times (5)_{10} = (50)_{10} = (3B)_{13}.$$

When we add the carry, we get

$$(6)_{13} + (3B)_{13} = (44)_{13}.$$

So we now have

$$\begin{array}{r} 58 \\ \times\, 3A \\ \hline 442 \end{array}$$

We continue along the same lines, and get

$$\begin{array}{r} 58 \\ \times\ 3A \\ \hline 442 \\ 13B \\ \hline 1822 \end{array}$$

which is the answer in base 13.

Exercises 8.4

1. Express the following numbers in base ten (*Note:* A, B, C, D, E, F represent digits 10, 11, 12, 13, 14, 15, respectively):

    a) $(10111.1)_2$ b) $(10111.1)_3$ c) $(10111.1)_5$

d) $(10111.1)_9$
e) $(10111.1)_{13}$
f) $(135.135)_6$
g) $(135.135)_{11}$
h) $(AB)_{12}$
i) $(AB)_{13}$
j) $(AB)_{16}$
k) $(97A.AB)_{12}$
l) $(A.BB)_{15}$
m) $(10000.01)_{17}$
n) $(3.3)_{14}$
o) $(757)_8$
p) $(ABCD)_{16}$
q) $(100A1.0A)_{12}$
r) $(101111111111111)_2$
s) $(0.1111111111)_2$
t) $(0.111111111)_4$

2. Perform these operations in the arithmetic of the indicated radix:

a) $(2011.2)_3 + (1012.2)_3$
b) $(59A)_{12} \div (477)_{12}$
c) $(423.05)_6 \times (22)_6$
d) $(7776)_8 - (17777)_8$
e) $(4096)_{11} - (3A62)_{11}$
f) $(103.22)_4 \div (2.21)_4$

8.5 OCTAL AND HEXADECIMAL NUMBER REPRESENTATION

Of all the number representation systems, there are four in particular which are of interest to us for use with computers. These are bases 2, 8, 10, and 16: base 2 because most computers actually operate in binary; base 10 because that's the system we (humans) happen to use; bases 8 and 16 because they are used by programmers for abbreviating binary numbers. (8 and 16 are both powers of 2: $8 = 2^3$, $16 = 2^4$). When a base is some integer power of another, conversion between the bases becomes very simple. This is because each digit in the larger base corresponds exactly to some number of digits in the smaller. If we have two bases, b_1 and b_2, and if

$$b_2 = b_1{}^n,$$

then each n digits in a b_1-number correspond exactly to one digit in b_2. Each three digits of a binary number correspond to one **octal** (base 8) digit. Similarly, each four binary digits correspond to one **hexadecimal** (base 16) digit. To illustrate, this is 219 in binary representation:

$$1\ 1\ 0\ 1\ 1\ 0\ 1\ 1$$

To convert to octal (base 8) representation, we group the digits into groups of three, beginning at the right. Note that we must add a leading zero:

$$011\quad 011\quad 011$$

Now we take each group of three digits and convert it to a single octal digit; $(011)_2 = (3)_{10} = (3)_8$, so we get

$$\underbrace{011}_{3}\ \underbrace{011}_{3}\ \underbrace{011}_{3}$$

or $(333)_8$. So $(11011011)_2 = (333)_8$. It's that simple. Let's try another:

$$\underbrace{110}_{6}\ \underbrace{111}_{7}\ \underbrace{011}_{3}\ \underbrace{011}_{3}\ \underbrace{101}_{5}$$

Thus $(110111011011101)_2 = (67335)_8$. Check for yourself by converting both to decimal. All we have to remember is that:

$$
\text{All three-digit combinations of binary digits}
\left\{
\begin{array}{ccc}
\text{Binary} & & \text{Octal} \\
000 & = & 0 \\
001 & = & 1 \\
010 & = & 2 \\
011 & = & 3 \\
100 & = & 4 \\
101 & = & 5 \\
110 & = & 6 \\
111 & = & 7
\end{array}
\right\}
\begin{array}{l}
\text{The eight octal} \\
\text{digits}
\end{array}
$$

When a radix point is involved, the process is the same. The grouping begins at the radix point and moves to the left *and* right. Take $(101001010.100111)_2$:

$$
\underbrace{101}_{5}\ \underbrace{001}_{1}\ \underbrace{010}_{2}\ .\ \underbrace{100}_{4}\ \underbrace{111}_{7}
$$

We see that $(101001010.100111)_2 = (512.47)_8$. The reverse conversion is just as simple. Each octal digit is converted to three binary digits. Here we convert $(4062.51)_8$ to binary:

$$
\begin{array}{cccccc}
4 & 0 & 6 & 2 & . & 5 & 1 \\
\downarrow & \downarrow & \downarrow & \downarrow & & \downarrow & \downarrow \\
100 & 000 & 110 & 010 & . & 101 & 001
\end{array}
$$

and we see that $(4062.51)_8 = (100000110010.101001)_2$.

Similar conversion can be used between binary and hexadecimal representations. Binary digits must now be grouped in fours rather than threes. The correspondence is:

Binary	Hexadecimal	Binary	Hexadecimal
0000	0	1000	8
0001	1	1001	9
0010	2	1010	A
0011	3	1011	B
0100	4	1100	C
0101	5	1101	D
0110	6	1110	E
0111	7	1111	F

Remember that A, B, ..., F are digits representing 10, 11, ..., 15, respectively in hexadecimal. Now we convert $(1100001101001001.00101111)_2$ to hexadecimal:

$$
\underbrace{1100}_{C}\ \underbrace{0011}_{3}\ \underbrace{0100}_{4}\ \underbrace{1001}_{9}\ .\ \underbrace{0010}_{2}\ \underbrace{1111}_{F}
$$

which is $(C349.2F)_{16}$. In some cases leading and trailing zeros must be added for the conversion. In converting $(101.1)_2$ to hexadecimal, we write

Add leading zero — 0101 . 1000 — Add these trailing zeros to complete group of four
5 . 8 binary digits

So $(101.1)_2 = (5.8)_{16}$.

Since many computers have rather large binary registers, we express their contents in octal or hexadecimal to reduce the lengths of the digit strings we have to examine.

Exercises 8.5

1. Convert the following binary numbers to octal representation:

   a) 10111   b) 10001   c) 11.001110
   d) 101.11111111111   e) 1.1   f) 100000.100001
   g) 1110111   h) 10.01

2. Convert the binary numbers in exercise 1 to hexadecimal representation.

3. Convert the following octal numbers to their binary representation:

   a) 7777   b) 1036.75   c) 111.111
   d) 223.402   e) 1234.5670   f) 3037.7073
   g) 7654321   h) 66677.771

4. Convert the following hexadecimal numbers to their binary representation:

   a) AB   b) 1013.7   c) 5AC.D3
   d) C00.0F   e) ABCDEF.111   f) 1.3
   g) E.E   h) 3C5.00D

5. Can you think of any way to convert octal numbers to hexadecimal representation? Try these:

   a) $(372.01)_8$ b) $(77.1)_8$ c) $(53)_8$
   d) $(460.02)_8$ e) $(11111.11)_8$ f) $(100001.00007)_8$

   How about hexadecimal to octal?

6. The method of radix conversion works for other bases as well. Can you convert these base 3 numbers to base 9?

   a) 102.2   b) 200
   c) 1111.1   d) 1112200.0211201

8.6 MEMORY

In most computers, as in FACET, the memory consists of a fixed number of memory registers, and each register of a fixed number of digit positions. The actual numbers involved vary from computer to computer. In most computers, the digit positions are binary. That means each position contains either a zero or a one. Such a binary digit is often called a **bit** (short for BInary digiT). The sign position also contains either a zero or a one, where zero means plus (+) and one means minus (−). We might depict a memory in a binary computer as shown in Fig. 8.3.

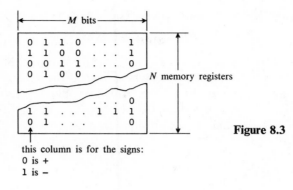

Figure 8.3

Typically, the memory may have from about 4000 locations (registers) in small computers to over a million in the very large ones.

As in FACET, each memory register has an address. These addresses are binary (rather than decimal) numbers. The number of bits needed for an address varies, depending on the size of the memory. If there are 4096 locations in the memory, for instance, then we need exactly 12 bits in an address, since the binary number $(111111111111)_2$ [12 ones] is $(4095)_{10}$, and we can have the following addressing scheme:

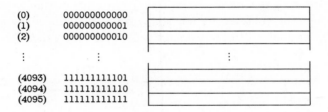

A memory word can have any number of bits. There are computers with many different "lengths" of memory registers, but usually the number of bits per register is a multiple of 6 or 8. The smallest word size of memory registers is 12 bits, and the largest about 60. Other computers have registers of 16 bits, 18 bits, 24 bits, 32 bits, 36 bits, as well as others.

As it is in FACET, a **word**, is a configuration of digits (binary, usually) which can fit exactly into one memory register. It is usually rather inconvenient to refer to or depict a word as a string of 12 or 32 or even 60 bits, since a long sequence of 0's and 1's is rather incomprehensible. The same goes for an address. Suppose we had a computer with a 4096-word memory (12-bit address) and 36-bit words. Then we might say

$$C(101111011011) = 010110110111011110100111011011000101$$

meaning "the contents of location such-and-such is word so-and-so." To avoid these unintelligible binary strings, they are often written in octal or hexadecimal representations. The previous statement, in octal, would be

$$C(5733) = 266736473305$$

This is an improvement. Of course, the machine works in binary, but frequently the assembler and the loader accept hexadecimal or octal strings written by the programmer and translate them to the equivalent binary.

Similarly, binary addresses and contents of binary registers can be (and are) expressed in hexadecimal. In the previous example, we could say (in hexadecimal):

$$C(BDB) = 5B77A76C5$$

Try the conversion yourself.

8.7 INTEGERS

A computer word can represent many different things. In FACET, a computer word can represent an integer, a floating-point number, a string of characters, or an instruction. This is also the case in other computers. Let us now see how integers are represented in binary computers.

Since memory registers consist of strings of bits (binary digits), one of these bits must serve to identify an integer as either positive or negative. This bit, usually the leftmost bit in the word, is called the **sign bit**. A zero in the sign bit means plus (+) and a one means minus (–). Positive integers are represented by a zero in the sign bit, followed by the binary representation of the integer in the remaining bit-positions. If our computer had 12-bit words, then this register

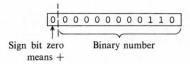

Sign bit zero   Binary number
means +

"contains" integer 6, since $(110)_2 = (6)_{10}$. Similarly, in a 24-bit computer, this register

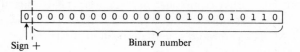

Sign +   Binary number

"contains" the integer 278, since $(100010110)_2 = (278)_{10}$.

Negative integers are represented differently in different computers. Two important methods of representation are employed: (a) signed magnitude, and (b) one's complement. **Signed-magnitude** integer representation is simplest, and is, in fact, the representation employed in FACET. The sign bit (or sign position in FACET) determines whether the integer is positive or negative, and the rest of the word represents the magnitude of the integer in binary.

Therefore

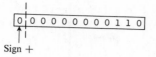

Sign +

represents $(+110)_2 = (+6)_{10}$ and

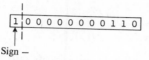

Sign −

represents $(-110)_2 = (-6)_{10}$.

One's-complement representation is more complicated. To find the representation of a negative integer in one's complement, we must take the representation of the corresponding positive integer and change all zeros to ones and ones to zeros. This is known as **complementing** a word. For instance, the representation of -6 in a 12-bit word would be 111111111001, which is computed by complementing the digits of $+6$:

$$\begin{array}{c} 0\ 0\ 0\ 0\ 0\ 0\ 0\ 0\ 0\ 1\ 1\ 0 \qquad (+6) \\ \downarrow\ \downarrow\ \downarrow\ \downarrow\ \downarrow\ \downarrow\ \downarrow\ \downarrow\ \downarrow\ \downarrow\ \downarrow\ \downarrow \\ 1\ 1\ 1\ 1\ 1\ 1\ 1\ 1\ 1\ 0\ 0\ 1 \qquad (-6) \end{array}$$

Note that the sign bit still tells us whether the word represents a positive or negative integer (0 for +, 1 for −). If an 18-bit register contains 111111111111001010, and one's-complement integer representation is used, we can tell which integer this word represents by complementing the word. We do this because the leftmost digit is 1, indicating a negative integer:

$$\begin{array}{c} 1\ 1\ 1\ 1\ 1\ 1\ 1\ 1\ 1\ 1\ 1\ 0\ 0\ 1\ 0\ 1\ 0 \\ \downarrow\ \downarrow\ \downarrow\ \downarrow\ \downarrow\ \downarrow\ \downarrow\ \downarrow\ \downarrow\ \downarrow\ \downarrow\ \downarrow\ \downarrow\ \downarrow\ \downarrow\ \downarrow\ \downarrow\ \downarrow \\ 0\ 0\ 0\ 0\ 0\ 0\ 0\ 0\ 0\ 0\ 0\ 1\ 1\ 0\ 1\ 0\ 1 \end{array}$$

Since $(110101)_2$ is $(53)_{10}$, the original word represents -53.

Why is one's-complement notation used? It simplifies the electronic circuitry needed to implement the addition and subtraction operations in the machine. Without going into any detail on this point, we can see this advantage working (in decimal instead of binary) if we recall some facts concerning arithmetic in FACET's index register. It was noted that DECX 002, for example, was equivalent to INCX 998. Here 998 is 1 greater than the nine's complement of 002, which is 997 (where the nine's complement is found by subtracting each digit from 9). Thus, instead of subtracting 002 from another positive number, you could *add* 998. Similarly, in binary arithmetic, subtraction circuitry could be entirely eliminated by using the addition circuits with appropriate modifications. For example, to add -4 and $+2$, the machine performs the following operations†:

$$
\begin{array}{ll}
\ldots 1\ 1\ 1\ 1\ 1\ 1\ 1\ 1\ 1\ 0\ 1\ 1 & (-4)\ \text{in one's complement} \\
+\ldots 0\ 0\ 0\ 0\ 0\ 0\ 0\ 0\ 0\ 0\ 1\ 0 & (+2)\ \text{in one's complement} \\
\hline
\ldots 1\ 1\ 1\ 1\ 1\ 1\ 1\ 1\ 1\ 1\ 0\ 1 & (-2)\ \text{in one's complement} \\
& \phantom{(-2)\ \text{in one's}}\text{is the result}
\end{array}
$$

Complementing can also be done (manually) in octal or hexadecimal. The operation corresponding to one's complementation in octal is seven's complementation. The octal representation of the 12-bit register containing $(+6)_{10}$ or $(000000000110)_2$ is

$$0\ 0\ 0\ 6$$

The seven's complement of an octal digit is the result of subtracting that digit from 7:

Digit	Seven's complement
0	7
1	6
2	5
3	4
4	3
5	2
6	1
7	0

Similarly, in hexadecimal we subtract from F (15) and get:

Digit	Fifteen's Complement	Digit	Fifteen's Complement
0	F	8	7
1	E	9	6
2	D	A	5
3	C	B	4
4	B	C	3
5	A	D	2
6	9	E	1
7	8	F	0

† Sometimes, when two numbers in one's complement representation are added, a carry of 1 is produced at the left. This does not always represent overflow. In certain situations, this carry must be added to the rightmost digit of the intermediate result to produce the correct final result. This process is known as an "end around carry."

The 24-bit word 000000000000100110111001 can be thought of as the octal word 00004671 or as the hexadecimal word 0009B9. We can complement the octal and hexadecimal words directly:

$$
\left.\begin{array}{ll}
\text{00004671} & \text{word} \\
\text{77773106} & \text{complement}
\end{array}\right\} \text{octal}
$$

$$
\left.\begin{array}{ll}
\text{0009B9} & \text{word} \\
\text{FFF646} & \text{complement}
\end{array}\right\} \text{hexadecimal}
$$

Octal and hexadecimal representations are important in machine and assembly language programming in most machines, since they are used by the programmer in place of binary. Memory dumps are generally printed in either octal or hexadecimal. If our 12-bit machine printed an octal dump, what integers would the following represent? (Cover the column on the right and try these for yourself.) Of course, we might get a different answer, depending on whether our machine used signed-magnitude or one's-complement representation. Assume that one's-complement representation is used:

If a memory location contained	Then an octal dump would print	The integer represented is
000000000000	0000	0
111111111111	7777	−0
000111111111	0777	511
111111111001	7771	−6
000000111000	0070	56
000000010000	0020	16
111110100111	7647	−88
100101011000	4530	−1703
001000001000	1010	520

Similar uses are made of hexadecimal representation.

Exercises 8.7

1. You receive an octal dump in an 18-bit signed-magnitude computer. What integers do these words represent? Note that you can tell the sign by the leftmost octal digit.

   a) 000001   b) 400001   c) 405311
   d) 777776   e) 000312   f) 000067
   g) 400022   h) 400000

2. You receive a hexadecimal dump in a 32-bit one's-complement computer. What integers do these words represent? Note that you can tell the sign by the leftmost hexadecimal digit.

   a) FFFFFFF3   b) 0000000A   c) FFFFFF29
   d) FFFF0000   e) 00000000   f) FFFFFFFF
   g) 00003BCD   h) FFFFF117

3. Represent the following (decimal) integers as 36-bit words, in one's-complement representation. Use octal representation.

a) 49

b) −73

c) 12

d) 0

e) −2

f) 512

g) −2048

h) 8193

8.8 FLOATING-POINT NUMBERS

Floating-point numbers are represented in most computers by partitioning words into sign bit, exponent part (often called the characteristic), and mantissa. Typically, between one-fifth and one-third of the word is devoted to the characteristic and the rest to the mantissa and sign bit:

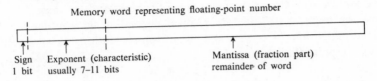

Memory word representing floating-point number

Sign   Exponent (characteristic)   Mantissa (fraction part)
1 bit   usually 7–11 bits   remainder of word

It is generally impractical to employ floating-point representation in computers with less than 24 bits per word, since the **precision** (number of significant digits in the mantissa) is not sufficient for most applications. This drawback is often overcome in short-word computers by storing a single floating-point number in two sequential memory registers. This procedure is known as **double precision**.

The mantissa is a binary fraction between zero and one. In normalized form, the first mantissa digit is nonzero, which means it is 1; so we have a fraction part (mantissa) of the form

$$0.1 \ldots,$$

meaning that it is a fraction between $\frac{1}{2}$ and 1 (why?). The characteristic has some **bias**, namely some value at which the mantissa is unaltered in its final interpretation. In FACET this value is 50 (decimal). Each computer employs its own bias and thereby determines the range of the floating-point numbers representable in that particular machine. Let's say a computer has an exponent bias of 1000000 in its 32-bit word. Then

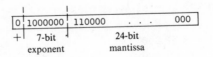

represents 0.11×2^0 or $(0.11)_2$ or $(0.75)_{10}$. Let's assume that we have just received a dump, and that some location is said to contain the following word (expressed in hexadecimal):

$$46E58000$$

What floating-point number does it represent? First, let's see what the binary register contains:

The mantissa is 0.11100101100. The exponent is 1000110, six larger than the bias 1000000. This means that the binary point must be moved six positions to the right (or, alternately, that the mantissa must be multiplied by 2^6):

$$(111001.01100\ldots)_2 = (57\tfrac{3}{8})_{10} = (57.375)_{10}.$$

Let's look at another example. Let's say we have a computer with a 60-bit word with an 11-bit characteristic and a bias of 01110000000. What floating-point number does this (octal) word represent?

$$16026314631463146314$$

16026314631463146314

The corresponding 60-bit word is

The exponent is two greater than the bias. The fraction (mantissa) is 0.1100110011001100..., and when the binary point is adjusted two positions to the right, we get

$$(11.00110011001100\ldots)_2 = (3.2)_{10} \qquad \text{(approximately)}.$$

What about negative floating-point numbers? Their representation depends on whether the particular computer employs signed magnitude, one's complement, or some other scheme. If the 60-bit computer in the last example employed one's complement, then

$$61751463146314631463$$

61751463146314631463

represents what floating-point number? The leading 6 is 110 in binary, so the first digit (1) is a minus sign. We complement the *entire* word, getting

16026314631463146314

which represents $(3.2)_{10}$; thus the original word represents -3.2. If the machine employed signed magnitude, then -3.2 would require only a change in the sign-bit from $+3.2$:

In octal this becomes 56026314631463146314; only the leading digit is changed.

Here's one last example. We have a 36-bit computer with an 11-bit exponent, one's complement, octal printout, and an exponent bias of 01000000000. What floating-point number does this octal number represent?

$$700227777777$$

The first digit, 7, is 111 in binary. The leading 1 tells us it's negative, so we complement the word:

$$077550000000$$

The corresponding machine word is:

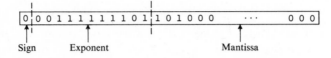

The exponent is 00111111101. When we subtract this from the bias 01000000000, we get

$$
\begin{array}{r}
01000000000 \\
-00111111101 \\
\hline
(00000000011)_2 = (3)_{10}
\end{array}
$$

The binary point of the mantissa must be moved three to the *left*:

$$(0.00010100\ldots)_2 = \tfrac{1}{16} + \tfrac{1}{64} = (\tfrac{5}{64})_{10} = (0.07812\ldots)_{10}.$$

Since the sign is negative, the number represented is $-0.07812\ldots$

Zero is represented as 00...000 in most machines.

There are various departures from the schemes presented in this and the previous section. Often, two's complement is used instead of one's complement, which means that to find the representation of a negative number, you complement the positive representation, and then add a 1 to the rightmost position, permitting the (possible) carry to propagate down the word.

Another notable departure from the traditional scheme is in the IBM 360 computers, which have a 32-bit word size. In the floating-point representation, a change of one in the (7-bit) exponent moves the binary point *four* positions to the left or right in the mantissa. Essentially, the mantissa is multiplied by some power of 2^4 or 16. A normalized mantissa therefore has a nonzero bit at least in one of the leftmost *four* positions.

The idea behind this section is to give you some familiarity with a variety of often-used representations. When you work with a specific machine, you must find out the details for that machine.

Exercises 8.8

1. Which (floating-point) numbers are represented by these hexadecimal numbers? Assume a 32-bit computer with a 7-bit exponent, one's-complement representation, and exponent bias of 0101000.

   a) 2C9C0000   b) 2C9D0000

   c) 27C00000   d) C77FFFFF

2. How would these numbers be represented in floating point? Assume a 36-bit machine with an 11-bit exponent (bias 10000000000), signed-magnitude representation.

a) -3.5 b) 4096 c) 0.0625

d) 500.01 e) -0 f) 12.3

8.9 CHARACTERS

As in FACET, memory locations in other computers cannot contain actual characters, since they merely contain strings of zeros and ones. However, characters can be encoded as combinations of binary digits; recall that in FACET characters are encoded as combinations of decimal digits. Either six or eight bits are usually used to encode a single character. Every computer has some such encoding scheme; for instance:

Character	Internal representation
0	000000
1	000001
2	000010
⋮	⋮
A	100000
B	100001
⋮	⋮
Z	111001
⋮	⋮
$	111100
⋮	⋮

Those machines in which a character is encoded as a string of six bits usually have machine words whose length is some multiple of six (such as 12, 18, 24, 36, 60). Similarly, machines employing 8-bit codes have memory registers whose length is a multiple of eight (notably IBM 360 with 32-bits per word). This permits an exact number of characters to be stored in a memory location; each character is said to be stored in a **field** (sometimes **byte**) in the word. A 48-bit computer (employing 8-bit characters) can therefore contain the representation of six characters.

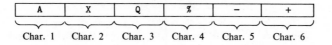

| A | X | Q | % | - | + |

Char. 1   Char. 2   Char. 3   Char. 4   Char. 5   Char. 6

The first field (first eight bits of the word) doesn't actually contain an A, but rather an 8-bit encoding of the character A.

A character string is stored in as many words as is necessary in the particular computer in question. A string of 70 characters in the above machine can be stored in 12 words (6 bytes × 12 words = 72 characters, two to spare).

Often internal representation of characters is given in terms of octal or hexadecimal digits. Two octal digits represent one 6-bit character and two hexadecimal digits represent an 8-bit character. Suppose, for a moment, that our machine employed the following 6-bit character representation

Character	Octal code	Character	Octal code	Character	Octal code
A	01	Q	21	6	41
B	02	R	22	7	42
C	03	S	23	8	43
D	04	T	24	9	44
E	05	U	25	+	45
F	06	V	26	−	46
G	07	W	27	*	47
H	10	X	30	/	50
I	11	Y	31	(	51
J	12	Z	32	)	52
K	13	0	33	$	53
L	14	1	34	=	54
M	15	2	35	blank	55
N	16	3	36	,	56
Ø	17	4	37	.	57
P	20	5	40		

Given this representation, determine the characters stored in this memory register:

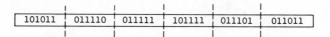

First, we translate to octal, keeping pairs of octal digits (individual characters) separated:

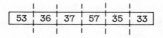

Then look up the correspondence:

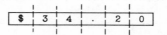

Note that, as in the FACET representation, this word has nothing whatsoever to do with the floating-point number 34.2 or the fixed-point integers 3420 or 34. It is merely a representation of a string of six characters. If the word were interpreted as either a fixed-point or a floating-point number, it would represent something entirely different.

Character strings are fairly easy to interpret in octal (or hexadecimal) memory dumps, given the correspondence table. For instance, if an octal dump indicated

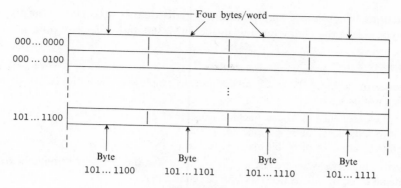

Figure 8.4

that six consecutive memory locations contained these six words

```
161722150114
552405221511
160124111716
551706550530
050325241117
165755555555
```

then those locations would contain the 36-character string

NØRMAL␣TERMINATIØN␣ØF␣EXECUTIØN. ␣␣␣␣

Check to see whether this is correct. Note that the actual message is padded on the right with blanks to fill in the last word.

In a 60-bit word-length computer with the same character codes this string can be stored in four machine words (10 characters per word):

NØRMAL␣TER	16172215011455240522
MINATIØN␣Ø	15111601241117165517
F␣EXECUTIØ	06553005300503241117
N. ␣␣␣␣␣␣␣␣	16575555555555555555

As in FACET, one usually doesn't have to know the internal representation codes, except possibly for interpreting dumps. In some machines, dumps are given both numerically and as character strings, so one never needs to know the actual codes. Despite this fact, knowledge of the internal character code can sometimes be used to advantage in writing fast-executing programs.

Some computers, notably the IBM 360, are character-oriented machines. In such machines, addresses correspond to characters rather than full words. In such a 32-bit word machine (4 bytes/word), for instance, the address of the first word is 00...000, the address of the second word is 00...100 [i.e., $(4)_{10}$], etc. Words have addresses in multiples of 4, and the intervening addresses refer to characters within words. This may be illustrated as shown in Fig. 8.4. Naturally, such machines have instructions which allow manipulation of individual bytes. Have you discovered that **byte** means the character unit in the IBM 360 and other computers?

Exercises 8.9

1. Encode the string ØUTPUT ØF ASSEMBLER by employing the 6-bit (2-octal-digit) code given in this section:
   a) into a sequence of 12-bit machine words;
   b) into a sequence of 36-bit machine words;
   c) into a sequence of 60-bit machine words:

2. What character strings are encoded in the following bit-strings, assuming the encoding scheme given in this section (six bits per character)?
   a) 100001100101010011001001011000101100011100011101
   b) 101011100000011110101111100010100100101000001100000010101111

8.10 REGISTERS AND INSTRUCTIONS

All computers have an operation cycle similar to that of FACET: There is a program counter† which contains the address of the instruction to be executed next—the cycle begins when that instruction is brought into an instruction register and executed; the program counter is then modified appropriately, and the cycle begins again. However, each computer has its unique configuration of special registers and its unique set of instructions. Small machines usually have only one or two accumulators, whereas larger ones may have eight or sixteen such registers. Often these registers are not called accumulators, instead, such names as **A-** (for arithmetic) **register** or **general register** are used.

Frequently computers have more than one index register; as many as 16 is not considered as too great a number. Recall that in FACET we were forced to continually bring numbers in and out of the accumulator and the index register. Much of this seemingly wasteful motion can be eliminated by use of multiple registers. To illustrate this point, we cite two examples. Consider the implementation of this flowchart box:

$$E \leftarrow (A+B) \times (C+D)$$

If we assume floating-point operations, we might implement this in FACET assembly language as follows:

```
LDAC    A
FADD    B
STAC    TEMP
LDAC    C
```

---

† The program counter is alternatively called the location counter, the instruction counter, the instruction address register, and other similar names in various computers.

```
FADD    D
FMUL    TEMP
STAC    E
```

If we had two accumulators, AC1 and AC2, we might have written something like this instead:

```
LDAC1   A       (AC1 ← A)
FADD1   B       (AC1 ← AC1 + B)
LDAC2   C       (AC2 ← C)
FADD2   D       (AC2 ← AC2 + D)
FMUL2   AC1     (AC2 ← AC2 × AC1)
STAC2   E       (E   ← AC2)
```

One instruction and two memory accesses (storing in location TEMP and retrieving from TEMP) are eliminated.

Multiple index registers provide an even clearer view of the kinds of program efficiency multiple registers introduce. Every program we have discussed that requires the use of the index register for more than one purpose, requires continual storing and reloading of pointers and loop indexes from and into the index register.

Recall the sorting program we discussed in Chapter 4. We had an array of 30 numbers called XYZ, and we wanted them sorted into ascending order. Two pointers, which we called P and Q, were needed. We had to use the single FACET index register for both P and Q. Let's assume we had had two index registers, X1 and X2, as well as two accumulators, AC1 and AC2. The following is a sequence of instructions which sorts the numbers in XYZ. X1 serves as pointer P and X2 as pointer Q. The algorithm (and flowchart) is the *same* as in Chapter 4, though many fewer instructions are required.

```
        ⋮
        LDX1      ZERØ      X1 ← 0
A       PX1X2               X2 ← X1
        INCX2     001       X2 ← X2 + 1
B       LDAC1*X1  XYZ       AC1 ← XYZ_{X1}
        SUB1*X2   XYZ       AC1 ← AC1 − XYZ_{X2}
        JNEG1     C         If AC1 < 0, jump to C.
        LDAC1*X1  XYZ   ⎫
        LDAC2*X2  XYZ   ⎪  Exchange XYZ_{X1} and XYZ_{X2}.
        STAC1*X2  XYZ   ⎬  (Note: 4 instructions instead of 9 or 10!)
        STAC2*X1  XYZ   ⎭
C       INCX2     001       X2 ← X2 + 1
        SX2EQ     THIRTY    If X2 = 030, skip to ⌐
        JUMP      B         Jump to B.          |
        INCX1     001       X1 ← X1 + 1    ⟵────┘
        SX1EQ     TWENT9    If X1 = 029, skip to ⌐
        JUMP      A         Jump to A.          |
        ⋮                              ⟵────────┘
```

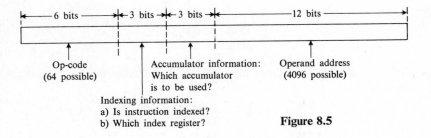

Figure 8.5

Some computers do not distinguish between index registers and accumulators. Their general registers serve as either, depending on their use in instructions. An instruction such as

              LØAD3,X5   GEØRGE

might mean "load general register 3 from array GEØRGE (in memory), indexed with general register 5." This approach is useful because of its flexibility—at times one might need many accumulators and few index registers; as other times, the reverse. General registers serve as both.

As in FACET, instructions are machine words broken into fields. Each field provides a different item of information. In FACET we had instructions like

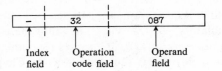

Each machine has its own scheme for interpreting an instruction. Figure 8.5 shows a possible scheme for a small, 4K†, 24-bit machine with multiple index registers and accumulators.

Many computers have variable-length instructions or, rather, different instructions of different lengths. In the 24-bit machine whose instruction we have just illustrated, there might be another instruction requiring only 12 bits. For example,

       HALT
       PX3AC2   AC2 ← X3
       FMUL5,AC3   AC5 ← AC5 × AC3 (floating point)

These instructions might possibly be implemented with 12 bits each, as shown in Fig. 8.6. Two 12-bit instructions appearing sequentially could be placed into one memory location, as shown in Fig. 8.7.

---

† K stands for 1000; 4K therefore means 4000. Since memory size is frequently a power of 2 and $2^{10} = 1024$, K is frequently used by programmers to mean 1024. A 4K-machine would therefore have 4 × 1024 or 4096 memory locations.

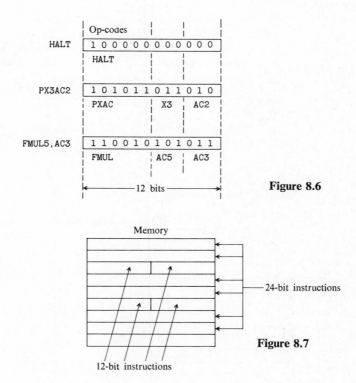

Figure 8.6

Figure 8.7

How can the instruction interpreter tell whether an instruction is short (half-word) or long (full-word)? By examining the op-code. This approach can be carried even further by a variety of lengths for instructions. Instructions which have a single memory address as operand are **one-address** instructions. **Two-address** instructions have two such operands; e.g.,

$$\text{ADD} \qquad \text{A,B} \qquad (\text{AC} \leftarrow \text{A} + \text{B})$$

The instruction might look like this

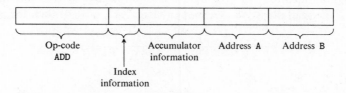

Three-address instructions are also possible, e.g.,

$$\text{ADD} \qquad \text{A,B,C} \qquad (\text{C} \leftarrow \text{A} + \text{B})$$

Here two numbers are taken from two memory locations and added together; the result is placed in a third memory location.

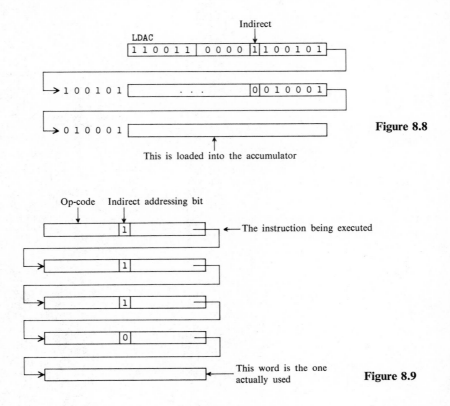

Figure 8.8

Figure 8.9

There is an important capability available in many computers which does not appear in the FACET machine. It is known as **indirect addressing**. A machine which has indirect addressing typically has a one-bit field in its instruction format indicating whether or not that particular instruction is to be executed with indirect addressing. When an instruction is executed with indirect addressing, it does not operate on the location indicated by the (effective) operand. Instead, it accesses the location indicated by the (effective) operand and determines the (effective) operand of *that* location. This address becomes the effective operand of the instruction. We shall illustrate. Let's say that 110011 is LDAC; then the instruction

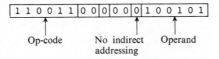

will place the contents of location 100101 into the (or some) accumulator. Let's say C(100101) = 101110100000010001; that number (564021 in octal) would be placed into the accumulator. But what if indirect addressing had been indicated?

For instance:

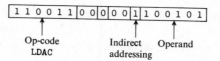

Then the contents of location 010001 would be placed into the accumulator, as shown in Fig. 8.8. The **depth** of indirect addressing here is *one*, because the actual operand (the memory location in which we are *really* interested) is *once* removed from the instruction. In some machines one is the limit; in others, greater depths are permitted. The indirect addressing bit, in such cases, determines the depth (Fig. 8.9).

An indirect addressing capability simplifies writing subprograms whose arguments are passed by name. For instance, let's say we have a program which calls a subprogram and passes some set of parameters by name:

```
        ⋮
     JSUB    WHICH
     ADRS    AAA    ⎫
     ADRS    BBB    ⎬  Parameter list
        ⋮          ⎪
     ADRS    XXX    ⎭
NEXT    ⋮
```

In FACET, each time we want to refer to the second parameter (BBB in this particular instance), we must place the address of the parameter list in the index register, retrieve the address of that second parameter, and finally retrieve the second parameter itself. In FACET, it looks something like this:

```
   ⋮
LDX     RETURN    place address of parameter list in XR.
LDX*    001       place address of second parameter in XR.
LDAC*   000       place second parameter into accumulator.
   ⋮
```

Three instructions such as these appear each time reference is made to some parameter. If we had indirect addressing, we could leave the address of the parameter list in the index register and write

```
   ⋮
LDAC*,IND    001    Load AC (with indexing and indirect addressing)
   ⋮
```

This causes the *contents* of parameter 2, C(BBB) in our example, to be loaded into the accumulator (rather than the *address* of parameter 2, in which we're not primarily interested.)

Indirect addressing, together with multiple-index-register use, also greatly simplify the passing and use of array parameters. Various approaches to passing array parameters are possible, and they are very hardware-dependent—i.e., dependent on the register configuration, indirect addressing, etc. Such approaches, as well as other uses of indirect addressing, will not be discussed here.

This discussion has given you some insight into a variety of machine configurations and outlined briefly some of the practices employed. It is not meant either to be complete or to point out "better" practices in any sense. It is sufficient, at this point, for you to keep your view of computers flexible, since the field is changing rapidly. The specific details of each machine therefore aren't as important as the ideas and the approaches employed.

Exercises 8.10

1. Can you think of a way to access (by name) elements of an array which have been passed to the subprogram you are writing? You may assume any arrangement of index registers and indirect addressing you wish.

2. How would you allocate index registers for use as loop indexes in a nested loop arrangement? Assume that there are n nested loops and m index registers, with $n > m$.

8.11 INPUT AND OUTPUT

The FACET computer has two devices attached to it through which it communicates with "the outside world"—a card-reader for input and a printer for output. Years ago, most computer facilities were set up with just a few such **peripheral devices**. Today, medium and large facilities consist of a **main frame** or **central processing unit** (the actual main computer) plus a large variety of peripheral devices. Some of these devices are input devices, some are output devices, and some can be used for both input and output. We shall describe a few such devices briefly. After reading this section, it would be helpful to take an excursion through your neighborhood computer center to actually familiarize yourself with these devices.

Following are listed some devices which are used solely for input:

1. **Card reader.** A device which reads punched cards. The card reader decodes the encoded characters and then re-encodes them into the machine's internal character-representation code.
2. **Paper tape reader.** This device reads a reel of paper tape in which characters are encoded by punched holes. The reader senses and decodes the hole combinations, then encodes them as the machine's internal representations for characters.
3. **Optical character reader.** A device which scans a paper for printed (sometimes even handwritten) characters and converts these for input into the computer.
4. **Magnetic character reader.** A device which senses specially designed characters printed on paper with special ink and converts these for input to the computer. These devices are often used in banks for reading information from checks.

Following are some devices which are used for output only:

1. **Line printer**. A device which receives a string of characters from the computer and prints it, an entire line at a time. This is the output device used by FACET.
2. **Card punch**. A device which punches holes in (originally blank) cards according to information it receives from the computer.
3. **Cathode-Ray tube display (CRT)**. A device which receives a string of characters from the computer and displays them for visual interpretation on a cathode-ray tube. The tube face bears resemblance to a television tube. Some CRT's can also be used for the output of arbitrary line drawings. Modifications to a CRT can make it suitable for input.
4. **Plotter**. A device which draws accurate line drawings based on commands from the computer. It is useful in creating computer-drawn maps, charts, graphs, and blueprints.

The following are devices which can be used for either input or output. Information from the computer may be output by use of these devices and stored; later, the same information may again be input. The media on which the information is actually encoded and stored is often called **secondary storage**, since these media are frequently used when the memory is not large enough to contain all the desired information. In contrast, the memory is sometimes called **primary storage**.

1. **Tape drive**. A device on which a reel of magnetic tape (similar to the kind used in home tape recorders) may be mounted and which can transfer information either from the computer onto the tape or in the other direction. Information is encoded on the tape by a process of magnetization of tiny spots on the tape in one of two directions, each spot represents one bit (0 or 1).
2. **Disk file**. A device which includes a stack of disks coated with magnetically sensitive material and a means for encoding and decoding information on these disks. The disks are usually spinning at a rapid rate, and read/write heads are positioned close to the disks so that the information transfer may be effected.
3. **Drum**. A device similar to the magnetic disk, except that the information is encoded on the surface of a rotating drum.

There is one other device of interest, the **typewriter terminal** (such as a teletype). This is a device which looks very much like a typewriter, except that it is (or can be) connected to the computer, either by direct connection or through telephone or other communication lines. When it is connected, the characters which are typed can be transmitted to the computer. The computer can also use the typewriter terminal as an output device, since it can send the typewriter a stream of characters which will also be typed.

Computers can also be connected to one another, either by direct wiring or by communications lines. At any particular time, one computer acts as an input device while the other acts as an output device.

Input and output (I/O) are by far the most complex operations in computers. These operations were greatly simplified in FACET specifically to allow us to study computing without getting too involved in I/O. The details of I/O vary so drastically from machine to machine that it is difficult to describe how I/O is done "in general." For this reason, we shall satisfy ourselves with a very cursory description. Basically, I/O operations take much longer than purely internal operations, because the internal operations require no mechanical movements. Execution of instructions like ADD or JUMP can typically take from a fraction of a **microsecond** (millionth of a second) to a few microseconds. Floating-point arithmetic might take somewhat longer. But to read a card takes about a tenth of a second, which makes this operation at least ten thousand times slower. Remember, a card must physically pass through some sensing device, and this physical movement takes time. Printers, card punches, and interactive typewriters similarly require lots of time. No physical movement occurs during purely internal operations—electrical pulses and magnetic fields are all that "move." It would not be wise to design a computer which waits for a card to be read before it does anything else. During that $\frac{1}{10}$ second, 10,000 non-I/O instructions could have been executed. To avert these inequities in distribution of time to I/O and non-I/O operations, machines often have instructions such as:

1. READ AND PRØCEED. This instruction starts the reading device, lets it operate on its own, and proceeds to the next instruction.
2. JUMP IF READ CØMPLETE. Later, this instruction tests the device to see if the read is completed. If it is, then the information is complete and can be used by the program. If not, the program sometimes waits in a loop until reading is completed.

Similar instructions are used for output.

Since computers are not built for specific I/O devices, and different configurations of such devices may be connected to a computer, there generally aren't specific instructions such as "read a card" or "write on magnetic tape." Instead, the I/O devices are connected to special purpose devices called **data channels**. Each channel and each device is thus identified as part of the operand of the I/O instructions. A configuration can be depicted as in Fig. 8.10. A computer I/O instruction would then actually be something like

READ   A,3   X

This might mean "read from device 3 on channel A (a tape drive in Fig. 8.10) into memory location (or array) X."

Some of these channels are rather sophisticated devices, actually small special-purpose computers; some can be programmed (with a special-purpose instruction set). The computer can activate many channels at once, and some channels (called **multiplexers**) can perform I/O through a number of devices simultaneously.

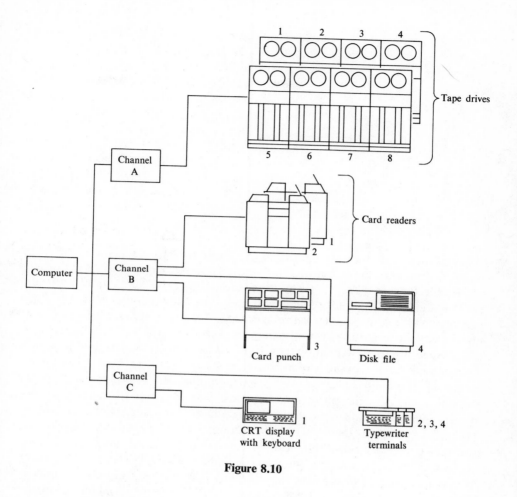

Figure 8.10

8.12 SOFTWARE PROCESSORS AND OPERATING SYSTEMS

You are already quite familiar with processors such as loaders and assemblers. In Chapter 5 we mentioned that such processors are *not* built into the computer, but are rather programs which perform these functions. There are many other processors employed in a large computer facility, all of which are programs. Some are translators; they translate from one computer language to another. We shall discuss these in the next chapter. Other types will be discussed in this chapter.

The memory is generally not large enough to contain all these processors at one time, since the user's programs must also fit into the memory. The procedure that is generally followed is to leave as much memory (primary storage) available as possible, and to store processors not in use in secondary storage, usually on a magnetic disk or tape. When a processor is required, it is read into the memory from disk or tape, and then executed. When the assembler is needed, for example,

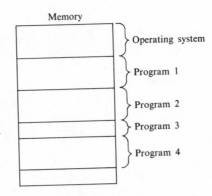

Figure 8.11

a special loader, also a program, reads the assembler into the memory, and then transfers control to the first instruction in the assembler.

Recall that in FACET there were special cards (START., LØAD., TRACE., EXECUTE., etc.) which "told" the computer what we wanted done. These cards are part of what is known as a **job control language**. They, too, are read by a program, known as the **executive system** or **monitor** or **operating system**. It is often a very complicated program, written by tens or hundreds of programmers, and requiring tens or hundreds of thousands of instructions. This operating system can do much for a user. It often has available to it many programs and subprograms. In many assembly languages the programmer doesn't actually write I/O instruction sequences, but rather calls on **system** subprograms (subprograms which are part of the operating system) to perform I/O functions. Usually only a portion of the operating system is **resident** (physically present) in the memory. As other portions are needed, they are read into the memory from disk or tape. A special type of programmer writes and modifies the operating system—the **systems programmer**. The typical programmer need not be acquainted with the inner workings of the operating system; he need only be familiar with the options it offers him and the job control language he uses to communicate with the system.

The operating system (or the resident portion of it) usually resides in the beginning of memory. For this reason, memory wrap-around is a feature usually not available to users. User programs are loaded elsewhere in the memory. Many larger facilities provide a **multiprogramming** environment; that is, a system in which more than one user program is resident in the memory at one time. The memory might, at some time, be configured as shown in Fig. 8.11.

At any given moment, one particular program is being executed. Whenever that program must perform an I/O operation, the appropriate channel and device are activated, and the program itself is interrupted. The operating system then allows another of the programs in memory to proceed with execution while the first program waits for its I/O operation to be completed. In this way the computer spends less time waiting for I/O operations. Imagine the complexity of an operating system which must deal with a number of programs simultaneously, some being executed, some being assembled, some waiting for I/O operations to be completed, and so on. It must keep track of all sorts of information, such as the identification of each user, the amount of time and memory each uses up (for accounting purposes), and the status of each program at any time.

Many computers have special hardware for **memory protection**. This hardware is controlled solely by the operating system. It often allows the operating system to allocate a **segment** or **field** of the memory (a contiguous sequence of memory locations) to a user. The user's program is then restricted to operate within this segment. If it attempts to execute an instruction whose operand is an address outside the segment (such as store information in, or transfer to some location outside the segment), the program is automatically interrupted. Control is then transferred to the operating system, which prints an appropriate error message and terminates the program.

The operating system is so important, that it is considered an integral part of the computer. It is provided by the manufacturer, who often remains responsible for its maintenance (correction of bugs, modifications). The efficiency and capabilities of an operating system are important considerations in choosing a computer—often more important than the efficiency and capabilities of the hardware.

Exercises 8.12

1. Does the computer (other than FACET) at your computer center have a multiprogramming capability? If so, find out how it works and describe it.
2. Describe the I/0 device and channel configuration of the computer at your computer center.

8.13 ADDRESSING SCHEMES

We have seen that an instruction consists of a number of fields, such as the op-code, indexing information, and an operand. The operand is often a memory address. Computers with very large memories require a very large operand field for a machine address. For instance, if our machine had 250,000 memory locations, then a complete memory address would require 18 bits, since addresses would run from 0 through 249,999, and

$$(0)_{10} = (000000000000000000)_2$$
$$(249,999)_{10} = (111101000010001111)_2$$

$$\longleftarrow \text{18 bits} \longrightarrow$$

A million memory locations would require a 20-bit address, and so on. Large memories are particularly important in computer systems with multiprogramming environments, since large user programs can easily take up 50,000 or 100,000 registers, and 5 or 10 user programs in the memory can require a million locations. However, if a large portion of each instruction is taken up with an address, either there would be little room for other important information (indexing, indirect

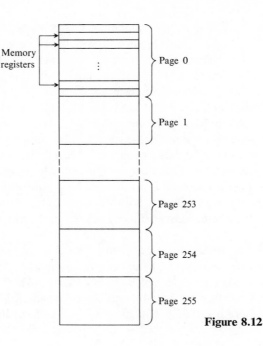

Figure 8.12

addressing, general registers) or words would be inordinately long. A number of addressing schemes which alleviate this problem are in use. We shall describe two of them briefly.

One possible approach is to segment the memory into a sequence of segments or **pages**. The memory might then look like Fig. 8.12. There might then be two types of instructions: one whose operand is an address *within* the page, and the other an absolute machine address. The locations within the page begin at address zero and are numbered sequentially. Each memory location therefore has two addresses—one within the page, requiring fewer bits, and the other a unique address within the memory. If the number of locations in a page is a power of two, then the absolute address of a location is just a composite of the page number followed by the address within the page. We shall illustrate using octal addresses. Keep in mind that each octal digit really represents three binary digits. Let's assume we have 256 pages, so they are numbered (in octal):

$$
\begin{array}{ccc}
0 & 0 & 0 \\
0 & 0 & 1 \\
0 & 0 & 2 \\
 & \vdots & \\
3 & 7 & 6 \\
3 & 7 & 7 \\
\end{array}
$$

Each page number is three octal (nine binary) digits. Let's also assume we have

4096 locations in each page, so addresses within a page (in octal) are

$$
\begin{array}{cccc}
0 & 0 & 0 & 0 \\
0 & 0 & 0 & 1 \\
0 & 0 & 0 & 2 \\
  & \vdots & & \\
7 & 7 & 7 & 5 \\
7 & 7 & 7 & 6 \\
7 & 7 & 7 & 7 \\
\end{array}
$$

Four octal digits (12 binary digits) are required for an address within a page. There are over 1 million registers in the memory:

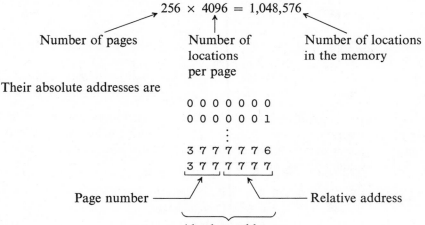

An arbitrary absolute octal address, such as 1245703, is in page no. 124 (octal), location within the page 5703.

   Some instructions can have 12-bit addresses—they refer to other locations within the page. Others can have full addresses (21 bits). Such instructions can (possibly) use two memory words; i.e., some instructions may have so much information that they cannot be "crammed" into one memory register. In machines with longer registers, the short-operand instructions can fit into part (a half or a quarter) of a word, and long-operand (full address) instructions can take a whole word.

   Another approach employed is the use of a **base-register**. This scheme provides the computer with an additional register known as a base register. When a program is loaded (read) into the memory, the full address of the first location of the program is placed into this base register. The program itself is written or assembled relative to address zero, as if the program were being loaded at the beginning of the memory (recall, that's the way the assembler works anyway—addresses are computed beginning with zero). The hardware of the machine takes care of the rest; when it executes an instruction, the address in the operand is added to the address in the

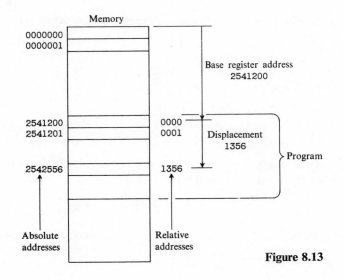

Figure 8.13

base register, and this is the address used. The base register acts as a pointer to the beginning of the program, and the operand gives the address within the program. If a program begins at octal location 2541200 and an operand contains address 1356, then the absolute address accessed is

$$
\begin{array}{r}
2\ 5\ 4\ 1\ 2\ 0\ 0 \quad \text{Base address} \\
+\qquad 1\ 3\ 5\ 6 \quad \text{Displacement} \\
\hline
2\ 5\ 4\ 2\ 5\ 5\ 6 \quad \text{Absolute address}
\end{array}
$$

The address actually comes in two parts. See Fig. 8.13. When indexing is used, the ultimate address is a composite of three addresses—base, displacement and index.

Exercises 8.13

1. Discuss the differences between the paging approach to memory addressing and the base register approach.
2. Find out and describe the addressing scheme employed by the computer (not FACET) of your computer facility.

8.14 IN REVIEW

Numbers are abstract objects. They are generally represented in the decimal number system. This is a fixed-radix, positional notation system in which there are 10 symbols called digits. These digits represent different numbers, depending on their position in the (written) string. The digits can be thought of as appearing in imaginary columns, each column having a "columnar weight." These weights are powers of ten, the base or radix of the system.

There are other ways of representing numbers. Specifically, computers generally employ binary (base two) representation and arithmetic. This choice is made because binary representation is more efficient and inexpensive to implement. Binary numbers are written as strings of zeros and ones, the two digits of the binary system. Columnar weights are powers of two rather than ten. The division between the integer portion and fraction portion of such a number is a dot known as the binary point (as opposed to decimal point in base 10).

Other bases can be used as well. Any positive integer greater than one can serve as a base or radix for a number representation system. Columnar weights are merely powers of that radix. Bases eight and sixteen are particularly important in computers; these two systems are called octal and hexadecimal, respectively. This is because conversion of binary numbers to and from either octal or hexadecimal is very simple, and long binary strings become more readable when printed as octal or hexadecimal strings.

The memory of most computers consists of a sequence of memory registers, each containing a fixed-length string of binary digits (or bits). Different computers have different length registers (but usually the length is a multiple of six or eight) and different numbers of registers in the memory. The registers are assigned binary addresses in sequence, beginning with zero. Some machines are character-addressable, in which case the characters are addressed in sequence rather than in the words of memory. The IBM 360 is an important example of a character-addressable computer.

There are a number of methods employed for representing integers in memory registers. The first (leftmost) bit indicates the sign of the integer, and is called the sign bit. Positive integers are represented in the binary representation system—a string of zeros and ones. Negative integer representation varies, depending on the representation scheme being used. In signed-magnitude representation only the sign bit changes when one converts a positive integer to the corresponding negative integer. In one's-complement representation, a negative integer is represented as the complement of the corresponding positive integer—that is, all zeros in the word are changed to ones, and ones to zeros. Two's complement is similar to one's complement, except that a one is added to the rightmost digit after complementation. One's- and two's-complement representation are used because implementation of arithmetic in the computer becomes more efficient.

Floating-point numbers are generally represented, as in FACET, by dividing the word into fields: a sign bit, a biased exponent (characteristic) and a mantissa (fraction part). These fields are binary rather than decimal, and the mantissa (fraction) is multiplied by a power of two rather than ten (i.e., the binary point is moved left or right an appropriate number of places). In one's- or two's-complement machines negative floating-point numbers are represented as the one's or two's complement of the corresponding positive floating-point number.

A single character is represented in a (binary) computer by a sequence of either six or eight bits. This sequence is often called a byte. An exact number of bytes (characters) usually comprise a word. Different computers have different internal representation codes for characters.

Many computers have more than one accumulator and/or more than one index register. Some computers have a set of "general registers" which can act as either accumulators or index registers. The instruction format in these multiple-register machines reflects the register configuration. A word which serves as an instruction is sectioned into a number of fields—for the op-code, the operand, indexing and general-register information, etc. Some machines have instructions with multiple operands (addresses in the memory). They are known as two-address machines, three-address machines, etc. (in contrast with one-address machines like FACET).

Indirect addressing is a capability built into some computers which allow a "chain search" for the actual operand. In this scheme, the address in the operand portion of an instruction points to a memory word which, in turn, points to still another. This capability is useful in subprograms in which parameters are passed by name.

Computers can generally be connected to a large variety of input-output (I/O) devices through a special-purpose intermediary device often called a channel. Some typical I/O devices are: line-printer, card reader, card punch, magnetic tape drive, disk drive, cathode-ray tube display, and interactive typewriter terminal. I/O instructions are rather complex; they vary greatly from computer to computer. Typically, an I/O instruction (READ or WRITE) takes 1,000 to 10,000 times longer to execute than does a purely internal instruction.

Assemblers and loaders are actually programs. There are many other processors in large computer systems, all programs. The program which controls the flow of user jobs is called the operating or executive system, or sometimes the monitor. The programmer communicates with the operating system via a job control language. He asks for assembly, loading, and execution in this language.

Some computers have a number of user jobs in the memory at one time. They are said to be multiprogrammed. Whenever a job or program requires an I/O operation, it is interrupted while a channel takes care of the I/O request, and another program executes. All this is controlled by a complex and sophisticated operating system.

Computers with very large memories must employ some memory addressing scheme in their instructions other than the one discussed previously. This is because addresses are so long (require so many bits) that too large a portion of the instruction would be taken up with a memory address under the usual scheme. Various methods are used for alleviating this problem. Most revolve around breaking up the address, and using only a portion of it in the operand (the rightmost bits) while placing the rest (the leftmost bits) in a special register, sometimes called a base register.

Chapter 9

HIGH-LEVEL LANGUAGES AND FORTRAN

9.1 INTRODUCTION TO HIGH-LEVEL LANGUAGES

Since Chapter 3 we have discontinued using FACET machine language and have used assembly language exclusively. This choice was based solely upon the greater convenience of assembly language. We found that by using a translator, in this case an assembler, programs could be written in a form more amenable to the programmer.

This approach suggests the possibility of further simplifying our programming efforts by increased exploitation of this translator concept. Specifically, can other languages be created which can also be translated to machine language and which can significantly improve our programming ease? In looking for an answer to this question, let us look at how we went from problem statement to final program. We found that after we discovered some algorithm to solve a problem, we specified that solution in a macro-flowchart. We then determined how the data could be represented in FACET, and we created a sequence of FACET operations necessary for that solution. Would it not be a great simplification to specify our program in a form as close as possible to the macro-specifications of the solution found in the flowchart?

Consider several typical ways we specify a macro-solution. If we are considering mathematical or scientific problems, we might see flowchart statements such as

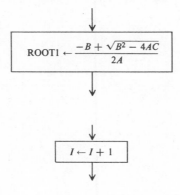

or

Would it not be convenient to have a language which closely corresponds to these flowchart statements in the following way:

$$\text{RØØT1} \leftarrow \frac{-B + \sqrt{B^2 - 4AC}}{2A}$$

and

$$\text{I} \leftarrow \text{I} + 1$$

The main question is whether arbitrary algebraic expressions (as seen on the right-hand side of the arrows) can automatically be translated to the corresponding FACET instruction sequence. If algebraic expressions cannot be translated algorithmically, then such statements could not appear in a programming language. It so happens, though, that the same rules we, as humans, use for translating algebraic expressions into FACET sequences can be formalized and built into an algorithm in a translator. Thus each algebraic expression can be used directly without reduction to its corresponding instruction sequence. One example of such use is in the **assignment** statements above (we are assigning a new value to the data location on the left-hand side of the arrow).

Another common use of algebraic expressions is when comparison is necessary. We might see in our flowcharts:

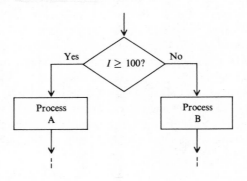

or

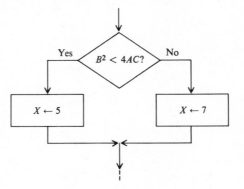

Would it not then be convenient to have a language which allows statements such as

IF I $\geq$ 100 THEN (DØ PRØCESS A); ØTHERWISE (DØ PRØCESS B)

or

IF B^2 < 4AC THEN LET X BE 5; ØTHERWISE LET X BE 7.

Again the determination of FACET instruction sequences which correspond to the above comparisons is straightforward and could be done by an algorithm in a translator.

Aside from the added convenience of specifying operations, and specifying tests, we might also expect a language to help us use specialized means of storing information peculiar to a particular problem area.

For example, we might be processing textual data and need a program to generate the index of a book. One portion of the program would scan the text for individual words. Another might store character strings of arbitrary length. Would it not be convenient if a language for text processing had a storage device which corresponded to our notion of a string? If we append additional characters to a string already in memory, the storage for the string could be expanded. If characters are removed, the storage shrinks in size. Thus in such a programming system the programmer could obtain a string by stating X STRING much the same way you now say X LØC, and he could then store an arbitrary number of characters in X. Here you may realize that more than simple translation is required. Depending on the data for the program, string X may be of different sizes during the execution of a program. Since it keeps changing during execution, a number of extra instructions, or possibly some special subprograms, would have to be added to the machine language translation. These instructions would somehow subtract memory locations from and add locations to arrays used for the various strings as needed.

Such a language for manipulating strings could have pattern-matching statements, such as

I = SCAN A FØR B

This might mean "scan string A to see if it contains string B as a substring. If it does, place into (integer) I the position in string A where substring B begins. If B is not a substring, place 0 into I." If A contains

THREE␣EGGS␣AND␣TWØ␣CUPS␣ØF␣FLØUR

and B contains

EGGS

then the scan statement causes 7 to be placed into I, since substring B begins at the *seventh* character of string A. All this is but one example of the *type* of statement we *might* want to implement in a string processing language.

One might be very concerned with format of output—printing reports and the like with appropriate spacing and messages. One might, in such an instance, create an editing capability. For instance, if whenever (floating-point) location X were printed, you would want it printed like this:

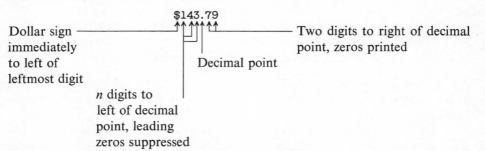

Dollar sign immediately to left of leftmost digit

n digits to left of decimal point, leading zeros suppressed

Decimal point

Two digits to right of decimal point, zeros printed

then you could identify the location X with a format:

```
X FØRMAT $ZZZZ.DD
```

where

Z   means decimal digit (leading zeros suppressed),
D   means decimal digit,
.   means decimal point, and
$ means dollar sign immediately to the left of the first nonblank character.

Thus whenever you write PRINT X, it would be printed something like this:

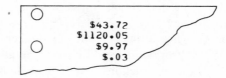

    Features similar to (but not identical to) these are actually built into many higher-level languages. Many classes of problems exist for which specialized high-level languages could be created. The major intent of these languages is to relieve the programmer of the task of reducing his solution, as he conceives it, to the level of the machine. Instead, he need only reduce his solution to the level at which algorithms can take over to complete the translation to machine language. These translators of high-level languages are called **compilers**. The problem classes handled by a specific language are generally quite large. For example, one has algebraic languages, symbol-manipulation languages, and business-oriented languages. More specialized languages naturally have a more limited use, and therefore their design and implementation costs are harder to justify economically. Also, a proliferation of specialized languages forces programmers into learning many more languages.

    Aside from the additional ease of programming in high-level languages, there are other advantages:

1. High-level languages are much more "readable" than assembly languages. This means that you will usually understand a lot more about how a program

works by examining, for equivalent lengths of time, the high-level language version of a program rather than the assembly language version. Two advantages ensue. First, less documentation is required for programs. Since documenting is often an essential activity which no one likes doing, this advantage is significant. Second, debugging programs and modifying them at a later time are greatly simplified.

2. Experimentation with different algorithms and programming techniques is encouraged by high-level languages because it is much easier to implement the new approaches in these languages.

3. Programs written in these languages are relatively **machine independent** in that they can be executed on any machine provided with a translator for that language. Consider the example presented earlier:

$$I \leftarrow I + 1$$

This would be translated into FACET assembly language as follows:†

```
LDAC    I
ADD     ØNE
STAC    I
```

This FACET sequence could be executed only on the FACET machine. The statement, I ← I+1, however, contains no machine-dependent operation codes or addresses and could therefore be translated into the machine language of almost any other computer. Thus programs written in such languages can be executed with comparatively little or no change on any computer with a translator for that language.

Due to these overwhelming advantages, the great majority of programming is done in high-level languages. Assembly language programming is used on machines too small to support compilers (e.g., FACET), for complicated programs for which no high-level language is suitable, and for **systems programming**. Systems programs are those programs usually written by computer manufacturers for use with specific machines they produce. Examples of such programs are operating systems, assemblers, loaders, and compilers. Assembly and machine languages are used in order to employ to advantage all the idiosyncrasies of the particular machine and its instruction set and thereby obtain the fastest possible execution speed for these frequently used programs.

---

† Many compilers translate directly to machine language; however, there are some which translate to assembly language.

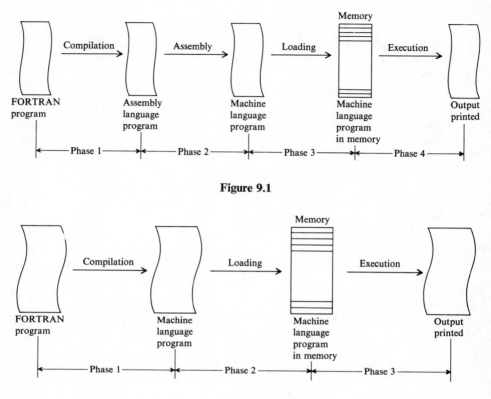

Figure 9.1

Figure 9.2

9.2 FORTRAN

FORTRAN is a higher-level language in widespread use today. Its name stands for FORmula TRANslation, and it was originally designed as a language for scientific and mathematical use. It has since been expanded to include other applications, such as text processing and business data processing. Most computers have FOR-TRAN compilers available. A FORTRAN compiler is a processor or program which translates (compiles) FORTRAN programs into machine or assembly language.

After you write a FORTRAN program, it undergoes a number of processes before it can be executed. It must be compiled (translated to, say, assembly language), assembled, loaded into the memory, and finally executed. This process can be viewed as shown in Fig. 9.1. Many FORTRAN compilers, however, compile directly into machine language, bypassing the assembly language step, as is illustrated in Fig. 9.2.

A FORTRAN program actually consists of a sequence of **statements**. In the remainder of this chapter we shall discuss many, though not all, of the statements available in FORTRAN.

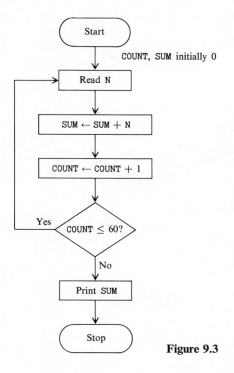

Figure 9.3

We punch our FORTRAN programs onto punched cards, as we did with the machine language and assembly language programs. Each FORTRAN statement is punched onto one card. The last card in the program is the END card (as it was in assembly language). This indicates to the compiler the physical end of the program.

We shall illustrate FORTRAN by writing a program which reads 60 numbers from 60 data cards, and prints their sum. Since we have already written similar programs in assembly language, we shall dispense with discussing the algorithm. The flowchart looks like that shown in Fig. 9.3. Now let's write the program. We start with these two statements:

```
INTEGER CØUNT, SUM, N
DATA CØUNT/0/, SUM/0/
```

These two statements are similar to assembly language pseudo-ops. They are not actually translated to machine instructions and are called **non-executable** statements. The first is similar to LØC, where locations are named (INTEGER means fixed point arithmetic). These locations are called **variables** in FORTRAN. This program has three variables: CØUNT, SUM, N. The second statement is like SET, and indicates that CØUNT and SUM are initialized to zero. Next we write

```
 5    READ 10, N        corresponding to
10    FØRMAT (I10)
```

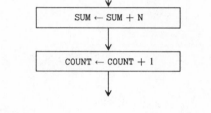

These statements specify that the fixed-point number in the first ten columns of the *next* data card (I10) should be read and stored in location N. Then we write

```
SUM=SUM+N            corresponding  to
CØUNT=CØUNT+1
```

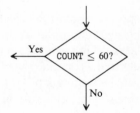

Note that the equals sign (=) in FORTRAN does not mean "equals," but "store into location" just like the flowchart arrow (←). Next we write

```
IF(CØUNT.LE.60)  GØ TØ 5      for
```

Here, note that .LE. means "less than or equal to" (≤) and that GØ TØ is a transfer or jump statement. Then

```
     PRINT 20, SUM        corresponding to
20   FØRMAT (10X, I12)
```

Finally, we write

STØP   for

and

END

as the last statement in the program. Like the INTEGER and DATA statements, it is non-executable. The entire program would then be written as follows:

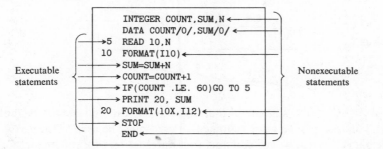

Several statements in this program are marked non-executable. These statements request the compiler to perform certain functions, such as storage allocation, setting of data types, and initialization of variables. All of these act as instructions *to the compiler*, and are performed entirely *before* loading and execution of the actual machine language program. They do not cause any machine language instructions to be generated, and they correspond to such assembly language statements as LØC, SET, and CHAR. When your program runs, only the **executable** statements, or rather their machine language counterparts, are actually being executed.

When the program is punched on cards, each statement is punched beginning in column 7, one statement to a card, like this:

Statements which are referred to by other statements are identified by **statement numbers**, which are punched in columns 1 through 5. These are eventually translated to machine addresses.

A statement may not extend beyond column 72 of the card. Columns 73 through 80 are ignored by FORTRAN compilers and are used by programmers for other information. Frequently a finished FORTRAN program has sequential numbers punched in those columns, so that if the cards are dropped they can be placed into the correct order by a mechanical sorting machine.

Blanks are ignored by FORTRAN compilers, so that, for instance, the statement CØUNT=CØUNT+1 can be punched as

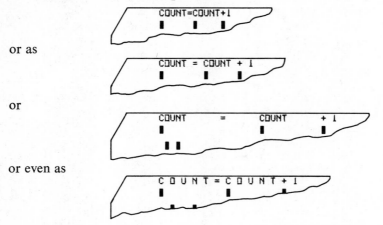

or as

or

or even as

If a FORTRAN statement requires more than 66 characters (columns 7 through 72), then one or more **continuation cards** may be used. Ordinarily, column 6 is left blank. When a card contains the continuation of a statement, a character other than zero or blank is punched in column 6 to indicate this to the compiler. So CØUNT=CØUNT+1 may be spread out onto four cards as follows:

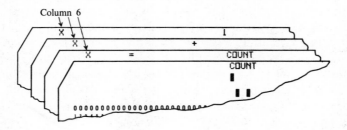

The FORTRAN compiler would consider these four cards as containing the single statement CØUNT=CØUNT+1. This procedure is syntactically valid, but silly unless the statement really does require extra cards.

The FORTRAN compiler usually **lists** your program as it compiles. A program **listing** is merely a copy of what you have on your punched cards printed on the line printer. This provides you with a "hard" copy of your program on paper— invaluable in documentation and debugging. If you want to insert comments on this hard copy, you may insert **comment** cards in your program deck. A comment card is a card which has a C in column 1. This is a signal to the compiler that the card is to be ignored in the compilation, but listed. Here's an example:

Comment cards are important in documenting programs properly. If you are writing a very long program (say 100 cards or more), the comments will be valuable to you during the debugging process. Frequently programmers who do not use comment cards are found saying, "Now what *did* I mean by these statements?".

The program we previously wrote might look like this if comment cards had been inserted:

```
                  ┌── columns 1–5
                  │     ┌────── column 6
                  │     │     ┌── columns 7–72
              ←───┼──→  ↓  ←──┼──────────────────────────────────→
                  │     │  │INTEGER CØUNT, SUM, N
              C   │     │  │
              C   │     │  │    INITIALIZE CØUNT AND SUM TØ ZERØ
              C   │     │  │
                  │     │  │DATA CØUNT/0/, SUM/0/
              C   │     │  │
              C   │     │  │    BEGIN MAIN LØØP FØR READING AND SUMMING
              C   │     │  │
                  │    5│  │READ 10, N
                  │   10│  │FØRMAT(I10)
                  │     │  │SUM = SUM + N
                  │     │  │CØUNT = CØUNT + 1
                  │     │  │IF(CØUNT .LE. 60) GØ TØ 5
              C   │     │  │
              C   │     │  │  PRINT SUM AND HALT
              C   │     │  │
                  │     │  │PRINT 20, SUM
                  │   20│  │FØRMAT(10X, I12)
                  │     │  │STØP
                  │     │  │END
```

Note that extra comment cards, blank in all columns except for a C in column 1, are inserted to set the comments off from the program in the listing. Although comments are hardly required in short programs like this one, it is a good idea to begin using them with your first program. This will help develop good programming habits.

When you submit a FORTRAN program at your computer facility, you must place control cards in front of and behind the program. Since the job control language varies at different facilities, no more will be said about these cards— find out about them from your instructor or computer center. These cards will identify you; cause the compiler (which is a program) to be loaded into the memory, read and compile your program; and then have the machine language translation of your program loaded and executed. If FACET had a compiler we *might* set up cards as shown in Fig. 9.4. However, it doesn't.

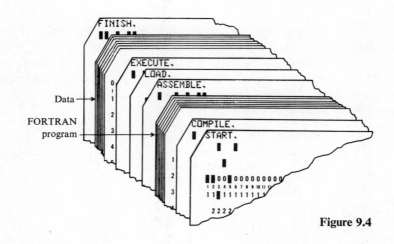

Figure 9.4

The remainder of this chapter will discuss how to write FORTRAN programs, some of the problems involved, and some of the algorithms by which FORTRAN is translated into machine or assembly language. The examples offered will show FORTRAN being translated to FACET assembly language, since we are familiar with it. In reality, FACET has no FORTRAN compiler.

The presentation of FORTRAN in this chapter and the next is fairly complete and self-contained. However, if you find yourself involved in extensive FORTRAN programming, you may find it worth while to examine the FORTRAN manual for the computer you are using. There you will find the idiosyncrasies and special capabilities of your compiler discussed. As you might expect, your FORTRAN programming proficiency will increase only with practice.

Exercises 9.2

1. What is an executable statement? a non-executable statement?

2. Why do we need continuation cards?

3. Why are there many different FORTRAN compilers? Why aren't they interchangeable?

4. Which statements require statement numbers?

5. In what ways are statement numbers and variables the same?

6. If a FORTRAN program were being translated to assembly language, how would the END statement be translated? the STØP statement?

7. What control cards are necessary at your computer facility for compiling and running a FORTRAN program? What does each card do? Are there separate cards for requesting compilation and execution? Why would you want to compile a FORTRAN program without executing it?

8. Why would one construct a FORTRAN compiler which compiles into assembly language rather than machine language?

9. What is the FORTRAN statement on the following card?

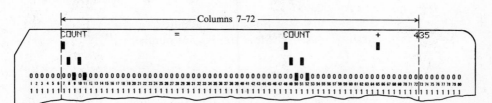

9.3 DATA TYPES AND DECLARATIONS

A computer program is usually placed in some contiguous sequence of memory locations. This happens in assembly language, and this also happens in FORTRAN —the assembler or compiler translates the program so that all our instructions and data are together in one block, with no "holes" or unused registers. The block has two sub-blocks of registers: instructions and data locations. In assembly language we sometimes mixed these sub-blocks, but FORTRAN compilers always keep them separate. (Even in assembly language we usually kept them separate.) Generally, all the instructions come first, followed by all the data locations, as shown in Fig. 9.5.

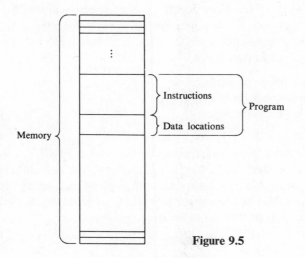

Figure 9.5

When we write assembly language programs, a data location can be used for either fixed-point or floating-point numbers, and sometimes even for both in the same program. Here's an illustration:

```
LDAC    CØUNT
ADD     ØNE        Fixed-point addition.
STAC    SUM        Store fixed-point number.
  ⋮
LDAC    X
FADD    Y          Floating-point addition.
STAC    SUM        Store floating-point number.
  ⋮
```

At one point, location SUM contains a fixed-point number, and at another, a floating-point number. This is *not* permitted in FORTRAN. Each data location is used *either* for fixed-point numbers *or* for floating-point numbers. Furthermore, the data locations are divided into **constants** and **variables**. Constants are those locations that contain specific numbers which are loaded with the program and never change. Variables are locations into which we may read numbers or place (store) numbers at execution time. In the sequence

```
          LDAC    CØUNT
          ADD     ØNE
          STAC    CØUNT
            ⋮
ØNE       SET     +00001
```

CØUNT is a variable and ØNE (1) is a constant. Both are fixed-point locations.

In FORTRAN, fixed-point locations and numbers are called **integer**, while floating-point locations and numbers are called **real**. An integer location is said to be of **data type** integer, while a real location is of **data type** real. So a FORTRAN program generally has four kinds of data locations:

1. integer (fixed-point) variables,
2. integer (fixed-point) constants,
3. real (floating-point) variables,
4. real (floating-point) constants.

The variables receive names exactly the way they did in FACET assembly language —one to six characters long, the first alphabetic, the rest either alphabetic or numeric. We begin our program with data **declarations**, which tell the compiler which of our variables will be integer (contain fixed-point numbers) and which will be real (floating-point). We do so by writing, for instance,

```
INTEGER X, CØUNT, I3
REAL ALPHA, BRAVØ, Q
```

This means that the three locations X, CØUNT, and I3 will contain integer numbers, and ALPHA, BRAVØ, and Q will contain reals. These declarations are needed to translate instructions properly. For example, if we later write

$$\text{C\O UNT} = \text{X} + \text{I3}$$

the compiler will translate this to

```
LDAC    X
ADD     I3        fixed-point (integer) addition
STAC    CØUNT
```

On the other hand,

$$\text{Q} = \text{ALPHA} + \text{BRAV\O}$$

will be translated as

```
LDAC    ALPHA
FADD    BRAVØ    floating-point (real) addition
STAC    Q
```

Note the syntax of declaration statements. This syntax can be described better if we introduce the term **list**. FORTRAN uses lists of various kinds. A list of variables is one of two things: either a single variable or a number of variables separated by commas. Thus X is a variable list, and A,B,C is, as well. Note that the commas are separators, and do not appear before the first or after the last variable. The syntax of an INTEGER declaration is therefore

INTEGER   (list of variables)

and the syntax of a REAL declaration is

REAL   (list of variables)

These declarations are placed at the start of the program.

The FORTRAN compiler forms a table for its own use of the data type associated with each variable. As it translates the program and needs to know the type of a variable appearing in some statement, it refers to the table.

Here are some integer declarations:

```
INTEGER    NØ1, NØ2, P3, P7
INTEGER    PØUNDS
INTEGER    A,B,C,D,E,F,G,H,I
```

These are real declarations:

```
REAL    RCPTS, BALNCE, TØTAL
REAL    INTRST
REAL    I33, I49, J72, LX5DP
```

A compiler might "translate" these declarations to assembly language by writing

NØ1	LØC
NØ2	LØC
P3	LØC
P7	LØC
RCPTS	LØC
BALNCE	LØC
TØTAL	LØC
⋮	

However, it would "remember" which are the integer locations and which the real, for later use.

FORTRAN provides another method for determining the type of a variable. If a variable appears in a program and has not been declared "explicitly" in a declaration statement, the compiler determines its data type according to the following rule:

First letter of variable	Type
A–H, Ø–Z	Real
I–N	Integer

For example, if the following variables had not been declared explicitly,

$$N, \ I, \ K5, \ MIN, \ MEDIAN$$

they would be classified as integers; and

$$CØST, \ SPEED, \ X, \ YPRIME, \ BETA7$$

would be classified as reals, based on the first letter of each name.

Integer and real constants are not declared, nor need we name them in FORTRAN programs. Their mere use in a FORTRAN statement is sufficient; the compiler takes care of the rest.

Integers can be written with leading zeros suppressed and with the plus sign suppressed. The following are valid FORTRAN integer constants:

$$0$$
$$-5$$
$$3462$$
$$-987654$$
$$31$$
$$+23$$

Real constants can be written in either of two ways. First, the exponent can be dropped entirely:

$$3.1416$$
$$0.$$
$$-2.0$$
$$-0.000123$$

Second, we can include the exponent when it is large or small:

$$.1E-6$$
$$-22.0E11$$
$$-0.398E-3$$
$$50.E+10$$

Note that for both ways the fraction part contains a decimal point and also that it need not be normalized. The plus sign may be suppressed from the fraction part as well as the exponent. Obviously, given our knowledge of floating-point internal representation, no decimal points are allowed in the exponent. Remember that the decimal point is essential in real constants because, for instance, if we consider the two FORTRAN constants 3 and 3., the first is of type integer (+00003) and the second of type real (+51300). Only the decimal point differentiates between them.

Both integer and real constants may appear in many places throughout the program. The FORTRAN compiler must recognize when an arbitrary character string is indeed such a constant and then translate it to its corresponding internal representation. So, for example, the statement Z = X + 3.69 should cause 3.69 to be translated to its internal representation, +51369, and stored in some location, either like

```
R1    FSET    +.369E+01
```

or like

```
R1    SET     +51369
```

The compiler would also generate the instruction

```
FADD    R1
```

at the appropriate point in order to implement the above FORTRAN assignment statement.

The maximum integer (variable or constant) allowable under the FORTRAN compiler you happen to be using is probably greater than 99999 (FACET's maximum). The maximum **precision** (number of significant digits) of a real number is almost certainly greater than three (FACET's maximum), since your computer probably has longer memory registers. Check with your instructor or examine the FORTRAN manual for the machine you are using to learn:

1. the maximum number of digits in an integer number;
2. the maximum precision (number of fraction digits) in a real number;
3. the minimum and maximum allowable exponents in a real number.

The IBM 360, for example, allows nine digits of precision in an integer, six to seven digits of precision in the fraction of a real number, and 10^{76} and 10^{-78} are the maximum and minimum exponents, respectively.

Recall that variable locations may be **initialized** in assembly language. If we want CØUNT to have an initial value of zero when execution begins, we would need a zero loaded into location CØUNT at load time. In such a case, we would write

CØUNT   SET   +00000

instead of

CØUNT   LØC

In FORTRAN, variables may be initialized by use of the DATA statement:

DATA   I/0/, X/.581E5/, A,B,C/-2., -2.5, -3./
DATA   I1, I2, I3, I4/4*1/
DATA   I1/1/, I2/1/, I3/1/, I4/1/

In the first statement I would be initialized to 0, X to .581E5, A to -2., B to -2.5 and C to -3. The second statement uses the form "$K \times$ constant" where K indicates a **replication** (repetition) number. Thus 4*1 is the same as 1,1,1,1, and the statement causes the same action that

DATA   I1, I2, I3, I4/1,1,1,1/

does. Each of I1, I2, I3, and I4 are initialized to (fixed-point, integer) one. The third statement has the same effect as the second, and the choice between the two alternatives is up to the programmer. Note that a variable must be initialized with its correct data type. Thus, if I is integer, we may write I/4/ but *not* I/4.0/.

The DATA statement has the same role as the SET and FSET pseudo-ops. They determine the value of a variable at the time execution *begins*. The value can be changed during execution, but there is no way to execute the DATA statement again to reinitialize it; it is non-executable. For example,

DATA   I/0/, X/.581E5/, A,B,C/-2., -2.5, -3./

might be compiled as

I	SET	+00000
X	FSET	+.581E+05
A	FSET	-.200E+01
B	FSET	-.250E+01
C	FSET	-.300E+01

The use of DATA statements does not relieve us of declaring variables. Here's an example of the beginning of a FORTRAN program where variables are declared and *some* are initialized:

INTEGER HQTR, EMPT, INT4
REAL MLST, MPTQ, R7A
DATA HQTR, R7A/300, -4.7E8/, MLST/-3.05/

This might be translated as

```
HQTR    SET     +00300
EMPT    LØC
INT4    LØC
MLST    FSET    -.305E+01
MPTQ    LØC
R7A     FSET    -.470E+09
```

Other data types exist in FORTRAN along with their corresponding declaration statements. They are called double-precision, logical, and complex. We shall discuss these in a later section.

Characters and character strings can be processed by FORTRAN. Character "constants" are written with an H- (**Hollerith**) field specification. The number of characters to be encoded is written before the H and the character string after the H. For example, 4HABCD encodes ABCD; 1H⌴ encodes a blank, and 10HAVERAGE⌴=⌴ encodes AVERAGE⌴=⌴. Note that blanks are significant in an H-field, in contrast with their treatment elsewhere in FORTRAN statements.

A special data type for characters and a corresponding declaration is not provided in FORTRAN. In their internally encoded form, character strings can be stored in either real or integer variables. For example,

```
REAL BLANK, X, AST
DATA BLANK/1H /,X/1HX/,AST/1H*/
INTEGER A,CØMP,ØNE,TWØ,THØUS
DATA A,CØMP,ØNE/1HA,4HCØMP,1H1/,TWØ,THØUS/1H2,4H1000/
```

A single variable can contain no more than the maximum number of characters which can be encoded into a memory word. In FACET, which holds at most two characters per word, the following statement

```
REAL A/1HA/,I33/2H33/,AAA/2HAA/
```

might be translated into the following pseudo-ops:

```
A       CHAR    02      A
I33     CHAR    02      33
AAA     CHAR    02      AA
```

Note that for A the field is padded with blanks on the right. In general, the FORTRAN compiler will pad a word with blanks on the right whenever fewer than the maximum number of characters are inserted in a word. For example, if our computer has a six-character word and we write

```
DATA SICK/ 3HILL/
```

then location SICK is initialized with the six characters ILL⌴⌴⌴.

In most cases it does not matter whether real or integer variables are used to store characters. However, one should be consistent; when both data types are used, you may find yourself writing statements which force the compiler to arithmetically convert character strings from one data type to another. We shall discuss this problem in Section 9.6.

Some compilers, but not all, permit a simpler specification of character constants by using delimiters. A single quote (') or an asterisk (*) is sometimes used. Thus, 4HLBS. could also be written 'LBS.' or *LBS.* on various computers. Here are two examples:

```
DATA    SPHINX/'SIT'/,RØC/'FLY'/
DATA    MØRT/*$100*/,GAGE/*.01*/
```

Exercises 9.3

1. Why must variables be declared in FORTRAN?

2. How does the compiler "know" if a constant is real or integer?

3. How might the following be translated to FACET assembly language?

```
INTEGER A,B,C
REAL M22, I75G
DATA A/407/, M22, D/-.00032, 53./
```

How does the compiler know the data type of variable D, which has not been declared?

4. How will real locations A1, A2, A3, ..., A10 be initialized?

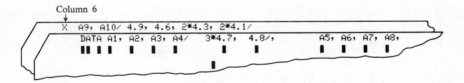

5. If the following DATA statement is included in a program, what will integer locations MIP and NIP and real locations SIC and TIC contain when the program begins executing (assume that a word contains eight characters):

```
DATA MIP, NIP, SIC, TIC/ 54, 2H54, .054E3, 6H.054E3/
```

Will any two locations contain the same word?

6. How might these FACET statements be written in a single FORTRAN statement?

```
HIJ    CHAR    02    ++
HIK    CHAR    02    +-
HIL    CHAR    02    -+
HIM    CHAR    02    --
```

7. Assume that your computer can have six characters encoded in each memory register. What do locations PIT, PAT, and PØT contain if they are initialized as follows:

> DATA PIT, PAT/3HPAT, 4HPUTT/, PØT/6H␣PETE␣/

Exhibit *all six* characters in each of the three locations.

9.4 INPUT AND OUTPUT†

Recall that input and output operations in FACET are rather primitive. In order to do a reasonable job of printing output in a "nice" readable format, many instructions are needed. Tabulation and carriage control statements, subprograms for suppressing zeros and plus signs, and character pseudo-ops are necessary for printing "reasonable" results like

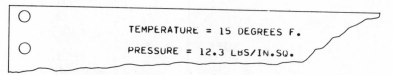

TEMPERATURE = 15 DEGREES F.

PRESSURE = 12.3 LBS/IN.SQ.

Similarly, input format is quite rigid in FACET. Fixed- and floating-point numbers can only be read in set formats, one number per data card. If an integer appears in columns 12–14 on a data card like

153

then we *could* write a sequence of instructions to read it (as a symbol string) and then convert it to a single FACET integer representation, but this would require quite a few FACET instructions.

The fact is that input and output are no simpler in other computers; usually they are more complex. Rarely are there instructions such as RNUM, PNUM, RFLT and PFLT. Everything must be read as strings of symbols and then converted to internal representations (in the case of numbers).

FORTRAN already has a set of subprograms which performs some rather fancy conversions and formatting for input and output. Your READ or PRINT statement is translated to a subprogram call which performs I/O functions. The FORTRAN statement for reading a card looks like this:

> READ 25, ALPHA, JX, N

It consists of the word READ, a statement number, and a list of variables. It causes the next card (of data) to be read and certain information from it to be placed into locations ALPHA, JX, and N (or whatever list of variables you have in the statement). The statement number refers to a FØRMAT statement, stating specifically which information from the data card should be placed into the variables. Note the comma following the statement number.

---

†   See Appendix F for FØRMAT specification summary.

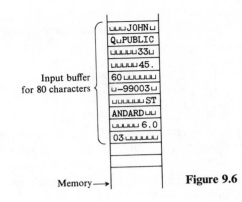

Input buffer
for 80 characters

Memory ⟶   **Figure 9.6**

Printing is similar. You write:

PRINT 177, A, B

This means "print a string of characters representing or depicting the contents of locations (in this case) A and B." Some FØRMAT statement labeled 177 contains further information specifying exactly how this information should be printed. These FØRMAT statements are non-executable and may appear anywhere in the program.

We shall examine reading first. When a READ statement is executed, the next data card is read into a block of memory called an **input buffer** as a string of 80 characters. In FACET, this buffer would be 40 words long, in other computers shorter. For instance, if our computer could store eight characters per word and we read the card

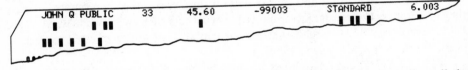

then our input buffer could be depicted something like Fig. 9.6. Note that all the characters on the card are read into the memory and stored in character representation—this includes the blanks.

Now the buffer is scanned, and the correct information placed into the appropriate memory registers—those variables named in the READ statement. The FØRMAT statement provides the information as to what to place into these variables. Let's assume that the card above was read with the following READ and FØRMAT statements:

READ 1045, C, B, J, K, X
1045 FØRMAT(10X, A3, 16X, F5.0, 7X, I3, I3, 8X, A4)

The list C,B,I,J,X is a sequence of five variables into which information will be placed. The associated FØRMAT statement contains a list in parentheses. Each item on its list defines a **field** on the card—a sequence of contiguous characters. Both lists are processed together from left to right. Here's how it would work in our example:

Item in *FØRMAT* *list*	*Item in* *variable* *list*	*Explanation*
10X	none	Skip the first 10 characters in the input buffer. In our case they are ⌴⌴⌴JØHN⌴Q⌴.
A3	C	The next three characters in the input buffer (PUB) are to be stored in variable C, left-justified, and right-padded with blanks. C now contains PUB⌴⌴⌴⌴⌴.
16X	none	Skip the next 16 characters in the buffer.
F5.0	B	The next five characters represent a floating-point number (45.60). Convert to internal floating-point representation and store in real variable B.
7X	none	Skip the next seven characters.
I3	J	The next three characters (−99) represent a fixed-point number. Convert to internal fixed-point representation and store in (integer) variable J.
I3	K	The next three characters in the input buffer (003) are to be converted to internal fixed-point representation and stored in integer variable K.
8X	none	Skip the next eight characters.
A4	X	The next four characters (TAND) are to be stored in variable X as characters, left-justified and right-padded with blanks.

To read a data card in FORTRAN you must know which fields on the card contain information you require. Further, you must know the form of that information: fixed or floating point, character, etc. Your FØRMAT statement essentially divides the card into fields:

X	for skip or ignore (e.g., 10X means ignore next 10 characters),
I	for integer (e.g., I5 means next five characters represent an integer),
A	for alphanumeric (e.g., A3 means next three characters *per se*),
F	for floating point (e.g., F5.0 means next five characters represent a real).

The X-fields are skipped, the others are converted to the appropriate internal representation and placed in the appropriate variables, from left to right down the variable list in the READ statement. We might visualize the card we just read (according to our READ and FØRMAT statements) as shown in Fig. 9.7.

Look over Fig. 9.7 until you are sure you understand how the READ statement, with its associated FØRMAT statement, works. Have you noticed the following points?

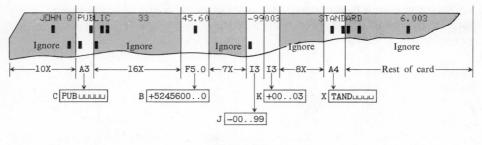

Figure 9.7

1. The FØRMAT statement by itself determines exactly which field will be read from the card (actually, from the input buffer) and which will be skipped. The FØRMAT statement further determines how the information will be converted for internal storage (fixed point, floating point, character). The READ statement merely lists the variables into which the results will be placed.
2. The A-field is a direct character transfer, but the sequence of characters placed into a variable is left-justified, with the remainder of character positions set to *blank*. The field should not be larger than the character length of a word (the number of characters that fit into a memory register). In our previous example, we could not have said A9. In FACET we should not say A4, since a word only stores two characters.
3. The field length specification is placed *before* the X in the skip-fields, but *after* the I, F, and A in those fields. For example: 12X—but I6, A2, and F7.0.
4. Note that the "point zero" in F7.0 or F5.0 does not affect anything. More will be said about its purpose later.

   Following are a few more illustrations. See if you can figure out what is placed into the variables during the execution of the READ statement *before* reading the answers.

```
      READ 44, FLXP, IIJJ, UNTD
  44  FØRMAT (F6.0, 7X, I4, 5X, A2)
```

```
      READ 1, I,J,K
   1  FØRMAT(I2,I2,I2)
```

```
      READ 999, X67, X68, X73, JUST
 999  FØRMAT(3X, A5, 2X, A3, 3X, A1, 3X, I1)
```

In the first illustration:

> real − .0005 is placed into FLXP,
> integer 5600 is placed into IIJJ,
> characters GR are placed left-justified into UNTD.

In the second illustration:

> integer −4 is placed into I,
> integer 44 is placed into J,
> integer −3 is placed into K.

In the third illustration:

> characters ⌄QUIC are left-justified in location X67, and right-padded with as
> many blanks as are necessary to fill out the word,
> characters BRØ are placed into X68 in a similar manner,
> character F is placed into X73 in a similar manner,
> integer 9 is placed into JUST.

An alternative method for reading floating-point numbers is in E-format, in which
the field is identified by an E (rather than an F). E fields must contain the exponent
explicitly. Here's an example:

```
      READ 2, A, B
  2   FØRMAT(F8.0, E12.0)
```

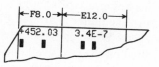

Note that E- and F-fields may have numbers represented *anywhere* in the fields
Integers in I-fields, on the other hand, should be right-justified in the field. When
they are not, many compilers fill in the rest of the field with zeros. For example:

```
      READ 6, Z, M
  6   FØRMAT (F10.0, I10)
```

Variable Z would have 0.5 (floating point) placed into it. Variable M, on the other
hand, might have 1200000 placed into it rather than 12, since the 12 is not right-
justified. It should have been punched like this if indeed 12 was the number
required:

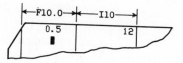

Now we can see that the FACET instructions

RNUM NUMBER　　and　　RFLT VALUE

can be written in FORTRAN as follows:

READ 4, NUMBER　　and　　READ 5, VALUE

4　FØRMAT(I6)　　　　　5　FØRMAT(E9.0)

Printing is sort of the reverse of reading. A block of memory is designated the **output buffer**. Information is placed into this buffer and then printed on the **line printer**. The line printer is a device which you've probably seen in your computer center—it prints an entire line of print at a time, usually either 120 or 132 characters across (of course, many of these characters may be blanks). Recall that in FACET we printed one or more characters at a time, not an entire line. In FORTRAN you can't print less than a line, so you must compute all the information required for an entire line before printing. Here's a print instruction in FORTRAN; we use the PRINT statement with its associated FØRMAT.

PRINT 80, DEL, INT

80　FØRMAT(10X, F12.4, 5X, I7)

Printing, like reading, is a two-step process. First the information in the variable list is converted to a character string and placed into the output buffer. Next the contents of this buffer are printed as an entire line on the line printer. All but the first character in the buffer is printed. This first character is known as the **carriage control** character. When this character is blank, the remaining characters in the buffer are printed on the next available line (the paper is positioned *one* line down). Other carriage control characters cause different positioning.

Let's see what happens in our example above. Assume that the variable DEL contains floating-point -89.03458 and INT contains integer 400. Again, the buffer is filled according to the FØRMAT statement. In this case, X means *blanks* (rather than skip, as in the READ statement). Here's what happens:

Item in FØRMAT list	Item in variable list	Explanation
10X	none	Fill the first 10 character positions in the output buffer with blanks.
F12.4	DEL	The next 12 character positions are to be filled with characters representing the floating-point number currently in variable DEL. Four places to the right of the decimal point are to be represented, and the numbers are to be right-justified in the field (ᵁᵁᵁᵁ−89.0346).
5X	none	Fill next five positions with blanks.
I7	INT	Next seven character positions should contain the character representation of the integer INT, right-justified with blanks at the left (ᵁᵁᵁᵁᵁ400).

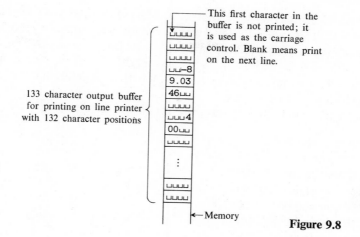

This first character in the buffer is not printed; it is used as the carriage control. Blank means print on the next line.

133 character output buffer for printing on line printer with 132 character positions

←— Memory

Figure 9.8

When the specification ends, the remainder of the output buffer is filled with blanks, and then the buffer is printed. Note that the first specification in the FØRMAT statement is 10X—only nine of the blanks will be "printed"—the first blank will be used for carriage control. Assuming that our computer has four characters per word, we could depict the output buffer as shown in Fig. 9.8 during the execution of that PRINT statement above. The printed line looks like this:

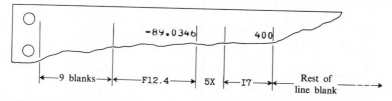

When printing, we must always make the print field large enough. Remember that decimal points and minus signs take up print positions as well as the digits.

We can use the E-format for printing as well; E17.5 means print a real in 17 character positions, 5 of them to the right of the decimal point, and the entire string right-justified with blanks at the left. The number is printed as a number between zero and one (in magnitude), with the exponent given as in FACET. Here are some examples:

If we print these numbers in E17.5 format,	then the following is printed, right-justified in the field of 17 characters.
300.9	0.30090E 03
− 0.000000007	−0.70000E−08
4444444.5555	0.44444E 07
1000.692	0.10007E 04
− 70.50339	−0.70503E 02
.00000000000000000005	0.50000E−19

Have you noticed that only 12 characters are required to print any number in E17.5 format? This means that five blanks will *always* be printed preceding the 12 characters of the number. In fact, an E-field specification need never require a field larger than the number of fraction digits plus seven. The extra seven characters are for the sign, the zero preceding the number, the decimal point, and four characters for the exponent.

Assume that the following variables are defined like this:

integer JACK contains 45
integer JILL contains −7002
integer JØHN contains 3285221
real XRAY   contains −0.000678
real XAVIER contains 7770.004318
real XACTØ   contains 50000000000000
real AAAAA   contains the characters BBBB
real AAAAB   contains the characters CDEF
integer I   contains the characters ⌴678

Then what would each of the following print statements print? Try yourself before checking with our results

a)   PRINT 46, JACK, I, JØHN
    46   FØRMAT(10X, I2, A3, I7)

b)   PRINT 11, XRAY, XAVIER, XACTØ
    11   FØRMAT (E14.6, F12.5, E8.1)

c)   PRINT 88, AAAAA, AAAAB, AAAAB, AAAAA
    88   FØRMAT (3X, A4, A3, A2, A1)

d)   PRINT 71, XAVIER, XAVIER, XAVIER, XAVIER
    71   FØRMAT (2X, F11.4, F11.5, F11.6, F11.7)

e)   PRINT 3, JACK, JILL, JØHN
     3   FØRMAT (6X, I5, 6X, I5, 6X, I5)

f)   PRINT 66, I
    66   FØRMAT(A4)

Here is what might be printed if these statements were executed consecutively:

```
        45 673285221
  -0.678000E-03  7770.00432 0.5E 14
     BBBBCDECDB
     7770.0043 7770.004327770.004318************
         45        -7002      *****
  678
```

This is the first character position

There are a number of rather important points you should note in the printing of these examples. We list the points explicitly:

1. You must make sure the **field-width** (the number of character positions designated for the printing of a certain variable) suffices for your specification. In (d), variable XAVIER could not be printed in F11.7 format, since it requires 12 character positions if seven digits to the right of the decimal point are to be printed. In (e), integer JØHN requires more than 5 characters. When this type of error occurs, many compilers merely fill the field with asterisks (∗) to indicate the error.

2. When you print in A-format, and require less than all the characters in a word to be printed, then the leftmost characters are printed. See how (c) is printed (the third printed line).

3. You need not specify a space (X) for carriage control. The first character in the output buffer is always chosen regardless of how it got there. In (b), the first character in the E14.6 field was a blank and that was used for carriage control. In (f), we asked that variable I be printed as four characters—the first being a blank. That blank was used for carriage control; the other three were printed.

4. Both integer and real variables may contain characters, and these can both be read and printed in A-format. See (c) and (f).

5. Variables may be repeated in the same print list, as in (c) and (d). Their formats may vary.

There is one other element we may place in the field specification list of a FØRMAT statement for printing—a sequence of characters. The specification is the same as in a data statement Hollerith constant, and the string may be as long as we like. For instance, say variable X contains floating-point 23.7, and we have just computed the pressure in this variable. We might want to print

```
  ◯
       THE PRESSURE IS 23.7 LBS./IN.SQ.
```

We can do this by writing

```
       PRINT 56, X
  56   FØRMAT(2X, 16HTHE PRESSURE IS , F4.1, 12H LBS./IN.SQ.)
```

Note that we have indicated four fields in the FØRMAT statement:

2X	meaning place two blanks in the first two character positions in the buffer (one for carriage control),
16HTHE PRESSURE IS	meaning the next 16 characters in the output buffer are to be THE␣PRESSURE␣IS␣,
F4.1	meaning the next variable (X) is to be printed in F4.1 format,
12H LBS./IN.SQ.	meaning that the next 12 characters are to be ␣LBS./IN.SQ.

As you can imagine, Hollerith fields are very important and useful in printing messages along with the output. Instead of storing messages in variables or arrays with CHAR pseudo-ops or DATA statements, we may now print messages without further bother.

Some compilers allow Hollerith fields in FØRMAT statements to be delimited by quotation marks or other marks, rather than in the standard way. The advantage of doing this is that the counting of the number of characters in a message is eliminated. We can rewrite the previous FØRMAT statement like this in such a case:

```
56    FØRMAT (2X, 'THE PRESSURE IS ', F4.1, ' LBS./IN.SQ.')
```

Make sure that your compiler allows this, and find out what the delimiters are (they aren't always single quotes).

The carriage control characters we have previously mentioned are as follows:

> blank   print on next line,
> zero   print two lines down (skip a line),
> one   print at top of next page.

Of course, any means you have of getting a carriage control character into the first character position in the output buffer is valid. The usual method for getting a zero or one there is by writing

```
1H0    or    1H1    or    '0'    or    '1'
```

If we wanted that previous line printed at the top of a new page, we could write

```
56    FØRMAT( 1H1, 1X, 16HTHE PRESSURE IS , F4.1, 12H LBS./IN.SQ. )
```

We can even write:

```
56    FØRMAT( 18H1 THE PRESSURE IS , F4.1, 12H LBS./IN.SQ. )
```

Do you know why this works? The first 18 characters in the output buffer are 1␣THE␣PRESSURE␣IS␣, and all but the first (the 1) are printed. The 1 is used for carriage control.

We can use Hollerith fields to print messages *without* reference to variables. For instance,

```
      PRINT 100
100   FØRMAT(1H1, 5X, 4HNAME, 10X, 4HRANK, 5X, 4HS.N.)
```

prints, at the top of a new page (why?), the following:

Note that the PRINT statement has no commas at all.

Let's say we had the following print statement:

```
      PRINT 47, A, B, C, D, E, F, G, H
 47    FØRMAT (4X, F6.3, 2X, F6.3, 2X, F6.3, 2X, F6.3, 2X, F6.3,
  1    2X, F6.3, 2X, F6.3, 2X, F6.3)
```

The FØRMAT statement is rather long but very repetitive. This statement can also be written

```
      47    FØRMAT ( 4X, 8(F6.3, 2X))
```

The 8 is a replication number, and whatever follows is to be repeated eight times. Similarly,

```
      92    FØRMAT (I10,I10,I10,I10,I10)
```

can be written

```
      92    FØRMAT (5I10)
```

Here the 5 is the replication number. This applies to FØRMAT statements for input (READ) as well.

If you wanted to print 10 numbers in a list, you might write

```
           PRINT 1, K1
      1    FØRMAT (3X, I7)
           PRINT 2, K2
      2    FØRMAT (3X, I7)
           PRINT 3, K3
                  :
           PRINT 10, K10
     10    FØRMAT (3X, I7)
```

But since more than one PRINT (or READ) statement may use the SAME FØRMAT statement, you can write

```
           PRINT 1, K1
           PRINT 1, K2
           PRINT 1, K3
                  :
           PRINT 1, K10
      1    FØRMAT (3X, I7)
```

What if you had just computed the pressure and temperature in variables PRESS and TEMP, and you wanted them printed on two lines like the following?

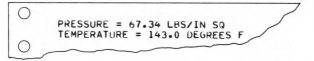

```
PRESSURE = 67.34 LBS/IN SQ
TEMPERATURE = 143.0 DEGREES F
```

Can you do this printing with *one* PRINT and *one* FØRMAT statement? Yes. The character string in a line of print or on a card is known as a **record**. Whenever you want to begin a new record in a FØRMAT statement, you merely use a slash (/). In the above case, it's done like this:

```
      PRINT 12, PRESS, TEMP
  12  FØRMAT (1X, 11HPRESSURE = , F5.2, 10H LBS/IN SQ/1X,
   1    14HTEMPERATURE = , F5.1, 10H DEGREES F)
```

The first slash is part of a Hollerith field, and doesn't count as "end of record"—
it is just printed. The next slash means "print the output buffer up till now and
begin filling it again." Note the new carriage control character after the end-of-
record slash.

Say we wanted to print variable M6, skip seven lines, and then print variable
Q45. We could do this:

```
      PRINT 885, M6, Q45
  885  FØRMAT (3X, I8////////3X, F8.3)
```

Note that there are eight slashes. The first ends the record, so M6 is printed. Each
additional slash causes a new record to be printed. Since each output buffer is
filled with blanks in all character positions not yet filled, each of these records is
printed as a *blank* line. This means seven blank lines are printed, or rather seven
lines are skipped.

Here's another way to do it:

```
  885  FØRMAT (3X, I8, 8(/), 3X, F8.3)
```

The slash may appear in a parenthesized expression for replication, just like any
other FØRMAT expression.

How does FORTRAN accomplish all this? Usually, it's done something like
this: Each time a READ or PRINT statement is encountered, it is translated as a call
to a subprogram. The parameter list for the subprogram might include:

a) the number of variables to be read in or printed out,
b) the addresses of the variables (they are called by name),
c) the address of the FØRMAT statement concerned.

The FØRMAT statements are stored as sequences of characters, and those characters
are *interpreted* at execution time by the I/O subprograms. For instance, if we write

```
      PRINT 25, A, B, C
  25  FØRMAT (10X,A3,F7.2,E10.1)
```

We might see a translation like this:

```
        JSUB    PRINT
        SET     +00003      Number of variables involved.  ⎫
        ADRS    A        ⎫                                  ⎪
        ADRS    B        ⎬ Variables passed by name.        ⎬ Parameter
        ADRS    C        ⎭                                  ⎪  list
        ADRS    ST25        Location of FØRMAT specs.      ⎭
          ⋮
ST25    CHAR    19          (10X,A3,F7.2,E10.1)
```

Special input/output subprograms take care of the actual I/O. However, the processes of reading from the card reader and printing on the line printer are but special cases of the general processes of **reading** and **writing**. *Reading* means placing information into the main memory from some external storage medium (punched cards, magnetic tape, disk, teletypewriter) and *writing* means placing information from the memory onto some external medium (paper, magnetic tape, cathode-ray tube display, punched cards, etc.). If you are interested in reading from (or writing onto) some device other than the card reader (and line printer), you may do so in FORTRAN by using a general form of the READ and PRINT statements. The general READ and WRITE statements are

```
READ (5, 100) ALPHA, BETA, GAMMA
WRITE(6, 200) ALPHA, BETA, GAMMA
```

In the parentheses following the word READ (or WRITE) are two numbers. The first (5 or 6 above) is the *unit* designation. Frequently 5 means card reader and 6 means line printer, but different facilities might have different unit designations. For instance, 7 might mean the card punch, and when you "write" on the card punch, each record is punched onto one card. Obviously, such a record has 80 characters. Consult your local facility for more information as to unit designations. Other I/O instructions are available in FORTRAN, such as the REWIND statement which is used in conjunction with a tape drive. After you've written on a tape, you might want the tape rewound. The second number in the parentheses is, of course, the FØRMAT statement identification.

In longer programs, many programmers place *all* the FØRMAT statements in the entire program either at the very beginning of the program after the declarations, or at the very end, immediately preceding the END statement. This makes the program more readable, and the FØRMAT statements do not interfere with the "flow" of the logic. Here's an example of a program which reads three numbers, finds their sum, and prints the numbers and the sum:

```
      INTEGER J, K, L, M
      READ 1, J, K, L
      M = J + K + L
      PRINT 2, J, K, L
      PRINT 3, M
      STØP
   2  FØRMAT(17H1THE NUMBERS ARE , 5X, I6/22X, I6/22X, I6)
   1  FØRMAT(I6/I6/I6)
   3  FØRMAT(11H0THE SUM IS, 9X, I8)
      END
```

Note that all the FØRMAT statements are at the end. They are in no apparent order, nor need they be. Note also the carriage control characters in the print FØRMATS (1 for new page, 0 for skip line). Did you notice that the output is formatted like this:

```
   THE NUMBERS ARE           780
                            1004
                             -56

   THE SUM IS               1728
```

Sometimes we must punch mountains of data onto data cards. If we happen to be punching numbers which must be read as reals (floating point), then much time can be saved in keypunching by leaving out the decimal point. For instance, assume that we have to punch 400 cards, each having 20 numbers of the form **xx.xx** (e.g. 44.78). If we required our keypuncher to punch merely **xxxx** (e.g. 4478) in a field of width 4, he or she saves 20 percent in keypunch time. How do we read 4478 and have it converted to floating-point 44.78? By reading with F-specification F4.2. This means "read a field of width 4, and place the decimal point 2 from the right." We've been reading with specifications like F4.0 or F10.0 until now. The digit beyond the decimal point in the FØRMAT specification is ignored *unless* there is no decimal point on the data card field. Thus the card

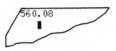

when read in F6.0 format, translates to real 560.08, but the card

when read in F5.0 format, translates to real 56008. When the second card is read in F5.3 format, it translates to 56.008. This works for E-format as well. The card

when read in E10.4 format, results in −1.0682E+16 (decimal point moved four to the left from the right end of the mantissa).

Input and output is rather complex in FORTRAN as it is in any other language. Many of the rules seem (and are) arbitrary, and a myriad of detail pervades. The presentation here has been concentrated and is incomplete. You have enough information to do some rather sophisticated I/O, but you do need lots of practice. More will be said about I/O in Chapter 10, after arrays have been introduced.

Exercises 9.4

1. Assume that the real variables   contain floating-point numbers

V	5.729
W	-370216.4
X	100.0
Y	4.09×10^{-17}
Z	$-44.09 \times 10^{+23}$

and integer variables   contain integers

I	100
J	0
K	-43
L	20007

and variables   contain character strings

A	E␣N␣␣...
B	UMB␣␣...
C	R␣IS␣...

what would the following PRINT statements print?

a)   PRINT 5, V, W, X
     5   FØRMAT(3E11.3)

b)   PRINT 16, I, V, J, W, K, X
    16   FØRMAT(3(5X, I3, 4X, F10.2/))

c)   PRINT 22, J, L
    22   FØRMAT(I1, I5)

d)   PRINT 100, A, B, C, K
   100   FØRMAT(3X, 2HTH, A3, A3, 1HE, A5, I3)

e)   PRINT 3, Y, Z
     3   FØRMAT(10X, F20.10, F20.10)

f)   PRINT 4, Y, Z
     4   FØRMAT(10H1ANSWERS—, 6X, 2E12.3)

g)   PRINT 11, I,J, K, L
    11   FØRMAT(4(I6))

h)   PRINT 12, I, J, K, L
    12   FØRMAT(4(I6/))

i)   PRINT 9
     9   FØRMAT(17H10 LITTLE INDIANS)

j)   PRINT 58, I, X
    58   FØRMAT(16H HUNDRED FIXED (, I3, 16H) AND FLØATING (, F5.1,
     1   2H).)

k)   PRINT 60, I, J, L
    60   FØRMAT(I3, I1, I5)

2. What would be the advantage of adding to FORTRAN a facility for accessing the contents of the input buffer *after* a READ statement has already been executed?

3. Give two instances which show that FORTRAN programs are, in general, not independent of the compilers and machines used in running them—namely, that different results, and even syntax errors might occur if you switch your program to another computer. [*Hint:* Think of (a) the number of characters in a word, and (b) the precision of number representation, i.e., the number of digits which can be stored in a word.]

4. Each of the READ statements below is used to read the card

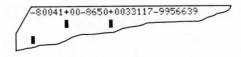
-80041+00-8650+0033117-9956639

In each case, what integers are contained in locations L, LL, LLL, and LLLL after the execution of the READ statement?

a)   READ 1, L, LL, LLL, LLLL
   1 FØRMAT(I6, 2I3, 6X, I1)

b)   READ 2, LLLL,LLL,LL,L
   2 FØRMAT(4I2)

c)   READ 3, LLL, L, LL, LLLL
   3 FØRMAT(I5, 3X, I1, I5, 8X, I8)

d)   READ 4, L, LLL, LL, LLLL
   4 FØRMAT(22X, 4I2)

5. Each of the following READ statements is used to read the card

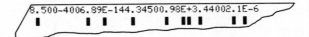
8.500-4006.89E-144.34500.98E+3.44002.1E-6

In each case, what do the real variables A, B, C, and D contain after the execution of the READ statement? Be sure to specify floating-point number or character. Assume 10 characters per word in this particular computer.

a)   READ 5, A, B, C, D
   5 FØRMAT (F5.0, E12.0, F6.0, E7.0)

b)   READ 6, D, C, B, A
   6 FØRMAT (30X, 4F2.0)

c)   READ 7, A, D, C, B
   7 FØRMAT (4(4X, A6))

d)   READ 8, A, C, B, D
   8 FØRMAT (2X, F3.2, F5.4, A5, 4X, F5.1)

e)   READ 9, A, B, D, C
   9 FØRMAT (10X, A6, F8.0, F3.0, A10)

f)   READ 10, B, A, C, D
  10 FØRMAT (A10, E6.0, 2F1.1)

6. Write and submit a FORTRAN program which reads five integers from a single data card and then prints them on a single line and also in a column. Choose your own format.

7. Write and submit a FORTRAN program which reads five reals from a single data card and then prints them: (a) in F-format; (b) in E-format.

8. Write and submit a FORTRAN program which reads three integers from a single data card, adds them together, and then prints the integers and the sum. Use a statement of the form

$$M = I + K + J$$

to add the integers together. Print messages with your output, such as THE NUMBERS ARE and THEIR SUM IS in the appropriate places.

9. Write and submit a FORTRAN program which reads the number −832.0054962 from a single data card, and then prints it in various formats. Try printing with various precisions (numbers of significant digits) by varying the E- or F-format.

10. Write and submit a FORTRAN program which reads a character string of at least 20 characters into a number of variables, and then prints the string at the top of a new page. Experiment with printing portions of the character string as well.

9.5 ARITHMETIC EXPRESSIONS AND ASSIGNMENT

Arithmetic expressions are expressions from which we can compute **values**. For instance, $a + b$ is such an expression. In order to **evaluate** $a + b$, we must know the value of both a and b. If a is 5 and b is 7, then

$$a + b = 5 + 7 = 12,$$

and the value of the expression is 12. Here are some other arithmetic expressions:

$$x + 3, \qquad s - t, \qquad (x^y)^3,$$

$$mx + b, \qquad \sqrt{1 - \frac{a + b}{a - b}}, \qquad 3.49a + \frac{4.2b}{1 + 3c/4d} - 5.2.$$

The "unknowns" are called **variables**. If we know the values of the variables in an expression, we can evaluate it.

Arithmetic expressions appear frequently in FORTRAN. They are written somewhat differently from the arithmetic expressions we encounter in mathematics. All the **operators** must appear explicitly. (An operator is something like $+$ or $-$.) In mathematical expressions we sometimes omit operators; for instance, ab means *a times b*. In FORTRAN we must write

$$A * B$$

where the asterisk is the multiplication operator. Note also that only capitals are used, since lower-case characters are not available. Also, x^y is written X ** Y in FORTRAN, where ** indicates exponentiation.

The FORTRAN operators are

+	addition
−	subtraction, negation
*	multiplication
/	division
**	exponentiation (raising to a power) •

The variables are merely locations which contain numbers, so they are named by any FORTRAN name, such as RADIØ or U45X or J3.

Here are some FORTRAN arithmetic expressions:

$$
\begin{array}{ccc}
\text{AXEL} & - & \text{BAKER} \\
\text{X} & + & \text{Z} \\
\text{II} & / & \text{JJ} \\
\text{MICKEY} & ** & \text{MØUSE} \\
3.7 & * & \text{HARRY}
\end{array}
$$

Parentheses are frequently used in longer FORTRAN expressions in order to preserve the order in which operations are performed. For example, it is clear in the expression

$$\frac{r}{s + 3.5},$$

that the addition should precede the division. In FORTRAN we would write this expression

$$R \ / \ (S + 3.5)$$

in order to ensure that the expression not be incorrectly interpreted as

$$\frac{r}{s} + 3.5$$

Here's another example of parenthesization. Can you write this expression correctly in FORTRAN?

$$\frac{a}{b + \dfrac{p}{r}}$$

Did you write A / (B + (P/R))? If you write just A/B+P/R, then it's not clear whether you mean

$$\frac{a}{b} + \frac{p}{r} \quad \text{or} \quad \frac{a}{b + \dfrac{p}{r}} \quad \text{or} \quad \frac{\left(\dfrac{a}{b + p}\right)}{r} \quad \text{or} \quad \frac{a}{\left(\dfrac{b + p}{r}\right)}$$

A FORTRAN arithmetic expression is translated to a sequence of (machine language) instructions for evaluating the expression. For example I + J might be translated (by the FORTRAN compiler) to FACET assembly language like this:

```
LDAC    I
ADD     J
```

and A/(B + (P/R)) might be translated to

```
LDAC    P
FDIV    R
FADD    B
STAC    TEMP
LDAC    A
FDIV    TEMP
```

After you convince yourself that the previous translation is correct in some sense, note the following points:

1. The value of the expression is in the accumulator at the end of the computation.
2. Temporary locations are sometimes necessary. They are used to store intermediate results, i.e., the values of **sub-expressions**. In the example, TEMP was used to store the value of the sub-expression B + (P/R).
3. The compiler has to know whether the arithmetic operations are to be performed in fixed-point or floating-point arithmetic. In evaluating I + J, the ADD instruction was used. FADD was used in the second example, as well as other floating-point operations.

The operators (+, −, *, /, **) can stand for different operations, depending on the data type of the variables, which are called **operands**. If location (variable) JIM contains, for instance, +51200 and location PETE contains +50400, then

```
JIM − PETE
```

can mean different things in the translation. If we had declared

```
INTEGER JIM, PETE
```

then the translation would be

```
LDAC    JIM
SUB     PETE
```

and the value in the accumulator would be (integer) 800 or +00800. If, on the other hand, we had declared

```
REAL JIM, PETE
```

then the translation would be

```
LDAC    JIM
FSUB    PETE
```

and the value would be 2.00 − 0.40 or 1.60 or +51160.

Now we shall give a few more examples of arithmetic expressions and their FACET assembly language translations. In these examples, and elsewhere in the chapter, variables beginning with the letters I, J, K, L, M, N will be considered integer, and others real, unless otherwise stated.

FORTRAN arithmetic expression	*FACET assembly language translation*	
I + (J*(K/L))	LDAC	K
	DIV	L
	MLS	J
	ADD	I
(A + B) * (C + D)	LDAC	A
	FADD	B
	STAC	TEMP
	LDAC	C
	FADD	D
	FMUL	TEMP
(TØMMY*CARL)+((FRED/BØB)*(SAM–STEVE))	LDAC	TØMMY
	FMUL	CARL
	STAC	TEMP1
	LDAC	FRED
	FDIV	BØB
	STAC	TEMP2
	LDAC	SAM
	FSUB	STEVE
	FMUL	TEMP2
	FADD	TEMP1

Have you noticed that each expression we have written so far consisted of variables of a *single* data type, either real or integer? Many FORTRAN compilers require this. Many others, however, allow mixing of data types in expressions; such expressions are called **mixed-mode** expressions. When a compiler (allowing mixed modes) encounters such an expression, it must translate correctly. This means it must make sure numbers appear in their appropriate representation for arithmetic operations. Here's an example:

$$I + A$$

Remember our convention—I is of data type integer, whereas A is real. If I is 52,200 (+52200) and A is −3,400 (−54340), then the translation

```
LDAC    I
ADD     A
```

is wrong. It gives us 52200 − 54340, or −02140 in the accumulator. This one,

```
LDAC    I
FADD    A
```

is also wrong. It results in 20.0 − 3,400 = −3,380, or –53338 in the accumulator. The correct translation is achieved by converting the value of I, once it is in the accumulator, to floating point. This is done with the assistance of a subprogram called FLØAT. FLØAT operates in different ways on different machines, but let's assume, for the moment, that it merely converts the word in the accumulator from fixed point to floating point, leaving the result in the accumulator. Then I + A could be translated like this:

```
LDAC    I          52,200 (+52200) in AC
JSUB    FLØAT      0.522 × 10⁵ (+55522) in AC
FADD    A          0.488 × 10⁵ (+55488) in AC
```

Now the (floating-point, real) result, 48,800, in the accumulator is correct. Mixed-mode FORTRAN compilers convert to floating point (real) only when the operands of an arithmetic operator are of different types. Thus the expression

$$(A*B) - (I/J)$$

is translated

```
LDAC    A
FMUL    B
STAC    TEMP1      A*B
LDAC    I
DIV     J          I/J (fixed point)
JSUB    FLØAT      Result floated
STAC    TEMP2
LDAC    TEMP1      A*B
FSUB    TEMP2      (A*B) − (I/J)
```

If A is 2.6, B is 1.5, I is 8 and J is 3, then the result is

$$(2.6)(1.5) - \frac{8}{3} = 3.9 - 2 = 1.9$$

fixed-point division!

The FLØAT operation is performed only when mixed data types occur during the evaluation. Following are two more examples; see if you can do the translation without looking at the columns on the right

$$(X * I) + J$$

```
LDAC    I
JSUB    FLØAT
FMUL    X
STAC    TEMP
LDAC    J
JSUB    FLØAT
FADD    TEMP
```

```
A − ((I + J) + C)    LDAC    I
                     ADD     J
                     JSUB    FLØAT
                     FADD    C
                     STAC    TEMP
                     LDAC    A
                     FSUB    TEMP
```

Constants may also be used in arithmetic expressions. A constant is a fixed- or floating-point number. When we want to write $3m + 4$ in FORTRAN, we write

$$(3*M) + 4$$

The compiler takes care of the rest. There are locations set up to contain the constants 3 and 4, and the translation might look like this:

```
            LDAC    CØNST1
            MLS     M
            ADD     CØNST2
              ⋮
CØNST1      SET     +00003
CØNST2      SET     +00004
```

Similarly, for the expression $0.00517(x + y)$ we could write

$$.00517 * (X + Y)$$

and get the translation

```
            LDAC    X
            FADD    Y
            FMUL    CØNST1
              ⋮
CØNST1      FSET    +.517E−02
```

The compiler differentiates between fixed- and floating-point constants by the presence or absence of the decimal point (dot). These are fixed-point constants:

```
        3           0
       15          43
   400000      +00001
       −1         −12
      444           2
```

These are floating-point constants:

```
    .004            4.9E−3
  −95.            −7000.E2
    4.32107         .000112E+14
−80241.0          73.85E+12
    0.              0.0E+00
     .0       −100000000.E−14
```

Note that an exponent part (E-notation) is optional and usually used for very large or very small numbers.

It is wise to use the constant of the appropriate data type in expressions. For example, if we write

$$(2 * X) + Y$$

then the compiler might well translate this to

```
         LDAC    CØNST1
         JSUB    FLØAT      convert from +00002 to +51200
         FMUL    X
         FADD    Y
            ⋮
CØNST1   SET     +00002
```

(although cleverly constructed compilers often detect and correct such ineffi-ciencies). On the other hand, if we had written (2.0 * X) + Y we would be assured of a compilation something like this:

```
         LDAC    CØNST1
         FMUL    X
         FADD    Y
            ⋮
CØNST1   FSET    +.200E+01
```

If your compiler doesn't allow mixed modes, you cannot mix integer constants with real variables, and you *must* write (2.0 * X) + Y.

There is one exception to mixing data types. *Every* compiler allows real variables and expressions to be raised to integer powers, like this:

$$X ** I \qquad\qquad \text{for} \qquad x^i$$

$$(A/B) ** (M + (2*N)) \qquad \text{for} \qquad \left(\frac{a}{b}\right)^{m+2n}$$

Only reals, however, may be raised to real powers:

$$GEØRGE ** XAVIER$$
$$(EGGS - SALT) ** 3.72$$

This is because raising to an integer power often is translated as repeated multi-plication:

```
W ** 2          LDAC    W
                FMUL    W

NANCY ** 3      LDAC    NANCY
                MLS     NANCY
                MLS     NANCY
```

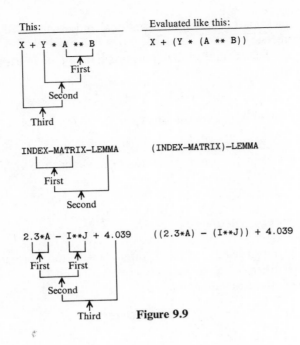

Figure 9.9

Whereas raising to a real power is usually implemented by logarithms:

$$x^y = \text{antilog } (y \log x).$$

Sub-expressions need not be parenthesized in FORTRAN. However, when they are not, the compiler performs the grouping according to predetermined rules. We can frequently avoid using parentheses by being familiar with the following rules:

1. First, perform all exponentiation.†
2. Next, perform all multiplication and division, from left to right.
3. Finally, perform all addition and subtraction, from left to right.

Some examples are shown in Fig. 9.9. Note in the last example that two operations (multiplication and exponentiation) are both at the "first level" of evaluation, since their order is immaterial. Parenthesized sub-expressions are always completely evaluated before being combined with other operands (Fig. 9.10).

Note how a parenthesis pair forms a sub-expression which must be entirely evaluated in order to produce its value. This value can be used as an operand for

---

† Do not use expressions such as K**L**M unless you are sure of the sequence in which the operations will be performed by your compiler. Parenthesize either as (K**L)**M or K**(L**M). See exercise 8.

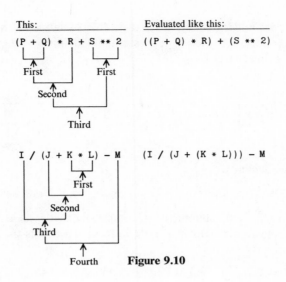

Figure 9.10

some operator *outside* the sub-expression, as in

$$A + (\ldots) \qquad or \qquad (\ldots)/X$$

For this reason, evaluation of expressions usually starts with the innermost parenthesis pair.

The **unary** minus sign is a minus sign used to negate (or change the algebraic sign of) an expression. This negation is performed after exponentiation but before multiplication and division. Thus

$$-A \;**\; 2 \qquad \text{is evaluated as} \qquad -(A**2)$$

but

$$-3.2 \;*\; B \qquad \text{is evaluated as} \qquad (-3.2) \;*\; B$$

Care must be taken in using this operator, since there is a FORTRAN rule stating that two operators may not appear in succession. So I $*$ – J is invalid and must be written

$$I \;*\; (-J)$$

The **arithmetic assignment** statement is a FORTRAN statement used for changing the value of a variable or location. It is written simply as a variable name, followed by an equals sign (=), followed by an arithmetic expression. Here are some examples:

```
I = I + 1
ANSWER = RATE * TIME + DIST
ALPHA = BETA ** 2 - 3*(JILL + TIM/FRANK3)
```

The equals sign does not mean "equals;" it means "assign value of expression on the right to the variable on the left." It is essentially identical to the left arrow (←). Recall that in our flowcharts we write

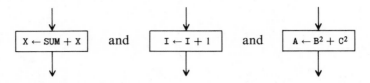

$$X \leftarrow SUM + X \quad \text{and} \quad I \leftarrow I + 1 \quad \text{and} \quad A \leftarrow B^2 + C^2$$

In FORTRAN we would write

X = SUM+X   and   I=I+1   and   A = B**2 + C**2

The arithmetic assignment statement is compiled exactly as is the arithmetic expression, with one additional instruction, STAC A (where A is the variable on the left). For instance

I = I+J	might be compiled as	LDAC	I
		ADD	J
		STAC	I
A = B*C+D	might be compiled as	LDAC	B
		FMUL	C
		FADD	D
		STAC	A

Of course, the original value of the assignment variable is lost. However, this original value may be used in computing the new value, as is obvious in the first illustration above (I = I + J).

Two very simple arithmetic expressions have been omitted from the discussion so far. They are

1) the single variable (such as I, X23, CØN, DEGREE);
2) the single constant (such as 5, 3.7, −4.2E+12, 0.0).

Such an expression rarely needs to be evaluated. The required value is already stored in the location either named by the variable name or denoted by the constant. So we can have assignment statements such as

I = 3   A = 5.7   TEX = GAMMA   MM = INCH

The first one is compiled like this:

```
              LDAC    CØNST
              STAC    I
                :
      CØNST   SET     +00003
```

Did this question occur to you: What happens in an arithmetic assignment statement when the expression to the right of the equals sign is of a different data type from the variable to the left? The answer is: FORTRAN takes care of the conversion. Thus, when we write A = I*J, we might expect compilation like this:

```
LDAC    I
MLS     J
JSUB    FLØAT      Convert result to floating point.
STAC    A
```

Similarly, FORTRAN employs another subprogram, called IFIX, for conversion from floating-point to fixed-point (real to integer) representation. Let's assume that in FACET this subprogram converts the contents of the accumulator from real to integer. In this case I = X/Y might be compiled as

```
LDAC    X
FDIV    Y
JSUB    IFIX      Convert result to fixed point.
STAC    I
```

The IFIX subprogram truncates the fraction portion of a floating-point number. In FACET, this would mean that

+51123 (1.23)	becomes	+00001 (1)
+52507 (50.7)	becomes	+00050 (50)
−52666 (−66.6)	becomes	−00066 (−66)

This conversion "across the equals sign" works in all compilers, regardless of whether or not mixed modes are allowed. "Mixed modes" refers only to mixing of data types *within* an arithmetic expression.

This conversion capability is important in compilers not accepting mixed modes. How, for instance, can we say X = I + A if the compiler does not accept I + A as a valid expression? We can employ an extra real variable, say Y, and convert prior to the addition:

$$\left. \begin{array}{l} Y = I \\ X = Y + A \end{array} \right\} \text{no mixed-mode expressions}$$

This would be compiled as:

$$\left. \begin{array}{ll} \text{LDAC} & \text{I} \\ \text{JSUB} & \text{FLØAT} \\ \text{STAC} & \text{Y} \end{array} \right\} Y = I$$

$$\left. \begin{array}{ll} \text{LDAC} & \text{Y} \\ \text{FADD} & \text{A} \\ \text{STAC} & \text{X} \end{array} \right\} X = Y + A$$

Here are some other examples of mixed-mode assignment statements and their counterparts with mixed modes eliminated:

Mixed modes	No mixed modes
I = A ** 2 + I ** 3	X = I I = A ** 2 + X ** 3
QUEST = SEEK*LØØK+FIND/2	SEARCH = LØØK QUEST = SEEK*SEARCH+FIND/2.0

Did you notice in the second example that the integer constant 2 was written as a real 2.0? This wasn't necessary in the first example, since reals may always be raised to integer powers.

Exercises 9.5

1. Write the FORTRAN equivalents for the following arithmetic expressions. Each variable has a single letter name. Assume that mixed mode expressions are permitted by the FORTRAN compiler, and that the naming convention for data types is employed.

   a) $ab + cd$ 　　　　　　　　　　　b) $a(b + c)d$
   c) $a^2 + b^2$ 　　　　　　　　　　　d) $2xy - 3w$
   e) $(3.5i - 4.7jkl)^2$ 　　　　　　　f) $a - b - c^3$
   g) $(x^y)^2$ 　　　　　　　　　　　　h) $(am + bn) - c$
   i) $s^2t^3u^4$ 　　　　　　　　　　　j) $(m + n + g)(p^{2.5})$

   k) $2.7 \times 10^{15} - 7.3 \times 10^{12}(d + j)$ 　　l) $\dfrac{ax + bg}{ay + bx}$

   m) $\dfrac{7.093v - 1.522 \times 10^{-3}w}{x^{(i+3)} + z^{(j-3)}}$

2. Which of the FORTRAN arithmetic expressions in exercise 1 would be considered syntactically incorrect by a compiler which does not allow mixing of data types?

3. Translate the following FORTRAN arithmetic assignment statements to FACET assembly language. Assume that mixed types are acceptable, and that variables beginning with I, J, K, L, M, N are integer, and the others real. Use subprograms IFIX and FLØAT, which presumably convert the contents of the accumulator from floating point to fixed point and from fixed point to floating point, respectively.

   a) I = J + K
   b) I = J + K/L
   c) I = J + K/X
   d) X = J + K/X
   e) X = Y * 3.7 + I ** 2
   f) ABLE = BAKER*(CHARLY + MASØN) - IBEX/JACK
   g) IBEX = JACK*(MASØN + BAKER) - CHARLY/ABLE
   h) BAKER = ABLE*(IBEX + JACK) - CHARLY/MASØN
   i) I = 3
   j) I = 3.0

   k) X = 3

   l) X = 3.0

4. Which of the statements in exercise 3 above are considered syntactically incorrect by compilers which do not allow mixed-data types in arithmetic expressions? Replace each with a sequence of FORTRAN expressions which are valid. For example:

   c) I = J + K/X is invalid, since K/X is a mixed-type sub-expression. You would have to say something like

$$X2 = J$$
$$X3 = K$$
$$I = X2 + X3/X$$

Now the expression to the right of the equals sign contains only real variables.

5. In a certain program, the following declarations and DATA statement appear:

```
INTEGER LBS, INCHES, PØUNDS, FEET, YARDS, MILES
REAL APPLE, PEAR, GRAPE, BANANA, PLUM, MELØN
DATA LBS,APPLE,MELØN,PØUNDS,YARDS,PLUM/2,2.5,-1.3,1,-3,+.3E1/
```

For each of the following assignment statements, determine the value assigned to the variable at the left of the equals sign (also indicate if the value is fixed or floating point).

   a) PEAR = LBS * 2.5/PLUM

   b) GRAPE = LBS/PLUM

   c) MILES = LBS/YARDS

   d) BANANA = (LBS + PØUND)/(MELØN + 0.3)

   e) INCHES = PLUM ** LBS + YARDS/MELØN

   f) FEET = 1.0 * PØUNDS/LBS +0.5

6. What would the following FORTRAN program print if it were submitted with these two data cards:

```
      INTEGER I, J, K, L
      REAL X, Y, A, B
      READ 1, A, B
    1 FØRMAT(A4, 9X, A7)
      READ 2, I, X, J, K, L, Y
    2 FØRMAT(I3, 5X, F2.1, 1X, 2I1, 3X, I2, F2.1)
      L = I - 125 + J * L + J ** K
      I = X
      X = I
      J = X * Y
      L = L + J
      PRINT 3, A, B, A, L
    3 FØRMAT(10X, A4, A7, A4, 3H⌴=⌴, I3)
      STØP
      END
```

7. Find out the largest fixed- and floating-point numbers that can be represented in your computer. Then write a program which:

   a) causes fixed-point overflow by addition or subtraction;
   b) causes fixed-point overflow by multiplication;
   c) causes floating-point overflow.

   Describe how your FORTRAN compiler handles these cases—does it terminate the program? print a warning or error message? What result is retained in each of the cases?

8. Write and submit a FORTRAN program which will help you discover whether your compiler compiles the expression K**L**M as

$$(K**L)**M \quad \text{or as} \quad K**(L**M).$$

9. Write a program which reads a single floating-point number from a data card, prints it, and then computes and prints the fraction part of the number (e.g., if the number is 13.47, the fraction part is .47).

10. Write and submit a FORTRAN program which will help you discover what your compiler does when you convert a large floating-point number to fixed point (i.e., a number which is larger than the largest integer that can be represented in your computer).

11. Write a simplified payroll program. It reads a single data card formatted as follows:

    columns 1–20   name of employee, a character string;
    columns 31–36   gross wage of employee, a real in F-format;
    columns 41–46   health insurance deduction, F-format;
    columns 51–60   the date, a character string.

    The data card might look like this:

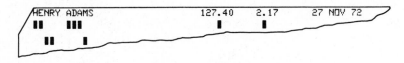

    The program prints a salary check for the employee. His net wage is computed as follows:

$$n = g - (w + h), \quad w = 0.08g,$$

    where g is gross wage, n is net wage, w is withholding tax, and h is health insurance. The output of your program should *look like* a check, possibly something like

```
 ***********************************************************
 *                        ARTHUR SMITH CO.
 *                                              27 NOV 7
 *
 *
 *     PAY TO THE ORDER OF --- HENRY ADAMS
 *
 *     THE SUM OF
 *
```

9.6   DECISIONS AND BRANCHING

Up to this point we have studied a number of FORTRAN statements in some detail. They are as follows:

Executable statements	*Non-executable statements*	
READ	INTEGER	FØRMAT
PRINT	REAL	END
Arithmetic assignment	DATA	

We've also seen and used the (executable) STØP statement,† which is analogous to the HALT instruction in FACET assembly language. We shall now consider branch or transfer statements.

To perform an unconditional branch in FORTRAN we use the GØ TØ statement:

$$\text{GØ TØ 80}$$

Its general form is

$$\text{GØ TØ } n$$

where n is the statement number of some executable statement. That statement will be the next one executed. The GØ TØ statement would be translated to a JUMP instruction in assembly language.

Decisions and their accompanying conditional branching statements are very similar to the decision boxes we use in flowcharts. In a single FORTRAN statement we can say something like

$$\text{IF(A .GT. 23.0) GØ TØ 59}$$

This is the same as the flowchart decision box

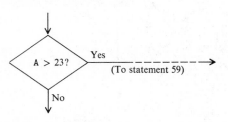

We already know how such a statement is translated to assembly language because we've already written assembly language programs to do this. In this particular case it would be something like

```
LDAC    TWENT3    Constant 23.0
FSUB    A
JNEG    ST59
```

---

†   In most computers STØP is translated to a sequence of instructions causing a transfer of control (a jump) to the operating system, so that the next job may be run.

Let us now take a look at the rules for writing these conditional statements. The specific statement we are discussing is called the **logical** IF statement and consists of three parts:

1) the word IF;

2) a **logical expression** enclosed in parentheses; such an expression has the value of either "true" or "false";

3) some executable FORTRAN statement *other* than an arithmetic or logical IF or a DØ statement† (such as READ, PRINT, STØP, GØ TØ, arithmetic assignment)— this statement is executed if (2) is true and bypassed (ignored) if (2) is false.

Let's look at some examples of logical IF statements, together with their flowchart counterparts:

```
IF(A+B .GT.  C+D) GØ TØ 50
```

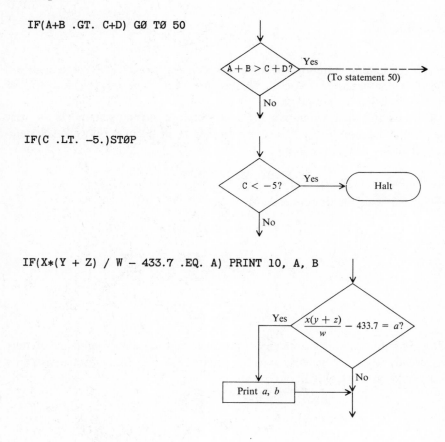

```
IF(C .LT.  −5.)STØP
```

```
IF(X*(Y + Z) / W − 433.7 .EQ. A) PRINT 10, A, B
```

---

† The arithmetic IF statement will be discussed next. The DØ statement is discussed in Chapter 10.

The logical expressions (in parentheses) are formed by placing a **relational operator** between two arithmetic expressions. There are six relational operators in FORTRAN:

FORTRAN	Mathematical symbol	Explanation
.EQ.	$=$	Equal to
.NE.	$\neq$	Not equal to
.GT.	$>$	Greater than
.GE.	$\geq$	Greater than or equal to
.LT.	$<$	Less than
.LE.	$\leq$	Less than or equal to

The following logical expressions show these relational operators in use:

$$3.0 \ .LT. \ X$$
$$4 \ .GT. \ 5$$
$$A+B \ .LE. \ A-B$$
$$A**2 + B**2 \ .EQ. \ C**2$$
$$E \ .EQ. \ M * C**2$$
$$PI \ .EQ. \ 3.14159$$
$$A+B+C+D+E \ .NE. \ (X - Y) * (Z + W)$$

Note that every logical expression has, at any time it is evaluated, the value of true or false. Here the true-false values correspond directly to the Yes-No labels placed on the outgoing arrows of the flowchart decision box.
Instead of writing

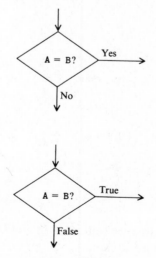

we could have written

Such a true-false value changes during execution. A logical expression is evaluated by computing the values of the two arithmetic expressions and comparing them according to the relational operator. In FACET this would be quite simple—we can easily subtract one arithmetic value from another and determine whether the result is positive or negative, or in some cases zero.

Let's see how some logical IF statements might be translated into FACET assembly language:

IF(A .EQ. B) GØ TØ 10

```
LDAC    A
FSUB    B
JZER    ST10
```

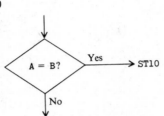

IF((I/J)*J .EQ. I) GØ TØ 222

```
LDAC    I
DIV     J
MLS     J
SUB     I
JZER    ST222
```

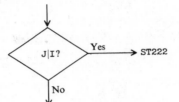

IF(I1 + I2 * I3 ** 2 .LT. JERRY − KAREN)
X   READ 15, X, Y, Z

```
LDAC    I3
MLS     I3
MLS     I2
ADD     I1
STAC    TEMP
LDAC    JERRY
SUB     KAREN
SUB     TEMP
JNEG    NEXT
JZER    NEXT
```
Instructions
reading into
locations X, Y, Z
. . .

NEXT

There is a second conditional statement in FORTRAN—the **arithmetic** IF. In an arithmetic IF, an arithmetic expression is evaluated, and then, depending on whether its value is

1) less than zero,   2) equal to zero,   3) greater than zero,

one of three flow-paths is taken. For example, if a flowchart contained

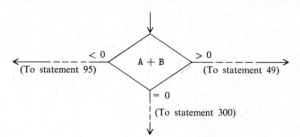

then we would write in FORTRAN

IF (A + B) 95, 300, 49

The arithmetic IF statement consists of

1) the word IF;
2) an arithmetic expression in parentheses;
3) a list of three statement numbers, one of which will be the next statement executed (depending on the value of the arithmetic expression).

Let's look again at

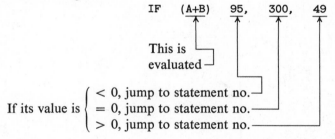

Translation of this statement to FACET assembly language might simply be

```
LDAC    A    ⎫ Compute arithmetic value.
FADD    B    ⎭
JNEG    ST95     Check for value < 0.
JZER    ST300    Check for value = 0.
JPØS    ST49     Check for value > 0 (this is the
                 only remaining possibility, so a
                 JUMP instruction would have
                 been acceptable as well).
```

Here are a few more examples of arithmetic IF statements. Look at the accompanying flowcharts, and see if you can write the FORTRAN statements and the corresponding assembly language instructions.

IF (I/17 + 3)100,101,102

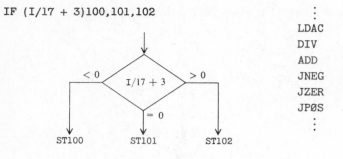

⋮		
LDAC	I	
DIV	SEVNTN	
ADD	THREE	
JNEG	ST100	
JZER	ST101	
JPØS	ST102	
⋮		

IF (X + 4.0) 159,159,59

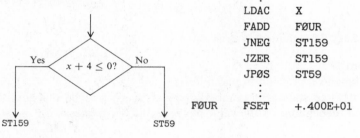

⋮		
LDAC	X	
FADD	FØUR	
JNEG	ST159	
JZER	ST159	
JPØS	ST59	
⋮		
FØUR	FSET	+.400E+01

IF (A)43,72,43

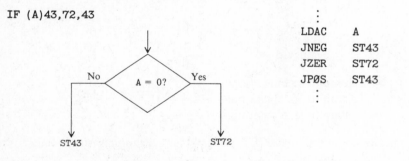

⋮	
LDAC	A
JNEG	ST43
JZER	ST72
JPØS	ST43
⋮	

Note that the same statement number may be used more than once. The FORTRAN compiler is usually quite mechanical, and does not simplify the translation (this is not true in all compilers, some do optimize). The last example could have been translated

```
LDAC    A
JZER    ST72
JUMP    ST43
```

This mechanical nature of compiling can be illustrated by other statements as well. The logical IF statement

IF (3 .GE. 2) STØP

would probably be translated something like

```
          LDAC    THREE
          SUB     TWØ
          JNEG    NEXT
          HALT
NEXT      ...     ...
```

where a translation accomplishing the same thing could have been

```
          HALT
```

Did you notice that the logical IF is used to perform a *two-way branch*? The decision box corresponding to this statement has two out-going paths. The outcome of the test (i.e., the decision) determines which of these paths is taken, the one marked *true* or the one marked *false*:

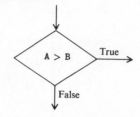

Similarly, the arithmetic IF performs a *three-way branch*. One of three paths is taken, depending on the outcome of the test:

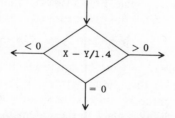

We sometimes come across algorithms which contain decisions with more than three possible outcomes. For example, suppose that a company classifies its employees into six groups, each identified by a number between one and six. If the company's payroll program must carry out a different instruction sequence for each employee classification, we might see a flowchart decision box like this:

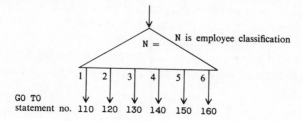

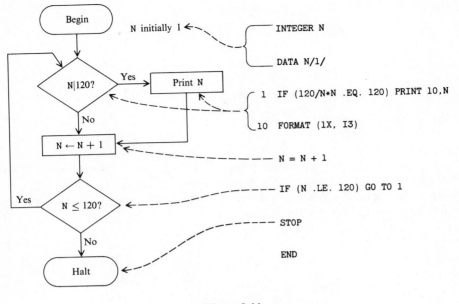

Figure 9.11

This represents a six-way decision box. Such a decision and six-way branch can be implemented by a *sequence* of arithmetic or logical IF statements.† However, it can also be performed by a single FORTRAN statement, the **computed GØ TØ**. This particular six-way branch would be written like this:

$$\text{GØ TØ (110, 120, 130, 140, 150, 160), N}$$

The computed GØ TØ is used, in general, for implementing n-way decisions. An integer variable must be set to a value between 1 and n. A list of n statement numbers enclosed in parentheses follows the words GØ TØ. If the value of the variable is k, then a branch takes place to the statement indicated by the kth statement number in the list. For example, if we execute

$$\text{GØ TØ (1, 15, 93, 1, 1, 600, 34, 112, 112, 34), KLASS}$$

and the value of KLASS is 6, then a jump takes place to statement 600, since 600 is the sixth statement number in the list.

Figure 9.11 shows a program for printing divisors of 120 (see Section 2.8). The program shown in Fig. 9.12 was discussed in Section 3.10. It prints the numbers between 1 and 20 and their squares and cubes.

We shall now discuss a program which demonstrates the use of the arithmetic IF. Let's assume there were three candidates running in a certain election: A,

---

†   See exercise 8.

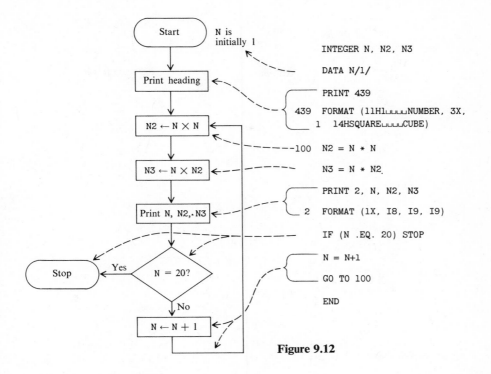

Figure 9.12

B, and *C*. Each vote is punched on a card, in columns 1 through 3, right justified. A vote for candidate *A* is encoded as a -1, for candidate *B* as a 0, and for candidate *C* as a $+1$.

All the cards are then gathered into a deck, and a special card with 100 punched in columns 1 through 3 is placed at the end. We now want to write a FORTRAN program which prints the election results. Each time our program reads a card, we want it to do one of three things, depending on the number read (-1, 0, or $+1$). The arithmetic IF is the logical statement to use for this branch. The flowchart and program are shown in Fig. 9.13.

Nothing has been said about mixing of data types. This is because most FORTRAN compilers these days take care of this problem automatically. Whenever a statement requires an arithmetic operation on two operands of different data types, such as REAL and INTEGER, such compilers will insert instructions or subprogram calls which convert one data type to the other. This is true in logical expressions as well as arithmetic ones. For example, suppose we have the following:

```
REAL X,Y
INTEGER I,J
    :
    :
IF (X+Y .GT. I-J) GØ TØ 27
```

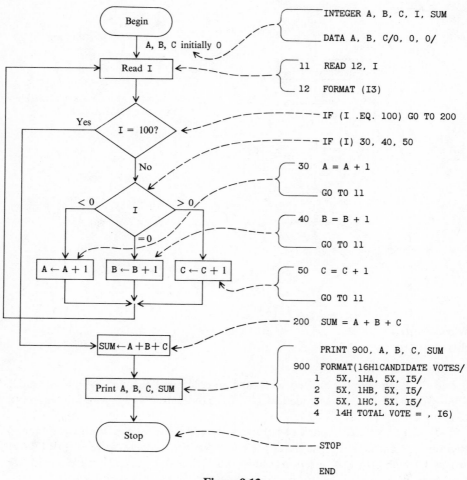

Figure 9.13

Most compilers would translate the logical IF statement as follows:

```
      ⋮
LDAC    X
ADD     Y
STAC    TEMP
LDAC    I
SUB     J
JSUB    FLØAT  ←
FSUB    TEMP
JNEG    ST27
      ⋮
```

{ This is the subprogram which converts the word in the accumulator from fixed- to floating-point representation.

Compilers which do not permit "mixed modes" would require the programmer to convert (by assignment statements):

```
REAL X, Y, Z
INTEGER I, J
    ⋮                                          ⎧ LDAC   I
Z = I - J  ←——————  This is compiled as  ⎨ SUB    J
IF (X+Y .GT. Z) GØ TØ 27                     ⎪ JSUB   FLØAT
                                             ⎩ STAC   Z
```

Note that even a compiler which does not compile mixed mode *expressions* does convert an expression of one data type at the right of an equals sign to the data type of the storage variable at the left. Find out about your compiler with regard to mixing modes before you try writing FORTRAN programs which use both REAL and INTEGER variables and constants in this fashion.

Characters may also be tested with FORTRAN conditional statements. Consider the following: We have just read a data card, and among other information, we have stored the characters in columns 1 and 2 in location Q:

```
        READ 17, Q, ...
17      FØRMAT (A2, 10X, ...)
```

We would now like to check whether those first two columns contained the characters Z+. We can do so as follows:

```
        INTEGER Q, S
        DATA S/2HZ+/
            ⋮
        READ 17, Q,...
17      FØRMAT (A2 ...)
        IF (Q .EQ. S) GØ TØ 100
            ⋮
```

This logical IF is translated to

```
        LDAC    Q
        SUB     S
        JZER    ST100
```

Although we are storing characters in those locations, the arithmetic IF works in equality tests. In FACET, for instance, Z+ is stored as +03643, so only if Q actually contains +03643 (i.e., only if the card read contains Z+ in columns 1 and 2), is the jump to statement 100 executed.

Note that both Q and S are declared integer. Be sure not to mix data types in character equality comparison. Let's say you did, and wrote

```
        IF (I .EQ. A) STØP
```

where I is integer and A real, and where both contained Z+ (or +03643 in FACET).

The FORTRAN compiler might translate this to:

```
       ⋮
LDAC    I
JSUB    FLØAT    (float contents of accumulator)
FSUB    A
JZER    STØP     (STØP is location containing HALT instruction)
       ⋮
```

But when +03643 is floated, it becomes +54364 (0.364×10^4) and the subtraction doesn't yield zero.

Exercises 9.6

1. Translate the following FORTRAN logical IF statements to FACET assembly language (assume that variables beginning with I through N are INTEGER, others REAL):

a) IF (I .LT. J) STØP
b) IF (A/(B + C) .GE. 4.72) GØ TØ 555
c) IF ((X + Y)*(I + J) .NE. K − 5) PRINT 10, L
d) IF (A .NE. B) GØ TØ 2333

2. Translate the following FORTRAN arithmetic IF statements to FACET assembly language (variables beginning with I through N are INTEGER, others REAL):

a) IF (A − 3.2) 44, 44, 55
b) IF (A ** 2 + B ** 3) 973, 247, 1
c) IF (I − (3 + B * Z/3.7)) 490, 70, 490
d) IF (X) 200, 400, 400

3. Translate the following FACET assembly language instruction sequence into FORTRAN IF statements (logical or arithmetic). In each case state what declarations must be made for the variables involved.

```
a)       LDAC    X            b)       LDAC    X
         SUB     Y                     FSUB    Y
         JNEG    ST34                  JZER    NEXT
                                       JUMP    ST687
                              NEXT      ⋮

c)       LDAC    A            d)       LDAC    A
         ADD     B                     FADD    B
         STAC    TEMP                  FSUB    C
         LDAC    W                     FDIV    D
         MLS     X                     JNEG    ST111
         SUB     TEMP                  JZER    ST112
         JZER    ST490                 JUMP    ST113
```

```
e)        LDAC   I              f)        LDAC   HILDA
          SUB    J                        FDIV   FPT3
          STAC   TEMP1                    STAC   TEMP
          LDAC   K                        LDAC   I
          ADD    L                        ADD    J
          STAC   TEMP2                    JSUB   FLØAT
          LDAC   I                        FADD   TEMP
          ADD    J                        STAC   TEMP
          MLS    TEMP2                    LDAC   K
          MLS    TEMP1                    MLS    L
          JSUB   FLØAT                    SUB    THREE
          FSUB   ØNE                      JSUB   FLØAT
          JNEG   ST155                    FSUB   TEMP
            ⋮                             JPØS   ST487
ØNE       FSET   +.100E+01                  ⋮
                                FPT3    FSET   +.430E+01
                                THREE   SET    +00003
                                           ⋮
```

4. Explain how you could write all your FORTRAN programs without ever using the arithmetic IF, i.e., how you could make the logical IF suffice. Make sure your explanation is complete. Demonstrate how the four arithmetic IF statements in exercise 2 above could be rewritten with the logical IF.

5. Explain how you could write all your FORTRAN programs without ever using the logical IF, i.e., how you could make the arithmetic IF suffice. Make sure your explanation is complete. Demonstrate how the four logical IF statements in exercise 1 above could be rewritten with the arithmetic IF.

6. Consider the following:

```
          REAL   R1, R2
          DATA   R1, R2/2HKJ, 2HTB/
            ⋮
10        IF (R1 .EQ. R2) STØP
            ⋮
```

What happens when statement 10 is executed? Consider the problem as though the compiler were translating to FACET machine language. What can you conclude about data types and character storage? You may find it necessary to trace a short FACET program to determine this.

7. Write and submit a FORTRAN program which reads 10 data cards. Each card has a number on it in FACET integer format—a sign and five digits. Have your program determine whether the number is

a) less than 50,
b) between 50 and 70,
c) between 71 and 85,
d) greater than 85.

Accordingly, print each number in one of four columns marked FAILING, PASSING, GØØD, and EXCELLENT.

8. Write a sequence of FORTRAN statements (other than the computed GØ TØ) which could be used to replace this statement in a program:

$$\text{GØ TØ (110, 120, 130, 140, 150, 160), N}$$

Does your solution employ the minimum number of statements possible? If you feel that it does, try to prove or justify your feeling.

9. Below is a list of programming exercises from previous chapters. They defined programs to be written in FACET machine or assembly language. Write one or more of these programs in FORTRAN. You may redefine the problems slightly to have the data and the printout appear in a more "reasonable" form. Try always to include headings and other messages in the FORTRAN programs you write. The exercises are:

2.7(1)	2.8(4)	2.11(2b)	5.5(2)	5.8(3)	6.7(1)
2.7(2)	2.8(5)	3.6(1)	5.5(3)	5.9(1)	6.7(2)
2.7(3)	2.8(7)	5.5(1)	5.6(1)	6.5(2)	6.7(4)

10. Exercise 2.8(9) defines a perfect number and asks you to find the next perfect number after six. Write a FORTRAN program which finds the next *three* perfect numbers after six. Do not try to find more than three! (Why?)

11. Design a payroll problem based on exercise 9.5(11). It should involve a file of employees (rather than a single employee), and it should print information about the entire payroll after the checks are printed (such as total wage paid, total withholding tax, etc.). Write a FORTRAN program to solve this problem.

12. You will receive a data deck of 25 cards, each containing a four-letter word punched in columns 1 through 4. Write a FORTRAN program which reads the data, prints them in a column, and prints, next to each word, the number of *different* letters in it. For example:

$$
\begin{array}{ll}
\text{PACK} & 4 \\
\text{DEED} & 2 \\
\text{KICK} & 3
\end{array}
$$

13. In each part of this exercise below, state the value of variable J immediately after the execution of the sequence of FORTRAN statements. Assume data types according to the implicit naming scheme. For example, in the sequence

$$
\begin{array}{l}
\text{X} = 7.8 \\
\text{J} = \text{X}
\end{array}
$$

J would have the value 7, since the fraction portion of a floating-point number is truncated by IFIX.

a)   J = 10
      J = 8
      J = 6

b)   K = 5
      J = K + 1/2 + 1/2

c) 1 J = 31
   2 J = J − 3
      IF(J − 14)3,1,2
   3 J = 2**(J/2)

d)   J = 2
      IF(3**2 .GT. 2**3)J = J + 1
      J = J − J − J

e)   J = −5
     5 J = J + 5 − 3*J
        IF(J .LE. 76) GØ TØ 5

f)   J = 14.789 + 1.905

g)   I = 67/178 + 1
        K = 54/I + 7
        L = I + K/I − K
        J = I + K + L/2

h)   J = 3
     6 GØ TØ (1,4,2,3,5),J
     3 J = J + 2
     4 IF(J .GT. 3)GØ TØ 2
     5 J = J + 4
     2 J = J − 1
     1 IF(J .LE. 5)GØ TØ 6

i)   J = 3
        I = 1
     8 J = J*2 + I
        I = I + 15
        IF(I .LE. 46)GØ TØ 8

14. THE FORTRAN statements listed here are not necessarily connected or from the same program. However, they all have something in common. Each has exactly one syntax error. Identify and describe these errors. Assume that mixed modes are allowed.

a)   555   (X) = (Y) + (Z)
b)   DATA A,B,C/9,0.000004,2H$$
c)   READ34 X, X1, X2
d) 2A2   IF(.4 − X*I)1,2,1
e) 47568   GØ TØ 477568
f)   INTEGER GEØRGE, MICHAEL, HARRY
g)   44   A = A*(B +C *(D + E*(F + G*(X + Y)))
h)   1   FØRMAT(3X,I10,F10.3, 4HEQUALS,I6)
i)   20   IF(X**2)STØP
j)   PRINT, 45, I, I
k)   998   A + B = C + D
l)   FØRMAT(///3X)
m)   IF(X.LT.X)END
n)   6   GØ TØ I + 5
o)   IF(A = B)A =B
p)   M .EQ. M + 1

15. In what way is FORTRAN basically different from machine and assembly language? It is more powerful in an obvious way—in one single FORTRAN statement we can say what would take many machine or assembly language instructions. But in another way, it is weaker—there are things we can do in assembly language that we *cannot* do in FORTRAN. What are they? Give an example of a sequence of assembly language instructions which cannot be the translation of a FORTRAN statement or a sequence of FORTRAN statements.

9.7 IN REVIEW

The translation concept employed in assembly language can be extended to higher-level languages. Programming languages have been created for use in general application areas such as business data processing, text manipulation, and mathematical problems. Programmers write their computer programs in these languages. These programs are then translated (compiled) into machine language for execution on a particular computer. Whenever a computer facility has a compiler (translator) for a particular language, programs written in that language may be compiled and run there. High-level languages for which there are many compilers on many computers are machine independent.

FORTRAN is one high-level language in extensive use. Most large computers have FORTRAN compilers. A FORTRAN program consists of a sequence of FORTRAN statements. Each statement is punched onto one card. The statement itself is punched in columns 7–72. Columns 1–5 may contain a statement number, and column 6 is usually blank. When a statement is too long for one card, it can be punched on a sequence of cards. Each card after the first in the sequence is a continuation card and has a character other than blank or zero in column 6. A statement may be punched in any of columns 7–72 since blanks are ignored by the compiler. There are two types of FORTRAN statements, executable and non-executable. Executable statements are translated to machine language instructions, while non-executable statements provide additional information for the compiler.

Variables are machine locations into which data may be placed or read by the program. Constants are machine locations which are loaded with specific numbers or characters; these numbers can be used, but not changed, by the program. Both variables and constants are associated with specific data types, usually real (floating point) or integer (fixed point). Variables are named by names comprised of one-to-six alphameric characters, the first of which is alphabetic.

The executable statements discussed are arithmetic assignment, READ, PRINT, GØ TØ, computed GØ TØ, arithmetic and logical IF, and STØP. The arithmetic assignment statement computes a value of an arithmetic expression and places it into a specified location (assigns a value to a variable). The READ causes one (or more) data card(s) to be read and certain information from the card(s) to be placed into one or more variables. The PRINT causes some information stored in variables to be printed on the line printer. GØ TØ is a jump instruction. The computed GØ TØ is a multiple branch instruction; the next statement executed depends upon the value of an integer variable. The arithmetic IF is a three-way branch, depending on the value of an arithmetic expression (negative, zero, or positive). The logical IF statement consists of a condition and an executable statement. If the condition is met, the statement is executed; otherwise it is bypassed. The STØP statement is equivalent to the assembly language HALT; it terminates execution of the program.

The non-executable statements are INTEGER, REAL, DATA, FØRMAT, and END. INTEGER and REAL are declaration statements. They are used to assign data types to variables used in the program. The DATA statement initializes variables in a manner similar to the SET, FSET, and CHAR pseudo-ops in FACET assembly language. The FØRMAT statement provides information for a READ or PRINT statement. The END statement is the last statement in a program. It informs the compiler that there are no more statements (cards) following.

In order to run a FORTRAN program on a particular computer, one must place some control cards before and after the program. These cards identify the programmer, invoke the FORTRAN compiler, and cause the resulting machine language program to be loaded and executed.

Chapter 10

MORE
FORTRAN

10.1 ARRAYS

We already know that much of our computing power depends upon the use of arrays. Without arrays we could not store sequences of numbers, or manage, sort, and merge files. In fact, most interesting and useful computations require arrays. FORTRAN provides a facility for defining and using arrays.

In FORTRAN, arrays have data types, as do ordinary variables, and they are defined in declaration statements. To construct an array of 10 words named ABC, of type REAL, we write

```
REAL ABC(10)
```

More than one array can be defined in a single declaration statement:

```
REAL Y1(50), Y2(50), YY(100)
```

The size of the array (the number of words or memory registers allocated) is given in parentheses immediately following the array name in the declaration. Array declarations can be interspersed with single variables:

```
REAL RATE, FUEL(8), DAY, BTU(25)
```

And, of course, integer arrays can be similarly defined:

```
INTEGER N(4), CØUNT, CHAR(80), GRADES(1000)
```

In these last two examples we have defined two real arrays named FUEL and BTU, of 8 and 25 locations, respectively, as well as three integer arrays, N, CHAR, and GRADES, of 4, 80, and 1000 locations. In assembly language we would ordinarily do this as follows:

```
RATE    LØC
FUEL    ARAY    008
DAY     LØC
BTU     ARAY    025
N       ARAY    004
  ⋮       ⋮       ⋮
```

Still another statement, the DIMENSIØN **statement**, can be used to define arrays in FORTRAN. This alternative technique provides no type information and is frequently used with the implicit naming scheme of FORTRAN. Thus the two declarations

REAL FUEL(8), BTU(25)

INTEGER N(4), MAX(150)

can be replaced by the single DIMENSIØN statement

DIMENSIØN FUEL(8), BTU(25), N(4), MAX(150)

Data types need not be declared, since the first letter of each name happens to correctly identify the desired data type in each instance. Whenever this is not the case, declarations must also be used. An array may be declared in the declaration and **dimensioned** in the DIMENSIØN statement, as follows:

INTEGER GRADES

DIMENSIØN GRADES(1000)

An array may not be dimensioned more than once. There is no need for uniformity in dimensioning. The following is perfectly adequate:

INTEGER N(4), GRADES

REAL MILL, BTU, FUEL(8)

DIMENSIØN GRADES(1000), MILL(23), BTU(25)

However, if the type declaration statements are used, there is really no need for the DIMENSIØN statement at all. We mention it so that you may recognize it in FOR-TRAN programs you see. Incidentally, *dimensioning* of an array means defining its size.

Recall, now, that during the execution of a program, an instruction could never refer to an entire array at once, but rather to some single element of that array. For example, the instruction:

ADD*   FUEL

meant "add to the accumulator the ith element of array FUEL," where i is in the index register, and the elements of FUEL are

$FUEL_0$, $FUEL_1$, $\ldots$, $FUEL_7$

This is important—because of the way the index register operates, we name array elements from zero to $n - 1$ (if there are n elements). In FORTRAN the **subscripting** is different; the subscripts run from 1 through n. For example, array N has four elements. In assembly language we think of the elements as being

N_0, N_1, N_2, N_3

In FORTRAN they are

N_1, N_2, N_3, N_4

and are written as follows:

N(1)   N(2)   N(3)   N(4)

The array in memory could be depicted as shown in Fig. 10.1.

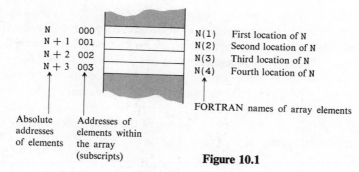

Figure 10.1

The FORTRAN subscripting convention was chosen because of the algebraic subscripting convention:

$$x_1, x_2, x_3, \ldots$$

Note that the FORTRAN subscript appears in parentheses after the array name exactly the same way as the array size. However, only in the declaration does the number refer to the array size or dimension; elsewhere in the program that number is a subscript. Here is an example:

```
REAL G(5), X, Y
    ⋮
X = G(5) + Y
```

The arithmetic assignment statement adds G(5) (or the *fifth* element of array G) to Y, placing the resulting sum in X, but G(5) in the declaration statement dimensions array G, i.e., declares an array of five elements. Do not let this ambiguous notation confuse you.

Integer variables may also be used as subscripts. Assuming that N is an integer array of four locations, what does this instruction sequence do?

```
        K=1
100     N(K)=K+5
        K=K+1
        IF(K .LE. 4) GØ TØ 100
```

Have you correctly deduced that integers 6, 7, 8, and 9 are placed into locations N(1), N(2), N(3), and N(4), respectively?

Of course, these variable subscripts should have a value in the range of valid subscripts for the array to which they refer. For example, array N has valid subscripts 1, 2, 3, and 4. If J is 30 and we write

$$N(J) = 3$$

this is undoubtedly an error. This sort of error is known as a **range error** since the subscript is out of the *range* of valid subscripts for the array. Such errors are difficult to detect, since most compilers cannot find them. A few FORTRAN compilers generate instructions which check subscript values at execution time. These instructions will cause an error message to be printed if an array subscript is out of range. However, most compilers do not make this check. Note that this is an execution time error, since at compilation time the compiler does not "know" the eventual value of the variable subscript (J in our example). If we do write N(J)=3, and J is 30, then frequently 3 is placed into the twenty-ninth location beyond the beginning of the array—surely one of the most difficult errors to debug.

This same error occurs in assembly language as well. If we write

```
              LDX      THIRTY
              STAC*    N
                :
          N   ARAY     004
```

then some location not in the array is similarly affected.

The compiler must make a special adjustment to compensate for the FOR-TRAN array notation, which begins with 1 instead of zero. It would be incorrect to generate for the statement

```
          K = N(I) + 6
```

the instructions

```
              LDX      I
              LDAC*    N
              ADD      SIX
              STAC     K
```

The error is in the effective operand of the instruction

```
              LDAC*    N
```

which loads the wrong array location into the accumulator. To see this, assume that I is 1. We therefore wanted N(1), the first array location. But

```
              LDX   I
```

places 001 into the XR, and when we execute

```
              LDAC*   N
```

the effective operand is N+001, the second location in the array:

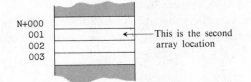

You might first suppose that the FORTRAN compiler handles this problem by always decrementing the index register by one, whenever an array reference is made. The compiled sequence would then be

```
LDX    I
DECX   001
LDAC*  N
ADD    SIX
STAC   K
```

This method would work, but a more efficient technique can be used. The above method requires an extra instruction to be executed every time any reference is made to an array location. The following method makes the necessary modification at compilation time, so that during the execution no additional instructions need be executed. Whenever we reference an array, we change the instruction operand from, say, N to N–001. In our example above, it would be from

```
LDAC*  N    to    LDAC*   N–001
```

Although N–001 is not a valid operand in FACET assembly language, most assembly languages permit such modification. N–001 would mean "the address of N minus 1," or the address of the location immediately preceding N. Now, if I is 1, indicating the first location in array N, and I is loaded into the XR (so XR=001), and we execute

```
LDAC*   N–001
```

then the effective operand is N–001 + 001, or N, which is the correct address of the first location of array N. The correct sequence could then be

```
LDX    I
LDAC*  N–001
ADD    SIX
STAC   K
```

Here's a simple program which employs an array. Assume that we have a data deck of 51 cards. Each card has an integer in columns 1 through 5. We want to print all the integers in the reverse order from which they appear in the deck. Here's the program—see if you follow it:

```
       INTEGER LIST(51), M          Declaration of variables, arrays.
       DATA M/1/                     Intialize M to one.
   30  READ 31, LIST(M)              Read a number into array.
   31  FØRMAT(I5)
       IF(M .EQ. 51) GØ TØ 77        Have we finished reading?
       M=M+1                         Increment index.
       GØ TØ 30
   77  PRINT 14                      Print heading.
   14  FØRMAT (14H1LIST REVERSED)
    6  PRINT 1006, LIST(M)           Print number.
 1006  FØRMAT (3X, I5)
```

```
M=M-1                          Decrement index.
IF(M .EQ. 0)STØP               Check for completion.
GØ TØ 6
END
```

Note that in FORTRAN we never refer to an index register; the compiler takes care of those "details." The program has two loops—one for reading and one for printing. A flowchart for this program might be as shown in Fig. 10.2.

Suppose, now, that we wish to find the **median** of the 51 numbers. The median is that number which has as many numbers greater than it as less than it (in the array or list). Let's further assume that all 51 numbers are different. Then we must find that number which has exactly 25 numbers *less* than it (or greater, if we wish). We already know how to read the numbers into array LIST. Here's a macro-flow-

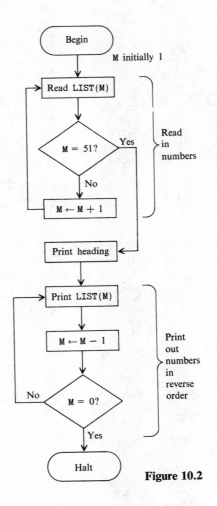

Figure 10.2

chart for finding the median:

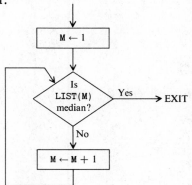

The decision box entails another loop, and this program therefore requires doubly nested loops. The inner loop must check each number in the list against LIST(M) and count those smaller than LIST(M). If there are exactly 25 numbers smaller than LIST(M), it is the median. The inner loop might look like that shown in Fig. 10.3.

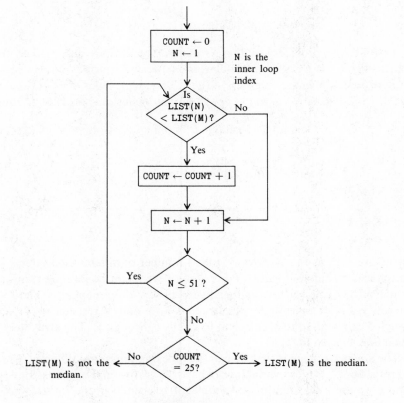

Figure 10.3

After you are convinced that these flowcharts "work," put together one complete flowchart and try to write the FORTRAN program for finding the median. The sequence for reading in the array is the same as in the previous program. The declaration would be:

```
INTEGER LIST(51), M, N, CØUNT
```

Here is the double-loop sequence for finding the median. Did you write a similar one without looking?

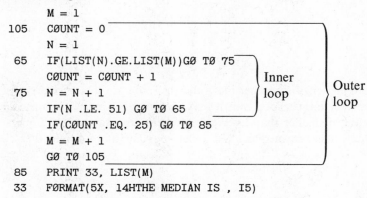

```
          M = 1
    105   CØUNT = 0
          N = 1
     65   IF(LIST(N).GE.LIST(M))GØ TØ 75
          CØUNT = CØUNT + 1
     75   N = N + 1
          IF(N .LE. 51) GØ TØ 65
          IF(CØUNT .EQ. 25) GØ TØ 85
          M = M + 1
          GØ TØ 105
     85   PRINT 33, LIST(M)
     33   FØRMAT(5X, 14HTHE MEDIAN IS , I5)
```

Inner loop · Outer loop

FORTRAN provides another structure for storing data, other than the ordinary array. It is called a **two-dimensional array**, and it has many columns of numbers (words, memory registers) instead of a single column as in the arrays we have discussed so far. We might depict a two-dimensional array as follows:

	Column 1	Column 2	Column 3	Column 4	Column 5
Row 1					
Row 2					
Row 3					

A structure such as this is used to store a number of different data items for *each* of a number of different cases. For example, we might be keeping records on the amount of hay eaten in five consecutive weeks by three elephants. Here we associate row 1, row 2, and row 3 with elephants 1, 2, and 3, respectively. Columns 1 through 5 can be used to correspond to weeks 1 through 5. The array itself will be named HAY, of type REAL.

The advantage here is that we can use indexing to refer to different locations in the array. Separate index variables can be used for rows and columns. For example, suppose we are interested in the amount of hay eaten in the fourth week by the third elephant. This amount is stored in the third row, fourth column of array

HAY, and can be referred to by writing

HAY (3, 4)

row no.⎯⎯⎯⎯⎯⎯ ⎣column no.

This may appear in such statements as

READ 1000, HAY(3,4)   or   CØST = HAY(3,4) * PRICE

or, in fact, any place where a single variable may appear, in arithmetic expressions, I/O statements, DATA statements, and so on. The row and column numbers may be integer variables, as in one-dimensional arrays:

HAY (I, J)

I contains the row number ⎯⎯⎯⎯⎯⎯⎯⎯ ⎣J contains the column number

If we are interested in the total hay eaten by elephant 2 during the entire five weeks, we are asking for the sum of *all* words (numbers) in row 2:

```
      TØTAL = 0.
      I = 1                        ┌──Week number
10    TØTAL = TØTAL + HAY(2, I)    Second row (elephant)
      I = I + 1
      IF (I .LE. 5) GØ TØ 10
```

where HAY and TØTAL are real. If we are interested in the total hay eaten during the third week by all three elephants, we might write:

TØTAL = HAY(1,3) + HAY(2,3) + HAY(3,3)

or we could have used a loop as in the former case. If we want to know the total hay eaten during the second through fourth weeks, inclusive, we could use a double loop (with two indices):

```
      J = 2  ⟵⎯⎯⎯⎯ Start with second week (column)
      TØTAL = 0.
10    I = 1  ⟵⎯⎯⎯⎯ Start with first elephant (row)
20    TØTAL = TØTAL + HAY(I, J)
      I = I + 1
      IF(I .LE. 3) GØ TØ 20
      J = J + 1
      IF(J .LE. 4) GØ TØ 10
```

Outer loop   Inner loop

These two-dimensional arrays are defined in declaration statements, as are the one-dimensional arrays. The number of rows and columns desired appear in the appropriate subscript positions. HAY would be declared:

REAL HAY(3,5)

The statement

INTEGER EVAL(30,7)

declares a two-dimensional array named EVAL, of type INTEGER, and containing 30 rows and 7 columns.

Two-dimensional arrays must be stored in the one-dimensional memory of a computer. FORTRAN stores them by columns, so that the first column is stored first, then the second column, and so on. Array BLT(4,3) with four rows and three columns would be stored as:

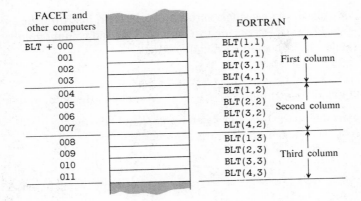

It is part of the job of the compiler to translate a FORTRAN reference to the corresponding machine address. For example, if BLT(3,3) is mentioned, the address BLT+010 must be computed. To obtain 010, first note that (3,3) is in the third column. Therefore there are two columns (the first and second), each four words long, stored ahead of BLT(3,3) in the memory, or $2 \times 4 = 8$ words altogether. Since BLT(3,3) is the third word in its column, there are two more words ahead of it in the memory, the first and second words in that column. Altogether there are $8 + 2 = 10$ words ahead of BLT(3,3) in the stored array. They are BLT+000 through BLT+009, so the address of BLT(3,3) is BLT+010, the eleventh word in the stored array.

In general, if A is a two-dimensional array with R rows, then for an arbitrary element A(I,J), its address within the array (in memory) can be computed as follows:

$$(J-1) * R + (I-1)$$

Thus for BLT(3,3), with R = 4, we get

$$(3 - 1) * 4 + (3 - 1) = 2 \times 4 + 2 = 10$$

and its address in memory is BLT+010. The subtraction in (I-1) can be skipped if one is subtracted from the array location at compile time, as it is in one-dimensional arrays. The statement

    IF(A(I,J) .LT. A(I,K)) GØ TØ 20

might be compiled as follows, assuming that integer RA contains the number of rows in array A:

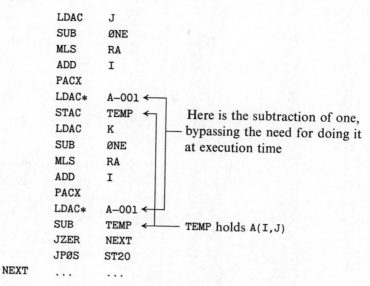

```
            LDAC    J
            SUB     ØNE
            MLS     RA
            ADD     I
            PACX
            LDAC*   A-001
            STAC    TEMP
            LDAC    K
            SUB     ØNE
            MLS     RA
            ADD     I
            PACX
            LDAC*   A-001
            SUB     TEMP
            JZER    NEXT
            JPØS    ST20
     NEXT   ...     ...
```

Here is the subtraction of one, bypassing the need for doing it at execution time

TEMP holds A(I,J)

Now we are about ready to write a more complex program. First, we shall need one more FORTRAN technique. An array name, without any subscript or parenthesized expression following it is an abbreviation for a sequential list of *all* the array elements. Thus, if N is an array of four elements, then N can be used in place of N(1),N(2),N(3),N(4) in a FORTRAN statement, notably in a DATA or I/O statement. For example,

                    DATA N/5,6,9,3/

can be used in place of

                DATA N(1),N(2),N(3),N(4)/5,6,9,3/

and

                    READ 33, I, N, X

can be used in place of

            READ 33, I, N(1), N(2), N(3), N(4), X

This use is applicable only when we want a list of *all* the array elements in their sequential order. The technique also works for two-dimensional arrays, but remember that "sequential order" is by columns, the same order in which the array is stored in the memory. Thus, if IT is an array of two rows and three columns,

                    PRINT 777, IT

is the same as

        PRINT 777, IT(1,1), IT(2,1), IT(1,2), IT(2,2), IT(1,3), IT(2,3)

Now, to our program. Noah has just received a government subsidy for feeding the animals on his ark. The animals are divided into five classes, and each class gets a certain percentage of its feed cost defrayed by the subsidy, according to the following table:

ID	Class	Percent defrayed
V	Very big	67
L	Less big	73
N	Neither big nor small	80
M	More small than big	82
S	Small	91

Since he must keep accurate records to qualify for the subsidy, Noah has a card punched with feed cost information for each pair of animals at the end of each week. The name of the animal is punched in columns 1–20, the size ID in column 25, and the feed cost for the week in dollars and cents in columns 41–48, like this:

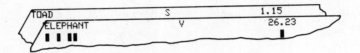

We are fortunate enough to be on board with Noah as his programming staff and are about to write a program which reads the week's cards, prints the information, and then computes and prints:

a) the total cost of feed,
b) the amount covered by subsidy,
c) the amount that must be covered by local contributions [sum (a) less sum (b)].

In order to do this, we shall keep a table in the memory as a two-dimensional array. There will be five rows for the five animal classes, and five columns for ID, percent defrayed, total cost for the week, amount subsidized, and remainder to be raised. We shall initialize this array as follows:

	1	2	3	4	5
1	V	.67	0.0	0.0	0.0
2	L	.73	0.0	0.0	0.0
3	N	.80	0.0	0.0	0.0
4	M	.82	0.0	0.0	0.0
5	S	.91	0.0	0.0	0.0

Noting that this must be a real array, we can write:

```
REAL TABLE(5,5)
DATA TABLE/1HV,1HL,1HN,1HM,1HS,.67,.73,.80,.82,.91, 15*0.0/
```

Recall that TABLE is an abbreviation for TABLE(1,1),TABLE(2,1),... TABLE(5,5). Our program's strategy is as follows: As we read the cards, we note the letter in column 25 of each card and search column one of the table for an identical letter. When we find that letter, say in row I, we add the feed cost onto column three of that row. By the time we have finished processing the cards, column three contains the total feed cost for each animal class. Using the information in columns two and three we can compute columns four (amount subsidized, column 2 times column 3) and five (column 3 minus column 4). Then we print the table. We shall assume that we don't know how many animals there are, so a blank card is placed at the back of the deck. When we are searching for the ID and do not find a match, we shall know that we've hit the end of the deck (since column 25 on that last card will be a blank).

Each time we read a data card, we must read a 20-character animal name. Let's assume our computer can store only four characters per word. Then we'll need five machine words to store the name. We can use a five-word array, called NAME. If we say

```
        READ 1, NAME
    1   FØRMAT(5A4)
```

it has the same effect as

```
    READ 1, NAME(1),NAME(2), NAME(3), NAME(4), NAME(5)
  1 FØRMAT(A4, A4, A4, A4, A4)
```

and if the first 20 columns of the data card read has

then our array would contain

DUCK
—BIL
LED⊔
PLAT
YPUS

The flowchart for our program is shown in Fig. 10.4. Note that the first (upper) loop entails a table search. This is very important in computing. We frequently want to search tables for certain entries, look across the appropriate row to find other entries, etc. Most files can be thought of as tables. Each record in the file is a

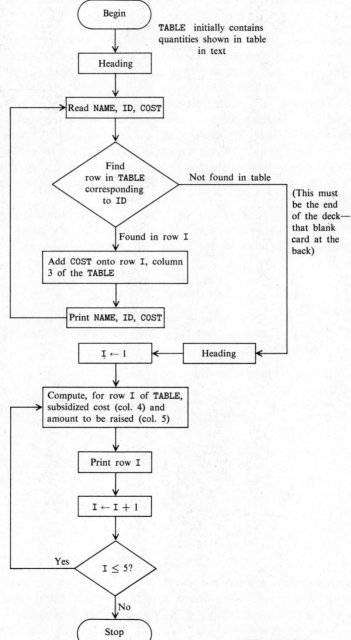

Figure 10.4

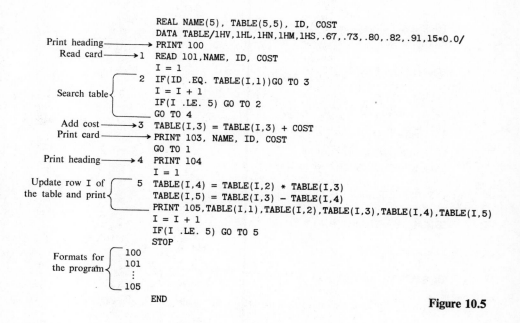

```
                            REAL NAME(5), TABLE(5,5), ID, COST
                            DATA TABLE/1HV,1HL,1HN,1HM,1HS,.67,.73,.80,.82,.91,15*0.0/
      Print heading ───────→ PRINT 100
      Read card ──────→ 1    READ 101,NAME, ID, COST
                            I = 1
                      ⎡  2   IF(ID .EQ. TABLE(I,1))GO TO 3
      Search table  ⎨       I = I + 1
                      ⎢       IF(I .LE. 5) GO TO 2
                      ⎣       GO TO 4
      Add cost ──────→ 3     TABLE(I,3) = TABLE(I,3) + COST
      Print card ─────→       PRINT 103, NAME, ID, COST
                            GO TO 1
      Print heading ──→ 4    PRINT 104
                            I = 1
   Update row I of    ⎡  5   TABLE(I,4) = TABLE(I,2) * TABLE(I,3)
   the table and print⎨       TABLE(I,5) = TABLE(I,3) - TABLE(I,4)
                      ⎣       PRINT 105,TABLE(I,1),TABLE(I,2),TABLE(I,3),TABLE(I,4),TABLE(I,5)
                            I = I + 1
                            IF(I .LE. 5) GO TO 5
                            STOP
   Formats for    ⎡   100
   the program    ⎨   101
                  ⎢    ⋮
                  ⎣   105
                            END
```

Figure 10.5

row in the table, with as many items as necessary. The number of columns in the table is the number of items in the record. The decision box marked "find row in TABLE..." is actually a nested loop for searching the table.

The program is shown in Fig. 10.5. Study it until you understand exactly what each statement does.

Exercises 10.1

1. What does this statement do?

$$XRAY(3) = XRAY(4)*XRAY(2)$$

Write a sequence of FACET assembly language instructions which perform the same task.

2. Following are fragments of eight FORTRAN programs. Each has an error. Find and explain these errors.

a) INTEGER A(5)
   REAL B
   DIMENSIØN B(7), A(5)

b) REAL HØAX(10)
   ⋮
   A = B − HØAX

c) REAL Q1, Q2, Q3, A(7)
   INTEGER AA, QQ, Q3(3)

d) INTEGER PENCIL
   REAL PEN(5)
     ⋮
   PENCIL(1) = PEN(3)

e) INTEGER I(5)
   DATA I,J/21,22,23,24,25,26/
   I(J) = 17.3

f) REAL QUERY(3),ANSWER(7)
   DATA QUERY, ANSWER/2*0.0,4*.2,1.,4*.7/

g) INTEGER SQUARE
   N = 3
   DIMENSIØN SQUARE(N,N)

h) REAL HALT(5,7)
     ⋮
   IF(HALT(I,6.0) .LT. 49.5)STØP

3. Fill in the FØRMAT statements in the program we wrote for Noah (Fig. 10.5).

4. Write a FORTRAN program which will address 27 envelopes. You may assume that each address is punched on a single card. The card contains a four-line address in columns 1–20, 21–40, 41–60, and 61–80. A typical card might be:

Each address line is left-justified in the 20-character field of the data card. Assume that the line printer has been supplied with envelope stock. Each time a "new page" carriage control is executed, a new envelope is inserted. Have your program print the address on four consecutive lines, ten lines from the top of the envelope and indented 30 spaces.

5. Write and submit a FORTRAN program that reads a single data card containing only decimal digits (0, 1, 2, . . . , 9) in all 80 columns and then prints that digit which appears the greatest number of times.

6. Cryptographers have a variety of methods for scrambling messages. Here is one way to scramble a message of no more than 36 characters. Place the message into a 6-by-6 square matrix, beginning with the top row, from left to right. Now "remove" the scrambled message by beginning at the lower left corner and taking successive diagonals, beginning at the upper left and moving to the lower right. Eliminate blanks from the message or replace them with X's. Any confusion should be cleared up by this example: Suppose we want to scramble

HOW DO I LOVE THEE, LET ME COUNT THE WAYS

We begin by placing it in the matrix, with blanks either eliminated or replaced by X's:

```
H  O  W  D  O  I
L  O  V  E  X  T
H  E  E  X  L  E
T  M  E  X  C  O
U  N  T  X  T  H
E  X  W  A  Y  S
```

The scrambled message is now "removed" from the matrix like this:

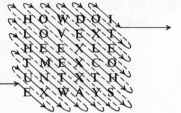

The scrambled text is

EUXTNWHMTALEEXYHOEXTSOVXCHWELODXEOTI

Such scrambled messages can, naturally, be unscrambled by reversing the original procedure. Schemes not unsimilar to this one are actually used by cryptographers. Write a FORTRAN program which reads a scrambled message, *un*scrambles it, and prints the unscrambled text. Have your program begin by reading the 36 characters from a single card (columns 1–36) into an array SCRAMB (one character per machine word), and then place it into two-dimensional array SQUARE. Begin like this:

```
      INTEGER ...
      REAL SCRAMB(36), SQUARE(6,6), ...
      READ 10, SCRAMB
   10 FØRMAT(36A1)
      ⋮
```

7. An integer array of length 100 called RSVP contains 100 integers. Write a sequence of FORTRAN statements which will:

   a) print out the numbers in even positions, i.e. RSVP(2), RSVP(4), ... RSVP(98), RSVP(100), all in a column;
   b) print out the array backwards in a column;
   c) print out the entire array, five numbers to a line;
   d) print out the entire array, four numbers to a line, five double-spaced lines to a page;
   e) print out the entire array in four columns (25 numbers in each column). The first column should contain RSVP(1) through RSVP(25), and so on. The columns should appear next to one another on the page.

8. Write a FORTRAN program which reads six consecutive data cards. Each card (which you will supply) contains an arbitrary string of 80 characters. For each card, the program should determine and print the following information:

   a) the number of asterisks (*) appearing on the card;
   b) the largest number of consecutive commas (,) on the card;

c) whether or not the two-character combination JB appears on the card;

d) the number of appearances of M between the first and second appearance of the character D;

e) the number of appearances of the character I neither immediately preceded nor immediately followed by a period (.).

10.2 DO LOOPS

Loops are so important and their use so frequent in programming, that a special structure is incorporated into FORTRAN to facilitate loop programming. This structure is called the DØ **loop**. Whenever a loop like this appears in a program

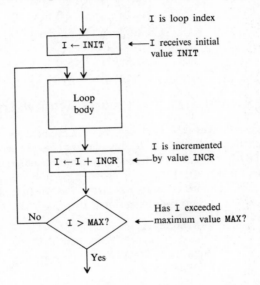

then a DØ loop may be employed in its FORTRAN implementation. Without the DØ loop, the loop illustrated above may be implemented like

```
      I = INIT
40
         Loop body

      I = I + INCR
      IF(I .LE. MAX) GØ TØ 40
```

The same loop may be implemented as a DØ loop like this:

```
      DØ 60 I=INIT,MAX,INCR
         Loop body

60    CØNTINUE
```

Note that there are two new FORTRAN statements involved, the DØ **statement** and the CØNTINUE **statement**. The loop body is "sandwiched" between them. The DØ statement consists of the word DØ, a statement number (indicating the end of the loop), the loop index (an integer variable), an equal sign, and a list of three integer variables (or constants)—the initial, maximum, and increment values. Here is a DØ statement:

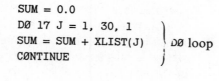

```
DØ 834 JACK = 5, MIX, LIB
Loop index
Initial value
Maximum value
Increment
```

The compiler sets up the instruction sequences for initializing, modifying, and testing the index.

Suppose that we want to add the 30 numbers in a real array XLIST. Then we might write

```
        SUM = 0.0
        DØ 17 J = 1, 30, 1        ⎫
        SUM = SUM + XLIST(J)      ⎬ DØ loop
   17   CØNTINUE                  ⎭
```

which implements

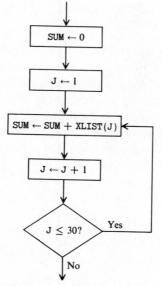

If we are interested in the sum of the alternate numbers in the array, XLIST(1) + XLIST(3) + XLIST(5) + $\cdots$ + XLIST(29), we could then use an increment of two:

```
        SUM = 0.0
        DØ 90 K = 1,29,2          or equivalently
        SUM = SUM + XLIST(K)
   90   CØNTINUE
```

```
        SUM = 0.0
        DØ 90 K=1,30,2
        SUM = SUM+ XLIST(K)
   90   CØNTINUE
```

If we want the sum of the first N elements of the array, the maximum value would be (integer variable) N. Furthermore, the CØNTINUE statement is not always necessary. When the loop always ends with the same executable statement, the DØ statement can name that statement (by its number) as the last in the loop. In effect, the CØNTINUE statement is a "dummy" statement, just placed there to hold the statement number. Here we add those first N numbers in XLIST:

```
          SUM = 0.0
          DØ 114 M = 1,N,1
114       SUM = SUM + XLIST(M)
```

Loops can't always end on that same last statement, so sometimes we need the dummy CØNTINUE statement. Here's an example: We want to find the sum of the positive numbers in XLIST as well as the sum of the negative numbers. Can you see why we *must* have the CØNTINUE statement in this case? Here's the DØ loop:

```
          SUMPØS = 0.0
          SUMNEG = 0.0
          DØ 88 NAP = 1, 30, 1
          IF (XLIST(NAP) .LT. 0.0) GØ TØ 57
          SUMPØS = SUMPØS + XLIST(NAP)
          GØ TØ 88
57        SUMNEG = SUMNEG + XLIST(NAP)
88        CØNTINUE
```

This is a very important point. In order to skip the *remainder* of the loop body, increment the index and continue with the next index value from the beginning of the body, we must jump to the *last* statement in the loop. If we don't have another statement we want executed, we use the dummy CØNTINUE statement. A jump to the DØ statement is incorrect, since that causes the loop to be re-initialized. Further, it is essential to begin a DØ loop by executing the DØ statement, otherwise the loop index may be "undefined", i.e., not initialized. Here is an incorrect way to jump to a DØ loop, together with the correct way:

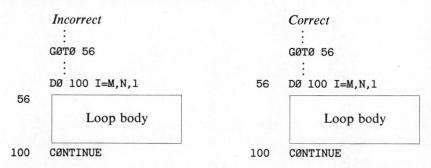

When the loop increment is one, the third item on the list (the increment) may be omitted. In this case, an increment of one is understood. The following is such an example, in which we want to find the sum of the numbers between 68 and 144

(i.e., $68 + 69 + 70 + 71 + \cdots + 143 + 144$):

```
        MANY = 0
        DØ 4 INDEX = 68, 144(   )←      ┤Increment omitted, understood
     4  MANY = MANY + INDEX            │to be one
```

The loop index may be *used* in any way in a DØ loop, but it should not be explicitly *changed*. The compiler has already set up instructions for modifying the index.

These uses of index are wrong   *These are acceptable*

```
        DØ 50 I=J,K,L                          DØ 50 I=J,K,L
            :                                      :
        I = I + 1                              X = Y**I
            :                                  N(I) = X/(I+1)
     50 CØNTINUE                                   :

                                               READ 56, N(I)
        DØ 50 I=J,K,L                          IF(N(I) .EQ. I+5)STØP
            :                                      :
        READ 75, I                             PRINT 83, K,L,I
            :                                      :
     50 CØNTINUE                             50 CØNTINUE
```

Nested loops may be implemented by use of nested DØ loops. Let's say, for instance, that we want to find the sum of columns 4–7 of real array PRICE, which has 20 rows and 13 columns. We might write

```
        TØT47 = 0.
        DØ 2 LARK = 1,20
        DØ 1 LISP = 4,7
        TØT47 = TØT47 + PRICE(LARK,LISP)   } Inner  } Outer
     1  CØNTINUE                             loop      loop
     2  CØNTINUE
```

Nested DØ loops may end on the same statement. The compiler will make sure that separate machine language instructions are generated for modifying and testing each of the loop indices in the correct order. The above illustration then becomes

```
        TØT47 = 0.
        DØ 1 LARK = 1,20
        DØ 1 LISP = 4,7
        TØT47 = TØT47 + PRICE(LARK,LISP)  } Inner  } Outer
     1  CØNTINUE                            loop      loop
```

We can even shorten this by eliminating the CØNTINUE statement:

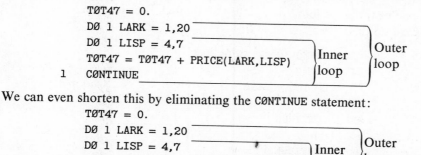

```
        TØT47 = 0.
        DØ 1 LARK = 1,20
        DØ 1 LISP = 4,7                    } Inner  } Outer
     1  TØT47 = TØT47 + PRICE(LARK,LISP)     loop      loop
```

There are a number of "don'ts" associated with DØ loops. These are not iron-clad rules, but rather rules of thumb to keep you out of trouble. Compiling algorithms vary significantly among the various compilers, and a violation of one of these "don'ts" might actually work to your advantage in a specific situation on a specific machine. However, it is wise to adhere to the "don'ts" while you are first learning FORTRAN.

Rule 1. Don't modify the index, initial value, maximum, or increment of a DØ loop in the body of the loop.

Rule 2. Don't use anything but simple integer variables and constants as initial, maximum and increment values. For instance,

don't do this ─────────────────┐   ┌───────── or this

```
              DØ 10 I = J, K*L, M(3)
```

Rule 3. Don't assign zero or negative values to the increment, initial value, or maximum of a DØ loop. For example,

don't do this ───────────────┐   ┌───────── or this

```
              DØ 95 I = 0, 27, -3
```

Rule 4. Don't jump *into* a DØ loop, bypassing the DØ statement. This is important— you cannot initialize the loop index with other statements—the DØ statement must initialize it. More will be said about this below.

Rule 5. Don't use the same index in nested DØ loops. For instance,

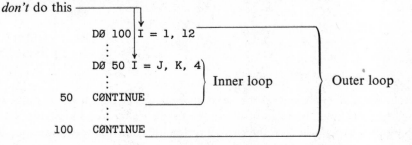

Rule 6. Don't overlap DØ loops unless they are nested. For instance, *don't* do this:

```
              DØ 50 INDEX1 = 5, MAX, 2
              ⋮
              DØ 100 INDEX2 = 1, 60
              ⋮
        50    CØNTINUE                      Loop 2
              ⋮
       100    CØNTINUE
```
Loop 1

Rule 7. Don't end a DØ loop on any of the following statements:

IF	STØP	DØ
GØ TØ	FØRMAT	RETURN (to be discussed)

Following are two examples of DØ loops in use. First, the nested loops for finding the median of a list of 51 numbers in array LIST, discussed in Section 10.1:

```
      DØ 80 M=1,51
      CØUNT = 0
      DØ 70 N=1,51
      IF(LIST(N) .LT. LIST(M))CØUNT = CØUNT + 1
70    CØNTINUE
      IF(CØUNT .EQ. 25) GØ TØ 90
80    CØNTINUE
90    PRINT 33, LIST(M)
```

Compare this sequence of statements to the one in Section 10.1 to see how the loops work. The next example is the one we discussed extensively in Chapter 4—sorting an integer array of 30 numbers. Here are the nested loops for performing the actual sort:

```
      INTEGER XYZ(30), P, Q, J, TEMP
         :
      DØ 1000 P=1,29
      J=P+1
      DØ 1000 Q=J,30
      IF(XYZ(P) .LE. XYZ(Q))GØ TØ 1000
      TEMP = XYZ(P)
      XYZ(P) = XYZ(Q)
      XYZ(Q) = TEMP
1000  CØNTINUE
```

Study these nested loops in conjunction with the flowchart in Section 4.7. Note that the CØNTINUE statement is required here. Why?

Sometimes the constraints of the DØ loop become too restrictive for our purposes. Let's say we want to evaluate a function in the range of -6 to -3 in increments of 0.1:

x	$f(x)$
-6.0	$\ldots$
-5.9	$\ldots$
-5.8	$\ldots$
$\vdots$	$\vdots$
-3.0	$\ldots$

Since we can't have a DØ loop index run from -6 to -3 in 0.1 increments, we can always resort to a loop of the ordinary kind:

```
            X = -6.0
   19       ┌─────────────────────────────┐
            │                             │
            │                             │
            └─────────────────────────────┘
            X = X + 0.1
            IF (X .LE. -3.0) GØ TØ 19
```

However, we *can* still use a DØ loop! The loop has 31 iterations, so we can write

```
   DØ 11 I = 1, 31                          DØ 11 I = 1, 31
   X = (I - 61.)/10.0    or equivalently    X = I/10.0-6.1
   ┌──────────────────┐                     ┌──────────────┐
   │                  │                     │              │
   │                  │                     │              │
   └──────────────────┘                     └──────────────┘
11    CØNTINUE                          11    CØNTINUE
```

We have performed a **linear transformation** on the index to give us the correct sequence of values:

I	X
1	-6.0
2	-5.9
$\vdots$	$\vdots$
31	-3.0

Similarly, we might want a loop in which the "index" takes on values 30, 29, 28, ..., 2, 1. For example, we might want to print an array backwards. Then we might perform the following index transformation (from DØ loop index I to new index J):

```
        DØ 44 I = 1, 30
        J = 31 - I
   44   PRINT 3, XLIST(J)
```

Note that

I	J
1	30
2	29
$\vdots$	$\vdots$
30	1

Rule 4 above warned us against trying to initialize a loop index outside the DØ statement. This means we *cannot* start halfway through the index range, for instance, like this:

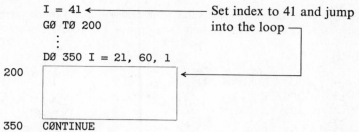

```
I = 41 ←─────────────────── Set index to 41 and jump
GØ TØ 200                    into the loop ─┐
    ⋮                                       │
DØ 350 I = 21, 60, 1                        │
200 ┌─────────────────────┐ ←──────────────┘
    │                     │
    │                     │
    └─────────────────────┘
350   CØNTINUE
```

Why can't we do this? Because the loop index of a DØ loop is generally stored, modified, and tested in an *index register*, and *not* in a memory location! The DØ loop above might be implemented something like this:

```
        LDX     TWENT1 ←─────────── Initialize index
ST200 ┌─────────────────────┐
      │     Loop body        │
      └─────────────────────┘
ST350   INCX    001 ←───────────── Modify index
        SXEQ    SIXT1 ←┐
        JUMP    ST200 ←┘─────────── Test index
```

The statement I = 41 puts integer 41 into location I, but does not initialize the appropriate index register. Implementations of FORTRAN vary widely, so be careful about using DØ loop indices in unorthodox ways. One thing we *can* do is jump out of a loop before completion and *use* the index. This is done in a table search. Here's the table search of the previous section (10.1), implemented with a DØ loop. Recall that we were looking in the first column of TABLE(5,5) for a match with the contents of location ID. When we find the corresponding row of the match, we use that row (I below) later, outside the loop:

```
        DØ 10 I = 1, 5
        IF(TABLE(I,1) .EQ. ID) GØ TØ 25
10      CØNTINUE
            ⋮
25      TABLE(I,3) = TABLE(I,3) + CØST
```

We can do this because FORTRAN always causes the loop index (in the index register) to be stored into the appropriate memory location before we jump out of the loop, with an instruction like

```
        STX     I
```

but we cannot generally effect the instruction

```
        LDX     I
```

without executing the DØ statement.

Exercises 10.2

1. In each case below, state the value of integer variable J immediately after the compilation and execution of the stated sequence of FORTRAN statements:

a)
```
      K = 3
      DØ 5 J = 1, 5
      IF(J .GT. K) GØ TØ 6
    5 CØNTINUE
    6 J = J + K
```

b)
```
      J = −1
      DØ 1 I = 15,41,13
    1 J = J + 1
```

c)
```
      INTEGER HARRY(997)
      DØ 23 J = 1, 10
      HARRY(J) = J
      IF(J/2*2 .EQ. J)HARRY(J) = J + 1
   23 CØNTINUE
      IF(HARRY(4).EQ.HARRY(5)) J = HARRY(6) + HARRY(7)
```

d)
```
      INTEGER WHAT(4,4),WHØ,WHY, WHEN
      DØ 99 WHØ = 1,4
      DØ 99 WHY = 1,4
      WHAT(WHØ,WHY) = WHY
      DØ 99 WHEN = 1,WHØ
   99 WHAT(WHØ,WHY) = WHAT(WHØ,WHY) + 1
      J = WHAT(3,4)
```

e)
```
      DØ 5 J = 76,92,19
    5 CØNTINUE
```

2. A real array called MØØN is of length 80 and contains a single character in each location (left-justified, padded with blanks on the right). R is real and I is integer; variables M, A, and N are real and contain the single characters M, A, N, respectively. For each of the following cases, write a program fragment (sequence of FORTRAN statements) which will:

a) place −1 into I if the characters M, A, N appear in consecutive locations anywhere in MØØN;
b) place into R the character which first appears in two consecutive locations in MØØN;
c) place a number representing the number of A's which appear between the second and third appearance of M in MØØN into I;
d) place the character which appears most frequently in MØØN into R.

3. Assume that you are provided with a data deck; each card contains an English word of 10 or fewer characters left-justified in columns 8–17. The last card contains the word FINISH, and this word appears on no other card in the deck. Write a FORTRAN program which will do the following:

a) print the words in the data deck, in order;
b) count and print, with an appropriate message, the number of cards (or words) in the deck;

c) count and print, with an appropriate message, the number of occurrences of the words CØMPUTER and FØRTRAN in the deck.

4. There are four (different) integers, all less than 24, such that the sum of the cubes of two of them is equal to the sum of the cubes of the other two. That is, if the integers are i, j, k, and m, then

$$i^3 + j^3 = k^3 + m^3.$$

Write a FORTRAN program which will help you find these numbers. Try to make the program somewhat efficient. For instance, do not have your program look at every possible combination of numbers. The fewer combinations your program tries, let's say, the more efficient it is. Is there more than one such set of numbers?

5. Below is a list of programming exercises from previous chapters. They defined programs to be written in FACET machine or assembly language. Write one or more of these programs in FORTRAN. You may redefine the program slightly to have the data and the printout appear in a more reasonable form. Try always to include headings and other messages in the programs.

4.5(3)	4.6(3)	4.7(2)	4.8(1)
4.6(2)	4.6(4)	4.8(2)	5.7(2)

6. There are versions of FORTRAN in which the statement I = I is reasonable and useful. Such a statement is used when I is the index of a DØ loop. Can you think of a reason for this?

7. Professor I. M. Clever has taught at a variety of universities in the past few years. His young son, Rather, is not exactly dull-witted, and has taught himself computer programming. Since he has lived in a number of cities, he has become familiar with quite a few "counting-out rhymes." These rhymes are universally used by children to select one child from a group.

In Philadelphia, Rather used a sixteen-beat rhyme:

> EEnie MEEnie MInie MOE
> CATCH a TIger BY the TOE
> IF he HOLlers LET him GO
> EEnie MEEnie MInie MOE

In New York, it was an eight-beat rhyme:

> ONE potato TWO potato THREE potato FOUR
> FIVE potato SIX potato SEVEN potato MORE

In London, an eleven-beat rhyme:

> INKy PINKy PEN and INK
> YOU go OUT beCAUSE you STINK
> ONE TWO THREE

The counting-out procedure works as follows: The participants stand in a circle. The leader begins the rhyme while pointing to one of the participants. For each successive beat of the rhyme he points to the next participant. The one he's pointing to when the rhyme ends is eliminated. The process repeats until one participant is left. He or she is "selected." *Note:* When an elimination occurs the rhyme begins with the next person in the circle.

Rather decides that since he is likely to move again, he will program the selection process in its general form. His FORTRAN program uses three parameters: the number of beats, the number of players, and the number of the person with whom the counting-out rhyme begins. The object of the program is to determine the winner of the selection process. Write such a program.

Your program should not only read the three items of information above, but also the names of the players (assume names of four or fewer characters, e.g., Joe, Pat, or Mark). The input should have the three integer parameters on a single card, and the names should follow on successive cards. Your output should be well presented. For example:

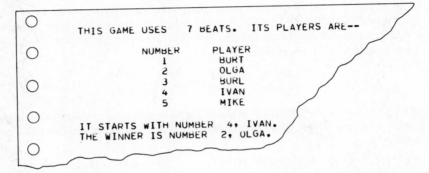

```
THIS GAME USES   7 BEATS.   ITS PLAYERS ARE--

        NUMBER        PLAYER
           1           BURT
           2           OLGA
           3           BURL
           4           IVAN
           5           MIKE

IT STARTS WITH NUMBER   4, IVAN.
THE WINNER IS NUMBER   2, OLGA.
```

Make sure you know how counting-out works before you begin. Check yourself by seeing if you get the same results as depicted here.

10.3 IMPLIED DO LOOPS

Frequently we are interested in creating lists of array elements for I/O statements. For instance, if we want to print the first ten elements of array Q, which has, say 100 elements, then we must write something like

```
PRINT 6, Q(1),Q(2),Q(3),Q(4),Q(5),Q(6),Q(7),Q(8),Q(9),Q(10)
```

The **implied** DO **loop** provides us with a convenient way to abbreviate long lists. Do not make the mistake of thinking that an implied DO loop is a FORTRAN statement or program structure. It is merely an *abbreviation* of a list, nothing more. It can be used where lists appear within FORTRAN statements, notably in READ, PRINT, and DATA statements.

The list

```
Q(1),Q(2),Q(3),Q(4),Q(5),Q(6),Q(7),Q(8),Q(9),Q(10)
```

can be abbreviated by writing

```
( Q(I), I=1,10 )
```

Note the syntax—the item we want plus the indexing information as it would appear in a DO loop. The usual rules about index, initial value, maximum, and increment apply in the implied DØ loop. We can write things like

$$(Q(I), I = J, K, L)$$

and

$$(TABLE(I, 5), I = 1, 5, 2)$$

and even

$$(A(J), B(J), C(J), J= 3, 6)$$

This last example illustrates that we can have more than one item in the set to be repeated. It is equivalent to

$$A(3),B(3),C(3),A(4),B(4),C(4),A(5),B(5),C(5),A(6),B(6),C(6)$$

We can even have the index as part of the list to be repeated:

$$(J, A(J), J=9,11)$$

If this "list" were used in a PRINT statement, then the list to be printed would be

$$J, A(9), J, A(10), J, A(11)$$

where the value of J, the index, is different each time it appears (it is successively 9, 10, and 11). Nonsubscripted variables may also appear in the list:

$$(B(K), X, K=1, 4)$$

This is the same as

$$B(1), X, B(2), X, B(3), X, B(4), X$$

Here's an example. In the Noah's ark program in Section 10.1, we printed a row of the two-dimensional array TABLE like this:

```
PRINT 105, TABLE(I,1),TABLE(I,2),TABLE(I,3),TABLE(I,4),TABLE(I,5)
```

Using the implied DØ, we can now write

```
PRINT 105, ( TABLE(I,J), J=1,5 )
```

Implied DØ's may also be nested. If we had wanted to print out the entire TABLE by rows, we could have written

```
PRINT 200, TABLE(1,1),TABLE(1,2),...,TABLE(5,4),TABLE(5,5)
```

but this would be easier:

```
PRINT 200, ((TABLE(I,J), J=1,5), I=1,5)
```

When we use the implied DØ, we frequently find ourselves reading and printing an undetermined amount of data. We may find, for instance, that we want to print the first N numbers in a real array, five to a line—but we don't know what N is. Well, we can write the PRINT statement:

```
PRINT 67, ( X(I), I=1,N)
```

but what about the FØRMAT statement? We can use the following:

                    67 FØRMAT(3X, 5F14.8)

Whenever we are printing, all the variables in our PRINT statement list are printed, regardless of whether or not there are sufficient specifications on the FØRMAT list. When all the FØRMAT specifications are exhausted, a line is printed and the same specification list is used again on the next line. In our present example, let's say N = 8. Then, essentially, we have the following correspondence in the two lists:

      X(1),   X(2),   X(3),   X(4),   X(5),   X(6),   X(7),   X(8)
       ↕   ↕   ↕   ↕   ↕
      (3X, F14.8, F14.8, F14.8, F14.8, F14.8)

X(1) through X(5) are printed on the first line. Then the same specification list is repeated for the rest of the variable list:

          X(6),   X(7),   X(8)
           ↕   ↕   ↕
      (3X, F14.8, F14.8, F14.8, F14,8, F14.8)

Now the last three values are printed. The last two specifications on the list must now be ignored, since there is nothing on the variable list matching. Can you now see why integer array CQ is printed in a column by this PRINT and FØRMAT statement?

              PRINT 3000, (CQ(L), L=1,M)
        3000   FØRMAT(1X, I10)

The FØRMAT specs are used over and over until the PRINT list is exhausted.† These rules also hold for READ statements. Each time the FØRMAT specification list is used over again, a new record is automatically started. Therefore M lines will be printed while this PRINT statement is being executed. Note that this is true despite the fact that more than one integer in I10 format can easily fit on one line. The same is true for reading. How many records (cards) are read by this statement?

              READ 2999, (CQ(L), L=1,21)
        2999   FØRMAT(3I7)

You are right if you said seven. Three integers are read from a card, exhausting the FØRMAT statement specs. Another card is then scanned in order to fulfill the requirements of the READ statement. This continues until the READ list is exhausted. How many records (cards) are read when this is executed?

              READ 2998 (CQ(L), L=1,19)
        2998   FØRMAT(3I8)

---

†   Beware! This use of the FØRMAT statement is universally valid only when there are no nested parentheses in the specification list. When such nesting does occur, as in FØRMAT (3X,I2,5(3X,I7)), different compilers act differently.

The answer is again seven. Only one number is used from the seventh card, since the READ list is then exhausted.

Clever use of the implied DØ can save us much anguish in outputting arrays (as well as reading into them). This is how we might print the first K elements of an array BIG, five numbers to a line until all the numbers are printed:

```
      PRINT 50, (BIG(J), J=1,K)
  50  FØRMAT(23X,5E14.7)
```

This is how we print the lower right quadrant of a square array SQUARE(40,40) by rows:

```
      PRINT 95, (( SQUARE(M,N), N=21,40), M=21,40)
  95  FØRMAT(10X, 10F12.3)
```

Review these examples carefully, and make sure you understand them all.

Exercises 10.3

1. RECT is a real rectangular (two-dimensional) array of 56 rows and 15 columns. Write a PRINT and FØRMAT statement which will print, in E-format, the upper left corner of RECT, 8 rows by 11 columns, in a rectangular arrangement on the page.

2. Write a FORTRAN program which reads 16 Roman numerals, prints them, and prints their Arabic equivalents. These are examples of Roman and Arabic numerals:

Roman	Arabic
CIX	109
MMLVII	2057
XIV	14

The data (which you will prepare yourself) consist of four cards; each contains four Roman numerals in columns 1–20, 21–40, 41–60, and 61–80, respectively. Each Roman numeral is left-justified and padded with blanks on the right within its field on the data card.

3. Describe some situations in which the implied DØ loop is practically indispensable; that is, in which it would be very difficult and cumbersome to get the same results without it.

4. FUNNY is an integer array containing numbers of no more than six digits. It is of dimension 1000. For each of the cases listed, write a sequence of FORTRAN statements. Make the sequences as short as possible.

   a) List the even-numbered elements of FUNNY in a column. That is, list FUNNY(2), FUNNY(4), ..., FUNNY(1000).
   b) List array FUNNY backwards in a column.
   c) List array FUNNY in ten parallel columns. The first column should contain FUNNY(1) through FUNNY(100), and so on.
   d) Print out the first 250 elements of FUNNY in as few lines as possible.
   e) Print, in three columns, FUNNY(M) through FUNNY(N).

10.4 COLLATING SEQUENCES

Suppose that two real locations, say X1 and X2, each contained a single character, left-justified and padded with blanks at the right:

X1   Q␣␣...␣

X2 $␣␣...␣

What happens when we execute this statement?

IF(X1 .LT. X2) GØ TØ 100

Does the jump take place? How does the compiler translate this logical IF statement? You have undoubtedly guessed that the compiler mechanically compiles code for subtracting X1 from X2 (or conversely) and for checking the sign of the result. It doesn't know that X1 and X2 will contain characters rather than floating-point quantities. Also, the words in X1 and X2 *are* floating-point quantities as well as character representations. One of them is surely less than the other. According to this scheme, each two characters have an inherent ordering, depending upon the internal codes used in representing them in a particular computer. In fact, all the characters are ordered by this choice of code, from the "smallest" to the "largest." This ordering is known as the **collating sequence**. Different computers have different collating sequences. The FACET computer has this sequence:

0123456789␣ABCDEFGHIJKLMNØPQRSTUVWXYZ)*(/=,+−$.

Thus the statement

IF(X1 .LT. X2) GØ TØ 100

would indeed cause a jump to statement 100 in FACET since X1 contains Q␣ and X2 contains $␣, and:

Q␣ is represented by +02710 ← this floating point number is less than
$␣ is represented by +04510 ← this floating point number

In Section 8.9 the internal representation of characters for another computer† was introduced. The collating sequence for this computer‡ is

56789+−*/()$=␣,.ABCDEFGHIJKLMNØPQRSTUVWXYZ01234

On this computer, that same logical IF statement would *not* cause a jump to statement 100, since $ falls *before* the Q in the collating sequence. Note that the alphabetic characters in each of these collating sequences are alphabetically ordered. This choice is no accident. It is the case in most computers that the alphabetic characters fall in either alphabetical order or in reverse alphabetical order in the collating sequence.

---

†   This is the character representation scheme of the CDC 6400-6500-6600.
‡   See exercise 1, at the end of this section.

Now consider this problem. We have a data deck of 100 cards. Each card contains an English word, left-justified in columns 1–20. We would like to write a FORTRAN program to read these data and print the words in alphabetical order. Since we shall have to examine individual letters during the alphabetizing, we shall store each character in a separate memory location. We can do this by storing the 100 words in a two-dimensional array of 100 rows and 20 columns, like this:

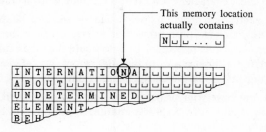

The data can be read in like this:

```
          REAL LIST(100,20)
          DØ 10 I = 1, 100
    10    READ 13, (LIST(I,J), J = 1, 20)
    13    FØRMAT(20A1)
            ⋮
```

The sorting algorithm of Chapter 4 (Section 4.7), with some modifications, suffices to sort the words. That algorithm requires that we look at two numbers, exchange them if they are in the incorrect order, but leave them if the order is correct. This time we shall look at two English words, each of which is "contained" in an entire row of array LIST. We exchange the two *rows* if the words are not in alphabetical order. Otherwise, we leave them. Suppose we are looking at these two rows in the array:

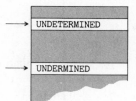

How shall we determine which row (word) belongs first alphabetically? We look at the first character in each English word. If they are the same ("equal" arithmetically), we look at the second character, and so on, until we find two "unequal" characters. Their order determines the order of the words. In this case, it is only when we look at the fifth character in both words, that we discover that UNDERMINED precedes UNDETERMINED alphabetically.

Although the program for alphabetization is not long, it has loops (probably DØ loops) nested to a depth of three.

Exercises 10.4

1. It is easy to see how we determined the FACET collating sequence. Explain why the second collating sequence presented,

56789+−*/()$=␣,.ABCDEFGHIJKLMNØPQRSTUVWXYZ01234

corresponds to the internal character representation scheme given in Section 8.9. (*Hint:* the left-most character position in a machine word includes the sign bit.)

2. Write the alphabetization program discussed in this section. Be sure to find out whether the alphabetic characters fall in normal or reverse order in the collating sequence of your computer. It also is important to note where the blank falls in the sequence, so that your program will place a word like ADD before, say, ADDRESS. Include ADD and ADDRESS in your list of test words for the program.

3. Do exercise 2, but have your program print, next to each word, the number of times that word appears in the list. Suppress multiple appearances of the word in the output list. Print the input list also.

4. Do exercise 2, but have each word be a last name (in columns 1–20). Let the rest of the card contain additional information, such as first name, address, telephone number, etc. Each data card is now a record of some sort. The program should alphabetize by last name, but print complete records.

5. Can you think of a way to do exercise 4 *without* exchanging records (entire rows of arrays) during the sort? (*Hint:* create and sort an array of pointers.)

6. Repeat exercise 2, but let the 100 words appear in **free format**. This means that they can appear anywhere on the card, more than one word may appear on a card, etc. The only restriction is that a single word appears entirely on one card with no intervening spaces, and two words on the same card have at least one intervening space. The data might look like this:

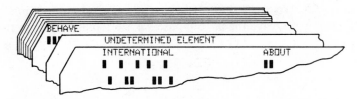

7. Can we alphabetize English words when more than one character is stored in each machine location? Explain.

8. Generally, real arrays are used for alphabetization. Why? (*Hint:* It has something to do with overflow. This problem doesn't show up in FACET, so think in terms of some other computer's internal representation scheme for characters and integers.)

10.5 SUBROUTINES

There are two kinds of subprograms in FORTRAN—the **subroutine** and the **function**. In this section we shall deal with the subroutine.

Suppose we are programming for the weather bureau and wish to produce a subprogram called STAT which finds the average, maximum, and minimum values of the real numbers in an array of arbitrary length. This subprogram could be used for taking daily, monthly, or annual statistics on any of a number of different sequences of temperatures, pressures, and other readings.

The parameters for STAT are defined as follows:

1) array name $\Big\}$ input
2) size of array

3) average

4) minimum $\Big\}$ output

5) maximum

Once we have written STAT as a subroutine in FORTRAN, we could find the average, minimum, and maximum temperatures of a sequence of N hourly temperature readings stored in array TEMP, and place the results in variables AVTEMP, MNTEMP, and MXTEMP. The FORTRAN calling sequence would be:

```
CALL STAT(TEMP, N, AVTEMP, MNTEMP, MXTEMP)
```

       a list of the parameters in the desired order

    the name of the subroutine

  the CALL statement for calling a FORTRAN subroutine

  begins with the word CALL

This CALL **statement** is a straightforward abbreviation of the corresponding FACET assembly language calling sequence, which might be produced by the compiler. This sequence might be:

$\vdots$

```
      JSUB    STAT
      ADRS    TEMP
      ADRS    N
      ADRS    AVTEMP
      ADRS    MNTEMP
      ADRS    MXTEMP
      (next instruction)
```

$\vdots$

Note that all parameters, including the last four, which are single variable locations, are passed by *name*. FORTRAN generally follows this technique of passing *all* parameters by name. Examine the FORTRAN and FACET versions of the call to see just how direct the correspondence between the two calling sequences is.

Subroutine STAT might be written in FORTRAN as follows:

```
      SUBRØUTINE STAT(X,LIM,AVRAGE,MIN,MAX)
      REAL X(LIM),AVRAGE,MIN,MAX,SUM
      SUM = X(1)
      MIN = X(1)
      MAX = X(1)
      DØ 20 I=2,LIM
      IF(MIN .GT. X(I)) MIN = X(I)
      IF(MAX .LT. X(I)) MAX = X(I)
```

```
20    SUM = SUM + X(I)
      AVRAGE = SUM/LIM
      RETURN
      END
```

Let's examine the SUBRØUTINE **statement** first:

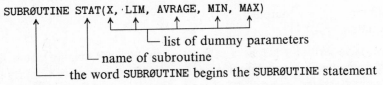

SUBRØUTINE STAT(X, ·LIM, AVRAGE, MIN, MAX)

— list of dummy parameters

— name of subroutine

— the word SUBRØUTINE begins the SUBRØUTINE statement

Such a statement always appears as the first statement of a subroutine. Its unusual feature is the **dummy parameter list**. This list is used by FORTRAN to provide a means to access the different parameters, frequently called **arguments**, in the **actual parameter list**. A correspondence is established between the actual and dummy parameter lists:

$$Actual \quad (\; TEMP, \quad N, \quad AVTEMP, \quad MNTEMP, \quad MXTEMP \;)$$
$$\updownarrow \qquad \updownarrow \qquad \updownarrow \qquad \updownarrow \qquad \updownarrow$$
$$Dummy \quad (\quad X, \quad LIM, \quad AVRAGE, \quad MIN, \quad MAX \;)$$

Any mention of a dummy parameter within the subroutine *stands for* the corresponding actual parameter. There are no memory locations allocated to the dummy parameters (*all other* variables do have memory locations allocated). Thus any appearance of LIM, the second dummy parameter, in the subroutine is understood to refer to the second actual parameter or argument, N.

Recalling the FACET techniques for passing parameters by name, we might expect to see the statement (third from the last in the program above)

$$AVRAGE = SUM/LIM$$

compiled as

```
STAT    STX     PARAM     address of parameter list stored in PARAM
        ⋮
        LDAC    SUM       AC ← SUM
        LDX     PARAM   ⎫
        LDX*    001     ⎬ AC ← SUM/(second parameter)
        FDIV*   000     ⎭
        LDX     PARAM   ⎫
        LDX*    002     ⎬ (third parameter) ← AC
        STAC*   000     ⎭
        ⋮
```

Do you see why SUM is mentioned explicitly in the first instruction? Because it is not a parameter, but rather an ordinary variable in the subroutine, a memory location is actually assigned to it. Can you also see why neither LIM nor AVRAGE appear as operands in any instruction? What appears in their place?

Note the declaration of array X in the subroutine REAL X(LIM), ... It dimensions X as an array with LIM elements, a **variable dimension**. This allows the subroutine to be general enough to operate on arrays of arbitrary size.† The SØRT subprogram defined in Chapter 7 is another example of the utility of variably dimensioned arrays. The compiler can accept such a declaration *only* in a subroutine or function and *only* where the array so dimensioned is passed as a parameter. This is because no actual memory locations are allocated to the array; it is a dummy parameter. The actual array to which it refers (TEMP in our example) must be dimensioned in the usual way in the calling program.

The RETURN statement causes control to return to the appropriate point in the calling program. In subroutine STAT, RETURN could be compiled as

```
LDX     PARAM   XR ← address of parameter list.
JUMP*   005     Jump to instruction following parameter list.
```

More than one RETURN statement may appear in a subroutine.

An END statement appears as the last physical statement in a subroutine. The main program and all the subprograms are compiled independently by most FORTRAN compilers, so these END statements are indispensable signals to the compiler:

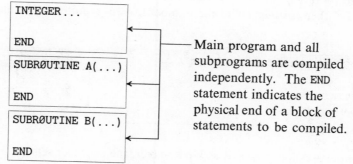

Main program and all subprograms are compiled independently. The END statement indicates the physical end of a block of statements to be compiled.

Of course, a subroutine may be called from different points in a calling program, and with different parameters:

```
REAL TEMP(24), AVTEMP,MNTEMP,MXTEMP, PRESS(360), AV,MN,MX
INTEGER LIM, ...
    ⋮
CALL STAT(TEMP, LIM, AVTEMP, MNTEMP, MXTEMP)
    ⋮
CALL STAT(PRESS, 360, AV, MN, MX)
    ⋮
END
```

---

† Only an array which is a dummy parameter in a subprogram may be variably dimensioned. The array in the calling program and all other arrays must be dimensioned with a constant, since storage must actually be allocated for them.

Did you notice that in the second call a constant (360) is passed as an actual parameter? In fact, any arithmetic expression can be passed as an *input* parameter to a subroutine. Let's suppose, for instance, that we have a subroutine called REFRIG which computes the amount of air-conditioning (in Btu.) required in a certain room. Its parameters are:

a) room area in square feet
b) height of room in feet   } input parameters
c) total window and door area in sq. ft.
d) number of Btu. required   output parameter

If we had an L-shaped room like (dimensions in feet)

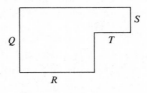

of height 14 ft 5 in., with five windows of dimensions $X \times Y$ ft^2 and a door of 22.5 ft^2, then we might find the number of Btu. required by calling REFRIG as follows:

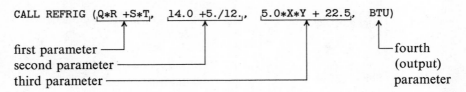

When an expression is passed as a parameter, the compiler sets up an instruction sequence which computes the value of the expression and stores it in a temporary location. This temporary location is then passed, by name, as the parameter. The call to REFRIG might therefore be translated like this:

```
      ⋮
    LDAC    Q        ⎫
    FMUL    R        ⎪
    STAC    TEMP1    ⎪  Compute value of first
    LDAC    S        ⎬  parameter, Q*R+S*T, and
    FMUL    T        ⎪  store in TEMP1.
    FADD    TEMP1    ⎪
    STAC    TEMP1    ⎭
    LDAC    CØNST1   ⎫
    FDIV    CØNST2   ⎪  Compute value of second parameter,
    FADD    CØNST3   ⎬  14.0 + 5./12. ; store in TEMP2.
    STAC    TEMP2    ⎭
```

```
LDAC    CØNST1  ⎫
FMUL    X       ⎪
FMUL    Y       ⎬  Compute value of third parameter,
FADD    CØNST4  ⎪  5.0*X*Y+22.5; store in TEMP3
STAC    TEMP3   ⎭
JSUB    REFRIG  ← Jump to subroutine.
ADRS    TEMP1   ⎫
ADRS    TEMP2   ⎪
ADRS    TEMP3   ⎬  Parameter list, passed by name.
ADRS    BTU     ⎭
(next instruction)
    ⋮
```

These expressions obviously cannot be used for *returning* values from the subroutine, since the programmer has no access to these temporary locations, which are, in fact, set up by the compiler.

All names used in a subprogram are meaningful only within the subprogram itself, since compilation is independent. Those names which are not the dummy parameters are called **local variables**. Local variables are variables which can be referred to *only* within the subprogram. If those same names appear elsewhere (e.g., in the calling program), they refer to different locations. Furthermore, statement numbers are local to subprograms, and may be repeated without confusion in other subprograms. To illustrate this, see if you can figure out what is printed by the following program.

```
          INTEGER A,C(6),B
          DATA A,B/6,100/
          CALL MIX (A, C)
          PRINT 10, A, C, B
    10    FØRMAT (I10)
          STØP
          END
          SUBRØUTINE MIX(C, B)
          INTEGER A, B(15), C
          DØ 10 A=1,C
    10    B(A) = 12
          RETURN
          END
```

Did you correctly deduce that this would be printed?

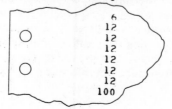

In the subroutine call, dummy parameters C and B stand for actual parameters A and C, respectively. Local variable A in the subroutine, the index of the DØ loop, has nothing to do with variable A in the main program. The two statement numbers 10 are perfectly valid, since they don't appear in the same subprogram or main program. The fact that array B in the subroutine is dimensioned 15 (rather than 6) does not affect anything, since there is no actual array B(15); B is merely used as the name of an array passed as a parameter. The 15 is not used† by the compiler; it merely indicates that B is an array.

We now summarize the points you should remember about the definition and use of a subroutine:

1. Its first statement is

      SUBRØUTINE NAME(N_1, N_2, ..., N_k)

   where NAME is the subroutine's name. N_1 through N_k are the dummy parameters of the subroutine. The parameter names must be nondimensioned variable names, since as dummy parameters they merely stand for actual parameters. If a dummy parameter stands for an array, it should be dimensioned in one of the subroutine's declaration statements. We shall shortly discuss the case in which a subroutine has no parameters. In such a case, the parameter list, as well as the enclosing parentheses are omitted.

2. A correspondence is established between the dummy and the actual parameter lists when a subroutine is called. For this correspondence to be meaningful, there should be the same number of parameters on each list. Further, corresponding parameters should be of the same data type. Those dimensioned in the calling program should be dimensioned in the subroutine (to indicate arrays). Nondimensioned dummy parameters may correspond to variables, array elements, or expressions in the actual parameter list. When an expression, such as 15 or J*3−II or X(5)+X(6), appears in a call, it is evaluated and the address containing its value is passed.

3. Names and statement numbers appearing in the calling program may be reused in the subroutine, since compilation is independent.

4. The return to the calling program is implemented by the RETURN statement. The last statement in a subroutine is the END statement.

5. The call to subroutine NAME is accomplished with the statement

      CALL NAME(P_1, P_2, ..., P_k)

   where P_1 through P_k are the actual parameters, satisfying conditions in 2 above.

---

† This is not always true. The subscript is used whenever the unsubscripted array name appears as an abbreviation for a list of all the array elements, as in PRINT 5, B. Also, if a dummy parameter is declared as a two-dimensional array, the row-dimension is used in computing the position of array elements in memory. If the row-dimension is not the same as in the calling program, array positions will not be correctly computed from subscript information. See page 350.

Here is another example of a subroutine:

```
      SUBRØUTINE EXCHG(ARRAY, R, C, I, J)
C
C
C        THIS SUBRØUTINE EXCHANGES RØWS I AND J ØF A 2-DIMENSIØNAL
C        ARRAY ØF R RØWS AND C CØLUMNS
C
      INTEGER R, C, I, J, K
      REAL ARRAY(R,C), TEMP
      DØ 7 K=1,C
      TEMP=ARRAY(I,K)
      ARRAY(I,K)=ARRAY(J,K)
    7 ARRAY(J,K)=TEMP
      RETURN
      END
```

Do you see how it works? Subroutines may be called from other subroutines. If we were writing a subroutine to alphabetize a list of words (see exercise 2 in Section 10.4), then SUBRØUTINE EXCHG would be useful for exchanging two rows when they are found to be alphabetically in the incorrect order. If those rows were I and J, we might write

```
      CALL EXCHG(LIST, 100, 20, I, J)
```

Exercises 10.5

1. Describe in whatever detail necessary what each of these subroutines does. Identify input and output parameters.

a)
```
      SUBRØUTINE WHAT(A)
      IF(A)1,2,2
    1 A = 0.0
    2 RETURN
      END
```

b)
```
      SUBRØUTINE HUH(I)
      RETURN
      END
```

c)
```
      SUBRØUTINE HØW(M,N)
      M = 1
      IF(N - 1)8,8,4
    4 DØ 6 I = 2,N
    6 M = M*N
    8 RETURN
      END
```

d)
```
      SUBRØUTINE HMM(J)
    1 READ 2, I, J
    2 FØRMAT(I1, 22X, I6)
      IF(I .NE. 5)GØTØ 1
      RETURN
      END
```

```
e)     SUBRØUTINE X(M,D)              f)     SUBRØUTINE WØW(Q)
       INTEGER D,I,J,K                       REAL Q, IT(2)
       REAL M(D,D),T                         DATA IT/3HYES,2HNØ/
       DØ 10 I = 2,D                         K = 1
       K = I - 1                             IF(Q .GT. 6.009)K = 2
       DØ 10 J = 1,K                         PRINT 4, IT(K)
       T = M(I,J)                     4      FØRMAT(10X, A3)
       M(I,J) = M(J,I)                       RETURN
10     M(J,I) = T                            END
       RETURN
       END
```

2. Write a subroutine which sorts a real array of arbitrary size into descending order. The subroutine has two arguments (what are they?).

3. A tic-tac-toe game in progress can be described completely by a 3-by-3 integer array called, say, BØARD. A 1 is placed into a location in BØARD whenever an X has been placed into the corresponding tic-tac-toe board position. A -1 is placed for the 0's, and a zero wherever no mark has yet been placed. For instance, if the board position is

X	X	O
	O	
	O	X

then array BØARD would be set to

1	1	-1
$\emptyset$	-1	$\emptyset$
$\emptyset$	-1	1

At any time, array BØARD is said to represent a tic-tac-toe configuration. Assume that player A has the X's and player B the O's.

a) Write a FORTRAN subroutine called WIN which receives BØARD as a parameter and prints

PLAYER A WINS	if the configuration shows player A winning;
PLAYER B WINS	if player B wins according to the configuration;
NØ WINNER YET	if neither player has yet won.

b) Write a FORTRAN subroutine called PICT which receives BØARD as an argument and prints a pictorial representation of the tic-tac-toe board, including X's, O's, and dotted or dashed lines to represent the board.

c) [difficult] Write a FORTRAN subroutine called DRAW, which again receives BØARD as an argument, and then prints

THE GAME IS A DRAW

if no one can win the game. Think carefully about an algorithm which actually works in all cases. For instance, will your algorithm declare the configurations

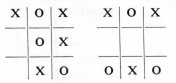

a draw? They are.

4. For the purpose of this exercise, we shall assume that a polynomial of degree n is represented by an array of its $n + 1$ coefficients:

$$a_n x^n + a_{n-1} x^{n-1} + \cdots + a_0 \qquad \text{is represented by}$$

a_0
a_1
a_2
$\vdots$
a_n

array of dimension $n + 1$

For each of the two subprograms below, write a short main program which supplies the subroutine with values.

a) Write a subroutine HØRNER which evaluates a polynomial at some point X. Begin as follows:

```
SUBRØUTINE HØRNER (PØLY, K, X, VAL)
INTEGER K
REAL PØLY(K), X, VAL
   ⋮
```

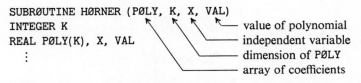

— value of polynomial
— independent variable
— dimension of PØLY
— array of coefficients

Note that PØLY represents a polynomial of degree K − 1. See exercise 2.11(2).

b) [For students who have had calculus.] Write a subprogram DERIV which differentiates a polynomial. Its output parameter is, of course, another polynomial. Begin as follows:

```
SUBRØUTINE DERIV (P, N1, PPRIME, N2)
REAL P(N1), PPRIME(N2)
   ⋮
```

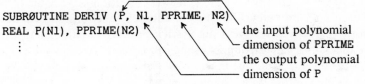

the input polynomial
— dimension of PPRIME
— the output polynomial
— dimension of P

10.6 FUNCTIONS

Another way of writing a subprogram in FORTRAN is by using a **function**. Functions differ from subroutines by a slight structural change in their implementation. However, a wide difference exists between the way subroutines and functions are used. Consider for a moment the parameters contained in a subroutine definition:

```
SUBRØUTINE A(AA, BB, CC, ... )
              ↑    ↑    ↑
```

Some are used for input, others for output. Still others might be used for both. Some might be simple variables, others arrays. Suppose one of these output parameters, one which returns a single value (rather than an array), is defined to be *the* value of the subroutine. Commonly this is done only when there is but one output parameter in the subroutine, so, in effect, we are therefore saying that the subroutine's output should be thought of as its value. The advantage of this quickly becomes apparent. Suppose we wrote a subroutine called SQRT which finds the square root of positive real values, and we wanted to use it to help calculate

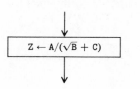

$$Z \leftarrow A/(\sqrt{B} + C)$$

We might then write

```
CALL SQRT (B, TEMP)        input parameter
Z = A/(TEMP + C)           output parameter
```

Here TEMP is the subroutine's output parameter. Once TEMP is set to $\sqrt{B}$, its value is used to compute Z. By singling out the computed $\sqrt{B}$ value as *the* value of the subprogram, we can avoid using a temporary location and an extra statement by writing

```
Z = A/(SQRT(B) + C)
```

When a subprogram is used in this way in FORTRAN, it is known as a **function**. The input parameters are the **arguments** of the function, and the output parameter is the **value**. Since this value is associated with the function as a whole, rather than with any particular parameter, it can be used in evaluating the arithmetic expression A/(SQRT(B)+C) without prior storage in some location or variable.

    The principal difference to observe between functions and subroutines is that functions themselves receive values, whereas output parameters of subroutines receive the output values. Suppose that we wanted a function ABS of one argument, a real, whose value would be the absolute value of the argument. We might write this function subprogram as follows:

```
FUNCTIØN ABS(X)
ABS = X
IF (ABS .LT. 0.0) ABS = - ABS
RETURN
END
```

Note that ABS, the name of the function, is used as a variable (an output parameter) within the function definition. The value contained in ABS when the RETURN statement is executed becomes the value of the function.

In assembly language, we might implement the function by returning the value of the function in the accumulator. This is, in fact, how FORTRAN functions are implemented on many computers. The arguments of the function are passed in a parameter list, just like subroutines. In fact, the entire compilation of a function is exactly like that of a subroutine, with the one exception that a value is returned in the accumulator. This is how ABS might be compiled (ABSLØC is the temporary location where the value of the function is stored):

```
ABS       STX       PARAM        FUNCTIØN ABS(X)
          LDX*      000       ⎫
          LDAC*     000       ⎬ ABS = X
          STAC      ABSLØC    ⎭
          LDAC      ABSLØC    ⎫
          FSUB      ZERØ      ⎪
          JPØS      ST10      ⎪
          LDAC      ABSLØC    ⎬ IF(ABS .LE. 0.0) ABS = −ABS
          FMUL      NEG1      ⎪
          STAC      ABSLØC    ⎭
ST10      LDAC      ABSLØC    ⎫
          LDX       PARAM     ⎬ RETURN
          JUMP*     001       ⎭
PARAM     LØC       ⎫
ABSLØC    LØC       ⎬ data area
ZERØ      FSET      +.000E+00 ⎪
NEG1      FSET      −.100E+01 ⎭
          END                     END
```

The compilation is illustrated statement by statement.† Note how the RETURN statement causes the value of the function (stored in ABSLØC) to be loaded into the accumulator before returning to the calling program. Thus the statement

$$Z = A/(\ SQRT(B) + C)$$

could be compiled as

```
   ⋮
JSUB      SQRT
ADRS      B              Argument of function SQRT
FADD      C
STAC      TEMP1          TEMP1 ← √B + C
LDAC      A              AC ← A
FDIV      TEMP1          A/(√B + C)
STAC      Z              Z = A/(√B + C)
   ⋮
```

---

† FORTRAN is usually compiled statement by statement, as in this example. Sometimes, as in this case, inefficient code is produced. See exercise 4.

Since the name of the function acts also as the name of an output parameter, we must have some means of declaring its type. Of course, the type must be the same in the function as in the calling program. ABS is known to be of type REAL by the implicit declaration scheme, since its first letter is A. If we wish to override the implicit type, we may do so as follows in the function's first statement:

INTEGER FUNCTIØN XYZ(...)

or

REAL FUNCTIØN IJK(...)

This establishes any appearance of XYZ or IJK within the function to be of type INTEGER or REAL, respectively. If other subprograms or the main program use the functions XYZ or IJK, they must also declare their types explicitly:

INTEGER XYZ, ...

REAL IJK, ...

Previously, we only declared variables and arrays. Functions must also be declared.

The solution to exercise 2.7(3), the rabbit problem, is called the Fibonacci sequence after the Italian mathematician Leonardo of Pisa, known as Fibonacci. This sequence is 1, 1, 2, 3, 5, 8, 13, 21,..., where the first two numbers in the sequence are both one, and each other number is computed by adding the two previous numbers. The numbers in this sequence are known as Fibonacci numbers. F_n is the nth Fibonacci number, so

$$F_1 = 1$$
$$F_2 = 1$$
$$F_3 = 2$$
$$\vdots$$

If we were interested in finding only a specific Fibonacci number, F_n, we might write a FORTRAN function:

```
      INTEGER FUNCTIØN FIBØ(N)
      INTEGER FIBØ1, FIBØ2, CØUNT
      IF(N .GT. 2) GØ TØ 10
      FIBØ = 1
      RETURN
10    FIBØ1 = 1
      FIBØ2 = 1
      DØ 20 CØUNT = 3, N
      FIBØ = FIBØ1 + FIBØ2
      FIBØ1 = FIBØ2
20    FIBØ2 = FIBØ
      RETURN
      END
```

Note explicit declaration of function data type in the FUNCTIØN statement.

Do you see how the function works? It must actually compute the entire Fibonacci sequence, through the nth Fibonacci number, to find F_n.† Note that FIBØ must be explicitly declared to be a function of type INTEGER. An explicit declaration must also appear in the calling program for FIBØ, since its name begins with F:

```
        INTEGER FIBØ, UNIT, WEIGHT, ...
               ⋮
        WEIGHT = UNIT * FIBØ(J)
               ⋮
```

Although the arguments of a function are *usually* input parameters, there is no reason why we cannot use them as output parameters as well. For instance, say that we want a function to find the median of an array of real numbers. We might call this function MEDIAN with two parameters—an array name and an integer giving the size of the array. While writing this function, we might find that the easiest way to find the median is to sort the array. Then whenever we invoke the function by writing something of the form

```
        X = MEDIAN(LIST, N)
```

not only do we get the median of array LIST into X, but we also get real array LIST *sorted*. While LIST serves as both an input and output parameter of function MEDIAN, the value of MEDIAN is still the median of LIST, the number placed into X in the statement above. Functions, as well as subroutines, may also perform I/O functions.

Following is a summary of important points to remember about FORTRAN functions:

1. The first statement of a FORTRAN function definition is

$$\text{FUNCTIØN NAME}(N_1, N_2, \ldots, N_k)$$

where NAME is the function's name, and N_1 through N_k are dummy parameters. A value should be assigned to the name during the execution of the function by some statement of the form

```
        NAME = ...
```

Since this name is treated as a variable, a type is associated with it. If implicit types are unsuitable, then use

```
        INTEGER FUNCTIØN ...    or    REAL FUNCTIØN ...
```

to assign an explicit type to NAME.

2. A function must have at least one dummy parameter. This contrasts with a subroutine, which may have none.

3. In other respects, a function is written and treated like a subroutine.

---

† This procedure is not necessary; see exercise 5.

4. The function is called whenever an arithmetic expression in which it appears is evaluated. For instance, function JINX is called when either of these two statements is executed:

$$X = A + JINX(4.5-Y, Q)$$
$$IF (JINX(A+B, A-B).GT. X**2) ST\text{\O}P$$

Functions are typically used with rather complicated expressions. Functions may appear in arguments of other functions. For instance, look at this formula for the cosine of an angle in terms of the sine:

$$\cos A = \sqrt{1 - \sin^2 A}.$$

If SIN is a function which computes the sine of an angle, and SQRT computes the square root, then we can write in FORTRAN:

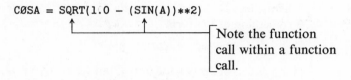

$$C\text{\O}SA = SQRT(1.0 - (SIN(A))**2)$$

Note the function call within a function call.

In this case, the SIN function call is said to be **nested** in the SQRT call. Note how the SQRT argument must be evaluated before a jump to the SQRT subprogram can take place:

JSUB	SIN	⎫
ADRS	A	
STAC	TEMP	TEMP ← sin²A
FMUL	TEMP	
STAC	TEMP	⎭
LDAC	FLT1	⎫
FSUB	TEMP	TEMP ← 1 − sin²A
STAC	TEMP	⎭
JSUB	SQRT	⎫
ADRS	TEMP	CØSA ← √TEMP
STAC	CØSA	⎭

In Chapter 7 we learned that subprograms need not be written by the programmer who writes the main program. In fact, a program may be parceled out to a number of programmers, each writing a subprogram to perform a portion of the task. The loader (or linkage editor) can load the separately compiled subprograms and link them together for execution. The same is true in FORTRAN. Even better, most FORTRAN compilers have access to standard subprograms which can be called upon by all FORTRAN users. These are in the form of functions, and are called FORTRAN **library functions**. The mere *use* of these functions in a FORTRAN program automatically causes them to be loaded with and linked to the remainder of the program, and executed as needed.

Some of the more common library functions, all of which accept one real argument and return a real result, are:

Function	Mathematical Name	Definition
SQRT(X)	square root	$\sqrt{x}$
SIN(X)	sine	sin x, x in radians
CØS(X)	cosine	cos x, x in radians
TAN(X)	tangent	tan x, x in radians
ATAN(X)	arctangent	$\tan^{-1}x$, result in radians
EXP(X)	exponential	e^x
ALØG(X)	natural logarithm	$\log_e x$
ALØG1Ø(X)	common logarithm	$\log_{10} x$
ABS(X)	absolute value	$|x|$

The absolute value function has an integer counterpart, which accepts an integer argument and returns an integer value:

IABS(I)	absolute value	$|i|$

The following two functions have already been discussed; they are used by the compiler whenever mixed-mode expressions must be evaluated. You can use them explicitly as well:

FLØAT(I)   converts from integer to real, accepts an integer argument, and returns a real value

IFIX(X)   converts from real to integer, accepts a real argument, and returns an integer value.

Note that in each of these library functions, sometimes called **built-in** functions, the type associated with the function name by the implicit declaration scheme agrees with the type of the result. For example, the two functions with integer results, IABS and IFIX, have names beginning with I. The other functions which return real values do not have names beginning with letters from I through N. Thus no explicit declarations are required in the calling program in order to use these functions.

FORTRAN does provide additional functions beyond the ones listed here. Check your computer's FORTRAN manual for the complete list.

Exercises 10.6

1. Under what conditions will this statement cause a program to stop?

$$\text{IF(X .EQ. FLØAT(IFIX(X))) STØP}$$

2. Write a FORTRAN program which computes and prints square roots of the integers between 1 and 100. Use the FORTRAN square root function SQRT. Print the results

something like this:

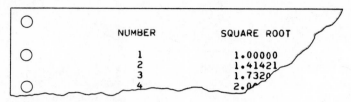

3. This is function GEØRGE:

```
INTEGER FUNCTIØN GEØRGE(M,N)
GEØRGE = (M + N + 1)/2
IF(M .GT. 5) GEØRGE = GEØRGE - 2
RETURN
END
```

What is the value of variable JUST after the execution of each of these statements?

a) JUST = GEØRGE(3,6)

b) JUST = GEØRGE(3,7)

c) JUST = GEØRGE(3,8)

d) JUST = GEØRGE(GEØRGE(-6,2),GEØRGE(7,4))

e) JUST = GEØRGE(37,GEØRGE(7,GEØRGE(7,7)))

f) JUST = SQRT(FLØAT(GEØRGE(IFIX(SQRT(35.)),3)))

4. The FACET assembly language translation of FUNCTIØN ABS given in this section is inefficient. The inefficiency comes about as a result of statement-by-statement compilation. The resulting instruction sequence requires 17 memory locations. Discuss where the inefficiencies occur. Rewrite the assembly language version of ABS. Nine or ten memory locations should suffice.

5. It is not necessary to compute the entire Fibonacci sequence $F_1, F_2, \ldots$ through F_n in order to determine F_n, as we did in INTEGER FUNCTIØN FIBØ. This is a formula for finding F_n directly:

$$F_n = \frac{\sqrt{5}}{5}\left[\left(\frac{1 + \sqrt{5}}{2}\right)^n - \left(\frac{1 - \sqrt{5}}{2}\right)^n\right].$$

Note, however, that floating-point arithmetic must be used in computing it. Write a program which employs this formula to find the first 30 Fibonacci numbers. Check it with FUNCTIØN FIBØ. Print the results of both computations in parallel columns, like this:

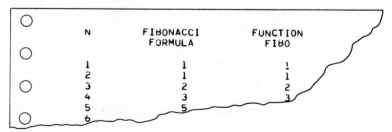

6. An integer function of one integer variable is defined as follows:

$$f(n) = 0, \qquad\qquad\qquad\qquad\qquad\text{when} \quad n < 2,$$
$$f(n + 2) = f(n + 1) + 2n(f(n) + 1), \quad \text{when} \quad 0 \le n \le 28,$$
$$f(n) = 1{,}000{,}000, \qquad\qquad\qquad\qquad \text{when} \quad n > 30.$$

Write a FORTRAN integer function named FUNC to compute this function.

7. Contrast the uses of subroutines and functions. Discuss when the subroutine is more useful, and in which type of application it is better to use the function subprogram.

8. It is possible, using only the constant π, the arithmetic operators $+$, $-$, $*$, $/$, and $**$, and the FORTRAN functions SQRT, IFIX, and FLØAT, to write an arithmetic expression with integer value. For instance, the expression

$$\text{IFIX}(\text{PI} * \text{PI}) + \text{IFIX}(\text{SQRT}(\text{PI}))$$

has the integer value 10, while

$$\text{IFIX}(\text{SQRT}(\text{PI}))$$

has the value 1.

Write a FORTRAN program which employs expressions of this type to compute and print the integers between 1 and 20. Minimize the number of appearances of π (PI) in the expressions (no more than four appearances are necessary in any expression). Your program might look something like this:

```
        INTEGER INT(20)
        DATA PI/3.14159265358979/
        INT(1) = IFIX(SQRT(PI))
        INT(2) = ...
           ⋮
        INT(10) = IFIX(PI * PI) + IFIX(SQRT(PI))
           ⋮
        INT(20) = ...
        PRINT 1, INT
   1    FØRMAT(I10)
        STØP
        END
```

Remember: the expressions may contain no variables or constants other than PI.

10.7 MORE DATA TYPES

FORTRAN has three more data types (besides REAL and INTEGER). They are LØGICAL, DØUBLE PRECISIØN, and CØMPLEX. We may declare logical, double-precision, or complex variables exactly as we declare reals and integers in type declaration statements. We may also declare arrays in this way:

```
        LØGICAL X, LS, YES, GØØD, A(10)
        DØUBLE PRECISIØN AAA, BLØCK(30), TIME(3,3)
        CØMPLEX Q99A(12), J4D, J5D, J6D
```

Double-precision variables are assigned two machine words each:

These are used for storing extra-precision floating-point numbers. The exponent or characteristic is usually the same as in REAL representation. The mantissa, however, extends through the second word.† The number

$$0.45327098 \times 10^{-15}$$

might be stored in the FACET computer as a double-precision number as follows:

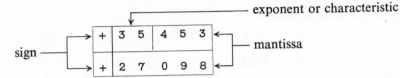

Naturally, a double precision array of 30 numbers, like BLØCK(30) above, is actually assigned 60 memory locations, two per array element. Double-precision constants are written as in E-notation, with a D replacing the E, like this:

$$43.0D{-}4 \qquad -1.0093211784D{+}20 \qquad 0.5D{+}0$$

Double-precision arithmetic is used when we require greater precision in our calculations than the particular computer we are using offers in ordinary floating-point (*single*-precision) representation. Some computers actually have hardware-implemented double-precision arithmetic. Others require subprograms to perform it. Most real FORTRAN library functions have double-precision counterparts:

	single-precision functions		corresponding double-precision functions
	SQRT	DSQRT	
	SIN	DSIN	
	ABS	DABS	
	ALØG	DLØG	

These functions have both double-precision argument and value. The functions should be declared in a calling program, along with the arguments:

```
DØUBLE PRECISIØN X, Y, DSIN, DABS, DLØG, ...
    ⋮
X = DSIN(DABS (Y)+ (X/Y — 4523.779D—8)) — DLØG(Y)/12.3D+2
```

---

† Frequently the mantissa only extends through the "mantissa portion" (right-most digits) of the second word. In such cases the characteristic portion of the second word stores redundant information about the exponent.

Double-precision I/O is accomplished with D-format specifications, which are similar to E-format specs. Here's a program which reads ten numbers representing areas of circles, prints them, and computes and prints the radius of each of the circles, all in double precision. We use the formula

$$\text{radius} = \sqrt{\text{area}/\pi},$$

where $\pi = 3.14159265358979323846\ldots$.

```
      DØUBLE PRECISIØN RADIUS, AREA, DSQRT  ←—— Note double-precision
      DØ 110 I = 1, 10                           square root function
      READ 5, AREA                               declared here
    5 FØRMAT(D25.0)
      RADIUS = DSQRT(AREA/0.314159265358979323846D+1)
  110 PRINT 6, AREA, RADIUS                      Square root function
    6 FØRMAT(3X, D25.17, 10X, D25.17)            used here
      STØP
      END                                 └— Note high-precision (many
                                             significant digits) retained
                                             in double-precision constant
```

Complex variables and constants are similarly assigned two words each. A complex number is a number of the form

$$a + bi,$$

where $i = \sqrt{-1}$. We shall not elaborate on the use of complex arithmetic. We shall merely mention that the usual arithmetic operators (+, −, *, /, **) perform complex arithmetic when the operands are of data type CØMPLEX. A variety of FORTRAN functions for complex arithmetic is available.

The four arithmetic data types form a hierarchy:

1. INTEGER
2. REAL   more complex   simpler
3. DØUBLE PRECISIØN
4. CØMPLEX

When an arithmetic expression is evaluated (by a compiler which accepts mixed modes), and the operands are of different data types, the simpler operand is converted to the data type of the more complex one, and then the appropriate operation is performed. For example, if variable X of data type REAL, variable D of data type DØUBLE PRECISIØN, and variable I of data type INTEGER appear in an assignment statement like

$$X = D * (X - I)$$

then the expression is evaluated thus:

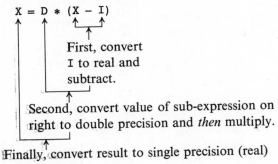

X = D * (X − I)

First, convert
I to real and
subtract.

Second, convert value of sub-expression on
right to double precision and *then* multiply.

Finally, convert result to single precision (real)
and store in X.

Logical variables are variables which have one of *two* values: true and false. There are two logical constants, .TRUE. and .FALSE., which are represented in various ways in different computers. Frequently the following representation is employed:

| 0000000000000000000 | .TRUE. |

| 1111111111111111111 | .FALSE. |

Recall that we previously defined expressions like the following one as logical expressions:

A+B .GT. X**2 − 3.5

Such an expression, when evaluated, is assigned the logical value of either .TRUE. or .FALSE. There are many other ways to write logical expressions. Here are the rules for forming such expressions:

a) A logical constant (.TRUE. or .FALSE.) is a logical expression.
b) A logical variable is a logical expression.
c) Two arithmetic expressions separated by a relational operator (.EQ., .GT.,...) form a logical expression.
d) The logical operator .NØT. followed by a logical expression is also a logical expression, e.g., .NØT.(A+B .EQ. SQRT(X)).
e) Two logical expressions separated by the logical operator .AND. form a logical expression, e.g., (X.EQ.Y) .AND. (G.GT.H+1.3).
f) Two logical expressions separated by the logical operator .ØR. make a logical expression, e.g., (A/B+C .NE. 7.3) .ØR. (0.5 .NE. 7.**Y).

The three logical operators .NØT., .AND., and .ØR. allow us to construct more complicated logical expressions from simpler ones. If L_1 and L_2 are logical expressions, then

1) The expression .NØT. L_1 is .TRUE. if L_1 is .FALSE., and is .FALSE. if L_1 is .TRUE.
2) The expression L_1 .AND. L_2 is .TRUE. only if *both* L_1 and L_2 are .TRUE., otherwise it is .FALSE.

3) The expression L_1 .ØR. L_2 is .TRUE. if either or both L_1 and L_2 are .TRUE. and it is .FALSE. if both L_1 and L_2 are .FALSE.

Rather complicated logical expressions can be constructed. Assume that LØG1 and LØG2 are logical variables, and that X, Y, and Z are reals. This would be a logical expression:

```
(LØG2 .AND.(.NØT.(LØG1.ØR.(X+3.7.GT.Y-4.3*2)))).ØR.(X**2.LE.4.2)
```

Only logical expressions may be used in logical IF statements:

```
IF((X.GT.3.0).ØR.(X.LE.-1.0))GØ TØ 104
IF(LØG1)RETURN
IF(LØG2.AND..NØT.LØG1)PRINT 5, X,Y
IF (M.GT.5) STØP
```

Logical expressions also appear in **logical assignment statements**, in which a logical value is computed and stored in a logical variable:

```
LØG1 = LØG2 .AND. (X*Y .LT. Z +17.5)
LØG2 = .FALSE.
```

Let's see how logical variables might be used in a program. Read the following expression, which is presumably part of an algorithm:

If *both* I and J are greater than 10, but only one of them is greater than 20; and K is either greater than M or less than N; then set I to zero.

We might break this procedure down into a number of FORTRAN statements, like this:

```
LØGICAL L1, L2, L3, L4
    ⋮
L1 = (I .GT. 10) .AND. (J .GT. 10)
L2 = (I .GT. 20) .ØR. (J .GT. 20)
L3 = (I .GT. 20) .AND. (J .GT. 20)
L4 = (K .GT. M) .ØR. (K .LT. N)
IF( L1 .AND. L2 .AND. (.NØT. L3) .AND. L4 ) I = 0
```

When a complicated logical expression is evaluated, the various sub-expressions are often parenthesized to tell the compiler the order of operations:

```
L3 .AND.((.NØT. L1).ØR. L2)
```

If a logical expression is *not* parenthesized, the compiler follows the following precedence hierarchy:

1. First, all arithmetic operations are performed, according to arithmetic precedence.
2. Next, all relational operators are evaluated together with their operands.
3. Then expressions preceded by .NØT. are evaluated.
4. Then expressions with .AND. are evaluated.
5. Finally, expressions with .ØR. are evaluated.

For instance,

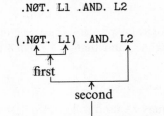

.NØT. L1 .AND. L2

is evaluated

and

X.EQ.Y+Z.ØR..NØT.A−B.GT.C.AND.L1

is evaluated

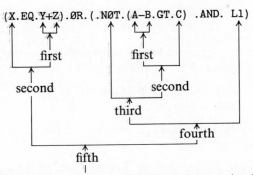

Logical, double-precision, and complex functions may be defined in the usual way:

```
LØGICAL FUNCTIØN GØØD(X, Y, Z)          DØUBLE PRECISIØN FUNCTIØN DD3(I, J)
REAL X, Y, Z, ...                        REAL I, ...
  :                                       DØUBLE PRECISIØN J, ...
GØØD = ...                                  :
  :                                       DD3 = ...
RETURN                                    RETURN
END                                       END
```

Whenever we do define such functions, we must make sure to declare them in calling programs:

```
LØGICAL L1,L2,L3,GØØD,...
DØUBLE PRECISIØN XQ3,R5,DD3,Y7,DSQRT,...
REAL A,B,C,Y,...
DATA L2,Y7/.FALSE.,1.ØD+0/
  :
L1 = L3 .ØR. GØØD(A,B,C*3.7−Y)
  :
R5 = DSQRT (Y7 + DD3(A, 3.ØD+07))
  :
```

Functions declared in appropriate data types, including FORTRAN library function DSQRT.

Note DATA statement with logical and double-precision variables initialized.

The functions are called.

Note also that all arguments in the calling-program function calls match the dummy parameter list as to data type.

Exercises 10.7

1. Why are single- and double-precision modes generally *not* mixed? For instance, if both X (real) and D (double precision) have the value $\frac{1}{3}$, and they are added, what can you say about the double precision result?

2. You get almost as high precision using real arithmetic on the CDC 6600 computer as you do using double-precision arithmetic on the IBM 360 computer. Investigate and explain this statement.

3. Explain what these subprograms do. Be explicit; describe input and output parameters.

a)
```
       SUBRØUTINE LØØK( ITEM, LIST,N,YES)
       LØGICAL YES
       REAL ITEM, LIST(N)
       YES = . FALSE.
       DØ 8 I = 1, N
       IF( ITEM.EQ.LIST( I))GØ TØ 9
   8   CØNTINUE
       RETURN
   9   YES = . TRUE.
       RETURN
       END
```

b)
```
       LØGICAL FUNCTIØN WHAT(A,NØ)
       DIMENSIØN A( NØ)
       INTEGER X, Y, Z
       X = NØ − 1
       WHAT = . TRUE.
       DØ 5 Y = 1, X
       Z = Y + 1
       IF(A(Z).LT.A(Y))WHAT = . FALSE.
   5   CØNTINUE
       RETURN
       END
```

4. Write a FORTRAN program which, when compiled and executed, prints an exact copy of itself. This program should contain no READ statements and it should not call on any subroutines or functions. Be sure you understand the problem—the compiler will, of course, list the program; we want the *output* of the program to list it again. *This is a difficult program.* You may also try this problem in FACET assembly language, i.e., an assembly language program which, when assembled and executed, prints a copy of itself.

5. Write a FORTRAN program which reads a sequence of English words, prints them, and prints them encoded in Pig-Latin. An English word is encoded in Pig-Latin by

taking all the consonants at the beginning of the word, placing them at the end, and adding the two letters AY. For example:

English words	Pig-Latin equivalents
WORD	ORDWAY
SPRINT	INTSPRAY
CHILDREN	ILDRENCHAY
ALWAYS	ALWAYSAY
QUEEN	EENQUAY

Note that words beginning with a vowel remain unaltered except for the addition of suffix AY and when words begin with QU, the QU is treated as a single consonant. Choose your own input format. Employ a logical function which tells the main program whether or not a character is a consonant.

10.8 COMMON

FORTRAN provides another technique (besides arguments and dummy parameters) for passing information to and from subprograms. Recall how all variables are local to either the main program or to some subprogram. These variables are allocated as a physical part of each independently compiled unit, as depicted in Fig. 10.6. When a subprogram is called, the information it needs is passed to it by giving it the addresses of the appropriate variables in the calling program.

In certain situations this method for transferring information becomes undesirable. Up to this point, we have pictured subprograms as carrying out general service processes which usually operate on different inputs each time they are called. In Chapter 7 another reason for using subprograms was given: to help organize a large, complex program. It is not unusual to design a program containing 20 or more subprograms, where each either represents a sequential phase of the larger process or serves some subsidiary service function. The essential characteristic of such a situation is that very often these subprograms operate on a common **data base**. In other words, they are performing different processes on the same data. When this is true, there is no need to pass these data as parameters, since their locations do not change from call to call. Instead, these variables can be placed in a separate physical block of memory called **common**. This block is accessible to all subprograms (Fig. 10.7).

Variables placed in common are no longer a physical part of the subprogram in which they are originally allocated. Any subprogram using a variable or array contained in common does not include that variable or array in its parameter list.

Variables are placed into the common block by including them in a CØMMØN statement:

```
CØMMØN C(80), INPUT(100), PARAM1, PARAM2, ØUT(20)
```

Every subprogram (and the main program) which needs access to common includes a CØMMØN statement after the declarations. The compiler treats common as one

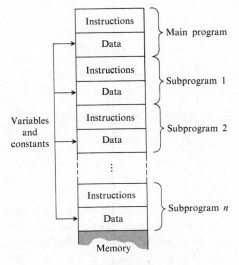

Figure 10.6

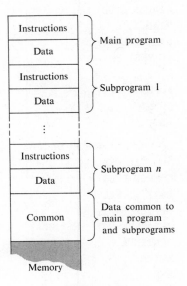

Figure 10.7

array. All variables placed into common are thought of in terms of their index within the array. In the CØMMØN statement above:

This variable	is located in these positions in common
C(80)	1–80
INPUT(100)	81–180
PARAM1	181
PARAM2	182
ØUT(20)	183–202

Therefore, the statement X = PARAM1 could be compiled as

```
LDX    ADRCØM
LDAC*  180        (180 is one less than the index of PARAM1)
STAC   X
```

where ADRCØM contains the address in memory of the beginning of the common block. Since the position of the common block is usually unknown at compilation time (remember, independent compilation of subprograms), the *loader* usually fills in ADRCØM with the correct address when it loads the entire program.

Following is an example of a program in which common is used. The example is admittedly contrived, for only large programs ever make efficient use of the common block. Can you figure out what the program does?

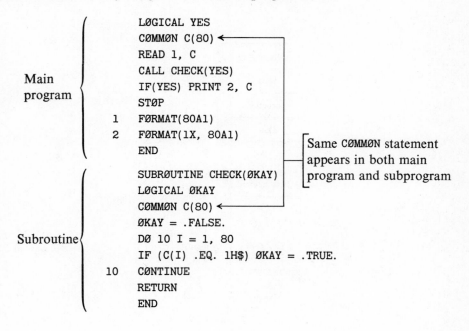

Main program

```
       LØGICAL YES
       CØMMØN C(80)
       READ 1, C
       CALL CHECK(YES)
       IF(YES) PRINT 2, C
       STØP
1      FØRMAT(80A1)
2      FØRMAT(1X, 80A1)
       END
```

Same CØMMØN statement appears in both main program and subprogram

Subroutine

```
       SUBRØUTINE CHECK(ØKAY)
       LØGICAL ØKAY
       CØMMØN C(80)
       ØKAY = .FALSE.
       DØ 10 I = 1, 80
       IF (C(I) .EQ. 1H$) ØKAY = .TRUE.
10     CØNTINUE
       RETURN
       END
```

The program reads the 80 characters from a data card into an array (in common), has subroutine CHECK see if a dollar sign ($) appears on the card, and prints the card if it does appear.

Note that we have dimensioned arrays in common within the CØMMØN statement. This procedure is not necessary. Such arrays can be dimensioned in a type declaration statement or a DIMENSIØN statement as well. The only thing you must remember about dimensioning is that an array may only be dimensioned *once* in any subprogram or main program. In our example above we could have written

```
REAL C(80)        DIMENSIØN C(80)       REAL C                REAL C
           or                    or   DIMENSIØN C(80)   or
CØMMØN C          CØMMØN C              CØMMØN C             CØMMØN C(80)
```

Since subprograms are independently assembled, there is no real need to name variables in common with the same names in different subprograms. It is often wise to do so, however, to avoid confusion. Look at this program:

```
    CØMMØN J, K            SUBRØUTINE MIX(K)
    CALL MIX(I)            CØMMØN I, J
    PRINT 5, I, J, K       I = 1
5   FØRMAT(3I3)            J = 2
    STØP                   K = 3
    END                    RETURN
                           END
```

What is printed? The following:

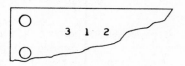

The reason is that names in the main program and the subprograms are independent, since compilation is independent. Subroutine MIX does the following:

a) It assigns 1 and 2 to the first and second locations in common, respectively.
b) It assigns 3 to its integer parameter.

Here is one last example. What does this program print?

```
    INTEGER A(3),B(3)       SUBRØUTINE PUT
    CØMMØN A, B             CØMMØN M, N(5)
    CALL PUT                M = 0
    PRINT 2, A, B           DØ 3 I = 1, 5
2   FØRMAT(3I2)          3  N(I) = 4
    STØP                    RETURN
    END                     END
```

Did you correctly deduce that the program prints

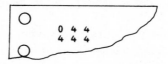

The layout of the common block can be assigned in any way whatsoever in the main program and subprograms, without any relation to layout elsewhere. Here, subroutine PUT has a different layout from the main program:

Location in common		Name in main	Name in PUT
first		A(1)	M
second		A(2)	N(1)
third		A(3)	N(2)
fourth		B(1)	N(3)
fifth		B(2)	N(4)
sixth		B(3)	N(5)

Note that subroutine PUT does not have any parameters at all. All the information it needs is in the common block. FORTRAN does not, however, allow you to define *functions* with no arguments at all.

Exercises 10.8

1. It is considered a syntax error in FORTRAN to have a variable in common appear in a DATA statement. Explain.

2. Frequently common is used for yet another purpose. Whenever different subprograms each require large chunks of memory for scratch-pad purposes (for intermediate results during a computation), common saves memory. Explain.

3. The FACET computer does not physically exist. It is simulated on the computer at your computer center. The simulation program was written in FORTRAN, and employs many subroutines. The FACET memory is merely an array, say MEM(1000), where FACET memory location 000 corresponds to MEM(1), 001 to MEM(2), and so forth. MEM is stored in common, possibly like this:

$$\text{CØMMØN MEM(1000)}$$

Memory words are stored as integers. For instance, if MEM(4) contains integer 349, then location 003 is considered to contain +00349.

a) Assume that NN contains the address of some FACET memory location and that ACC represents the FACET accumulator (both are integers). Assume also that logical variable ØVF represents the overflow indicator (.TRUE. if on, .FALSE. if off). Write a sequence of FORTRAN statements which perform the FACET instruction

$$\text{ADD   NN}$$

You may employ additional variables if you need them.

b) Write and test a FORTRAN subroutine called READNØ which reads a data card containing a sign and five digits in columns 1–6, and places the number thus represented into memory. Start like this:

```
SUBRØUTINE READNØ(NN, ERRØR)
LØGICAL ERRØR
CØMMØN MEM(1000)
      ⋮
```

NN is the address of the FACET memory location into which the number should be read, and ERRØR should be set to .FALSE. if the card actually contains a sign and five digits in columns 1–6 otherwise it should be set to .TRUE.. (*Hint:* The data card must be read as a string of characters rather than in I6 format. Why?)

10.9 BINARY COMPUTERS, DECIMAL FORTRAN

By this point, you have noticed that everything about FORTRAN is decimal (base 10). Both real and integer constants are specified in decimal representation, and all numbers are read and printed in decimal. Yet the computer itself operates in binary arithmetic. Every number is internally represented in binary. When you read an integer, say 19, into variable K, the data card might specify

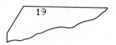

but the memory location you call K will contain

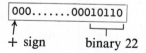

When you add 3 to that location, it then contains not 22, but

But, when you now print K, say in I3 format, the output will be

All this happens because the compiler *converts* your decimal (fixed- or floating-point) constants to binary when it compiles. Further, the I/O **routines** (subprograms) perform conversion, both decimal to binary and binary to decimal, during the execution of your program. To all purposes, you can think of the computer as a *decimal* computer when you program in FORTRAN—well, *almost*.

There are times when you would be hard-pressed to explain the results of certain computations if you assumed a decimal computer. For example, let's say you write

$$X=0.8$$

Location X is assigned a (floating-point) value of 0.8. In FACET (*really* a decimal computer), we would have

$$X \quad \boxed{+50800}$$

But $\frac{8}{10}$ is not expressible (exactly) in binary representation. Recall that it is

$$0.\overline{1100} = 0.11001100110011001100\ldots$$

If our computer had a 24-bit mantissa, 0.8 might be represented like this, with the infinite sequence of digits truncated:

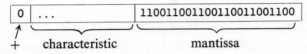

Neither of these is an exact representation of 0.8.

The first case represents

$$0.7999999537058\ldots$$

And the second represents

$$0.8000000119209\ldots$$

If we now ask the contents of location X to be printed in, say, F8.5 format, we would probably get, as output

$$0.80000$$

regardless of representation, because the conversion results (this time, binary to decimal) are probably rounded.

But, if we print in F12.9 format, we just *might*† get either

$$0.799999954 \quad \text{or} \quad 0.800000012$$

In itself, this is not a problem; we don't expect the machine to store more significant digits than are available to it. However, this conversion error can propagate to the left during arithmetic operations. For instance, try writing a FORTRAN program which adds $0.8 + 0.8 + \cdots + 0.8$, 10,000 times.

---

†   The actual printed result depends on how the particular conversion routines work.

Then print the result, in, say, F12.3 format. Is the result as follows?

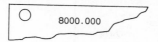

8000.000

Now try the same thing, but use double precision (use appropriate D-formats for printing). Has the result improved? Why?

These conversion errors rarely interfere with programs, but in some rare cases they do. Here's an example of the type of program in which such an error *might* interfere. We say *might* because the whole matter is highly dependent upon both the hardware (representation scheme of fractions) and software (binary-decimal conversion routines) of your particular computer.

```
              ⋮
          X = 0.0
      3   Y = F(X)
          PRINT 20, X, Y
          X = X + 0.01
          IF(X .EQ. 1.0) STØP
          GØ TØ 3
              ⋮
```

The program increments X in steps of $\frac{1}{100}$ (which cannot be represented exactly). In FACET, or any other *decimal* computer this would work. In your binary computer it might not, since X will never be exactly one. It will possibly be 0.99999... and then 1.00001... This type of error cannot be illustrated and doesn't exist in decimal computers, since the internal representation is in the same radix as the FORTRAN representation.

One way to avoid this kind of error is to avoid comparing floating-point numbers for exact equality. In the previously illustrated program, we can change the logical IF statement to

```
          IF(X .GE. 1.0) STØP
```

If you must have an equality comparison, leave some tolerance for conversion errors (or, in fact, truncation, rounding, and other errors). If we want to see if Z is 55.7, we might write

```
          IF(ABS(Z - 55.7) .LT. 0.0001) GØ TØ ...
```

When the logical expression is true, we are assured that Z is *very close* to 55.7. The exact tolerance you choose is both problem- and computer-dependent.

Exercises 10.9

1. Write a short program which displays an anomaly, similar to the ones discussed here, due to conversion errors on your computer.

2. When two quantities must be compared for equality within a certain tolerance, what factors are involved in the choice of tolerance? What limitations are there in this choice?

10.10 IN REVIEW

Arrays may be defined in FORTRAN in type declaration or DIMENSIØN statements. Array elements are indexed by unsigned integer constant or variable subscripts. Two-dimensional arrays can also be defined; these are stored in the one-dimensional memory by columns. These two-dimensional arrays are useful for storing tables and files.

Program loops can be implemented by the DØ loop, a program construct which begins with a DØ statement and usually ends with a CØNTINUE statement. The loop body is enclosed between the two. The loop parameters are all defined in the DØ statement. Compilers frequently employ an index register to store the DØ loop index, although the programmer merely assigns an integer variable as loop index. The implied DØ loop is a convenient method for creating lists of variables, usually array elements. Implied DØ's are useful in I/O and in DATA statements.

A collating sequence is an ordering of the character set of a computer. The order is determined by the numerical order of the internal representations of the characters. The alphabet usually appears in ascending or descending order in the collating sequence so that English words may be alphabetized.

There are two implementations of subprograms in FORTRAN, the subroutine and the function. These are implemented in similar ways, but are used differently. One important difference is that functions return a designated value to the calling program. The parameters of subprograms are called arguments. Dummy parameters in the subprogram definitions serve as place-holders for actual parameters. Both subroutines and functions are independently compiled. A subroutine is called by a CALL statement, whereas a function is called whenever it appears in an expression. There are a number of frequently used functions, FORTRAN library functions, which need not be written by the programmer. Reference to a FORTRAN library function in a program causes it to be loaded with the program. Examples of such functions are SIN (sine), ABS (absolute value) and SQRT (square root).

There are three other data types which commonly appear in FORTRAN— logical, double precision, and complex. Logical variables and constants take on one of two values, .TRUE. and .FALSE. There are a number of operators which convert arithmetic expressions to logical expressions, and others which operate on logical expressions. Double-precision variables and constants are similar to reals, except that two machine locations are assigned to each variable or constant, extending the precision of the numbers represented. Complex variables and constants represent complex numbers. The usual arithmetic operations of addition, subtraction, multiplication, division, and exponentiation can be used in double-precision and complex expressions. The compiler will correctly identify the type of operations intended, and will translate into appropriate instruction sequences.

Logical, double-precision and complex arrays and functions may be defined. The FORTRAN library contains double-precision and complex functions corresponding to most of the real library functions.

Variables and arrays are made common to all subprograms and the main program whenever they appear in a CØMMØN statement. They are then assigned to a block of memory called common. Common is an alternative method for passing information between subprograms.

Decimal fractions cannot, in general, be represented exactly in binary computers. FORTRAN is essentially a decimal language and the compiler provides routines for decimal-to-binary and binary-to-decimal conversion. Conversion errors can be avoided by refraining from requiring exact equality of quantities.

Appendix A

THE FACET INSTRUCTION SET

Instruction type	Mnemonic code	Opera-tion code	Explanation of instruction	Page No.
Halt	HALT	00	Halt.	11
Instructions for moving data	LDAC	11	Load number from memory into accumulator.	10
	STAC	12	Store number from accumulator into memory.	11
	LDX	13	Load 3 digits from memory into index register.	91
	STX	14	Store index register in 3 digits of memory.	91
	PACX	15	Put 3 digits from accum. into index register.	91
	PXAC	16	Put index register into 3 digits of accum.	92
Fixed-point arithmetic	ADD	21	Add memory register into accumulator.	11
	SUB	22	Subtract memory register from accumulator.	39
	MLS	23	Multiply, retain 5 least significant digits.	39
	MMS	24	Multiply, retain 5 most significant digits.	39
	DIV	25	Divide, retain integer quotient.	39
Transfer (jump) instructions	JUMP	31	Unconditional transfer.	20
	JNEG	32	Jump if accumulator negative.	23
	JPØS	33	Jump if accumulator positive.	23
	JZER	34	Jump if accumulator zero.	23
	JØVF	35	Jump if overflow indicator ON.	45
	JXZR	36	Jump if index register zero.	94
	SXEQ	37	Skip instruction if index register equal.	94
	JSUB	38	Jump to subprogram.	196
Input/ output instructions	RNUM	41	Read number from next data card.	32
	PNUM	42	Print number in next tab field on paper.	10
	RSYM	43	Read string of characters from next data card.	151
	PSYM	44	Print string of characters on paper.	133
	TAB	45	Tabulate to next print field.	76
	CRGC	46	Carriage control.	76
	RFLT	47	Read floating-point number from next card.	177
	PFLT	48	Print floating-point number in next tab field.	177

Instruction type	Mnemonic code	Operation code	Explanation of instruction	Page No.
Digit manipulation instructions	LEFT	51	Shift accum. digits left; sign unaffected.	143
	RGHT	52	Shift accum. digits right; sign unaffected.	143
	EXTR	53	Extract accumulator digits using mask.	142
Index register modification	INCX	61	Increment index register.	93
	DECX	62	Decrement index register.	93
Floating-point arithmetic	FADD	71	Floating add memory register into accum.	170
	FSUB	72	Floating subtract memory register from accum.	171
	FMUL	73	Floating multiply memory register into accum.	171
	FDIV	74	Floating divide memory register into accum.	171

Appendix B

THE
FACET
PSEUDO-OPERATIONS

Mnemonic code	Description of pseudo-operation	Page No.
ADRS	Store address of label operand into digits 3–5 of a memory register.	212
ARAY	Reserve a sequence of locations in the memory (an array).	87
CHAR	Encode a string of characters and place into a sequence of locations in the memory.	138
END	End of program.	57
FSET	Reserve a single location in the memory and initialize it to a floating-point value.	179
LØC	Reserve a single location in the memory.	57
SET	Reserve a single location in the memory and initialize it to a fixed-point value.	60

Appendix C

THE FACET CONTROL CARDS

Shaded areas indicate fields that are ignored by the job control processor.

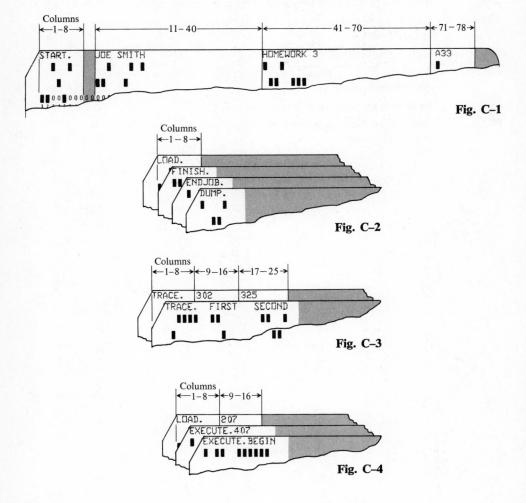

Fig. C–1

Fig. C–2

Fig. C–3

Fig. C–4

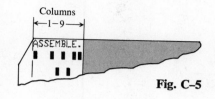

Fig. C–5

Appendix D

FACET
JOB
CONTROL
LANGUAGE

Machine language program:

```
START.
DUMP.          ┐ Optional,
TRACE.         ┘ in any order
LØAD.
┌─────────────────┐
│ 101    +41207   │
│  ⋮              │ ←Program
│ 503    +00012   │
└─────────────────┘
EXECUTE.101
┌─────────────────┐
│ +00227          │
│ +00015          │ ←Data, if any
│  ⋮              │
│ +00221          │
└─────────────────┘
FINISH.†
ENDJØB.
```

Multiple programs:

```
START.    ┐
  ⋮       │ Program 1, machine
FINISH.   ┘ or assembly language
START.    ┐
  ⋮       │ Program 2, machine
FINISH.   ┘ or assembly language
  ⋮
START.    ┐
  ⋮       │ Program n, machine
FINISH.†  ┘ or assembly language
ENDJØB.
```

Assembly language program
for assembly only:

```
START.
ASSEMBLE.
┌─────────────────┐
│ A   RNUM    X   │
│     PNUM    X   │ ←Program
│      ⋮          │
│     END         │
└─────────────────┘
FINISH.†
ENDJØB.
```

Assembly language program
for loading and execution:

```
START.
DUMP.          ┐ Optional,
TRACE.         ┘ in any order
ASSEMBLE.
┌─────────────────┐
│ A   RNUM    X   │
│     PNUM    X   │ ←Program
│      ⋮          │
│     END         │
└─────────────────┘
LØAD.
EXECUTE.
┌─────────────────┐
│ +00237          │
│   ⋮             │ ←Data, if any
│ −01111          │
│ +00221          │
└─────────────────┘
FINISH.†
ENDJØB.
```

† FINISH. card may be omitted when immediately followed by ENDJØB. card.

Appendix E

SYNTAX
OF
FORTRAN
STATEMENTS

The following FORTRAN statements are not necessarily meant to be related in any way. They are listed here as examples of correct FORTRAN syntax.

Type of statement		Sample statements	Page references
Declarations and dimensioning		INTEGER A15, NUMBER, LIST(50) REAL CØST, XYZ(20), MAX, MIN, A(10,20) LØGICAL L, PØSTIV, ØK DØUBLE PRECISIØN DX, DY(5) DIMENSIØN X(25,5), Y(25), CØST(40), Q(2)	288–294, 341–343, 349, 391
CØMMØN		CØMMØN LIST, CØST, NUMBER(100)	398–402
DATA		DATA A, B/3.8, −.6E−8/,NAME/4HMARC/,SUM/0.0/ DATA (X(I),I=1,5)/−3.1,−2.2,−1.8,0.4,2.5/	292–294, 351, 368– 371
Arithmetic assignment	35	I=I+5 ANS = X + SIN(X2+X3) − XYZ(J)**2	311–324
Logical assignment	7878	LØG1 = X .NE. Y L5=L4.ØR.L3.AND..NØT.(L1.ØR.L2)	394–395
Arithmetic IF	4	IF(B**2 − 4.*A*C)90,130,200 IF(J−5)25,25,60	328–331

Logical IF	10	IF(A*B−C .LE. 100.0)GØ TØ 85
		IF(ABS(X) .LT. EPS)RETURN
		IF(X.LT.3.7.ØR.Y.GT.5.8)R(K)=R(KK)−4.9E−7
			325–328,
			334

GØ TØ		GØ TØ 75	325
Computed GØ TØ		GØ TØ (60, 85, 90, 70), N	331–332

Type of statement		Sample statements	Page references
Input/output		READ 1025, K,X(K),VAL	295–308,
		READ (5, 1000) X, Y	351,
		READ 99, (INPUT(N), N=1,K)	368–371
	40	PRINT 2050	
		PRINT 2000, ((TABLE(I,J),J=1,20),I=1,K)	
		WRITE (6,49) I,J,K	
	500	FØRMAT(1H⊔,16HTHE⊔ANSWER⊔IS⊔=⊔)	
	1025	FØRMAT(10I5, 15X, I10)	
	97	FØRMAT(5H1X⊔=⊔, F11.4)	
	155	FØRMAT (6(I4,2X,2E12.4,3X,D23.12/)//1H1)	
DØ		DØ 95 I=2,K,3	358–365
	14	DØ 150 INDEX = 1, 30	
CØNTINUE	150	CØNTINUE	358–365
Program exit		STØP	283
Subprogram definition		SUBRØUTINE FIXIT	375–381,
		SUBRØUTINE CØMP(A,B,I)	384–389
		FUNCTIØN F(X)	
		REAL FUNCTIØN INTERP(Z1,Z2)	
		LØGICAL FUNCTIØN EQUAL(R,S,J)	
Subprogram exit		RETURN	375–381, 384–389
Subprogram call		CALL FIXIT	375–381
	55	CALL CØMP(X, 6.3E–4, K)	
		Z = INTERP(X,Y) + 3.7	
		ABC = F(100.0 – SIN(Q**2))	
END		END	283, 377

Appendix F

FORTRAN FORMAT SPECIFICATIONS

INPUT SPECIFICATIONS

I-format

When this input field	is read with this format specification	then this fixed-point integer is placed into memory
⊔⊔⊔⊔⊔⊔	I6	0
⊔⊔⊔−10	I6	−10
⊔⊔−10⊔	I6	−100
−10⊔⊔⊔	I6	−10000
⊔⊔⊔⊔2479	I8	2479
⊔⊔2⊔4⊔79	I8	204079
247⊔⊔⊔⊔9	I8	24700009

Note: Trailing and intercalated blanks are interpreted as zeros.

F-format

When this input field	is read with this format specification	then this floating-point number is placed into memory
153⊔⊔	F5.0	15300.0
153⊔⊔	F5.3	15.3
⊔⊔153	F5.0	153.0
⊔⊔153	F5.2	1.53
⊔⊔153	F5.4	0.0153
⊔⊔153	F5.7	0.0000153
⊔⊔−9.57⊔	F8.0	−9.57
−9.57⊔⊔⊔	F8.0	−9.57
−9.57⊔⊔⊔	F8.4	−9.57
−9.57⊔⊔⊔	F8.8	−9.57
−9.5⊔7⊔⊔	F8.0	−9.507
−9⊔.⊔5⊔7	F8.0	−90.0507

Note: Trailing and intercalated blanks are interpreted as zeros; the F-specification determines the placement of the decimal point only when a dot does not appear in the input field. Some compilers consider specifications of the form Fm.n where n > m to be a syntax error.

E-format

When this input field	is read with this format specification	then this floating-point number is placed into memory
␣␣␣1.092E+00	E12.0	1.092
␣␣−1.092E␣00	E12.7	−1.092
␣␣␣1.092E−␣1	E12.0	0.1092
␣␣−1.092E−06	E12.0	−0.000001092
␣␣−1.092E−1␣	E12.0	−0.0000000001092
␣␣−1.092E−10	E12.0	−0.0000000001092
1.092␣␣␣␣␣E0	E12.0	1.092
1.092␣␣␣␣␣E4	E12.0	10920.0
1.092E␣␣␣␣␣4	E12.0	10920.0
1092E␣␣−␣␣␣3	E12.0	1.092
1092E␣␣␣␣␣␣3	E12.0	1092000.0
1092E0␣␣␣␣␣␣	E12.0	1092.0
1092E␣␣␣␣␣␣0	E12.0	1092.0
1092␣E␣␣␣␣␣0	E12.0	10920.0
1092␣␣␣␣␣E␣0	E12.0	109200000.0
1092␣␣␣␣␣E␣0	E12.5	1092.0
1092␣␣␣␣␣E␣0	E12.10	0.01092
␣␣␣␣␣1092E␣0	E12.4	0.1092
␣␣␣␣␣1092E−8	E12.4	0.000000001092
␣␣␣␣␣1092E20	E12.20	1092.0
␣␣␣␣␣1092E2␣	E12.20	1092.0
1␣0␣9␣2␣E␣2␣	E12.20	10009020.0

Note: The character E in the input field divides that field into two fields; the one on the left is interpreted as an F-field, and the one on the right as an I-field (for the exponent). Trailing and intercalated blanks are treated as zeros in each of the fields. Some compilers do not accept intercalated blanks or specifications of the form Em.n with n > m.

A-format

When this input field	is read with this format specification	in a computer with this character capacity per memory word	then this character sequence is placed into the memory location
)+(	A3	4	)+(␣
)+(	A3	6	)+(␣␣␣
)+(	A3	10	)+(␣␣␣␣␣␣␣
FØXY−LØXY	A9	4	LØXY
FØXY−LØXY	A9	6	Y−LØXY
FØXY−LØXY	A9	10	FØXY−LØXY␣
PRØGRAMMING	A11	2	NG
PRØGRAMMING	A11	6	AMMING
PRØGRAMMING	A11	8	GRAMMING

Note: Characters are placed into memory locations from the left, padded with trailing blanks at the right. If the input field is greater than the character capacity, the word is filled with the rightmost characters of the input field.

OUTPUT SPECIFICATIONS

I-format

When this integer in memory	is printed with this format specification	then these characters are printed in the appropriate columns
3	I1	3
3	I3	␣␣3
3	I10	␣␣␣␣␣␣␣␣␣3
−3	I1	*
−3	I3	␣−3
−3	I10	␣␣␣␣␣␣␣␣−3
47209	I3	***
47209	I5	47209
47209	I10	␣␣␣␣␣47209

Note: Integers are printed right-justified with leading zeros and plus sign suppressed; asterisks indicate that the print field is not sufficient (does not have enough character positions) to print the integer in question.

F-format

When this floating-point number in memory	is printed with this format specification	then these characters are printed in the appropriate columns
−14.85703	F10.5	␣−14.85703
−14.85703	F10.3	␣␣␣−14.857
−14.85703	F10.1	␣␣␣␣␣−14.9
−14.85703	F10.6	−14.857030
−14.85703	F10.8	*.85703000
5.7×10^{20}	F15.2	␣␣␣␣␣␣␣␣␣␣␣*.00
5.7×10^{-20}	F15.10	␣␣␣0.0000000000

Note: The last digit of the fraction portion is appropriately rounded; asterisks indicate that the field width is insufficient to contain the integer portion of the number. Some compilers fill the *entire* field with asterisks when it is too small.

E-format

When this floating-point number in memory	is printed with this format specification	then these characters are printed in the appropriate columns
287.0934	E14.7	␣0.2870934E␣03
−287.0934	E14.7	−0.2870934E␣03
0.0002870934	E14.7	␣0.2870934E−03
−0.0002870934	E14.7	−0.2870934E−03
0.0002870934	E13.7	0.2870934E−03
287.0934	E14.2	␣␣␣␣␣␣0.29E␣03
287.0934	E14.10	**************

Note: If the format specification is Em.n, then m should be, in general, at least seven greater than n; otherwise there may not be sufficient character positions to print—as indicated by one or more asterisks in the print field. Slight variations in printing E-format numbers are found among the various compilers.

A-format

When a memory location contains exactly these characters	and is printed with this format specification	then these characters are printed in the appropriate columns
ABCDEF	A1	A
ABCDEF	A3	ABC
ABCDEF	A6	ABCDEF
ABCDEF	A9	␣␣␣ABCDEF

Note: If the format specification is Am and a memory word contains, in the computer being used, n characters, then (a) if $m \leq n$, the m leftmost characters in the word are printed, and (b) if $m > n$, $m - n$ blanks are printed, followed by the n characters of the word.

Appendix G

GUIDE TO DEBUGGING

Finding and correcting bugs in a computer program is sometimes a challenging task. FACET (and other computers) provide two *debugging aids* which assist you in this process: the memory DUMP and the program TRACE. Following are some general guidelines to debugging, some specific suggestions concerning the use of the DUMP and TRACE, and finally some techniques for debugging high-level languages such as FORTRAN, where the DUMP and TRACE are much less useful.

A program may contain bugs even though its execution terminates *normally* (when the HALT instruction is the last instruction executed in the program). You must therefore *always* verify the results printed by your program. To do this, you must have a good idea of what the correct printout should be. Even though such verification may be tedious, since it involves hand computation of results produced by a complex algorithm, it must be done. Otherwise, your results may be entirely wrong.

Suppose, however, that your program terminates *abnormally*. In this case, an error message will be printed and execution terminated. Some computers print a code of a few characters which stands for the message; in such cases an explanation of the error may be found in a manual. FACET prints error messages in English. Your first task in debugging is: *read* and *understand* that message. If necessary, consult texts, manuals, and instructors in order to obtain that understanding. Remember, it is futile to look for a program error if you do not even know which kinds of errors could have generated the particular error message printed. Sometimes the error message includes additional helpful information such as the location of the instruction which produced the error. Typical causes for abnormal termination are:

a) attempted division by zero,
b) incorrect information on data card during attempted read,
c) attempt to read beyond the last card of the data deck,
d) program is in endless loop and runs out of time (or jumps in FACET),
e) too many lines printed.

If the error message itself proves insufficient for locating the cause of the problem, we may use the memory DUMP. This facility prints the contents of the accumulator(s), the index register(s), and all memory locations containing your program or used by your program, when *execution terminates*. The DUMP is printed, when requested, regardless of whether execution ends normally or abnormally.

We can observe the use of the DUMP by considering a simple example.

Suppose we are interested in writing a FACET assembly language program to read ten numbers from ten data cards and print their sum. Assume we have already constructed the following flowchart:

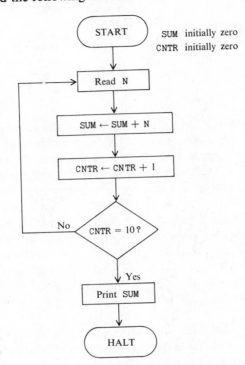

SUM initially zero
CNTR initially zero

Suppose, further, that we incorrectly translated the flowchart as follows:

```
LØØP      RNUM    N        READ A NUMBER
          LDAC    SUM      INCREMENT
          ADD     N          THE
          STAC    SUM          SUM
          LDAC    CNTR     MØDIFY THE
          ADD     ØNE        CØUNTER
          SUB     TEN      TEST CØUNTER
          JZER    PRINT    PRINT IF CNTR = 10
          JUMP    LØØP       ØTHERWISE REPEAT LØØP
PRINT     PNUM    SUM
          HALT
N         LØC
CNTR      SET     +00000
SUM       SET     +00000
ØNE       SET     +00001
TEN       SET     +00010
          END
```

If you examine the program, you might discover that the error is that the newly-computed value of CNTR (in the accumulator) is not stored in the memory after incrementation. What will happen if this program is run? Execution will terminate abnormally because the loop exit does not take place; the program will attempt to read beyond the tenth (and last) data card and will encounter the FINISH card. The error message generated claims that the "read instruction" at location such-and-such attempted to perform an illegal read by reading a data card which isn't there. The message doesn't really narrow our search to a fault with CNTR, the *real* problem. If we are stumped, we might turn to the DUMP.

How should we use the DUMP to help locate the problem? The general strategy is to examine *all* data locations to see if they contain their expected values. What are the expected values in this case? If the program were operating correctly, N should contain the value of the tenth data card, CNTR should be ten, and SUM should be the SUM of all ten data numbers. In order to locate N, CNTR, and SUM on the DUMP, we must know their memory addresses. We glance back to the "output of the assembler" which reads in part:

N	LØC		011		
CNTR	SET	+00000	012	+00000	NØ
SUM	SET	+00000	013	+00000	NØ

Locations 011 through 013 were assigned by the assembler. Let's suppose loading begins in location 200, so all addresses were modified by 200, and the actual addresses in memory are:

N	211
CNTR	212
SUM	213

Now we are ready to look at the DUMP. Location 211 (N) contains the last data number, which is as it should be. In location 213 we find the correct sum, but in location 212, corresponding to CNTR, we find +00000. This is the initial value of CNTR and not the expected value, ten. Immediately our attention centers on every instruction and instruction sequence dealing with CNTR, and soon we discover that we omitted the instruction

STAC   CNTR

immediately after incrementation.

We have used the DUMP by scanning final values in data locations. This process often leads to the discovery of a location containing a value it should not have, narrowing our search for bugs to those instructions dealing with the location in question.

Most computers provide a DUMP facility as a debugging aid. A TRACE facility is less frequently found and costlier to use. It is therefore to your advantage to develop proficiency in the use of the DUMP. There are, however, cases in which the bug is so stubborn that you would request a TRACE. The program TRACE prints a record of your program *as it executes*. Each time an instruction is executed, a line is printed relating all pertinent information about the instruction, machine registers, and so on. The initial portion of the TRACE for our program (including the error) is depicted on page 425. The column headers are:

PC program counter containing the address of the instruction currently being executed;

INSTR this is the instruction itself, the one currently being executed—it is the contents of the memory location whose address is in the PC;

ACCUM the contents of the accumulator *after* the instruction is executed;

INDEX contents of the index register (XR)—printed only if the instruction uses, modifies, or tests the index register;

ØPERAND the effective operand of the instruction;

CØNTENTS printed only when the effective operand refers to some memory location—if so, it is the contents of that location;

ØVERFLØW gives the value of the overflow indicator when it is being set or tested.

The error in our program would probably have been detected in the TRACE on the second iteration through the loop. When LDAC CNTR is executed the second time, we would probably notice that +00000 is placed into the accumulator (see the second appearance of instruction +11212) where CNTR should now be +00001. This should indicate to us that STAC CNTR was not executed on the previous iteration, and must therefore be inserted.

Not that both DUMP and TRACE evidence is easily overlooked. The error will never appear in flashing neon lights. You must actively search for those items printed by the DUMP and TRACE which do not agree with what you believe ought to have been printed if the program were operating properly.

Debugging high-level languages is different because it is difficult, if not impossible, to use the DUMP and TRACE. This is because they can only be understood and used at the machine-language level; you, on the other hand, are writing in some high-level language. You may not even know the machine language of the particular computer in question. You probably don't know how your compiler translates to machine language. So another technique is called for.

The most widely used technique employed by high-level language programmers is the insertion of extra PRINT statements in their programs. These statements print the intermediate values of variables suspected of being in error. The PRINT statements are removed when debugging is complete. The extra information printed acts in lieu of a TRACE, since the programmer can observe the progress of the program with each newly computed and printed value of a variable.

An example of this debugging technique can be seen in the following FORTRAN program. It is again a program for summing ten numbers, and employs the same flowchart as our assembly language program. Do you see the error?

```
        INTEGER CNTR, SUM, N
        DATA CNTR, SUM/0,0/
   20   READ 100, N
  100   FØRMAT(I10)
        SUM = SUM + N
        CMTR = CNTR + 1
        IF (CNTR .NE. 10) GØ TØ 20
        PRINT 101, SUM
  101   FØRMAT(12H1THE␢SUM␢IS␢, I10)
        STØP
        END
```

The error is, of course, that CNTR is misspelled as CMTR on line 6 of the program, to the left of the equals sign. The incremented counter is stored in the wrong location (one called CMTR), and this error has the same effect as the one in our assembly language program—CNTR remains zero. A similar error message would be printed. To help debug this program, the following might temporarily be inserted between lines 6 and 7 of the program:

```
  C       REMØVE THIS CØMMENT AND STATEMENTS 10000 AND 10001
  C       AFTER THE PRØGRAM IS DEBUGGED...
 10000   PRINT 10001, N, SUM, CNTR
 10001   FØRMAT( 3(5X, I12))
```

When the program is run with these statements inserted, we have a record of the values of the important variables *each* iteration. We quickly notice that CNTR remains zero, and this should immediately lead us to our error.

Many programmers insert such PRINT statements into their programs as a *precautionary measure* when they first write their programs. They assume that there will be some bugs as a matter of course and that they might as well be prepared. This procedure is recommended.

D Y N A M I C   T R A C E

PC	INSTR	ACCUM	INDEX ØPERAND	CØNTENTS	ØVERFLØW
200	+41211		211	+01000	
201	+11213	+00000	213	+00000	
202	+21211	+01000	211	+01000	ØFF
203	+12213	+01000	213	+01000	
204	+11212	+00000	212	+00000	
205	+21214	+00001	214	+00001	ØFF
206	+22215	−00009	215	+00010	ØFF
207	+34209	−00009	209		
208	+31200		200		
200	+41211		211	−00060	
201	+11213	+01000	213	+01000	
202	+21211	+00940	211	−00060	ØFF
203	+12213	+00940	213	+00940	

204	+11212	+00000		212	+00000	
205	+21214	+00001		214	+00001	ØFF
206	+22215	−00009		215	+00010	ØFF
207	+34209	−00009		209		
208	+31200			200		
200	+41211			211	+00099	
201	+11213	+00940		213	+00940	
202	+21211	+01039		211	+00099	ØFF
203	+12213	+01039		213	+01039	
204	+11212	+00000		212	+00000	
205	+21214	+00001		214	+00001	ØFF
206	+22215	−00009		215	+00010	ØFF
207	+34209	−00009		209		
208	+31200			200		
200	+41211			211	−00300	
201	+11213	+01039		213	+01039	
202	+21211	+00739		211	−00300	ØFF
203	+12213	+00739		213	+00739	
204	+11212	+00000		212	+00000	
205	+21214	+00001		214	+00001	ØFF
206	+22215	−00009		215	+00010	ØFF
207	+34209	−00009		209		
208	+31200			200		
200	+41211			211	−00006	
201	+11213	+00739		213	+00739	
202	+21211	+00733		211	−00006	ØFF
203	+12213	+00733		213	+00733	
204	+11212	+00000		212	+00000	
205	+21214	+00001		214	+00001	ØFF
206	+22215	−00009		215	+00010	ØFF
207	+34209	−00009		209		
208	+31200			200		
200	+41211			211	+00021	
⋮	⋮			⋮	⋮	

INDEX